New Directions
P.O. Box 80611,
Lansing, MI 48906

Become
a Pen Pal

Bind Them
Upon
Your Heart Forever

366 Daily Devotions

By David Meengs

Bind Them Upon Your Heart Forever
By David Meengs
English

Copyright 2008
1st printing November 2008
2nd printing March 2011
3rd printing January 2018
4th printing September 2021

Biblical Counseling Worldwide

All rights reserved. Written permission must be secured from the publisher to use or reproduce any part of this book, except for brief quotations in critical reviews or articles.

All Scripture quotations are from the NIV unless otherwise mentioned.

ISBN - 81-7916-009-2
ISBN - 13-978-81-7916-009-1

Published and distributed by:
    Biblical Counseling Worldwide
    P.O. Box 547
    Caledonia, MI 49316

    e.mail: bcworldwide@hotmail.com

Printed by Sheridan Publishing Grand Rapids, Inc.

Dedication

This book is dedicated to
our dear children and grandchildren
whom the Lord has graciously blessed us with
and are a source of joy to us.
These devotionals are God's way of living
and may they be a guide for the Christian life
He calls each of us to.

"Bind them upon your heart forever;
fasten them around your neck.
When you walk, they will guide you;
when you sleep, they will watch over you;
when you awake, they will speak to you."

Proverbs 6:20-21

Bind Them Upon Your Heart Forever
366 Daily Devotionals

Thank You

There have been many efforts to get this devotional book out. I just wanted to acknowledge those who have helped. Mary, my dear wife of 51 years has spent hundreds of hours over the past years going over this material. She has corrected mistakes and has given good advice when something was not said as well as it could have been. Mandie Wierenga was so helpful in corrected my improper English Daughter Becky and Mary's sister, Donna, have also spent hours looking over the material and checking references, to find the mistakes before you do. The whole staff in India has been a huge blessing. They have taken care of so many day to day details, so that my wife and I could concentrate on writing these devotionals and other books. Particular thanks to Sherine, the manager of The Biblical Counselling Trust of India and to Jansy, who did so much to get this publication out.

Above all, we want to thank our God who has established a relationship with us so that we might be devoted to Him. He has blessed us and encouraged us. May His Name be lifted up!

The Author,
David Meengs

January

February

Day	Text	Title of the Devotional
1.	Ephesians 6:4	Provoking our children to wrath
2.	1 Corinthians 13:4a	*"Love is patient"*
3.	1 Corinthians 13:4b	*"Love is kind"*
4.	1 Corinthians 13:4c	Love *"does not envy"*
5.	1 Corinthians 13:4d	Love *"does not boast"*
6.	1 Corinthians 13:4e	Love *"is not proud"*
7.	1 Corinthians 13:5a	Love *"is not rude"*
8.	1 Corinthians 13:5b	Love *"is not self-seeking"*
9.	1 Corinthians 13:5c	Love *"is not easily angered"*
10.	1 Corinthians 13:5d	Love *"keeps no record of wrongs"*
11.	1 Corinthians 13:6a	*"Love does not delight in evil"*
12.	1 Corinthians 13:6b	Love *"rejoices with the truth"*
13.	1 Corinthians 13:7a	Love *"always protects"*
14.	1 Corinthians 13:7b	Love *"always trusts"*
15.	1 Corinthians 13:7c	Love *"always hopes"*
16.	1 Corinthians 13:7d	Love *"always perseveres"*
17.	1 Corinthians 13:8a	*"Love never fails"*
18.	Luke 2:40	The leadership training of Jesus
19.	Luke 2:52	The leadership skills Jesus learned
20.	Luke 22:32a	God's Son prays for you!
21.	John 9:1	Jesus *"saw a man"*
22.	James 1:27	Religion that God accepts
23.	Philippians 2:14-15	Complaining and arguing is insanity!
24.	Matthew 28:19a	The Great Commission stalled
25.	Jeremiah 5:30-31	Evil prophets and priests
26.	John 10:4b-5a	Do you recognize false shepherds?
27.	2 Timothy 2:15	Do we have our ATG degree?
28.	Romans 8:17	*"Co-heirs with Christ"*
29.	Psalm 35:9	*"Shall be"* - words of hope

March

Day	Text	Title of the Devotional
1.	Isaiah 58:6-7	Lent begins – a proper fast
2.	Mark 9:12	Why did Christ suffer? - Part 1
3.	Hebrews 2:17	Why did Christ suffer? - Part 2
4.	Isaiah 53:2b	How did Christ suffer? - Part 1
5.	Isaiah 53:5a	How did Christ suffer? - Part 2
6.	Isaiah 53:7b	How did Christ suffer? - Part 3
7.	Isaiah 53:12b	How did Christ suffer? - Part 4
8.	1 Peter 2:20b-21	Why and how we must suffer Part 1
9.	1 Peter 1:6-7	Why and how we must suffer Part 2
10.	Matthew 4:4a	The answer to temptation
11.	John 13:1b	Jesus *"showed"* His love by serving
12.	Luke 22:60b-61a	"The look" that melted Peter's heart
13.	Exodus 20:3	Identifying our idols
14.	Isaiah 49:16a	Is your name written on Christ's hand?
15.	Judges 6:15	God still uses common people!
16.	Mark 14:6	People will mock you!
17.	Jeremiah 17:9-10	What our hearts are really like
18.	Proverbs 15:8b	5 ways we're not "upright" in prayer
19.	Mark 11:24	A prayer that moves mountains
20.	Genesis 4:7b	How close can I get to sin?
21.	1 Timothy 1:15	Are you satisfied spiritually?
22.	Exodus 12:43a	The Passover
23.	Leviticus 23:6	The Feast of Unleavened Bread
24.	Leviticus 23:9-11	The Feast of First Fruits
25.	Deut. 16:9-11a	The Feast of Weeks or Pentecost
26.	1 Timothy 2:15	The high calling of motherhood
27.	Proverbs 15:27	Is our greed killing us?
28.	Job 31:1	Why is lust idolatry?
29.	Proverbs 6:6-8	What is so wrong with laziness?
30.	Ecclesiastes 2:24a	Do I love and enjoy my daily work?
31.	1 Samuel 17:47b	*"The battle is the LORD's"*

April

Day	Text	Title of the Devotional
1.	John 12:13	Why do we have a Palm Sunday?
2.	Luke 23:34	The 1st of 7 sayings on the Cross
3.	Luke 23:43	The 2nd saying on the Cross
4.	John 19:26b-27a	The 3rd saying on the Cross
5.	Matthew 27:46	The 4th saying on the Cross
6.	John 19:28b	The 5th saying on the Cross
7.	John 19:30a	The 6th saying on the Cross
8.	Luke 23:46	The 7th saying on the Cross
9.	Matthew 26:59	Liars, the 1st voice by the Cross
10.	Luke 12:8-9	Deniers, the 2nd voice by the Cross
11.	Matt. 27:41-42a	Mockers, the 3rd voice by the Cross
12.	John 19:24b	Gamblers, the 4th voice by the Cross
13.	Luke 23:39	Blasphemers, the 5th voice by the Cross
14.	Luke 23:42	Repenters, the 6th voice by the Cross
15.	Matthew 27:38	Robbers, the 7th voice by the Cross
16.	Matthew 1:20b-21	Why Jesus had to be God and man
17.	Hebrews 1:14	Angels work for God & bless believers
18.	Acts 12:23b	Angels bring mercy as well as justice!
19.	Revelation 12:7-9	Angels who hate God and believers
20.	1 John 4:19	Why can we love God and others?
21.	Matthew 6:33	From self-esteem to Christ-esteem
22.	Romans 5:12	Total Depravity, the T of TULIP
23.	Ephesians 1:3-5a	Unconditional Election, the U of TULIP
24.	Psalm 65:4	Limited Atonement, the L of TULIP
25.	John 5:25	Irresistible Grace, the I of TULIP
26.	2 Timothy 4:18	Perseverance of the Saints, P of TULIP
27.	2 Samuel 9:13	Am I a Mephibosheth?
28.	Luke 12:10	The unpardonable sin
29.	Lamentations 3:40	When our love grows cold
30.	Titus 2:1	Is my life teaching "sound doctrine"?

May

Day	Text	Title of the Devotional
1.	Matthew 7:3-5	*"Take the plank out of your own eye"*
2.	Matthew 22:35-40	A brief summary of the Bible
3.	Ephesians 5:29	Can you hate yourself?
4.	1 Peter 3:15	The reason for our hope
5.	2 Cor. 1:3-4a	Testimonies
6.	Romans 6:6	*"Slaves to sin"*
7.	Romans 6:17-18	*"Slaves to righteousness"*
8.	1 Corinthians 10:13	*"God is faithful"*
9.	Hebrews 4:15-16	Mercy *"in our time of need"*
10.	James 1:2-4	*"Count it all joy"*
11.	Hebrews 12:2	How to endure trials
12.	Genesis 50:20	Trials are for our good
13.	Psalm 119:165	The secret to peace
14.	Ezekiel 36:26	Are we responsible to change others?
15.	Luke 24:50b-51	The benefits of Christ's ascension
16.	Matthew 5:1-2	Why "The Beatitudes"?
17.	Matthew 5:3	*"Poor in spirit"*
18.	Matthew 5:4	*"Mourn"*
19.	Matthew 5:5	*"Meek"*
20.	Matthew 5:6	*"Hunger and thirst for righteousness"*
21.	Matthew 5:7	*"Merciful"*
22.	Matthew 5:8	*"Pure in heart"*
23.	Matthew 5:9	*"Peacemakers"*
24.	Matthew 5:11-12	Persecuted and falsely accused
25.	Matthew 5:13	*"The salt of the earth"*
26.	1 Timothy 6:10	The deceitfulness of riches
27.	Malachi 3:8	God's blessings if we tithe
28.	Genesis 1:26a & 27	Am I normal?
29.	1 Peter 5:7	How big is our God?
30.	Psalm 66:18	When God doesn't hear prayer
31.	2 Corinthians 4:18	Everything in this world is temporary

June

July

August

Day	Text	Title of the Devotional
1.	Genesis 2:15	What is a bridegroom and husband?
2.	Genesis 2:18	What is a bride and wife?
3.	Genesis 2:22	Why did God make a wife from a rib?
4.	Genesis 2:15	How is a man created different?
5.	Genesis 2:20 & 3:16b	How is a woman created different?
6.	Genesis 34:12	What about paying a dowry?
7.	Numbers 12:1 NKJV	What about crossing caste to marry?
8.	2 Corinthians 6:14	How to determine a marriage match
9.	2 Cor. 6:15-16b	Why not marriage to an unbeliever?
10.	1 Samuel 25:2-3	Can we change him or her?
11.	Genesis 1:28	Biblical reasons to get married
12.	Genesis 2:18a	Preparing for marriage or singleness
13.	Numbers 30:3-5	Decisions in the home
14.	Proverbs 11:14 NKJV	Seeking help to find a spouse
15.	Genesis 2:24 KJV	*"Leaving"* to establish a covenant
16.	Genesis 2:24 KJV	*"Leaving,"* a command to parents
17.	Genesis 2:24 KJV	*"Leaving,"* a command to newlyweds
18.	Genesis 2:24b	Newlyweds not *"leaving"* spiritually
19.	Ephesians 5:22-24	Why is headship necessary?
20.	Ephesians 5:25-27	A husband must love like Christ
21.	1 Peter 3:1	The importance of submission
22.	1 Peter 3:1a	*"In the same way"*
23.	1 Peter 3:7	Are you a "considerate" husband?
24.	1 Peter 3:7b	When husbands are sledge hammers
25.	Ephesians 5:33b	*"Respect,"* a one-word summary
26.	Philippians 3:18-19	The sin of gluttony
27.	Genesis 9:3	Eat meat or be vegetarian?
28.	Proverbs 12:10	Are you *"kind"* to animals?
29.	Deuteronomy 5:11	What is swearing?
30.	Genesis 4:6-7	How jealousy destroys us
31.	1 Corinthians 6:11	People with addictions can change!

September

Day	Text	Title of the Devotional
1.	Jonah 1:3	Are we running away?
2.	Philippians 2:14-15	Beware of self-pity!
3.	1 John 4:18	The perfect love that drives out fear
4.	Matthew 25: 25-26a	Fear doesn't build relationships!
5.	Matthew 6:27-30	Why is "worry" so wrong?
6.	Psalm 38:1-2	David's depression
7.	Psalm 32:3-4	How does God see depression?
8.	Psalm 32:8-9	A recipe for depression
9.	Genesis 4:5b-7	Why was Cain depressed?
10.	Romans 15:4	Follow Elijah's eyes to see his problem
11.	Psalm 77:3b-4	Asaph, Peter, and Job depressed
12.	Proverbs 12:25	Is a chemical imbalance the cause?
13.	1Timothy 4:7b	Getting serious with our daily schedule
14.	Genesis 4:7	A depressed ministry worker
15.	James 1:22	A depressed student or housewife
16.	Philippians 4:4	"Rejoice in the Lord always"
17.	Philippians 4:5	"Gentleness... to all"
18.	Philippians 4:6	Pray "with thanksgiving"
19.	Philippians 4:7	God's "peace" will guard us!
20.	Philippians 4:8	Learning to "think" God's way
21.	Philippians 4:9	Are we practicing Christians?
22.	Philippians 4:11b	How Paul "learned" contentment
23.	Philippians 4:12b	A true test of God's blessings
24.	Leviticus 23:24b-25	The Feast of Trumpets
25.	Hebrews 9:7-8	The Day of Atonement
26.	Leviticus 23:33-34	The Feast of Tabernacles
27.	Proverbs 28:14	Jesus, the solution to a right attitude
28.	2 Corinthians 3:5-6	God's sufficiency
29.	Song of Songs 2:3a	Is your husband an "apple tree"?
30.	Song of Songs 2:2	Is your wife a "lily among thorns"?

October

November

December

JANUARY

"Oh, the depths and the riches of the wisdom
and knowledge of God! How unsearchable His judgments,
and His paths beyond tracing out! Who has known the
mind of the Lord? Or who has been His counselor? Who
has ever given to God, that God should repay him? For
from Him and through Him and to Him are all things.
To Him be the glory forever! Amen."
Romans 11:33-36

January 1

"Blessed is the man who does not walk in the counsel of the wicked or stand in the way of sinners or sit in the seat of mockers. But his delight is in the law of the LORD, and on His law he meditates day and night. He is like a tree planted by streams of water, which yields its fruit in season and whose leaf does not wither. Whatever he does prospers."
Psalm 1:1-3

Why Devotions?

This year-long series of daily devotions were written to be of practical use in developing a closer relationship with God. In our text, we see that there are blessings associated with being devoted to God. We also see that there are curses when we are not. But what does it really mean to be devoted to God? Does being devoted to God, mean having Bible reading and prayer every morning before we begin our daily work? Yes, but is this devotional time in the morning or evening more of a spiritual activity than the rest of the day? Not really! When we finish our devotion time, we must now put into practice and <u>show</u> our devotion to God and to others.

We can't come to Jesus in the morning and call Him "Lord" and "Master," and then live the day, demanding to be the master of our life. It is quite easy to be devoted to God when we are in prayer! But how will we react when someone cheats us or lies to us? Believing in Jesus must include our daily walk, or we really don't believe in Jesus! Then the curses that follow our text will be ours.

If we are not "changed" people, God will not bless us. *"Not so the wicked! They are like chaff that the wind blows away. Therefore the wicked will not stand in the judgment, nor sinners in the assembly of the righteous. <u>For the LORD watches over the way of the righteous, but the way of the wicked will perish</u>,"* Psalm 1:4-6.

Prayer: Most Holy Lord, we praise You for Your promises and protection. Help us delight in Your law and meditate on it. Help us in our daily responsibilities and relationships to be faithful, so that Your Kingdom grows. We want to be this tree that is *"planted by streams of water, which yields its fruit in season and whose leaf does not wither."* In Christ's name we pray. Amen.

January 2

"From one man He made every nation of men, that they should inhabit the whole earth; and He determined the times set for them and the exact places where they should live. God did this so that men would seek Him and perhaps reach out for Him and find Him, though He is not far from each one of us." Acts 17:26-27

Why are we here?

The Apostle Paul noticed that in Athens the people had an altar: "TO THE UNKNOWN GOD." In Acts 17:22-34, Paul tells them and us, *"The God who made the world and everything in it is the LORD of Heaven and earth and does not live in temples built by human hands,"* Acts 17:24.

God lives in the hearts of His people. God in His wisdom and power put us all, in *"the exact places"* and *"determined the times"* He specifically wanted us here on this Earth. *"God did this so that men would seek Him and perhaps reach out for Him and find Him, though He is not far from each one of us,"* Acts 17:27. We are here in the world, with a purpose, that is, to find God, to know God. And once again, He does not exist in temples or church buildings, but individual lives, in our hearts.

Jesus said, *"Seek and you will find; knock and the door will be opened to you. For everyone who asks receives; he who seeks finds; and to him who knocks, the door will be opened,"* Matthew 7:7b-8.

Why is it important to find God and His will for us? Because God *"commands all people everywhere to repent. For He has set a day when He will judge the world with justice by the Man He has appointed. He has given proof of this to all men by raising Him from the dead,"* Acts 17:30b-31. Do we have a necessary *"seek"* and *"find"* mentality?

Prayer: Knowable Lord, You tell us; *"Seek the LORD while He may be found; call upon Him while He is near. Let the wicked forsake his way and the evil man his thoughts. Let him turn to the LORD, and He will have mercy on him, and to our God, for He will freely pardon,"* Isaiah 55:6-7. Lord, we need Your mercy and pardon to even repent! We are so thankful that You are willing to give us new hearts that have a new power to repent! Lord, have mercy on our souls for Jesus' sake. Amen.

January 3

"Fulfill your vows to the Most High, and call upon Me in the day of trouble; I will deliver you, and you will honor Me." Psalm 50:14b-15

The keeping of vows

It is common to have a New Year's resolution to live differently. We need to lose weight; draw closer to God; be a blessing to the family; work more faithfully, and the list goes on. Vows are good, but they should be taken carefully and prayerfully because a vow is a voluntary pledge to fulfill an agreement. Once made, a vow is binding. *"When you make a vow to God, do not delay in fulfilling it. He has no pleasure in fools; fulfill your vow. It is better not to vow than to make a vow and not fulfill it,"* Ecclesiastes 5:4-5.

A vow actually has curses if it is done foolishly. In 1 Samuel 14, *"The men of Israel were in distress that day, because Saul had bound the people under oath, saying, 'Cursed be any man who eats food before evening comes, before I have avenged myself on my enemies!'"* Later, the army was out in the woods and came across some honey, *"but Jonathan had not heard that his father had bound the people with the oath,"* and he ate some. Because the selfish King Saul made a rash oath, the soldiers were faint from hunger, and after that, some of the soldiers even ate raw meat because they were starved! Saul would have killed his own son for breaking the vow, but the more righteous soldiers rescued his son.

A vow has benefits if done wisely. *"Jacob made a vow, saying, 'If God will be with me and will watch over me on this journey I am taking and will give me food to eat and clothes to wear...then the LORD will be my God...and of all that You give me I will give You a tenth,'"* Genesis 28:20-22. Jacob kept his vow, and God blessed him greatly!

Prayer: Covenant-keeping Lord, we are grateful to You for giving us wisdom concerning vows. It is our desire to serve and love You more faithfully. We have so much to be thankful for! We praise You with words from King David in Psalm 22:25. *"From You comes the theme of my praise in the great assembly; before those who fear You will I fulfill my vows."* In Christ's name we pray. Amen.

January 4

"Thus says the LORD: 'Let not the wise man glory in his wisdom, let not the mighty man glory in his might, nor let the rich man glory in his riches; but let him who glories glory in this, that he understands and knows Me, that I am the LORD, exercising loving-kindness, judgment, and righteousness in the earth. For in these I delight,' says the LORD."
Jeremiah 9:23-24 NKJV

Who is God? What is He like?

To know God, we must know His character, also called His attributes. We also need to know God to trust Him and to worship Him sincerely! We can learn about the perfect character of God because He is personal and is knowable. He is not like other gods who are impersonal and unknowable. Jesus Himself became flesh to identify with us, so that we could love Him and follow Him. Do we not need to know God, to enjoy Him now and forever? The Holy Spirit, also fully God, lives in us, walks with us, guides us, protects us, and keeps us close to our gracious and loving Lord.

We cannot possibly learn everything there is to know about our infinite God. We can only learn what God has chosen to reveal to us, through His Word and Spirit. Meditate too, on how much God delights in us knowing Him.

Another good reason to study the attributes of God is that many people have made out the character of God to be different from what the Bible tells us about Him. Some teach much about the love and grace of God and little about His justice. Others teach much about the justice of God and little of His love and grace. We really do need a Biblical balance of law and grace.

When we go through great trials at various times in our lives, it is critical to know and depend on God's character. How can we pray sincerely if we don't know what God can do and wants to do for us? For this reason, we need to study who God is and have a close relationship with Him before our trials in life come.

Prayer: Wise and loving Lord, we want to worship You more, for You created us for that purpose! Help us to learn about You so that it impacts how we live. In Jesus' name we pray. Amen.

January 5

"In the beginning God." Genesis 1:1a

The Self-existence of God

Faith involves trust and hope in the God of the Bible. It is quite impossible to trust in God if we do not know anything of His holy character points. For this reason, we study the attributes of God. We will try not to emphasize one attribute of God above another, as that can develop a wrong idea of who God is. We will begin where the Bible does.

The Self-existence of God - Our text is the first four words in the English Bible. In the original Hebrew, the first word in the Bible is El Elohim, our covenant-keeping God. In fact, there really was no beginning for God because He always existed. Thus, God is outside of time. God was neither created nor made. God existed by Himself, independent from anything else. It is hard to imagine, but at one time, there was no earth and no heavens. There was no sun, no moon, and no stars. There were no angels. God existed all alone. He did not exist for a day or for a year, but for eternity. During this eternity, God was self-contained, self-existing, self-sufficient, self-satisfied, in need of nothing and no one. God is still like this today. He does not need you and me! He is fully self-existent.

The internal completeness of God is shown in the words "*I am that I am.*" This not only means that God does not need you or me in any way to complete Him, but that the opposite is true! We the creature, need God the Creator to complete us. What kind of God would we have if we somehow needed to complete Him? God is self-existent in Spirit form only. To the Samaritan woman Jesus said, "*God is spirit.*" No one has ever seen God in a body, other than God the Son, Jesus Christ.

Prayer: Perfect Lord, we stand in awe of the fact that You have always existed perfect and complete. We who are incomplete, need You who are complete and eternal. How humbling it is that You shower Your love upon us, to establish a present and lasting relationship with us. Lord, we desire more than anything, to know You better, to love You more! Bless our study of Your divine character. In Christ's name we pray. Amen.

January 6

*"For there are three that bear witness in Heaven: The Father, the Word, and the Holy Spirit; and these three are one."*1 John 5: 7 NKJV

The doctrine of the Trinity

The Trinity is not really an attribute of God, but it is important to know God better. God reveals Himself as one God, yet existing in three persons, in Trinity. Granted, this is hard to understand. It will take a faith that submits to the mind of God to believe in the Trinity. <u>Faith believes what God says, even if we cannot fully understand it.</u> That is the nature of faith. Unbelief on the other hand, is not submitting our mind to what God has revealed to us in the Bible. An attitude of faith stands under and submits to the Word of God. Some say that the Trinity should not be believed because it cannot be understood. That's bad reasoning! Any god that we can totally understand is surely not greater than us! If we put logic before belief and faith, then the virgin birth and resurrection are a myth.

God existed in Trinity before creation, because in Trinity, God made all things. *"God said, 'Let <u>Us</u> make man in <u>Our</u> image, according to <u>Our</u> likeness,'"* Genesis 1:26 NKJV. In Matthew 3:16b while being baptized, Jesus *"saw the <u>Spirit</u> of God descending like a dove."* Also, *"a voice came from heaven, saying, 'This is My Beloved <u>Son</u>, in whom I am well pleased,'"* Matthew 3:16c-17 NKJV. The Father, Son and Spirit, are present in one place, at one time. The command, *"Go therefore and make disciples of all the nations, baptizing them in <u>the name</u> of the Father and of the Son and of the Holy Spirit,"* Matthew 28:19 NKJV. I underlined "the name," because in the original Greek, this is a definite article, first person, singular, meaning one God. Our God is not <u>a god</u>, like there are others. He is <u>the God</u>, one and only! This is a very important distinction.

Prayer: Lord, we worship the Father who planned our salvation, the Son who accomplished our salvation, and the Holy Spirit who is sent to sanctify, preserve, and glorify us. Your Trinitarian benediction in 2 Corinthians 13:14 also blesses us! *"May the grace of the Lord <u>Jesus Christ</u>, and the love of <u>God</u>, and the fellowship of the <u>Holy Spirit</u> be with you all."* In Christ's name we pray. Amen.

January 7

"Oh, the depth of the riches of the wisdom and knowledge of God! How unsearchable His judgments, and His paths beyond tracing out! Who has known the mind of the Lord? Or who has been His counselor?"
Romans 11:33-34

The Wisdom of God

God knows everything, past, present, and future. In fact, His wisdom has a perfect understanding of all that is or might be. This means it is impossible for God to learn even one thing that is new. How can God learn anything if He infinitely knows all things? If anyone could tell God something new, then God would not know everything! Paul calls Jesus *"the wisdom of God"* in 1 Corinthians 1:24. The Bible is also God's wisdom. Know *"the Holy Scriptures which are able to make you wise for salvation through faith in Christ Jesus,"* 2 Timothy 3:15a. So then, Christianity is wisdom for the believer that is bound up in a relationship with God through Christ and His Word. With this relationship, we can learn much about the wisdom and will of God.

God the Holy Spirit opens our eyes to real wisdom. *"No one knows the things of God except the Spirit of God. Now we <u>have received</u>, not the spirit of the world, but the Spirit who is from God, that we might know the things that have been freely given to us by God,"* 1 Corinthians 2:11b-12 NKJV. With this in mind, nominal Christians or non-Christians may have knowledge, but certainly not wisdom. The problem is, *"The natural man (unconverted person) does not receive the things of the Spirit of God, for they are foolishness to him; nor can he know them, because they are spiritually discerned,"* 1 Corinthians 2:14 NKJV.

There are two questions that will echo into eternity: Will we seek God and His wisdom? Or, will we seek the world's wisdom?

Prayer: Wise and loving Lord, Your Word tells us that, *"There is a way that seems right to a man, but in the end it leads to death,"* Proverbs 14:12. Lord, we do not want death, but eternal life. Help us to *"Trust in the LORD with all your heart and lean not on your own understanding; in all your ways acknowledge Him and He will make your paths straight,"* Proverbs 3:5-6. In Jesus' name we pray. Amen.

January 8

"Ah, Sovereign LORD, You have made the Heavens and the earth by Your great power and outstretched arm. Nothing is too hard for You."
Jeremiah 32:17

The Omnipotence of God

God's omnipotence is His infinite ability or power to instantly bring to pass that which He wills. When God created the world, His power made everything from absolutely nothing. God simply spoke and the sun, moon, and stars were made. He put it all into a perfect orbit, and kept it there, all by His power. God has all wisdom to go with His power. If God had all power, but no wisdom, He would be a lunatic. If God had all wisdom but no power, He would be frustrated. The attributes of God fully complement each other for His glory and our good!

It is God's power that gives a limited amount of power to man. In Psalm 2, we read that God's power sets up authorities and kings everywhere. *"There is no authority except from God, and the authorities that exist are appointed by God,"* Romans 13:1b NKJV. How foolish then, for us to fight against even the authorities that God has placed over us. It is also foolish for the authorities to fight against God and not recognize that His power placed them there.

We must be careful about questioning God's power. Job could only say, *"I am unworthy how can I reply to You? I put my hand over my mouth."* Job also said, *"I know that You can do everything, and that no purpose of Yours can be withheld,"* Job 42:1 NKJV. Jesus' mother believed in the power of God. When Mary was told that she would give birth to the Christ Child, she said, *"Nothing is impossible with God,"* Luke 1:37. In answer to the question, "Who then can be saved?" Jesus said, *"With man this is impossible, but with God all things are possible,"* Matthew 19:25b, 26b. Corrie Ten Boom said in response to these two verses, "If all things are possible with God, then all things are possible to him or her who believes in God."

Prayer: Most Powerful Lord, we cannot even begin to understand the depths of Your power. You created the world out of nothing and put us here also. We worship You for Your Almighty power. In Jesus' name we pray. Amen.

January 9

"I the LORD, do not change." Malachi 3:6a

The Immutability of God

God's character never changes. That is what the word immutable means. Our God is the same yesterday, today and forevermore. God cannot change for the better! He is already perfect, and always has been. His power will never fade. His glory will always shine. His divine perfections will always be the same.

God's Word never changes! Some say the Old Testament no longer applies to us. How wrong! The Old Testament and the New Testament both point to Christ as the only Mediator. What was true in the past, is true in the present, and will always be true. *"The plans of the LORD stand firm forever, the purposes of His heart through all generations,"* Psalm 33:11.

How God deals with people never changes! The stories of Adam, Moses, Ruth, David, Elijah, and Paul may seem ancient to us. But, it is right here that the doctrine of "the immutability of God" needs to tie our two worlds together. God never changes how He relates to men and how we are to relate to Him and others. God will never change the principles for living, shown to us in the lives of Bible characters.

God's purpose for us never changes! It will always be God's will that conforms us to the image of Christ, Romans 8:28-29. Everything in our lives is geared to that end. If God could change, we would not know how to pray. If God could change, worship would be impossible. If God could change, salvation would be questionable as we could lose it tomorrow. If God could change, Heaven would be a dream, and Hell would be a lie. How horrible Hell is going to be in the hands of an unchanging God.

Prayer: Dear Lord who never changes in our uncertain world. You are beautifully predictable, always. Your character promises that your love and salvation will never ever change. We believers are already with You forever! There will never be a day when You will leave or forsake us. You are so unchanging that we can stand firm, certain of Your promises. May we always trust in Your unchanging care for us. In Jesus' name we pray. Amen.

January 10

"O LORD, You have searched me and You know me. You know when I sit and when I rise; You perceive my thoughts from afar. You discern my going out and my lying down; You are familiar with all my ways. Before a word is on my tongue You know it completely, O LORD."
Psalm 139:1-4

The Omniscience of God

The omniscience of God is that part of His character that sees or has perfect knowledge of everything in the Heavens and on the Earth. He saw everything that has ever happened in the past, sees everything that is happening in the present, and will see everything that will happen in the future. Nothing will ever escape His all-seeing eye. *"Nothing in all creation is hidden from God's sight. Everything is uncovered and laid bare before the eyes of Him to whom we must give account,"* Hebrews 4:13. We should think twice before we choose to sin!

The omniscience of God is important for our prayer life. God clearly sees every event in our life. Thus, we should never use prayer to give God a history lesson or a weather report. He not only sees all, but He either plans or allows it. We need His eyes to see how to respond with obedience and faith in the present and in the future.

The omniscience of God opens our eyes to the truth of Scripture. Without God's Spirit, we are blind and not able to understand spiritual things. *"No one knows the thoughts of God except the Spirit of God. We have not received the spirit of the world but the Spirit who is from God, that we may understand what God has freely given us,"* 1 Cor. 2:11b-12. Paul further explains: *"The man without the Spirit does not accept the things that come from the Spirit of God, for they are foolishness to him, and he cannot understand them,"* 1 Corinthians 2:14a. God helps us to see what the rest of the world is unable to see.

Prayer: Amazing Lord, what a huge blessing and comfort it is that nothing will ever escape Your loving eye. Such knowledge is too wonderful to even fully understand. O Lord, You see us when we lie down, when we rise, wherever we are. How poor are our eyes that look at You, yet how perfect is Your eye on us. We praise You for watching over us. In Jesus' name we pray. Amen.

January 11

"'Can anyone hide in secret places so that I cannot see him?' declares the LORD. 'Do I not fill Heaven and earth?' declares the LORD." Jeremiah 23:24

The Omnipresence of God

The omnipresence of God is the attribute by which He, in Trinity, fills all parts of the universe by being present everywhere at once. No one can hide from God. Nor can anyone be any place where God cannot reach him or her. God's everywhere presence in a believer's life must fill us with great hope and comfort. If God is so for us, who can be against us? Fear, worry, and depression must be a short experience in a believer's life as we look to our ever-present and loving God!

David said, *"Where can I go from Your Spirit? Where can I flee from Your presence? If I go up to the Heavens, You are there; if I make my bed in the depths, You are there. If I rise on the wings of dawn, if I settle on the far side of the sea, even there Your hand will guide me, Your right hand will hold me fast. If I say, 'Surely the darkness will hide me and the light become night around me', even the darkness will not be dark to You; the night will shine like the day, for darkness is as light to You,"* Psalm 139: 7-12.

The omnipresence of God must cause us to fear sin! Since God is everywhere, there's not a place in the world that God is not there. God's presence everywhere is eternal. His holy wrath is always present in Hell. His love is always present in Heaven.

The omnipresence of God must cause us to trust Him. If God had all power, all wisdom and loves us, but was not everywhere, He might still miss us. But our God is everywhere, thus He is trustworthy. What other god is like this? What other god placed us in this world to watch us, to love us, and to protect us? What other god will we stand before in the Judgment? The answer is none except You, O my God.

Prayer: O Perfect Lord, how thankful we are that You are everywhere present in the universe. No matter where we are, You are there. And then to think, You are our Father in Jesus Christ also. Even when we sin You are always there to convict us by Your Holy Spirit to draw us back into Your presence. Our words cannot express our gratitude. May Your most holy name be praised! In Jesus' name we pray. Amen.

January 12

"God is love." 1 John 4:8

The Love of God - Part 1

"God is love" describes the very essence of God's being. Love is His overall plan behind all that He does in saving us. Our love for God grows as we understand Him. At times we will doubt God's love, yet even our doubts can never destroy God's love any more than our faith can create it. The reason is: love originates in God. To help remember how *"God is love,"* we'll use an acronym, PERFECT.

The love of God is Personal. *"We love because He first loved us,"* 1 John 4:19. Jesus is a very personal Savior, for He is not calling every person to Himself, in a saving way, that is. Even though God gives life to dead sinners, He does not give life to all dead sinners. *"Jacob have I loved, but Esau I have hated,"* in Romans 9, is an example of a much wider truth. God saving Rahab was very personal, when we see that the rest of Jericho was destroyed. What is true of Rahab is true of every real Christian. Jesus said, *"I am the Good Shepherd, the Good Shepherd gives His life for the sheep."* He did not give His life for both the sheep and the goats. It is a mystery as to why God saves some, but that makes His love personal.

The love of God is Essential. Pull the love of God away from our lives, and all that remains is the wrath of God. If it were not for God's love, we would not even breathe our next breath.

The love of God is Relational. If we want absolute proof of God's love for us, look at the Cross! God relates to us because of our relationship with Christ, not because of any good in us. In Christ, we are adopted, relatives and co-heirs with Him.

Prayer: Personal and relational Lord, we praise Your perfect love with a favorite song. "Could we with ink the ocean fill, and were the skies of parchment made, were every stalk on earth a quill, and every man a scribe by trade, to write the love of God above, would drain the ocean dry, nor could the scroll contain the whole, tho' stretched from sky to sky." Chorus: "O love of God, how rich and pure! How measureless and strong! It shall forevermore endure, the saints and angels song." In Jesus' name we pray. Amen.

January 13

"God is love." 1 John 4:8

The Love of God - Part 2

<u>The love of God is Familial,</u> meaning, a covenant family. A covenant is an agreement of love and protection that a king gave to his subjects with a single condition, they must love, obey, and be loyal to him in return. Earthly covenants are patterned after that first covenant God gave to Adam. However, Adam didn't keep his covenant obligations and thus did not receive "life forever," the reward for obedience, Genesis 2:17. Where humanity failed, Christ, the last Adam fulfilled the righteous requirements of the covenant, (1 Corinthians 15:45.) All who are "in Christ" are in the covenant, along with their children per 1 Corinthians 7:14. This makes children privileged to hear and see the Gospel. Familial means God sees our children as a special child of His special child (us), and of His special child (Christ). God loves His sheep and their lambs too. We are all His family.

<u>The love of God is Eternal.</u> God saves us forever. Peter said we have *"an inheritance that can never perish, spoil or fade, kept in Heaven for you,"* 1 Peter 1:4. Paul said, *"God's gifts and His call are irrevocable,"* Romans 11:29. Jesus said, *"I give them eternal life, and they shall never perish; no one can snatch them out of My hand,"* John 10:28. God's amazing love in Christ is eternal!

<u>The love of God changes us.</u> We were all *"slaves to sin"* in Romans 6:6. God's loving grace changed us to *"slaves to righteousness"* in Romans 6:18. In this process of change, we now put off the old nature and then put on the new, as in, Ephesians 4:22-24. When we fail to put off the old and sin, God the Holy Spirit, in love, gives us guilt so we will change. When we are faithful and put on new behavior, the Holy Spirit, in love, gives us peace and joy. God continues to change us.

<u>The love of God Transforms us.</u> Through Christ, we are transformed from being mortal, to immortal, 1 Corinthians 15:50-57. The love of God is indeed P.E.R.F.E.C.T.

Prayer: Perfect Lord, we thank and praise You that Your love is so personal that it changes us from sinners to saints. Without Your love we perish. How amazing, You loved us even though there was no good in us! We praise You! In Jesus' name we pray. Amen.

January 14

"The wrath of God is being revealed from Heaven against all the godlessness and wickedness of men who suppress the truth by their wickedness." Romans 1:18

The Wrath of God - Part 1

<u>The wrath of God is not an imperfection in His divine character</u>. His wrath flows from the fact that He is holy and just. God cannot turn His back on sin. The doctrine of the wrath of God should move us to praise Him, for that is what Jesus saves us from! If the Father, Son and Spirit were not holy, we could not be made holy either. To not believe in the wrath of God is to say that we know more than God does about His holy and just character. God is not a grandfather sitting on a cloud, waiting to bless us. There are more verses on God's wrath than there are on His love and mercy.

<u>The wrath of God is different than the wrath of man</u>. Man's anger flows out of the imperfection of his sinful nature. God's wrath flows out of the perfection of His holy nature. We should never use the holy wrath of God as an excuse to be angry. The reason is, *"The wrath of man does not produce the righteousness of God,"* James 1:20 NKJV. To see a more complete picture of just how detestable our sin of anger is to God, note the deeds of the flesh in Galatians 5:19-21. Eight different expressions of man's wrath, among others, if regularly practiced, will condemn a soul to Hell to face the full wrath of God.

<u>The wrath of God is horrible to experience</u>. Jesus, in pure agony on the Cross, fully experienced the wrath of God. With the sin of every believer upon Him, Jesus prayed, *"If it is possible, let this cup pass from Me."* His last dreadful cry was a Hell-scream, *"My God, My God, why hast Thou forsaken Me?"* These verses show what fearful apprehension Jesus had, and what it was like to experience God's wrath. Poor sinners may well cry out, "Lord, who shall stand," for even the Son of God trembled under the weight of God's wrath!

Prayer: Just and holy Lord, cover us with Christ's perfect blood and save us from Your present and eternal wrath. What a great deliverance Your salvation is. Lord, also give us a burden in our hearts for the lost souls who are still under Your wrath. In Christ's name we pray. Amen.

January 15

"Whoever believes in the Son has eternal life, but whoever rejects the Son will not see life, for God's wrath remains on him." John 3:36

The Wrath of God - Part 2

<u>The wrath of God is important for evangelism</u>. Today many tell the unsaved that God loves them, as if this will draw them to Christ. God loves only those "in Christ." *"Whoever believes in the Son has* (a present tense verb meaning already today) *eternal life, but whoever rejects the Son will not see life,* (future tense) *for God's wrath <u>remains</u> (present and future tense) on him,"* John 3:36. The wrath of God is both present and future! *"The wrath of God <u>is being revealed</u> from Heaven against all the godlessness and wickedness of men who suppress the truth by their wickedness,"* Romans 1:18. Until we flee to Christ, we are under the wrath of God.

<u>The wrath of God is important for our gratitude and service to God</u>. Gratitude is all about attitude, which is so essential in the Christian life. Israel wandered in the wilderness for 40 years, ungrateful that God had delivered them from sin, from Egypt, and from 400 years of slavery. As Christians, we too have been delivered from sin and from God's eternal wrath. We were slaves to sin, just like Israel was in Egypt. Then Christ came along and pardoned our death sentence for His glory and good pleasure. What gratitude we must have when we consider the wrath that we are saved from! If we are not grateful, then we are quite dead spiritually speaking. God's grace and mercy to us in salvation, makes no sense until we understand that it saves us from the wrath of God, and from our sin.

Prayer: O Lord, we thank You for showing us how important Your wrath is for the Gospel message. To think that Jesus fully saves us from Your present and future wrath is quite incredible. No wonder, *"The wicked will not stand in the judgment,"* Psalm 1:5. If we have not yet fled to Christ for refuge, then push us there! Help us to listen to Jesus in Matthew 3:7, *"<u>Flee from the wrath to come.</u>"* Help us to see that there is no escaping Your righteous wrath, unless Your wrath is poured out on Your perfect Son in our place! In His name we pray. Amen.

January 16

"Know therefore that the LORD your God is God; He is the faithful God." Deuteronomy 7:9

The Faithfulness of God

The faithfulness of God is His absolute reliability, His firm constancy, His steadfast love, and His absolute loyalty. God's faithfulness stands in contrast to the world's unfaithfulness. It is the very nature of God to be faithful. God's faithfulness is a covenant promise, by which God proves to Christians, they are not subject to fate, luck, or chance. All that happens to God's children is bound up in the divinely planned faithfulness of God! His storehouse of blessings would be nothing if He were not faithful in giving them to His children! Because of God's "faithfulness," Joseph, after 14 years of slavery and imprisonment, could say to his brothers without bitterness, *"Ye meant evil against me; but God meant it unto good,"* Genesis 50:20 KJV.

Our suffering is also the faithfulness of God. The purpose of it is exactly the same as Joseph's suffering. It is *"for the saving of many lives,"* Genesis 50:20b. When we see this clearly, the faithfulness of God becomes much clearer. Our suffering helps us to look like Christ much quicker, so that God can use us for *"the saving of many lives."*

Even in the midst of difficult trials, we can fully rely on the faithfulness of God. The truth is, *"No temptation has overtaken you except such as is common to man; but God is faithful, who will not allow you to be tempted beyond what you are able, but with the temptation will also make the way of escape that you may be able to bear it,"* 1 Corinthians 10:13 NKJV. Based on the faithfulness of God, this verse is a promise for every single believer! God is always *"faithful."*

Prayer: Faithful Father in Heaven, we praise You. If You were not faithful, we would not even be able to pray to You right now. What a beautiful compliment Your faithfulness is to the rest of Your attributes. Your power, wisdom and all-seeing eye would be of little benefit to us if You were not faithful in loving us. Lord, forgive us for not properly modeling Your faithfulness in our relationships. Change us, and use us for Your glory. In Jesus' name we pray. Amen.

January 17

"Give thanks to the LORD, for He is good; His love endures forever."
Psalm 118:29

The Goodness of God - Part 1

The goodness of God is not the righteousness or the holiness of God. Neither is this goodness really the grace of God either. "Goodness" is God's general blessings to all. A.W. Tozer said:

> "The goodness of God is that which causes Him to be kind, cordial, and benevolent toward men. He is tenderhearted and of quick sympathy and His unfailing attitude toward all moral beings is open, frank and friendly. By His nature He is inclined to bestow blessedness and He takes holy pleasure in the happiness of His people."

Think of what God's "goodness" means for us. He is not cold or distant from us! He is not unapproachable or uncaring, but very personal. God is knowable! Other gods (little g) are impersonal, unknowable, unapproachable, and are not "good."

God's "goodness" is infinite, perfect, eternal, powerful, omniscient, and omnipresent. Because God is infinite, His "goodness" has no limit. Because God is perfect, His "goodness" is always pure. Because God is self-existent, His "goodness" had no beginning. Because God is eternal, His "goodness" has no end. Because God is all-powerful, He can give His "goodness" in any situation. Because God always sees us, His "goodness" is never blind to our need. God's perfect goodness is never given out based on someone's social status, money, or good looks. May we learn character points for ourselves from God's perfect "goodness."

Prayer: Most perfect and loving Lord, how wise You are. For when we are ignorant, Your "goodness" gives us wisdom. When we are sick, Your "goodness" comforts us and makes us well. When You withhold Your "goodness" from us, it is only because it is not safe for us to have a blessing from Your good hand! We would be more proud if You blessed our arrogance. Lord, keep us humble so we may have more of Your goodness. In Jesus' name we pray. Amen.

January 18

"They will celebrate Your abundant goodness and joyfully sing of Your righteousness." "The LORD is good to all; He has compassion on all He has made." Psalm 145:7&9

The Goodness of God - Part 2

It is because of God's *"goodness"* that even the worst sinner can approach Him without fear. Even if we had committed every sin in the world, God's *"goodness"* still welcomes us to come to Him for forgiveness. God's Son is alive, sitting on a throne, reigning with the Father dispensing goodness. He is our sympathetic High Priest. It is important to better understand the *"goodness"* of God so that we can pray to God through Jesus. *"You are forgiving and good, O LORD, abounding in love to all who call to You,"* Psalm 86:5.

Because God is *"good,"* we must be *"good."* The author of Hebrews says, *"Remember those in prison as if you were their fellow prisoners, and those who are mistreated as if you yourselves were suffering,"* Hebrews 13:3. Later, the chapter concludes, *"And do not forget to do good and to share with others, for with such sacrifices God is pleased,"* Hebrews 13:16.

Satan pressed Adam and Eve in the garden to doubt God's *"goodness."* As children of Adam, it is also our natural sinful tendency to doubt the goodness of God. To question the goodness of God implies that we know more about what is good for us than God does. This is simply, idolatry. Lord, forgive us!

In times of great trials, we must especially think on the *"goodness"* of God. If God is for us, who can be against us? Even when we sin, our good God forgives, cleanses, and restores us!

Prayer: O Lord our God, we confess that we have been much like the prodigal son, who proudly demanded his father's goodness. We have been like the Pharisees. In self-righteous ways, we have demanded Your good blessings. How often You have told us, if we will just humble ourselves and pray, You will give out of Your goodness. Lord, humble us to see that like the prodigal we are hungry, dirty, wretched and in need of Your divine goodness! In Jesus' our Savior's name we pray. Amen.

January 19

"For it is by grace you have been saved, through faith — and this not from yourselves, it is the gift of God — not by works, so that no one can boast. For we are God's workmanship, created in Christ Jesus to do good works." Ephesians 2:8-10a

The Grace of God - Part 1

To see the grace of God, it is easier to tell you a story. James was a robber who spent 10 years in prison for stealing. Upon release, no one would take him in. But a kind bishop invited him to sleep the night in his house. While the bishop slept, James took his gold and silver. The police caught James and returned him to the bishop's house. The bishop welcomed him back. After the police laid out all the gold and silver, the bishop said to James the robber, "You forgot to take this gold watch that I gave you along with the other things." James was shocked! When the policemen left, the bishop told James, "I want you to keep this gold watch as a reminder to be an upright man." Because of his grace, James became an honest man.

What can we learn from this story? James saw grace and forgiveness <u>before</u> he even repented. James received what he <u>needed</u>: grace, not what he <u>deserved</u>: imprisonment and death. <u>Grace</u> changed James when nothing else in life had. The bishop's grace moved him to <u>repentance</u>!

In our text, we can see that the grace of God is a gift to those He saves! God moved towards us when we were still His *"enemies,"* Romans 5:10. Since *"the wages of sin is death,"* Romans 6:23, that is what we deserve. Also, since no work from a sinner is acceptable to God, He, totally in grace, of His own free will, sacrificed not gold or silver, but His own sinless and precious Son. Jesus payed our huge sin debt that we could never pay.

Prayer: Gracious Lord, we thank You for exercising Your will in saving us. We were actually sinning and were completely Your enemies when Your grace selected us! You have truly given us the forgiveness we needed, instead of the death we deserved. You even planned all this before the world was created. Lord, in light of Your grace, help us live for You now. In Jesus' name we pray. Amen.

January 20

"The LORD God made garments of skin for Adam and his wife and clothed them." Genesis 3:21

The Grace of God - Part 2

After sinning, Adam and Eve *"realized that they were naked"* in Genesis 3:7a. Their sin (and ours) separates us from God. Adam and Eve knew the pain and shame of their separation. That's why *"they sewed fig leaves together and made coverings for themselves,"* Genesis 3:7b. Immediately, Adam and Eve tried to get back into fellowship with God. They tried to do some "good work," picking fig leaves, to cover their sin. That didn't work! Why? Man's good works to earn salvation are the opposite of the grace of God. How many people today are still trying to do "good things" so God will accept them?

Our text shows how God came to Adam's rescue. He graciously covered Adam's sin. God killed an innocent animal. God made the first death of any kind happen, to pay for the guilt of Adam and Eve. God shed innocent blood. Why? *"For the life of a creature is in the blood and I have given it to you to make atonement for yourselves on the altar; it is the blood that makes atonement for one's life,"* Leviticus 17:11. God later provided the blood of His sinless Son so that we might personally be saved from His wrath. His grace alone saves us!

The grace of God is also needed for our sanctification, our growing up in Christ. We cannot possibly live our daily life in our own strength. Paul clearly said, *"Are you so foolish? After beginning with the Spirit, are you now trying to attain your goal by human effort?"* Galatians 3:3. This is exactly why so many people are failing in life. We can't live life without God! Christ invites us to come to the throne of grace for our daily strength! May we understand more fully that we need to meet with the Savior every day to renew our fellowship with Him. The Christian life is a <u>relationship</u> that needs to be sustained.

Prayer: O Lord, thank You for Your grace that woke us up when we were dead and still sinning. We deserve death, but You give us life. We deserve Your wrath, but You give us mercy. We deserve the fires of Hell, but You give us the glories of Heaven. May we be gracious to others, as You have been to us, evidence that Your grace is in us! In Jesus' name we pray. Amen.

January 21

"I saw the LORD sitting on a throne, high and lifted up, and the train of His robe filled the temple. Above it stood seraphim; each one had six wings: with two he covered his face, with two he covered his feet, and with two he flew. And one cried to another and said: "Holy, holy, holy is the LORD of host; the whole earth is full of His glory!"
Isaiah 6:1b-3 NKJV

The Holiness of God - Part 1

The holiness of God is a complete absence of sin or moral blemish. Stephen Charnock said, "Power is God's hand or arm, omniscience is His eye, mercy His bowels, eternity His duration, but holiness is His beauty." Holiness is not a divine perfection that God somehow worked up to. God always was holy, and always will be. We are fallen creatures who are born in sin, to sin, and will die sinners, because *"the wages of sin is death,"* Romans 6:23.

God's holiness sent Adam and us out of the Garden of Eden. God's perfect holiness cannot look at even one sin. Like Adam, we cannot expect to see God's face, unless we are sinless and holy. We cannot be sinless and holy without Christ's perfect, holy, atoning blood. Praise God, that through Christ, we can become holy!

The holiness of God is seen in creation. Everything was created holy and good. The world, man, even Satan, were once holy according to Ezekiel 28:15. In rebellion, Satan, then man, lost their holiness. Now we are in bondage to Satan. In salvation, God rescues us from our slavery to sin and makes us holy once again! It is only through God's holiness that we can reclaim what we formerly lost.

The holiness of God is seen in the law. God gave us His perfect law to guide us to holy living in a lawless world. If you think God's holy law is a burden, then pray for the eyes to see how it directs us to Christ. Meditate on how each person of the holy Trinity calls us to holiness, for God said, *"Be holy for I am holy,"* 1 Peter 1:16b.

Prayer: Beautiful Lord, we thank and praise You for Your holy character. Because You are holy we too can be holy. You cover our sin by the holy blood of Your perfect Son. We worship You for giving us Your holiness or we would be forever lost. In Jesus' name we pray. Amen.

January 22

"Exalt the LORD our God, and worship at His footstool;
He is holy." Psalm 99:5

The Holiness of God - Part 2

<u>The holiness of God is seen in the Cross</u>. When you see a Cross, think about God's holiness. See the bloody and marred face of Christ. It was because of God's holiness, that He poured out His wrath against sin, on Christ. Because of God's holiness, Jesus cried out, *"My God, My God, why hast thou forsaken me?"* Know this about the Cross. God forgives sinners, but He does not forgive sin! God's perfect holiness can't forgive sin. Sin must be punished, and Christ took that punishment.

<u>God's holiness makes His grace necessary</u>. If it were not for God's holiness, the Cross and grace would not have been necessary. If God were not holy, Jesus' blood would be common blood. God's holiness is the first attribute He gives to us as Christians. We can be holy, only because He is holy. Do you see why we will be forever praising God in Heaven for His holiness? Jesus Christ alone makes us holy and acceptable to God.

<u>The holiness of God is seen in the work of the Holy Spirit</u>. God gives us His Holy Spirit by leading us to salvation in Christ. Then the Holy Spirit walks with us every day. The Holy Spirit seals our redemption, keeping us in the faith, meaning God will never take His holiness away from us! In fact, God's holiness is given to us as an *"irrevocable"* gift in Romans 11:29.

The Spirit of God is not a common spirit, but is the Holy Spirit. The Holy Spirit gives us guilt when we sin, John 16:7-8. Why? To drive us back to holiness, so that we might remain holy! The Holy Spirit also gives us peace and joy in the Christian life when we are obedient. Why? So that we might see the need to remain holy. God's holiness is exalted more than any other attribute in the Bible. We will eternally praise God for His holiness. We should begin to do it today!

Prayer: O Lord, we exalt You our God, and worship at Your footstool, for You are holy! Help us who are blind, to see that Your holiness cannot accept sin in any form. Help us to see that Your forgiveness makes us perfectly holy, without which no one will see the Lord. May holiness be our constant pursuit! In Jesus' name we pray. Amen.

January 23

"Now may the God of patience and comfort grant you to be like-minded toward one another, according to Christ Jesus."
Romans 15:5 NKJV

The Patience of God - Part 1

The patience of God in the original Hebrew is described as God being slow to anger against sinners who have offended His holiness. <u>God's "patience" is His ability to sustain or endure great insult and injury without immediately avenging Himself</u>. God's *"patience"* shows His complete control over His character. It is because of God's *"patience"* that His mercy has time to work.

The *"patience"* of God is meant to produce *"patience"* in us. In the love chapter, 1 Corinthians 13:4-8, *"patience"* is listed first for a very good reason. As new believers, our love now becomes *"patient."* The reason is that God the Father, Son, and Holy Spirit have put new graces in us — changing our hearts. The attribute of *"patience"* opens up the way for other necessary changes in our personalities. *"Patience"* gives us the ability to bear trials without grumbling because we now see what God is doing.

Many verses show us why and how to be *"patient."* *"Do not be overcome with evil, but overcome evil with good."* It takes God's Spirit in our spirit to replace our anger and bitterness with forgiveness. God, forgiving our sin, comes with a new responsibility to be gracious to others. We can do that if we are *"patient."* We all have relationship problems that need fixing. *"When you stand praying, if you hold anything against anyone, forgive him, so that your Father in Heaven may forgive you your sins,"* Mark 11:25. If it were not for the *"patience"* of God in us, we would never have the desire or ability to forgive those who do not deserve it!

Prayer: Beautiful Lord, we worship You for Your patience. Forgive us for not following Your loving example by being patient to others. Lord, have mercy on us and move us to be more patient! We realize that it is only through the *"patience"* of the Father, the Son and the Spirit that we too can have *"patience."* We pray to You in the name of our patient Savior, Jesus Christ. Amen.

January 24

"What if God, choosing to show His wrath and make His power known, bore with great patience the objects of His wrath – prepared for destruction?" Romans 9:22

The Patience of God - Part 2

In our text, we learn that God did not in His eternal plan intend to give salvation to every person in the world. Paul teaches us how God's *"great patience"* works in a world filled with unbelievers.

Paul began this chapter saying, *"I tell the truth in Christ, I am not lying."* Then for five verses Paul explains how *"the covenants,"* *"the law,"* *"the promises,"* and *"the patriarchs"* did not fail when some were not saved. In verse six he concludes, *"It is not as if God's Word had failed."* Why? *"For not all who are descended from Israel are Israel."* Not all are Christian. Paul shows how God intended to save Jacob but not Esau. Then in verse 14-15, Paul answers our objections. *"What shall we say? Is God unjust? Not at all! For He says to Moses, 'I will have mercy on whom I have mercy, and I will have compassion on whom I have compassion.'"*

In verse 17, Paul shows God's great *"patience"* in bringing King Pharaoh into the world, only to defeat and destroy him. *"For the Scripture says to Pharaoh: 'I raised you up for this very purpose, that I might display My power in you and that My name might be proclaimed in all the earth.'"* Paul teaches us, in vs. 21, *"Does not the potter have the right to make out of the same lump of clay some pottery for noble purposes and some for common use?"* God here is *"the potter"* and we are the *"clay."* God making *"some pottery for noble purposes,"* is His gift of saving grace to us.

We see the depth of the *"patience"* of God with unbelievers. *"What if God, choosing to show His wrath and make His power known, bore with great patience the objects of His wrath – prepared for destruction?"* Romans 9:22. This is the height of the *"patience"* of God. He puts up with a lifetime of foolishness from those who are headed for Hell. How great is God's grace to us who believe!

Prayer: Sovereign Lord, we thank You for helping us understand Your *"patience."* May this encourage us to be patient to our enemies! Help us to display Your attributes. In Jesus' name we pray. Amen.

January 25

"Oh, give thanks to the LORD, for He is good! For His mercy endures forever." Psalm 136:1 NKJV

The Mercy of God - Part 1

The mercy of God is different than His providence and love. God's providence is His inexhaustible and eternal storehouse of everything a believer needs both spiritual and physical. His love is why He gives the storehouse to us. God's mercy now, is His commitment in giving His inexhaustible supply to us who do not deserve it.

God's "mercy" is eternal. If God's *"mercy endures forever,"* it has to be eternal. There will never be a time when God fails to be merciful to those whom He caused to believe. God cannot help but be merciful because that is His character. Our text gives thanks for God's never-ending mercy to His true believers.

God's mercy is judicial. God the Eternal Judge gives mercy to us by taking away our death sentence. Mercy is a judicial term for when a judge gives a guilty offender a lesser sentence than what is deserved. When God gives us eternal life instead of eternal death, that is judicial mercy to the greatest possible degree!

God's mercy is limited, thus very personal. God's mercy is not given to everyone! Salvation is a gift. If an earthly judge were to pardon every prisoner, would not their mercy then cease to be mercy? By definition, the word mercy has to be limited and personal. Why do some of us have a problem with this? Our problem has to be that we think everyone deserves salvation. Not true. Everyone deserves death! *"The wages of sin is death."* Even John 3:16 that so many misquote, is teaching that God saves some people from every tribe, tongue and nation in the world, but not every single person in the world.

Prayer: Most holy and loving Lord, we praise You for giving us Your judicial mercy when we deserved spiritual death. We stand in awe of Your tender mercy that is given simply because of Your good pleasure and nothing at all that is within us! That is why we will lovingly sing for all eternity, "Worthy is the Lamb!" In Jesus' most merciful name we pray. Amen.

January 26

"Blessed be the God and Father of our Lord Jesus Christ, who according to His abundant mercy has begotten us again to a living hope through the resurrection of Jesus Christ from the dead."
1 Peter 1:3 NKJV

The Mercy of God - Part 2

We have already seen that the mercy of God is eternal, judicial and limited. But God's mercy also endures. We sinners resist God, but His mercy still endures. It keeps on working. We have been disobedient and have broken every law, but His mercy endures! The last day of the life of every unbeliever is coming, but God's mercy still endures until the day of our death! Spurgeon said of God's mercy:

> "Do not dream of asking God for justice, for justice will be your ruin. But get hold of this word, 'Lord, I ask for mercy.' And if something whispers, 'Why, you have been a hardened sinner,' say 'Lord, it is true. But I ask for mercy.' 'But you have been a backslider.' Reply, 'Lord, that I have been, but I ask for mercy on that account.' 'But you have resisted and rejected grace.' 'Lord, that is very true. But I shall want all the more mercy because of that.' 'But there is nothing in you to argue for forgiveness.' Say, 'Lord, I know there is not, and that is why I ask for Your mercy.'"

God's mercy must also move us to pray, to give thanks, and to worship Him. How much we need to meditate on the mercies that are ours by faith through Christ! Think how God was merciful to Daniel's three friends and saved them from the fiery furnace. Think how God saved Queen Esther from the wicked killer Haman, just in time! Think of how God gave King Hezekiah 15 more years to live. This is our God who still gives us "*mercy*" when we need it most.

Prayer: Merciful Lord, open our eyes to see that You are as merciful today as You were to those in Bible times. Lord, we deserve Your eternal wrath, but "*mercy*" is what we need. May the "*mercy*" You give, create "*mercy*" in us, not the wrath we often show! Lord, we cannot properly thank You for Your "*mercy*." We praise Your "*mercy*" now, and in all eternity. In Jesus' name we pray. Amen.

January 27

"When times are good, be happy; but when times are bad, consider: God has made the one as well as the other."
Ecclesiastes 7:14a

The Sovereignty of God - Part 1

Jerry Bridges defines the sovereignty of God as "His constant care for and His absolute rule and control over all of His creation for His own glory and the good of His people." The sovereignty of God does not allow for anything in our life to be fate or chance. Romans 8:28 says that for a believer, God works all things for our good and for His glory. This is the sovereignty of God at work, for which we must, *"Give thanks in all circumstances,"* 1 Thessalonians 5:18.

It is common for us to talk about the sovereignty of God when "good" things happen. We do not doubt the sovereignty of God then! But when "bad" things happen, we say it was fate, chance or bad luck. Not so, <u>the sovereignty of God is His constant care for and absolute rule over all of creation including us</u>. If there is a single event anywhere in the history of the world that is outside the sovereign will of God, then God is not totally in control of everything. Could we trust God, if He was not in total control?

If we can't trust God to the events of our everyday life now, then how can we trust that God will care for us in eternity? *"Many are the plans in a man's heart, but it is the LORD's purpose that prevails,"* Proverbs 19:21. Revelation 3:7 says about God *"what He opens no one can shut, and what He shuts no one can open."* With these things in mind, can someone curse us, trouble us or do great harm to us apart from the will of God for us? With the doctrine of the sovereignty of God in mind, the answer to such questions is a big "NO." Lamentations 3:37 is clear, *"Who can speak and have it happen if the LORD has not decreed it?"*

Prayer: Dear faithful and all-powerful Lord, our faith is tested to see if we will trust in Your sovereignty. Help us to understand Your sovereignty more so that we can learn to trust You more! Help us to see You are always true to Your Word and character. In Jesus' name we pray. Amen.

January 28

"Look at the birds of the air; they do not sow or reap or store away in barns, and yet your Heavenly Father feeds them. Are you not much more valuable than they?" Matthew 6:26

The Sovereignty of God - Part 2

The sovereignty of God teaches us that no detail in our life is small or unimportant to God! If the sovereignty of God feeds a sparrow, He will surely feed us. If God clothes a lily in the field, surely will He clothe us too. Learning to trust in the sovereignty of God is learning to live *"by faith and not by sight."* If God in all of His sovereignty is for us, who can be against us?

The lives of Esther and Ruth show us the depths of God's sovereignty in the affairs of our lives. It was God's sovereign will to destroy Haman, Esther's enemy, and God's also. A main reason God did this is to show us something! We know from Romans 15:4, an absolute truth; *"Everything that was written in the past was written to teach us, so that through endurance and the encouragement of the Scriptures we might have hope."* God still looks out for His own children. God is showing us His sovereignty in accomplishing His will. Thus, God's power and rule is not in any way dependent on our actions.

The sovereignty of God teaches us to endure suffering. Paul, in the midst of great suffering could say, *"For I know whom I have believed and am persuaded that He is able to keep what I have committed to Him until that day,"* 2 Timothy 1:12. When our hearts are aching, when our bodies are racked with pain, we can keep our eyes of faith on God. We can see the big picture of His sovereignty working all things for our good. We can see that God is conforming us to the image of Christ. We can see that in His sovereign love, God knows best how to make us spiritually much more beautiful. Faith accepts God's sovereignty with trust and joy, not fear.

Prayer: Amazing Lord, we worship Your sovereign will that supplies us spiritually, physically, mentally, socially, and financially. Paul was right! *"My God will supply all your needs, in Christ."* Lord, we praise You for Your sovereignty that selected us in Ephesians 2:1, sends us in Matthew 28:19, and equips us in Matthew 28:20. How great Thou art! In Jesus' name we pray. Amen.

January 29

"For in Christ all the fullness of the Deity lives in bodily form, and you have been given fullness in Christ, who is the head over every power and authority." Colossians 2:9-10

The Attributes of Christ complete us

"You have been given fullness in Christ," means that a believer participates in the divine nature, fully. Christ's attributes become ours, as His character is formed in us. His forgiveness makes us forgiving. His grace makes us gracious. His omniscient eye gives us a different view of God, others, and even ourselves. Because of God's indwelling Spirit we are much more patient. Our unfaithfulness is now transformed by His faithfulness! We do not change our mind every day because of His unchangeableness. His unlimited knowledge gives us real truth. We are able to love and enjoy God and others because of His love in us.

His wisdom is our compass. His knowledge is our instruction. His power is our protection. Because Christ took our guilt, His divine justice is satisfied and is forever guaranteed. His unlimited mercy is our eternal peace. His providence is our inexhaustible supply that meets our every need. His sovereignty is always on the throne to move mountains for us if necessary. The fullness of Christ gives us limited *"power and authority."*

"You have been given fullness in Christ." Notice what comes next! *"Who is the head over every power and authority."* In Christ, every single believer has a Christ given crown. In Christ, we too have power over Satan and his demons. Ascended, our Jesus is now above the angels and demons, not a little lower than them. Meditate on the implications of that beautiful truth.

Prayer: O powerful Lord, You are our everything and our all. We are so complete in You! We were incomplete, but You completed us. How blessed we are. Your amazing grace found us. And if that were not enough, You gave us *"fullness in Christ."* We praise and worship You for giving us the strength to live the Christian life. *"We are more than conquerors through Him who loved us."* We are delighted beyond words to express our love to You. In Christ, our amazing Savior's name, we pray. Amen.

January 30

"Go and enjoy choice food and sweet drinks, and send some to those who have nothing prepared. This day is sacred to our LORD. Do not grieve, for the joy of the LORD is your strength."
Nehemiah 8:10

"The joy of the LORD is your strength"

The Lord gives joy. The people respectfully stood before God in the public square as Ezra the priest read the law from morning till noon. For six hours, they stood before God, respectfully, as a servant stands before his master. Those who formerly ignored God's law and covenant said, *"Amen,"* and wept before God as they heard His law read. They were convicted of their wayward ways, and then forgiven of their sins. These words are for us; *"Do not grieve."* Rejoice, keep your head up, don't grumble. Paul said twice, *"Rejoice in the Lord,"* Philippians 4:4. Israel tried to find their joy in idols and drifted from God. Do we? The people came back to God and *"rejoiced."* So can we!

"Enjoy choice food and sweet drinks." The Lord spreads a table before us. We prayerfully thank God for His providence of good food. Then while we eat, we often complain about His providence in the rest of our lives. What happened to our *"Joy of the Lord"*? When we gave thanks, did we really see God, the giver?

Think about the taking of the Lord's Supper! We don't worship the elements that represent Christ's body as though they save us, but what they are a memorial of: Jesus as our Savior. We must never be so pleased with the way God cares for us, than we are for who He is. God is pleased and honored to save us. Are we pleased with Him?

"Send something to those who have nothing prepared." Give spiritual food to those who need it. Are we yet convicted to help others learn what we have learned? Our grace and salvation from God comes with responsibilities. Jesus says, *"Go,"* with gratitude.

Prayer: Lord, our joy, we know that You are our joy and strength. Forgive us for looking in other places for it. Help us to desire You more than money or a better reputation, and the list goes on. Forgive us for not looking to You first, for You are the fountain of all joy. May we die to selfishness and live for You. In Jesus' name we pray. Amen.

January 31

"Do not be overcome by evil, but overcome evil with good."
Romans 12:21

Are we better than a terrorist?

It is not just a terrorist that overcomes evil with more evil! When someone wrongs us, we, too often, want to "get even." This is natural for sinners. If we in the church are busy dishing out slander, gossip and hurting others, are we any better than a terrorist? We are worse. We know better. We have God's wisdom and strength. *"Do not repay anyone evil for evil. Be careful to do what is right in the eyes of everybody. If it is possible, as far as it depends on you, live at peace with everybody. Do not take revenge, my friends, but leave room for God's wrath, for it is written: 'It is Mine to avenge; I will repay,' says the Lord,"* Romans 12:17-19. Our "repay" attitude is a lack of faith in God! Our responsibility is to "overcome evil with good."

Start forgiving people. Being angry or bitter is evil. Forgiveness is the opposite of being angry and bitter and it is the "good" God demands from His children. We must forgive people in our hearts as well as with our actions too.

Plan ways to be a blessing to others. How and when will we show kindness to the one who has hurt us?

Pray. Those whom we pray for become dear to us. Jesus said, *"Pray for those who spitefully use you and persecute you, that you may be sons of your Father in Heaven,"* Matthew 5:44b-45a NKJV.

Stay in the Word of God. *"Do not be overcome with evil but overcome evil with good."* Jesus said, *"In this world you will have trouble. But take heart! I have overcome the world,"* John 16:33b. Jesus overcame the world with right responses to those who hurt Him. May the Lord help us to overcome evil His way.

Prayer: Gentle Lord, help us to "overcome evil with good." Thank You for Your Holy Word and Your Holy example. We would never know how to "overcome evil," if You didn't tell us, show us, and then give us the heart to live well. We worship You for Your perfect goodness. In Jesus' name we pray. Amen.

FEBRUARY

"Dear friends, let us love one another,
for love comes from God.
Everyone who loves has been born of God
and knows God.
Whoever does not love does not know God,
because God is love."
1 John 4:7-8

February 1

"Fathers, do not provoke your children to wrath, but bring them up in the training and admonition of the Lord." Ephesians 6:4 NKJV

Provoking our children to wrath

In the next 19 lessons we will focus on Biblical leadership in the home, business, church, and school. These are the four discipleship areas concerning our relationships and responsibilities. God's principles of leadership are the same in all four. To *"provoke our children to wrath,"* is the same as tempting them to be angry or bitter. That's wrong because such behavior is the opposite of the Biblical love or grace that God expects to flow from us. Why? Because grace is what God poured into us in salvation. Now, grace must come out. If God's grace is not flowing out of us, it is not in us!

All children are lovingly commanded, *"honor your parents in the Lord, for this is right."* They will be blessed if they do. Parents and leaders make it much harder for a child or any disciple to keep this command if we tempt them to be angry! True, the cause of anger is always in the heart of a person, but we must not provoke or tempt others to sin, *"that it may go well with you."* Blessings follow obedience for us, our children, workers, students, and church members also.

The command *"do not provoke,"* is especially to fathers because they are *"the leader"* in the house. Mothers are also spiritual leaders in the home. Any leader who manages or models their discipleship efforts with wrath, they are teaching others to be angry also. *"Love one another"* is the echo of the Bible. Wrath or anger does not show love! In fact, James tells us *"the wrath of man does not produce the righteousness of God,"* James 1:20 NKJV. If you and I are trying to justify our *"wrath,"* we will find people who will agree, but God will not.

To see the many ways we provoke others to wrath, we will study the "love chapter," which is 1 Corinthians 13:4-8a.

Prayer: Holy and loving Lord, You tell us in Proverbs 19:19, that *"A man of great wrath will suffer punishment."* We also see in Proverbs 21:9 that an angry woman drives others out of the house. Lord, forgive us and direct us in the upcoming studies to model gracious leadership skills with Your kind of love. In Jesus' name we pray. Amen.

February 2

"Love is patient." 1 Corinthians 13:4a

All leaders provoke wrath in others when they/we are not *"patient."* We do not live in a *"patient"* world. Most people want fast food, fast men, fast women, and fast everything else. If we are waiting for the world to teach patience to those we are responsible to disciple, it will not happen. God's truth in His Word is exactly what we need in our impatient world.

"Patience," is that calm, rational spirit in how a person reacts to the sinful behavior of others in his or her daily living. "Patience" is the first loving virtue listed here in the "love chapter," which teaches about Biblical love. "Patience" is so important that without it, we will not have the peace of mind to put into practice the other virtues listed here in the love chapter.

Being *"patient"* in life is saying we need a right attitude every day. We know from Romans 8 that God works all things for the good of those who are His children. Should we not then be *"patient"* while He works these things out? If we are going to "grow in grace," (what the love chapter teaches) then we need to be *"patient."*

The Scriptures show the patience of Jesus as a perfect man. As His believers, God is certainly conforming us to His image! The disciple James said, *"Let patience have its perfect work, that you may be perfect and complete, lacking nothing,"* James 1:4 NKJV.

Impatience is poor parenting. I am "impatient" when I am more concerned about my needs, my rights, and my agenda than I am about the needs of others. I am "impatient" when I am not gracious or flexible to meet the needs of my children. I am "impatient" when I do not give a worker time to change. I am "impatient" when I give a student a task that is beyond his capability to perform. I am also "impatient" when I am rude. I am "impatient" when I am angry or bitter, refusing to forgive.

Prayer: Gracious Lord, forgive us for not demonstrating a *"patient"* attitude in how we relate to You and to others. Lord, Your wisdom and ways are so practical and necessary for us to live for You. Lord, equip us with Your Spirit to be patient. Make us like Jesus, who was so meek and mild. In His precious name we pray. Amen.

February 3

"Love is kind." 1 Corinthians 13:4b

We provoke wrath in others when we are not *"kind."* Being *"kind"* covers a wide range of how we treat others. Being *"kind"* is to be sweet and gentle to another person in the face of adversity. *"Kind"* is the same as being nice, and the opposite of being nasty. Being *"kind,"* willingly respects and blesses others, regardless of their age, sex, religion, or their station in life. Respect is the one thing that all people need! If a leader is not willing to give respect, a disciple will find it elsewhere, even if it is with the wrong crowd.

Being *"kind"* is to sacrificially protect others from outside dangers. Above all, being "kind" is to teach others in the ways of the Lord. *"Kindness"* is the willingness to openly tell the truth, with love. Being *"kind"* is to <u>quietly and privately</u> rebuke someone when they are wrong. Proud rebukes are more like doing surgery on someone without anesthesia. *"Kindness"* is essential to be able to live out the rest of the love chapter.

Jesus is the number one *"kind"* person ever! Jesus is so loving and kind that it is said, *"He will not quarrel nor cry out, nor will anyone hear His voice in the streets. A bruised reed He will not break and a smoking flax He will not quench"* Matthew 12:19-20a NKJV. Jesus is a gentle shepherd and so must we shepherd others, just like our Master.

We do not show *"kindness"* when we provoke others to wrath. Kindness does not discipline anyone in front of others. Kindness does gossip about other people's problems to those who are not able to help. It is self-centeredness and insecurities that keep us from being kind to others.

Prayer: Kind and loving Lord, we are convicted by Your Word that love does not do cruel things to others. We need to hear this because we have been nasty at times, affecting our ability to build relationships. We say things that should not be said. We say things that are correct, but without kindness! Lord, forgive us, and help us to repair our relationships with You and with others. Help us to be like Jesus, who was so kind and loving. In His name we pray. Amen.

February 4

Love *"does not envy."* 1 Corinthians 13:4c

"Love never is envious nor boils over with jealousy," (The Amplified Bible). To *"envy,"* is to sinfully desire what others have, which can lead to trying to deprive them of it. *"Jealousy,"* is similar to envy and the two words are used interchangeably. If we selfishly want others good looks, their ability, or money, how can we love them?

"Envy" is called *"hateful"* in Titus 3:3, *"demonic"* in James 3:15 and indicates a depraved mind in Romans 1:28-29. *"Envy"* charges God with being unfair. *"Envy"* is a deed of the flesh in Galatians 5:19-21. *"Those who live like this will not inherit the kingdom of God."* *"Envy"* is serious in God's eyes, harmless in Satan's eyes.

Because of *"envy,"* Joseph's brothers sold him into Egypt. Because of *"envy,"* in Acts 17:5, the religious leaders persecuted the church by hiring mobsters to cause trouble. Because of *"envy,"* church members and leaders today elbow for position. When we *"envy,"* we are not content with what we have. *"Envy"* places the advancement of self before the love of our children, church members, students and workers, and most importantly, God. When we stop our *"envy,"* we will also stop the fruit that grows on it , which is lying, cheating, and stealing. *"Envy"* quickly leads to many sins!

"Envy" breaks the 10th Commandment: *"You shall not covet your neighbor's house; you shall not covet your neighbor's wife, nor his male servant, nor his female servant, nor his ox, nor his donkey, nor anything that is your neighbor's."* *"Envy"* is idolatry, thinking we know more than God does about what is good for us. Lust is *"envy,"* as it wants more than God has given us. *"Envy"* destroys unity in our lives! Psalm 37 shows us we cannot put on *"trusting in the LORD,"* *"delighting in the LORD,"* and *"resting in the LORD,"* until we put off the sin of *"envy."*

Prayer: Lord, we have envied other people's money, looks, position in life, their spouse, even their house and vehicle. Because of our *"envy"* we have not been thankful, trusting in You to provide for us. Lord, forgive us and help us to understand how *"godliness with contentment is great gain."* In Christ's name we pray. Amen.

February 5

Love *"does not boast."* 1 Corinthians 13:4d

The Collins Dictionary describes boasting as: "to speak in excessively proud terms of one's possessions, skills or superior qualities." Boasting does not love others, because it primarily pats self on the back. Real Biblical love is focused on God first (commandments 1-4) and others second (commandments 5-10). When we put self in the first position of importance, we have our love life completely out of order. Self-first, including selfish boasting is a serious mental and spiritual problem!

Consider the *"boastful"* life of Nebuchadnezzar, King of Babylon. In Daniel 4:30-31a. He said, *"Is not this the great Babylon I have built as the royal residence, by my mighty power and for the glory of my majesty?"* *"The words were still on his lips"* when God made him live like an animal for seven years. After these years, Nebuchadnezzar *"raised his eyes to Heaven,"* (vs. 34) and God restored him. The king then wisely said, *"Now I, Nebuchadnezzar, praise and exalt and glorify the King of Heaven, because everything He does is right and all His ways are just. And those who walk in pride He is able to humble,"* Daniel 4:37.

We are not to boast of our faith either! *"For it is by grace we are saved, through faith – and this not of yourselves, it is the gift of God – not by works, so that no one can boast,"* Ephesians 2:8-9. Not only is our faith a *"gift of God,"* but so are the works we do. *"For we are God's workmanship, created in Christ Jesus to do good works, which God prepared in advance for us to do,"* Ephesians 2:10. Since God planned our faith and even prepared our works, He alone deserves the glory and praise for them! How great is the grace of God to us sinners who deserve His wrath, not His love.

Prayer: Great and awesome Lord, please forgive our boasting, for it works to put You and others second to our selfish ambitions. We have torn others down for the purpose of lifting ourselves up. You clearly tell us in Proverbs 27:2; *"let another man praise you, and not your own mouth."* We have not listened. Our boasting also teaches our children and others to follow our bad example. Lord, help us to understand why *"the law of faith"* in Romans 3:27, excludes boasting. Lord, help us to change! In Christ Jesus' name we pray. Amen.

February 6

Love *"is not proud."* 1 Corinthians 13:4e

We provoke wrath in others when we are *"proud."* *"Pride goes before destruction and a haughty spirit before a fall,"* Proverbs 16:18. Why do we think this truth does not apply to us. Is it because we know that many others are even worse than we are? *"The LORD detests all the proud of heart. Be sure of this: They will not go unpunished,"* Proverbs 16:5. Why does God hate pride so much?

God put each of us in this world, specifically to worship Him, and to be a blessing to others. A proud person wants self to be glorified! *"In his pride the wicked does not seek Him, in all his thoughts there is no room for God,"* Psalm 10:4. Whether it is our looks, money, status, abilities or spiritual growth, it has been given to us from Him alone. Claiming the glory for these is plainly wrong because, quite simply, it is idolatry. God alone deserves the thanks and praise, not us!

We provoke or encourage someone to be proud by promoting them too quickly. <u>We should never grant privileges to anyone before they display faithfulness</u>. If we want to spoil someone, especially children, just give them lots of privileges without expecting faithfulness! God warns us not to put a recent convert into a leadership position in the church. Otherwise, they will *"become conceited and fall under the same judgment as the devil,"* 1 Timothy 3:6.

Pride is what caused Satan to fall from Heaven. Even today, *"A man's pride will bring him low, but the humble in spirit will retain honor,"* Proverbs 29:23 NKJV. *"The LORD will destroy the house of the proud,"* Proverbs 15:25a NKJV.

Prayer: O Lord, our Creator and Sustainer of life, we have exalted ourselves to the neglect of praising You who alone is worthy of praise! Jesus clearly said, *"Blessed are the poor in spirit for theirs is the kingdom of Heaven."* Lord, if You are not blessing us today, it is surely because it is not safe for us to have it. For then, we would be even prouder! If You were to let our *"proud"* spirit win a victory for Your Kingdom, we would steal the crown for ourselves! Lord, forgive us and make us like the perfect man, Jesus. In His name we pray. Amen.

February 7

Love *"is not rude."* 1 Corinthians 13:5a

We provoke wrath in others when we are *"rude."* "Rude" in the dictionary is "insulting, discourteous, impolite and lacking refinement." The word *"rude"* covers a range of behavior that is not respectable or loving. When a father is *"rude"* to the mother, the children learn how to be *"rude."* After fifty years, a cousin told my sister, "I never knew what a loving family was until I stayed at your house. I thought that the way my father treated my mother and us was normal behavior." In the same way, when a mother is disrespectful or *"rude"* to the father and the children, the children are in the process of learning how to be *"rude."* When a manager is *"rude"* to a worker, they promote the opposite of customer service!

Being "gracious" is the opposite of being *"rude."* *"Let us have grace, by which we may serve God acceptably with reverence and godly fear,"* Hebrews 12:28b NKJV. *"Godly fear"* is to have godly respect. We are not only called to reverence God, but also to reverence man who is created in the image of God. *"If anyone says 'I love God' yet hates his brother he is a liar. For anyone who does not love his brother, whom he has seen, cannot love God whom he has not seen,"* 1 John 4:20.

Being *"rude"* is a threatening, fear-based leadership style, not love-based. Fear-based leadership works, but it is short lived and not God's way of managing any relationship. Loving leadership not only works in this world, but it leads to the next. *"Happy is the man who is always reverent,"* Proverbs 28:14a NKJV. When we respect God and others, we find true joy. It is the Holy Spirit (God) who fills us with this joy when we are following His loving commands, John 15:10-11.

In the end, being *"rude"* forfeits rewards! Peter writes, *"Finally, all of you, live in harmony with one another; be sympathetic, love as brothers, be compassionate and humble. Do not repay evil with evil or insult with insult, but with blessing, because to this you were called so that you may inherit a blessing,"* 1 Peter 3:8-9. Obedience has rewards.

Prayer: Humble Lord, we have been *"rude"* at times to our family and friends, basically to those we are called to disciple. Forgive us for our foolish words and actions. Strengthen us to be respectful and loving. In Christ's name we pray. Amen.

February 8

Love *"is not self-seeking."* 1 Corinthians 13:5b

"Self-seeking" or selfishness, is idolatry. Biblical love is God first, others second, and self last, as Jesus taught in Matthew 22:37-40. We need to repeat this fact often, because so many, even in the church, have been so affected by those who teach that we need to love self more to overcome our problems in life. Recently, a professor in a Biblical denomination told me, "College students need to love themselves more to come out of their depression." What foolishness! Is this what our text and Jesus taught? Did David need to love himself more to get over his depression from adultery and murder? Or, did David need less selfishness and to humble himself before God, confessing his *"self-seeking"* sin in Psalm 32 and in Psalm 38?

Is there any command, anywhere in the Bible to love ourself more? No. Since Adam's sin, that is our nature. It is the world and Satan that preach we must love self more before we can love others. *"Everything in the world - the cravings of sinful man, the lust of his eyes and the boasting of what he has and does — comes not from the Father but from the world. The world and its desires pass away, but the man who does the will of God lives forever,"* 1 John 2:16-17.

"For <u>no one ever hated his own flesh</u>, but nourishes it or cherishes it, just as the Lord does the church," Ephesians 5:29 NKJV. We need to teach what Jesus teaches! *"If anyone would come after Me, he must deny himself and take up his cross daily and follow Me. For whoever wants to save his life will lose it, but whoever loses his life for Me will save it. What good is it for a man to gain the whole world, and yet lose or forfeit his very self?"* Luke 9:23-25.

Paul wrote, *"But mark this: There will be terrible times in the last days. <u>People will be lovers of themselves</u>, lovers of money, boastful, proud, abusive, disobedient to their parents, ungrateful, unholy, without love, unforgiving, slanderous, without self-control, brutal, not lovers of the good, treacherous, rash, conceited, lovers of pleasure rather than lovers of God,"* 2 Timothy 3:1-4. We have arrived!

Prayer: Merciful Lord, help us self-centered sinners who have believed the world's theology. Lord, forgive us and help us to put our 'love life' in the right order. In Jesus' name we pray. Amen.

February 9

Love *"is not easily angered."* 1 Corinthians 13:5c

We tempt others to be angry when we ourselves are angry. We all lie when we say that, "others make me angry." In Matthew 15:18-19, God says that anger comes from the heart of a man. It is true that others <u>tempt</u> us to be angry, yet the <u>cause</u> is always in our hearts! Anger is perhaps the most unconfessed sin known to man. We justify our anger when we say: 1. I get over it quickly. 2. I was born like that, or 3. Jesus was angry so I can be angry too.

Our holy God clearly tells us, *"My dear brothers, take note of this: Everyone should be quick to listen, slow to speak and slow to become angry,"* James 1:19. God also says, *"For man's anger does not bring about the righteous life that God desires,"* James 1:20. Who is right? Is it God who says man's anger is not righteous, or man who says it is?

The acts of our sinful nature are clear in Galatians 5:19-21. Here we see eight kinds of anger listed with *"murder,"* *"adultery,"* *"idolatry"* and *"drunkenness."* God's Word is a double edged sword right here. Paul wrote: *"I warn you, as I did before, that those who live like this will not inherit the kingdom of God."* The KJV says, *"Those who practice such things will not inherit the kingdom of God."* The real question is: Are we *"easily angered"*? If God and others see the regular *"practice"* of being angry in us, then we do *"live like this."* The sad result is that we *"will not inherit the kingdom of God."*

By being *"easily angered,"* we actually teach anger to others, provoking them to be angry also. Many people and places teach anger management classes. Does God ever tell us to manage our anger? No. God tells us to get rid of *"all"* of our anger in Ephesians 4:31.

Prayer: O holy Lord, we have *"provoked our children"* and others we disciple, *"to wrath."* Lord, our anger has hurt You and the building of Your kingdom. It has hurt all the relationships in our lives. It has hurt our own spiritual life. We are grateful to You, that You tell us the truth about anger so that we can confess it, put it off, and start loving others. Help us to replace our anger by listening to others as you teach us in James 1:19. Lord, help us to repair our relationships instead of destroying them. It is only in Christ that we can have the heart and power to do this. In Jesus' name we pray. Amen.

February 10

Love *"keeps no record of wrongs."* 1 Corinthians 13:5d

Keeping a *"record of wrongs,"* about anyone is essentially about evil bitterness! *"Pursue peace with all men, and holiness, without which no one will see the Lord: looking diligently lest anyone fall short of the grace of God; lest any root of bitterness springing up cause trouble, and by this many become defiled,"* Hebrews 12:14-15 NKJV. Bitterness is the opposite of the grace of God, and it defiles many.

Bitterness is *"demonic,"* in James 3:14-15. Demons promote and provoke wrath, never peace and love. Ephesians 4:31 says, *"get rid of all bitterness, rage and anger."* To do that, we must first replace it with forgiveness. When God forgives us, He doesn't remember our sin against us in three ways! 1. He never brings our sin against us again personally! 2. God doesn't tell others about our sin! 3. God doesn't dwell on our sins either! God commands us: *"Be kind and compassionate to one another, forgiving each other, just as in Christ God forgave you,"* Ephesians 4:32.

Love, *"keeps a record of wrongs"* when we focus on a child's faults and failures, without noticing their good points. How long can we live without encouragement and not be frustrated? When any person, spouse included, is given unrelenting criticism, anger is provoked in them because that is what is shown to them!

God's grace changed us, who deserved His wrath, into vessels of mercy. Now, God demands that we are to be merciful to others when they do not deserve it. If we expect others to prove their love to us before we will forgive them, we do not yet understand what Biblical forgiveness is all about! *"Keeping a record of wrongs"* is an evil attitude in us that demands perfection in others before we will accept them.

Prayer: Gracious Lord, we are so thankful that You did not make us prove our love to You before You forgave us! We, dead sinners, couldn't possibly do it. And then we expect others, even our children, to earn our love before we will forgive and love them. We have so much to learn! In Mark 11:25, You even tell us, *"If you hold anything against anyone, forgive him, so that your Father in Heaven may forgive you your sins."* Thank You Lord for making it so clear! In Jesus' name we pray. Amen.

February 11

"Love does not delight in evil." **1 Corinthians 13:6a**

To *"delight in evil"* is to be enslaved to certain sins without turning from them. Anytime we love a sin more than we love God, we *"delight in evil."* In the home, church, school and business, we push people away from God when we teach one thing, and then we live a different way. In 1 Timothy 3, it is very clear that it is the way we live, not the degrees we have behind our names, that is the main requirement to be a leader of any kind.

• We *"delight in evil"* when we are addicted to gambling, drinking, anger and the deeds of the flesh listed in Galatians 5:19-21.
• We *"delight in evil"* by proudly telling stories of our past sins.
• We *"delight in evil"* when we neglect to read the Bible and pray for those we are responsible to care for.
• A wife *"delights in evil"* when she gossips about her family to others who have no reason to know.
• A husband *"delights in evil"* when he demands that his family "keep the family name pure," while he embraces a lust problem.
• Teachers *"delight in evil"* when they demand that the children are prepared for class when they themselves are not.
• A business leader *"delights in evil"* when he/she takes a bribe and then tells the workers not to cheat or steal.
• A pastor *"delights in evil"* when he demands that the people repent when he is not serious about repentance in his own life.

   If we laugh at the "naughtiness" of a child, or smile at the evil actions of any person, then we too reward *"evil for good."* The result will be that, *"evil will not depart from his house,"* Proverbs 17:13 NKJV.

Prayer: O Lord, we have not spent much time in prayer, and little in Your Word. We have not put off the deeds of the flesh as we should. Forgive our evil hearts for doing so much *"evil."* Cover our sin by Christ's blood that we might be forever changed. Strengthen us to be good examples of a true believer, living Your way. In Jesus' name we pray. Amen.

February 12

Love *"rejoices with the truth."* **1 Corinthians 13:6b**

In God's process of Biblical change, and *"delight in evil"* in the last lesson, was what we need to put off. That change process is still not complete until we replace it with this put-on, *"rejoice with the truth."* If we do not *"rejoice with the truth"* then we are not replacing the evil in our lives. In today's world, we are in a real battle for truth. To *"rejoice in the truth,"* we need to love what God loves. That is, to *"pursue righteousness, godliness, faith, love, endurance and gentleness,"* 1 Timothy 6:11b. The word *"pursue,"* is important to change Biblically.

To be able to *"rejoice in the truth,"* we need to know *"the truth."* One of the greatest problems in the church is that many people know about the Truth (Jesus), but they do not know the Truth, personally that is. Christianity is a relationship, much more than head knowledge or a feeling. Jesus must be the most important Person in our life in order to *"rejoice with the truth."* Do we have a close personal relationship with Him? If not, then we do not rejoice in the truth.

To *"rejoice in the truth,"* we also need to strive to keep God's holy commands. It is possible to know about the commandments and the truth of God, and still live a lie. Little children, workers, students and church members are frustrated and greatly provoked to do evil, if their "leadership" says one thing but does another. The truth is, we only believe what we practice. If we say we do not believe in adultery, but then commit adultery, we believe in adultery. Hypocrites are bad examples! May we love the Lord with all of our heart, soul and mind, proving that we do *"rejoice with the truth."*

Prayer: O God of all truth, You sent Your Son Jesus to show us what truth looks like. We so often pursue other things, instead of following Jesus' example. We look for our joy in other things, instead of looking for our joy in You! Forgive us. For Jesus clearly said, *"If you obey My commands, (His truth) you will remain in My love, just as I have obeyed My Father's commands and remain in His love. I have told you this so that My joy may be in you and that your joy may be complete,"* John 15:10-11. Lord help us, for we are weak and prone to wander. In Jesus' name we pray. Amen.

February 13

Love *"always protects."* 1 Corinthians 13:7a

When a mother hen sees danger, she immediately spreads her wings to *"protect"* her little chicks. When a shepherd sees danger, he also *"protects"* his sheep. David, the shepherd boy, killed a lion and a bear with his hands to protect his sheep. Loving parents or leaders in the home, church, business or school, see the attacks on those that we are responsible for, and seek to help them.

• When we as a parent allow the TV to openly display shame and bad language, does that lovingly *"protect"* our children?
• When we as a parent allow the children to dress as the world does, by showing more and more skin, does that *"protect"* them?
• When we as a pastor, teacher, parent or businessman are enslaved to lust and adultery, what are others being led towards? God shows us from David's life how it can pass on to others.
• If a leader in business cheats and steals to get ahead, does he/she *"protect"* the workers, or encourage them to do the same?
• If a father does not have a close relationship with his little daughter who is so "relationship oriented," and she looks elsewhere to get her affection needs met, does dad really *"protect"* her?
• If a mother does not teach her son to be gentle, will he learn how to be a gentleman, and *"protect"* him from being abusive?
• Do we *"protect"* ourselves when we gossip about all the wrong things in other people's lives? God said, "Whoever *secretly slanders his neighbor, him I will destroy,"* Psalm 101:5a NKJV.
• In Matthew 7:3-5, can we see clearly to reach out to others, if we do not first remove the plank or sin from our own life?
• Will God hear the prayers of any of us, if we hang on closely to sin in our own life according to Psalm 66:18 and 1 Peter 3:7?

Prayer: O holy Lord, we can see that we can't warn others of evil when we cling to it ourselves. Lord, be merciful to us sinners. Help us to change our living habits to lovingly "protect" those we are leading. May we become more like our gentle Shepherd. In Jesus' name we pray. Amen.

February 14

Love "*always trusts.*" 1 Corinthians 13:7b

We all need to "*trust*" two specific ways in our relationships. First, we must "*trust*" fully in God who is perfect in knowledge and in power, perfectly holy, and perfectly everywhere at once. We must "*trust*" in God, that He will keep His promises and be true to His Word. A Biblical faith means that we must, "*Trust in the LORD with all your heart and lean not on your own understanding; in all your ways acknowledge Him and He will make your paths straight,*" Proverbs 3:5-6.

Secondly, we must "*trust*" those we are called to disciple. We must believe in them to do good, not evil. In other words, we need to believe that our disciples will do the right thing. For example, we need to tell our growing children, the difference between love and lust. We need to tell them how a life of lust leads to Hell. Then, "*trust*" that they will do the right thing, under the control of the Holy Spirit. If there is not a trusting environment in the home, church, school or business, it will be a very negative place!

If we do not "*trust*" in our children to take on some important responsibility in the home while they are still young, how will they be able to be equipped to lead their own homes someday? If we do not delegate responsibilities by "*trusting,*" how will we ever develop leadership in the home, church, school or business?

There is nothing trusting about our anger and bitterness, for then, we are pushing people away. Who wants to be around an angry or bitter person? When we talk gently, in a friendly open way, then we can discuss issues with both God and with man. Ask others that we trust serious questions. "*Where there is no counsel, the people fall; but in the multitude of counselors there is safety,*" Proverbs 11:14 NKJV.

The opposite of "*trust*" is worry, called "*little faith*" in Matthew 6:30b. The opposite of "*trust*" is also fear, called "*wicked and lazy*" in Matthew 25:26. Satan loves it when we "*trust*" little, for then we believe little, and then work little for the kingdom of God!

Prayer: O Lord, our "*trust*" level is not what it should be. Forgive us Lord for not working on better relationships with You and with others. Lord help us to trust in others, expecting them to do what is right, by the leading of Your Spirit. In Jesus' name we pray. Amen.

February 15

Love *"always hopes."* 1 Corinthians 13:7c

No one can live long, or well, without *"hope."* Those who are struggling in life have one thing in common, they lack *"hope."* As Christians, we are called to *"give a reason for the hope that is in us"* in 1 Peter 3:15. The world's hope is dependent on people, possessions or changing circumstances. The *"hope"* a Christian has is not dependent on these created things, but on the Creator of everything. A Christian's *"hope"* is in God the Father, His Son, and His Spirit, sincerely trusting in His ability to keep His promises.

"Hope deferred makes the heart sick," Proverbs 13:12. Those who are without *"hope,"* get sick! Evangelism includes giving Biblical *"hope"* to others in their daily living! If we don't give God's *"hope,"* then we are failing God and others too. In our contact with others, nothing steals hope quicker than our silence or being critical without giving any encouragement. Who can live well in this kind of environment and have a good attitude, without the hope that God gives?

We are tempted to lose *"hope"* when someone in our life won't change. But if our *"hope"* remains in God to change them, while we continue to faithfully love them, then we will wait for God, with a good attitude. When Jesus suffered, *"He made no threats. Instead He entrusted Himself to Him who judges justly,"* 1 Peter 2:23b. If we do not understand that only God can change a human heart, then we will try many weird things to change people and be upset when they don't.

Apart from a changed heart from the Lord, we cannot have, or give *"hope."* Job in the Bible had *"hope,"* because he trusted in God! In a great trial Job could say, *"I know that my Redeemer liveth." "In my flesh I shall see God."* Job had eternal hope! Do we have this hope?

Prayer: Caring Lord, we have lacked *"hope."* We have walked around with a sad face, as if our service to You was slavery instead of true worship! Lord, help us to consider it pure joy whenever we face trials of many kinds, knowing that the testing of our faith develops perseverance. We want to be mature and complete, not lacking anything. We praise You who always work all things for our good. In Jesus' name we pray. Amen.

February 16

Love *"always perseveres."* 1 Corinthians 13:7d

We provoke wrath in others when we do not *"always persevere."* To *"always persevere,"* is to lovingly continue in our relationships, regardless of the circumstance. Paul in 1 Corinthians 15:58b expresses it well. *"Stand firm. Let nothing move you. Always give yourselves fully to the work of the Lord."*

1. The process of "persevering" follows how God perseveres in the life of a believer. When we sin, God in love doesn't give up on us! He lovingly confronts us with His Holy Spirit. He gives us a little guilt, John 16:7-8, to drive us to the Cross where we find forgiveness and hope. The big question is, do we give up on people just because they have some sin in their life? Think of a marriage relationship. When a man and woman marry, they commit to love one another in sickness or in health, for rich or for poor, as long as they both shall live. Then soon after the marriage ceremony, one or both of the members will do something sinful. Suddenly they will think or say, "I no longer have 'feelings' for my spouse." That is not "persevering" in love.

2. The process of "persevering" involves reconciliation. We are responsible to confess our sin, ask for forgiveness, and promise to repent. When we are humble and obedient in this, we will persevere because, in a nutshell, this is the daily Christian life!

3. The process of "persevering" involves overcoming evil *"with good."* By nature, we want to return evil for evil. That is not *"persevering."* Paul had the right idea when he said, *"I can do everything through Him who gives me strength,"* Philippians 4:13. It will take an *"I can"* attitude to "persevere." So often we say "I can't" in difficult circumstances, when the truth is, "I won't." We are told in Revelation 21:8, *"cowards"* will be in Hell. Their love did not persevere. It is those who *"overcome"* in Revelation 21:7 that inherit Heaven. God gives us much incentive to have a love that *"always perseveres!"*

Prayer: O Author and Finisher of our faith, You clearly show us that love does not give up on others. Forgive us where we have given up. Lord, strengthen our faith and obedience to You and to others. It is in Jesus' name that we pray. Amen.

February 17

"Love never fails." 1 Corinthians 13:8a

Every spiritual gift will fail without *"faith, hope and love." "But the greatest of these is love,"* 1 Corinthians 13:13. We can understand our "love failures," by seeing how God's love never fails.

God promises us, *"Never will I leave you; never will I forsake you,"* Hebrews 13:5. God saved us *"while we were still sinners"* according to Romans 5:8. As Christians, God the Holy Spirit continues to convict us when we sin, all in love. God's Spirit gives us peace and joy when we are obedient. Does our love for others reach out to them in the same way? Do we love sinners by forgiving them?

God's love is so great that, *"If God is for us, who can be against us?"* Romans 8:31b. Do we have such an undying and dedicated love towards those we are with? If we don't, then our love *"fails."* God asks us, *"Who shall separate us from the love of Christ?"* Romans 8:35a. Can *"tribulation, or distress, or persecution"* separate us from those we are called to disciple? If it can, then our love *"fails."* No *"created thing, shall be able to separate us from the love of God,"* Romans 8:39b NKJV. Is there a relationship, money, or other "created things" separating us from others? If so, our love "fails."

Dr. John Stott said, "The authority by which the Christian leader leads is not power but love, not force but example, not coercion but reasoned persuasion. Leaders have power, but power is safe only in the hands of those who humble themselves to serve."

Are we willing to lovingly serve others? Jesus willingly washed His disciples' feet to prove that His love never failed. Do we willingly serve others? If we are not willing, then our love *"fails"*!

Prayer: Most loving Lord, we thank and praise You, Father, Son and Spirit, that Your love to us *"never fails."* What a beautiful example You are to us, every day, for all eternity! We know that many of our failures add up to the fact that we have been selfish and preoccupied with serving ourselves, rather than serving You and others. Dear Lord, forgive us. Help us to change our love life, so that *"our love never fails."* Create in us clean and willing hearts, O God! In Christ Jesus' name we pray. Amen.

February 18

"And the Child grew and became strong; He was filled with wisdom; and the grace of God was upon Him." Luke 2:40

The leadership training of Jesus

Jesus had 30 years of leadership training. A two-year-old, Hebrew child was expected to learn and recite daily the Shema, that followed the giving of the Ten Commandments. *"Hear, O Israel: The LORD our God, the LORD is one. Love the LORD your God with all your heart and with all your soul and with all your strength. These commandments that I give you today are to be upon your hearts. Impress them on your children. Talk about them when you sit at home and when you walk along the road, when you lie down and when your get up. Tie them as symbols on your hands and bind them on your foreheads. Write them on the door frames of your houses and on your gates,"* Deuteronomy 6:4-9.

The following observations can be made from Jesus' training:

Jesus learned that leadership is about obedience. Telling others to "do right," is not enough. Leaders must "do right." Doing right must be "upon their hearts." Leaders need a reverence for the commandments, including: respecting all in authority, don't lie, don't cheat, don't steal, don't commit adultery, and don't covet. Jewish men kissed the commands of God when they entered their houses. Jesus did this too.

Jesus learned that leadership is about relationships. A leader who is more interested in personal goals than in the advancement of their disciples, is more inclined to "privileged leadership," than "sacrificial servant hood." Leaders need to be, absolutely need to be, with those they are leading. Absent leaders who claim that "quality time," is a good substitute for much time, are not in time with Jesus! Leaders must "sit" and "walk" with those they were leading. Jesus' leadership example was more about individual attention, than group meetings. Jesus was <u>with</u> His disciples.

Prayer: O Lord, we have not followed Your perfect example. We have been more interested in self-advancement than in advancing those we are discipling. Lord, forgive us for not working on the relationships in our lives. Implant in our hearts the strong desire to glorify You and edify others! In Jesus' name we pray. Amen.

February 19

"And Jesus grew in wisdom and stature, and in favor with God and men." Luke 2:52

The leadership skills Jesus learned

As a young carpenter, Jesus learned how to work. Jesus knew the importance and satisfaction of hard, sacrificial, physical work for the benefit of others. Today, too many leaders don't know how to work!

As a young carpenter, Jesus already learned how to establish a working relationship to accomplish a common goal. Too many leaders today manipulate people to advance their own kingdom.

As a young carpenter, Jesus learned about the work process. He learned how to take wood, metal and stone from its rough original shape, and mold it into a finished product for the customer. Using the very same process, Jesus used another raw product, "rough fishermen." He shaped them into vessels for The King.

As a young carpenter, Jesus learned the importance of character. Today, many leaders learn something about books, little about character. As a result, many leaders have knowledge without wisdom, resulting in pride instead of humility.

As a young carpenter, Jesus learned to manage well. He had a product, His time, and limited resources. With these He learned to schedule, budget, prioritize and constantly evaluate. Later on, Jesus had a tight schedule - three years. He had a limited budget - a stone for a pillow, and little food to feed many. He prioritized events to teach the right things, in the right order. He constantly evaluated His disciples using a gentle rebuke and steady encouragement.

As a young carpenter, Jesus was given the opportunity to display His skills and delegate responsibilities. Today many leaders hang on to absolute control and then think that they understand discipleship. As a result, leaders pretend to care about multiplying disciples and "developing their gifts," but rarely encourage them to use them!

Prayer: O wise and loving Lord, forgive us for learning leadership from the world instead of from You. For You are the Way, the Truth and the Life. Your methods of leadership are timeless. Help us to use them to make Your kind of disciples, in all walks of life. In Jesus' name we pray. Amen.

February 20

"I have prayed for you, Simon, that your faith may not fail."
Luke 22:32a

God's Son prays for you!

Every Christian could put their name in the place of Simon's here. Simon Peter was about to have a very "bad day." He did not know it, but his Lord and Savior did, and Christ was already praying for Peter. Jesus was about to be crucified, yet still, He prayed for Peter's big trial that was coming. What a comforting thought for us. Jesus is praying for us in our difficult trials! The text does not say, "I thought of praying for you, Peter." It does not say, "I will pray for you, Peter." The text is clear, *"I have prayed for you."* And if this is not enough, look at the content of Jesus' prayer for us all: *"That your faith may not fail."*

We know from other passages like 2 Timothy 4:18, that saints persevere in the faith. Our text shows us why! *"I have prayed for you."* Jesus knew that Peter would turn back to Him. Jesus even said, *"When you have turned back, strengthen your brothers,"* Luke 22:32b. It is the powerful prayers of Christ and His tender love that keeps the believer safe.

Peter listened to Jesus. He did strengthen his brothers. The once weak and fearful Peter later wrote, *"Dear friends, do not be surprised at the painful trial you are suffering, as though something strange were happening to you. But rejoice that you participate in the sufferings of Christ, so that you may be overjoyed when His glory is revealed,"* 1 Peter 4:12-13.

Do we fear? Jesus prays for our faith today and heads off Satan. Jesus stops our evil desires, keeping us from sinning. Do we encourage others who do not understand the wonderful grace of Jesus?

Prayer: Precious Lord, we praise You for praying for us. We see more clearly how Satan desires to have us, to control us, and to hurt us. But You, our Lord and Savior, cut off Satan's desires like a stalk of sugar cane at harvest time. Lord, thank You for protecting us. Thank You for preserving us in the faith and leading every believer to an eternity with You. May we tell many others about Your storehouse of mercy and grace! We pray in the name of our eternal High Priest, Jesus Christ. Amen.

February 21

"As He went along, He saw a man blind from birth." John 9:1

Jesus *"saw a man"*

What an awesome statement this is! Other religious leaders simply *"went along"* on their daily comings and goings, not seeing people and their needs. Jesus *"saw a man"* as He *"went along."* Jesus was not so busy doing "ministry" that He did not "see" individual people. The parable of the "Good Samaritan" is a good example of this. Jesus was that "Good Samaritan." Ministry is not primarily about programs, it's about people. Jesus noticed, and then comforted the afflicted.

Jesus *"saw a man blind from birth."* This man was not just physically blind! He was born spiritually blind also! This blind man actually had a big advantage over the Pharisees and us. He knew he was blind. Do we know that we are born spiritually blind also? Or, are we one of those who think that we were born righteous, because we were born into a Christian family? We would not be the first to believe this! The children of Israel thought like this for years. They wandered in the wilderness, never reaching the promised land. They thought their covenant status would somehow save them. After all, they were the children of Abraham, Isaac and Jacob. What about us? Do we think our Christian family history save us?

The amazing grace of Jesus comforts the afflicted! The blind man in our text is us, not seeing or seeking Jesus! It was Jesus who notices us and pours His grace into us. Jesus later asked the blind man, *"Do you believe in the Son of Man?"* John 9:35b. *"Then the man said, 'Lord, I believe,' and he worshiped Him,"* John 9:38.

Jesus also afflicts the comfortable. Through His Word and Spirit, Jesus convicts us of our wayward ways. When we repent, Jesus forgives us and heals us. Then He says to us, *"Go and sin no more."* Jesus makes us beautiful and holy because He sees us and rescues us. This formerly blind man is we who now believe.

Prayer: O Lord, the Light of the world, we praise You for showing us our blindness. By Your grace alone, we can say with this blind man, *"I was blind but now I see,"* John 9:25b. You alone open our eyes to see You! Lord, we are so grateful that You *"have come into this world, so that the blind will see,"* John 9:39b. In Jesus' name we pray. Amen.

February 22

"Religion that God our Father accepts as pure and faultless is this: to look after orphans and widows in their distress and to keep oneself from being polluted by the world." James 1:27

Religion that God accepts

To be acceptable to God, people do strange things in the name of religion. People roll their bodies down the road for miles to "get holy." Others carry rice on their heads for thousands of miles, to dump their sins into the Ganges River. It is not just pagans who do these things to be acceptable to God! Some think pure religion is going to church on Sunday, only to live like a child of Satan the rest of the week. Some think that if they fill their head with "right doctrine" and know the right things, they are *"pure and faultless."* Still others give money, sing songs or take communion to be *"pure and faultless."*

Not long ago, two ducks flew right through the church when I was teaching. They entered as ducks and exited as ducks. God cuts through our "formal" external religion and gets to the heart of the matter. Those who have real grace in their hearts act gracious! They care for *"orphans and widows,"* because God in His grace does! Truth is, *"If anyone says, 'I love God', yet hates his brother, he is a liar. For anyone who does not love his brother, whom he has seen, cannot love God, whom he has not seen,"* 1 John 4:20.

"To look after orphans and widows in their distress," is to care about what God cares about. *"Orphans and widows"* are crying out to God, who is gracious and compassionate. However, God chooses to work through His redeemed children to help the *"orphans and widows."* God could have rained down money on the orphans and widows! Instead, we are to love the hurting with His love! Will we go to them? When the orphans and the widows see our love, they will praise God.

Prayer: Holy and loving Lord, in The Judgment, many will plead with Jesus to allow them into Heaven. But Christ will rebuke them saying, *"I was hungry and you gave Me nothing to eat, I was thirsty and you gave Me nothing to drink, I was a stranger and you did not invite Me in..."* Matthew 25:42-43a. Lord, even with these warnings, we are still more concerned with our kingdoms than with Yours! Forgive us and change us! In Jesus' name we pray. Amen.

February 23

"Do everything without complaining or arguing, so that you may become blameless and pure, children of God without fault in a crooked and depraved generation, in which you shine like stars in the universe."
Philippians 2:14-15

Complaining and arguing is insanity!

We are directed by God to do *"everything without complaining or arguing!"* The reason is, *"complaining and arguing"* is evil living. When we complain and argue, we question God's ability to govern our life. We think we deserve more than we are getting. What exactly do we deserve as sinners? Romans 6:23 says, *"the wages of sin is death."* That is what we all deserve.

Think of the life of Joseph. When he was 16 years old, his very own brothers sold him as a slave to Egypt. He spent seven years as a slave. Then, he spent the next seven years in prison. Finally, the Lord led him out to be second in command in the land of Egypt. When his starving brothers came for food, they found Joseph in charge. They fell down and begged for their lives. But Joseph said to them, *"You intended to harm me, but God intended it for good to accomplish what is now being done, the saving of many lives,"* Genesis 50:20. Joseph learned to trust in the hand of God through all of his troubles. His faith did not complain! Joseph was like Jesus. Are we yet learning this?

Do we realize that to grumble and complain is to say that we know better than God does about how our life should be? It is hateful idolatry to look down on God, as if He is a servant who must answer to us. God is never impressed with our pride and will not bless such an insane attitude! If God were to bless our pride, we would be even more proud.

Prayer: O Perfect Lord, You said in Romans 8:28, *"that in all things God works for the good of those who love Him, who have been called according to His purpose."* We have not trusted in Your goodness. We, the creature, have accused You, the Creator, of not doing good to us in *"all things."* Lord, forgive us for being so proud. Help us to be, *"blameless and pure, children of God without fault in a crooked and depraved generation."* In Jesus' name we pray. Amen.

February 24

"Therefore go and make disciples of all nations." Matthew 28:19a

The Great Commission stalled

Jesus said, *"All authority in Heaven and on earth has been given to Me,"* Matthew 28:18b. Just before Jesus went back to Heaven, He gave His authority to the disciples and then to others in ministry. We read in Ephesians 4:11, *"It was He who gave some to be apostles, some to be prophets, some to be evangelists, some to be pastors and teachers."* Christ gave teaching and preaching gifts to believers. Why? *"To prepare God's people for works of service, so that the body of Christ may be built up until we all reach unity in the faith and in the knowledge of the Son of God and become mature,"* Ephesians 4:12-13a.

Then why has the Great Commission failed in so many churches? First, too many people are looking for decisions instead of working on making disciples! Jesus clearly told us, *"go and make disciples."* Second, practical Christ-centered discipleship is rare because we have emphasized knowledge to the lack of teaching obedience. Head knowledge without obedience, makes a rebel, not a disciple of Christ. James 1:22, says such a person is *"deceived."* Fallen Satan has much knowledge, yet he has no obedience!

Third, too many pastors and evangelists, think discipleship is their job alone. A certain pastor complained he was too busy. I suggested he take a promising young man in his church and train him to help teach. He replied, "Then what would I do?" This pastor's inflated ego was far more interested in building his own name and his kingdom, instead of the kingdom of God.

To pass on the faith to *"all nations"* we need to have more people faithfully discipling others, so that they in turn can disciple others also. Twelve common fishermen did much because they were given the power and the encouragement to go out. That same power is there today, but are church leaders preparing and encouraging those in the pew to go out? It is every Christian's job to be involved in the process of discipleship.

Prayer: O Lord, forgive our lazy habits concerning discipleship! Help us to be faithful to the Great Commission that You gave to all who confess Christ. May Your kingdom come. In Jesus, name we pray. Amen.

February 25

"A horrible and shocking thing has happened in the land: The prophets prophesy lies, the priests rule by their own authority, and My people love it this way. But what will you do in the end?" Jeremiah 5:30-31

Evil prophets and priests

In almost every book in the Bible, God warns us about evil church leaders, and this is still a problem. We see corruption and power struggles in many churches. God is not being glorified and people are not being edified. The *"priests,"* and many *"people"* too, are busy hugging the deeds of the flesh in Galatians 5:19-21, not putting them off. Why? There is only one answer. Where there is little affection for God, there is little commitment to God. How can such *"priests"* and *"people"* lead others to God?

In Jeremiah, we read of God's reaction to an apostate church. Even though the times are different today, God's principles against evil in the Church are for all generations. He was angry with both the *"priests"* and the *"people."* God's judgment of evil in the Church are the curses God promised in Deuteronomy 28:15-68. He will act, if we do not keep covenant with Him. God always judges His covenant people more severely for their lack of faith and repentance. *"Their rebellion is great and their backslidings many. Why should I forgive you? Your children have forsaken Me and sworn by gods that are not gods,"* Jeremiah 5:6b-7a. God was looking in the churches!

God was, and is, so clear: *"I supplied all their needs, yet they committed adultery and thronged to the houses of prostitutes. They are well-fed, lusty stallions, each neighing for another man's wife."* This pretty much describes our growing problem of lust and porn in the Church. *"'Should I not punish them for this?' declares the LORD,"* Jeremiah 5:7b-9a. God was looking in the churches! It is a serious matter for us to examine our hearts to see if we are following Christ and His humble ways of leadership, especially in our Christian institutions.

Prayer: O holy Lord, Your Word tells us the blind cannot lead the blind as both will fall into the ditch. We have seen many falling, and we pray for the leaders in our churches to be Your kind of servants. May Christ crucified be central in all of our hearts. In Jesus' name we pray. Amen.

February 26

"His sheep follow Him because they know His voice. But they will never follow a stranger; in fact, they will run away from him."
John 10:4b-5a

Do you recognize false shepherds?

The Bible warns about false shepherds in so many places. Why is it then, that so many in the church don't see false shepherds for who they are? Why can't they see the power games and the manipulation that these false shepherds are doing in the name of "ministry?" John 10 opens our eyes to the "why." Jesus was clear, false shepherds are only recognized by sheep! *"Sheep,"* are the true believers. So then, Jesus is telling us that if we really are a Christian, we will recognize false leaders.

"The man who does not enter the sheep pen by the gate, but climbs in by some other way, is a thief and a robber," John 10:1. The *"sheep pen,"* is the true church. The *"gate"* is Jesus. A *"thief and a robber"* is a false shepherd. In John 10: 2-4, if a leader in the church does not go through the *"gate,"* which is Jesus, they only come in to steal — for money purposes. As we look around, what do we see? So many are "in ministry," trying to get money, but for whose kingdom? If a pastor collects a big salary but is not really even a Christian, he is a thief.

Now we come to John 10:5, a verse that has been on my mind. *"They will never follow a stranger; in fact, they will run away from him."* *"They"* again are the *"sheep,"* or true believers. *"Sheep"* will never follow a false shepherd! More than that, *"they will run from him."* We need the spiritual eyes to recognize a *"false shepherd,"* before we can *"run."* We also need patience for those who are not real sheep. They will not recognize the false shepherds until they become believers, instead of just "church goers."

Prayer: Dear Lord, our Good Shepherd, thank You for teaching us about false shepherds in both the Old and New Testament. It pains us, and surely You more, that so many are being led astray by *"strangers"* to Your grace. Open our eyes and give us the courage to speak Your Gospel message along with a loving warning. We are grateful that You are the Shepherd of the true Church and that through Your Spirit we can see the truth. In Jesus' name we pray. Amen.

February 27

"Be diligent to present yourself approved to God, a worker who does not need to be ashamed, rightly dividing the Word of truth."
2 Timothy 2:15 NKJV

Do we have our ATG degree?

There is one degree in this world that is worth more than any other. It cannot be purchased with money. It involves more commitment than studying for a master's degree. The degree is, *"Approved to God."* Our text really drove Jim Elliot, who became a martyred missionary. He knew this verse from the King James version; *"Study to shew thyself approved unto God."* Jim Elliot knew he was first of all accountable to God who calls all of His children to be faithful and skillful concerning His Word. That takes study and application by each of us.

Whose "approval" do we seek? The answer to this question will determine who we will work for, God or man. Is the denomination we belong to and their rules more important than the Bible? Is even our ministry itself our idol? God knows the answer. Whose 'approval" do we seek? Whoever that person is, even if it is money that we seek, then that is what or who we will live for. If we are *"approved to God,"* our idols have been exposed and our real problems have been identified. *"Approved to God,"* we are dying to sin. Are we? Whose *"approval"* is it that we seek the most?

"Rightly dividing the Word of truth." There is a truth of God that runs through everything. Are we seeking the wisdom of God in the Bible? Are we willing to call sin: sin? Are we willing to speak plainly about Heaven and Hell? Are we willing to teach others the Gospel of grace clearly? Are we teaching about confession, forgiveness and repentance, the "big three" needed to have reconciliation between God and man? If we are not, then we are majoring in the minors and minoring in the major things in life, not *"approved to God."*

Prayer: O Lord, the Author and Perfecter of our faith, how we need Your approval more than anything! Forgive us for seeking approval from man before You our God. Lord, help us to march to the beat of Your drum. For Yours is the kingdom, the power and the glory forever. In Jesus' name we pray. Amen.

February 28

"Now if we are children, then we are heirs - heirs of God and co-heirs with Christ, if indeed we share in His sufferings in order that we may also share in His glory." Romans 8:17

"Co-heirs with Christ"

What an amazing truth to meditate on. When I took a Biblical counseling test the question, "What does it mean that we are co-heirs with Christ, really moved me. Being *"co-heirs with Christ"* is an inclusion by God Himself, to the blessings and privileges of Christ. God's love to us is always, "in Christ." Just as God's love to His Son cannot change, His love to us cannot change either. Why? Because we are "in union" with the One that He loves. God never looks within us for a reason to love us. He loves us because we are *"co-heirs with Christ,"* clothed in His righteousness.

As *"co-heirs,"* Christ has commuted our death sentence so that we are no longer guilty of our sin. Our sin no longer has a hold on us. We are now, without excuse for a pattern of disobedience. As *"co-heirs,"* we are connected with Him in purpose. We are to live a life worthy of that calling to which we have been called. There is never an excuse for our lives to be in neutral in our growing up in Christ. As Christ has completed His sacrificial life, we too have a selfless pattern to follow in dying to self and sin.

"If God is for us, who can be against us? He who did not spare His own Son, but delivered Him up for us all, how shall He not with Him also freely give us all things? Who shall bring a charge against God's elect? It is God who justifies. Who is he who condemns? It is Christ who died, and furthermore is also risen, who is even at the right hand of God, who makes intercession for us," Romans 8:31b-34 NKJV. It is amazing how Christ entered this world for us, died for us, arose for us, ascended for us and now, presently, intercedes to the Father for us!

Prayer: O Lord, how precious is the present and future reality that in Christ, we are holy, just as if we never sinned. How amazing that we redeemed sinners are *"co-heirs,"* sharing in all that belongs to Christ. But Lord, help us to see that for now, in this world, we also need to share in Christ's sufferings. May we not complain, but rejoice, and work for the building of Your kingdom. In Christ's name we pray. Amen.

February 29

"My soul shall be joyful in the LORD; it shall rejoice in His salvation."
Psalm 35:9 NKJV

"Shall be" - words of hope

Do we think too much of our present trials, and not enough about what we *"shall be"*? Our troubles, our relationship problems, our striving with sin are all very temporary. Today, we are mocked and persecuted. It will not always be like this. In the very near future, we believers will be in Heaven, with the Church of all ages, rejoicing! The song is right, "It will be worth it all when we see Jesus." Thus, we must not fix our eyes on the temporary trials we are going through, but on how our temporary trials fit into the bigger picture of what we *"shall be."*

Do we doubt that we *"shall be,"* sanctified or cleansed because we still sin? David said, *"Purge me with hyssop, and I shall be clean; wash me and I shall be whiter than snow,"* Psalm 51:7 NKJV. David confessed his sin and was made righteous and clean. Suddenly, the *"shall be"* is today, in the present, not just in the future. *"The righteous shall be glad in the LORD, and trust in Him. And all the upright in heart shall glory,"* Psalm 64:10 NKJV.

"The LORD knows the days of the upright, and their inheritance <u>shall be</u> forever," Psalm 37:18 NKJV. The Lord who knows us today, will know us tomorrow. He will never forget even one of His children. If our God knows every hair on our head, can He forget our soul? Surely, if we are covered by the blood of Christ, we are clean. Then we can say, *"As for me, I will see Your face in righteousness; I <u>shall be</u> satisfied when I awake in Your likeness,"* Psalm 17:15 NKJV.

Prayer: O Lord, what hope the two words *"shall be"* give us. By Your Son, and Spirit we *"shall be like a tree planted by the rivers of water,"* Psalm 1:3 NKJV. Even if You were to come back today, *"then we who are alive and remain <u>shall be</u> caught up together with them in the clouds to meet the Lord in the air. And thus we <u>shall always be</u> with the Lord,"* 1 Thessalonians 4:17 NKJV. Lord, help us to wrap our minds around the reality of the words, *"<u>shall be.</u>"* Use us to tell others about You so they too, *"<u>shall be</u>"* in Your kingdom also. In Jesus' name we pray. Amen.

MARCH

*"Dear friends, do not be surprised
at the painful trial you are suffering,
as though something strange were happening to you.
But rejoice that you participate in the sufferings of Christ,
so that you may be overjoyed
when His glory is revealed."*
1 Peter 4: 12-13

March 1

"Is not this the kind of fasting I have chosen: to loose the chains of injustice and untie the cords of the yoke, to set the oppressed free and break every yoke? Is it not to share your food with the hungry and to provide the poor wanderer with shelter - when you see the naked, to clothe him, and not to turn away from your own flesh and blood?"
Isaiah 58:6-7

Lent begins - a proper fast

The Lord starts out in Isaiah 58 saying, *"Declare to my people their rebellion,"* Isaiah 58:1b. God was disgusted on how the people were insulting Him. They were fasting, but the problem was that it was not connected to holy living. Today, people still do weird things in the name of "fasting." Some give up certain kinds of meat for Lent. Jesus said, *"Don't you see that whatever enters the mouth goes into the stomach and then out of the body? But the things that come out of the mouth come from the heart, and these make a man 'unclean.' For out of the heart come evil thoughts, murder, adultery, sexual immorality, theft, false testimony, slander,"* Matthew 15:17-19. God's questioning is clear. "Is our fasting improving our Christian walk?" If not, then something is wrong, and that is exactly what was happening.

God said: *"Day after day they seek Me out; they seem eager to know My ways,"* Isaiah 58:2a. The people asked God, *"Why have we fasted... and You have not noticed?"* Isaiah 58:3a. The LORD saw that there was no repentance in their life! *"Your fasting ends in quarreling and strife, and in striking each other with wicked fists. You cannot fast as you do today and expect your voice to be heard on high,"* Isaiah 58:4b.

Fasting is not about forsaking foods! It is about praying and then giving what we have to others! *"If you spend yourselves in behalf of the hungry and satisfy the needs of the oppressed, then your light will rise in the darkness,"* Isaiah 58:10a. Jesus added, *"Blessed are the merciful, for they will be shown mercy,"* Matthew 5:7. If and when we fast, we must also be merciful to others.

Prayer: Holy Lord, we may beat our bodies so You would love us, but You have already beaten Christ's body because You love us. We so quickly want a form of religion, instead of changing our hearts to love what You love. Forgive us dear Lord! In Jesus' name we pray. Amen.

March 2

"The Son of man must suffer much and be rejected." Mark 9:12

Why did Christ suffer? Part 1

As we go through Lent and Good Friday, it is good to think about how the suffering of Christ should affect us. We know that there is much suffering in the world, and that we also suffer ourselves. But why? We see that man did not suffer until after sin. God told Eve that she would suffer in childbirth and that Adam would suffer in much hard work. Our suffering came as a result of sin. Yet, is it right to teach, that our suffering is sin? No, Christ suffered more than anyone, yet He was without any sin! So why then did Christ suffer?

God the Father caused Jesus to suffer. *"It was the LORD's will to crush Him and cause Him to suffer,"* Isaiah 53:10a. *"He was despised and rejected by men, a Man of sorrows, and familiar with suffering,"* Isaiah 53:3a.

Jesus suffered because of the holiness of God. When you see a Cross, think of God's holiness. God is not cruel, but holy. Starting with Adam, not one sin could be in His presence. The New Testament cross is like the Old Testament sacrifices. Both show the holiness of God in pouring out His wrath against the sacrifice, all for our salvation so we can be made holy.

Christ had to suffer to take the guilt of our sin. *"The LORD makes His life a guilt offering,"* Isaiah 53:10b. Jesus did what we could not do with our own blood, sweat, and tears. We could not earn salvation by our own work, so Christ did the perfect work for us!

Christ had to suffer to heal us. *"By His wounds we are healed,"* Isaiah 53:5. This is not primarily a physical healing, although God is the Great Physician. Christ suffered to heal us spiritually, which is our biggest need. The best healing crusade in the world is where the faithfully preached Word of God changes hearts!

Prayer: Gracious Lord, You clearly saw our problem and came to our rescue. You suffered greatly, to satisfy the righteous requirements of God's holy and perfect law. We praise You for so graciously suffering for us so we can live. May we love You more. In Christ Jesus' name we pray. Amen.

March 3

"For this reason He had to be made like His brothers in every way, in order that He might become a merciful and faithful High Priest in service to God, and that He might make atonement for the sins of the people." Hebrews 2:17

Why did Christ suffer? Part 2

Christ had to suffer to be our perfect priest. We can see in our text, *"He had to be made like His brothers in every way, in order that He might become a merciful and faithful High Priest in service to God,"* Hebrews 2:17a. Was there ever a priest who humbled himself more to completely identify with our need?

Jesus as perfect man, suffered to help us in our temptations. *"Because He Himself suffered when He was tempted, He is able to help those who are being tempted,"* Hebrews 2:18. What a loyal, hard-working High Priest we have in Jesus our Lord!

Christ had to suffer to learn obedience. *"Although He was a Son, He learned obedience from what He suffered and, once made perfect, He became the source of eternal salvation for all who obey Him,"* Hebrews 5:8-9. We too must learn obedience through our suffering! If we do not learn in our painful trials, our suffering is in vain!

Christ had to suffer before He could be glorified. *"Did not the Christ have to suffer these things and then enter His glory?"* Luke 24:26. Why do we complain so much about our suffering? We too need to suffer as Peter said, *"for a little while"* to prepare us for an eternity where there is no sin, sickness, pain or suffering!

Christ had to suffer before He could rise again from the dead. Jesus said, *"This is what is written: The Christ will suffer and rise from the dead,"* Luke 24:46a. Should it be any different for us?

Prayer: Dear *"Merciful and faithful High Priest in service to God,"* how amazing that You had to be made like us *"in every way."* You completely understand our temptations and sufferings as You went through more than we ever will. You now help us in our time of need. We worship You for Your hard work and dedication to the kingdom of God. Forgive us for complaining about our sacrifices for Your kingdom! In Jesus' holy name we pray. Amen.

March 4

"He had no beauty or majesty to attract us to Him, nothing in His appearance that we should desire Him." Isaiah 53:2b

How did Christ suffer? - Part 1

We now look at how Jesus suffered, so we can worship Him for what He sacrificially did for us. By knowing how Christ suffered, we can understand more clearly, how we too are expected to suffer. The following points mostly follow the outline of Isaiah 53.

"He had no beauty or majesty to attract us to Him." Christ humbled Himself so much, that He placed Himself in a body that was weak and unattractive. We walk around wanting more outward beauty so that everyone will adore us! Our humble Lord deliberately put Himself in an unattractive body! "He *had no beauty or majesty to attract us to Him."* Christ pointed us to God, not to Himself in any way. God, help us to do the same!

Christ was *"despised and rejected by men."* The disciples not only left Him in His hour of need, but Peter even denied that he knew Him! We should expect the same, even from our close friends. Do not be surprised if what happened to Christ, happens to us also.

He was, *"a Man of sorrows."* His whole life was one of sorrow. It is not recorded that Jesus laughed. Jesus lived in misery. Why? "We *do not have a High Priest who is unable to sympathize with our weaknesses,"* Hebrews 4:15a.

Christ was *"familiar with suffering."* "*Suffering*" was always Christ's companion. Jesus begged for food, had a stone for a pillow and washed filthy feet. His own Father even planned His death. Why do so many foolish "preachers" tell us, "Come to Christ and He will give you money, big houses, etc... all here and now." The glory and the mansions are in Heaven. The point is this: who will suffer for a few short years here on earth for an eternity of glory in Heaven?

Prayer: Lord our Teacher, we do not think enough about how You suffered to redeem us. We cannot imagine intentionally placing our self in a body that is not attractive. How wonderfully You pointed people to worship God. You were so selfless, and we are so selfish! O Lord, forgive us. In Jesus' wonderful name we pray. Amen.

March 5

"He was pierced for our transgressions." Isaiah 53:5a

How did Christ suffer? - Part 2

"We hid, as it were, our faces from Him," Isaiah 53:3c NKJV. In our fallen state, we cannot see the inner beauty of Christ. And since all outer beauty in Christ was lacking, *"we hid, as it were, our faces from Him."*

"We esteemed Him not." We whom He came to save, rejected Him! He is the stone we refused. Uncaring, we looked the other way as He suffered for us! Do not be surprised when we too suffer for Christ and people do not seem to care. This will happen.

"He took up our infirmities." Christ not only had His own sorrows, He bore ours upon His body also! Are we willing to "take" other people's burdens? We can hardly "take" our own. God, give us strength!

He *"carried our sorrows."* Fallen man has many sorrows because of sin. Jesus willingly *"carried our sorrows."* He did not shrink from this responsibility, nor did Jesus sink from the load. He *"carried"* it until His work was finished. We do not think enough about how hard Jesus worked for us! Nor do we thank Him much. Shame on us! Jesus did not just take our sorrows, He *"carried"* them!

He was, *"smitten by God."* God's holy wrath was poured out on Christ to pay for our sin. When Christ saved us, He did far more than save us from our sin! He saved us from God's wrath! God struck His Son with all of His wrath. The Father beat the only Son He ever had. He beat the Son He loved! The very wrath we deserved, fell on Christ. When is the last time we willingly took a horrible beating for even one person?

He was *"afflicted."* Every insult imaginable was thrown at Jesus. Every one of them was a lie! He was beaten on the inside as well as on the outside. It was us who deserved His horrible beating!

Prayer: Suffering Lord Jesus, You were *"pierced for our transgressions."* You were made sin for us. Because of that You had to live out the sentence our sin put on You. You took our spear in Your side! Your Father spared Abraham from spearing his son, but He did not spare You, His only Son. It cost You so much to bear our sin. May we think twice before we sin, knowing what it cost You. In Christ's name we pray. Amen.

March 6

"He was led like a lamb to the slaughter." Isaiah 53:7b

How did Christ suffer? - Part 3

"He was crushed for our iniquities." The crown for Jesus' head had thorns. His feet were pierced with nails. From head to toe there were bruises. Every one of them ours. And He took our beating from His own Father!

"The punishment that brought us peace was upon Him." The punishment that Christ took, gives us the peace that we so desperately need. It is often said; a dog won't bite the hand that feeds him. Yet while our Redeemer prepared the banquet of all banquets for us, spiritually speaking, we bit Him.

"By His wounds we are healed." Christ primarily heals us of our spiritual sin disease. He heals us from the inside out! By Christ's wounds and shed blood, we are so completely healed that God can look at us as if we have never sinned.

"The LORD has laid on Him the iniquity of us all." Only God has the power to lay our sins on Christ. It was God we have sinned against and God alone must determine the penalty for our sin. No one could live a perfect life, so God sent His perfect Son, who was fully human, to do what we could not do. How gracious are we to others?

"He was oppressed." Christ was appointed by God to be our sin-bearer. Why then do we sinful people put ourselves through many self-denials to try to become acceptable to God? If we could do any good work to "impress" God, Christ would not have been "oppressed."

"He was led like a lamb to the slaughter." Slaughterhouses often use a Judas goat to lead the sheep up a ramp to be slaughtered. But the goat turns off through a small gate just before the killing floor. Jesus allowed Himself to be led by Judas, to be the Lamb of God. But, Christ knew He was going to be slaughtered, and He went willingly.

Prayer: Amazing Lord, *"as a sheep before her shearers,"* You were *"silent."* As You suffered for us, You did not even open Your mouth or struggle in the hands of the shearers. You are a gracious contrast to our anger and bitterness when people shear us! May we copy Your holy character. In Christ's name we pray. Amen.

March 7

He *"was numbered with the transgressors."* Isaiah 53:12b

How did Christ suffer? - Part 4

"By judgment He was taken away." If we accept God's gracious gift of Christ's righteousness for our sin, our very own *"judgment"* from God is fully *"taken away."* We are no longer under the curse of the law because of God's grace through Christ.

"He was cut off from the land of the living." Like a branch of a tree, Jesus was cut off so we could be grafted in. Just as a seed must die for it to give life, Jesus died so He could give life.

"He was assigned a grave with the wicked." Adam's disobedience earned us all a place in the grave. Since then, *"the wages of sin is death,"* Romans 6:23, Jesus had to die for our sin, taking our penalty.

"He poured out His life unto death." Think of Leviticus 17:11 to see what God did for us; *"For the life of a creature is in the blood, and I have given it to you to make atonement for yourselves on the altar; it is the blood that makes atonement for one's life."* What blood is more powerful than Christ's blood?

"He was numbered with the transgressors." Jesus humbled Himself so much that He placed Himself in the middle of the worst murderers and thieves. Even the guilty Barabbas was released, just so Jesus could keep His divine appointment with death! If you are a Christian, this Barabbas is you! As a Christian, you are released from eternal death! Jesus *"was numbered with the transgressors"* to make intercession to God for *"transgressors."* Jesus' perfect blood is crying out to God for mercy, not vengeance! All for us vile sinners!

Jesus as the Creator of all life, even grew the tree He would be crucified on. So deeply did He plan our redemption! Then, He carried that tree all the way to Calvary. So complete and great is the grace of God for our salvation!

Prayer: Most compassionate Lord, we can see Your body was bloody, beaten and broken on the Cross! Lord, may Your death not just be a historical fact, but may it affect us personally, all of our life! You are the Lamb of God that takes away the sin of the world! In Jesus' name we pray. Amen.

March 8

"If you suffer for doing good and you endure it, this is commendable before God. To this you were called, because Christ suffered for you, leaving you an example, that you should follow in His steps."
1 Peter 2:20b-21

Why and how must we suffer? - Part 1

In our text, we see three points on the how and why we must suffer as Christians. It is *"commendable before God"* to suffer. We are *"called" by Christ"* to suffer. Suffering for doing good follows His example. *"You should follow in His steps."*

1. Since our suffering is *"commendable,"* *"Dear friends, do not be surprised at the painful trial you are suffering, as though something strange were happening to you,"* 1 Peter 4:12. If by God's grace we are given the name of Christian, suffering comes with it. *"Do not be surprised,"* but rather, expect suffering. It is *"commendable"* before God. If we do not expect to suffer, we will not do the next point.

2. Since you are *"called"* to suffer, have a joyful attitude towards suffering. *"Consider it pure joy, my brothers, whenever you face trials of many kinds,"* James 1:2. We must have a right response, or a right attitude to what we face in life! That is mature Christian living. We are *"called"* to suffer with Christ! Being angry or bitter, to anyone in any situation, is a wrong response that will hurt us more than what that "someone" did to us. Like Peter, we must learn to praise God for suffering because, *"to this you were called."*

3. Since *"you should follow in His steps,"* start walking in them! We must not complain and say, "I can't," but we should take up our bed and walk. Stop the cries of self-pity concerning our situation! We have God the Father, the Son, and the Holy Spirit comforting and leading us through the valley of death. Spurgeon said, "As sure as God puts His children in the furnace, He will be in the furnace with them." Daniel's three friends were seen "walking" in the fiery furnace with Christ. They came walking out, as will we, if we *"follow in His steps."*

Prayer: Perfect and holy Lord, thank You for giving us a godly pattern for suffering. Help us to have the right attitude towards our suffering in Your name, for it is *"commendable."* Lord, thank You for helping us to grow in grace. In Jesus' name we pray. Amen.

March 9

"In this you greatly rejoice, though now for a little while you may have had to suffer grief in all kinds of trials. These have come so that your faith, of greater worth than gold, which perishes even though refined by fire, may be proved genuine and may result in praise, glory and honor when Jesus Christ is revealed." 1 Peter1:6-7

Why and how must we suffer? - Part 2

God in His mercy and wisdom, allows us to suffer to prove whether or not our faith is *"genuine."* A goldsmith knows gold is *"refined,"* when he can see his face clearly in the pot of gold. We too are *"refined,"* when God clearly sees Christ formed in us. Note that God chose us to suffer for *"a little while"* only! Even as we suffer, we know what is coming, an eternity in Heaven! Do we yet understand it? The glory is in Heaven, not so much here! Who is willing to suffer here, *"for a little while,"* for an eternity of glory with Christ in Heaven?

God uses our sufferings to mature us in the faith

James knew by experience, *"perseverance must finish its work so that you may be mature and complete, not lacking anything,"* James 1:4. We are all born selfish, going our own way. As God's child, we need to now go His way and persevere in the going. For example, faith, not fear or worry must lead us. God gives us many trials to learn Christ-likeness. Why do we learn so slowly?

We suffer so God can use us in ministry

Joseph suffered seven years as a slave, and then seven years in prison. His words to his brothers, who sent him into these 14 years of suffering, are very instructive for us. *"You intended to harm me, but God intended it for good to accomplish what is now being done, <u>the saving of many lives</u>,"* Genesis 50:20. Christ's and Joseph's sufferings were for *"the saving of many lives"* Our suffering as a Christian is also for, *"the saving of many lives."*

Prayer: Dear Lord, it is good that You teach us about our suffering so that we develop the right attitude towards it. Forgive us for complaining about our suffering when You use it to make us more like Christ! Lord, may we trust in You more! In Jesus' name we pray. Amen.

March 10

"It is written." Matthew 4:4a

The answer to temptation

Immediately after Jesus was baptized, He was *"led by the Spirit into the desert to be tempted by the devil,"* Matthew 4:1. Jesus' serious trial in the wilderness was also a test from God to prove His faithfulness. All new Christians will be tested to see if their faith is the real thing. In fact, we should expect intense temptation. If God's Son needed to overcome temptation (and to be faithful to God's test) as He began His ministry, how much more do we need to do the same! Jesus passed the test, overcame temptation, to show us how to do the same!

Jesus had to do what Adam did not do, and He is often called the second Adam. The first Adam fell three different ways to Satan's temptations. It was, *"The cravings of sinful man, the lust of his eyes, and the boasting of what he has and does,"* 1 John 2:16b. Jesus was also tempted three times, in the same ways Adam was, and so are we. Jesus overcame temptation by pointing to the Word of God saying, *"It is written."* Jesus' three-time response to temptation must be ours! Jesus not only listened to God's Word, but He also broke the power that sin can have on us when He defeated Satan.

We have God's will for our lives written down so that we too can see for ourselves what the will of God is for us. The same Spirit that wrote the Word of God speaks to our spirit. The Reformation cry was "sola Scriptura" (Scripture alone), and many lives were changed! When the words of the Bible take root in our heart, God speaks and we change.

Recently wheat was found in the hand of a 5000-year-old Egyptian mummy. When planted, it sprouted and a beautiful bearded wheat plant came to life. So too, the written Word sprouts when it is planted in the hearts of men and women, thousands of years after it was written.

Prayer: Perfect Lord, we praise You for Your written Word. David said about Goliath's sword in 1 Samuel 21:9b, *"there is none like it; give it to me."* We say, there is none like Your Holy Word, give it to us by Your Spirit! In Christ's name we pray. Amen.

March 11

"Having loved His own who were in the world, He now showed them the full extent of His love." John 13:1b

Jesus *"showed"* His love by serving

We have here, a deathbed scene. Jesus knew that He was going to die the next day. In these situations, the most important messages are communicated to our loved ones. Suddenly, sports or a nicer car are just background noises to the more important issues. It is interesting and instructional that Jesus *"showed"* them His love. He chose to preach an important message by simply showing them how to love one another.

True love is serving others. The disciples are gathered with Jesus for "the Last Supper." Jesus *"got up from the meal, took off His outer clothing, and wrapped a towel around His waist. After that, He poured water into a basin and began to wash His disciples' feet, drying them with the towel that was wrapped around Him,"* John 13:4-5. The Lord of all Heaven and earth *"got up"* from a nice meal and washed dirty fisherman's feet. Can you imagine everything they stepped in?

A know-it-all man brutally controlled his wife and children. He demanded perfection in them, while acting the part of a bully. The family was greatly tempted to be angry and bitter, and they were. That man needs to show his love and be gracious!

Are we too proud of our education or social status to serve others? Our high opinion of ourselves disqualifies us from ministry, not qualifies us for it! How can we go to the lost and share God's Word with a proud heart? Consider Isaiah 58:7b, God asks us this question about serving others, is is not *"to provide the poor wanderer with shelter, when you see the naked, to clothe him?"* How can we do this if we are not willing to serve them? We need to stop thinking we are so righteous and start *"showing"* it, like Jesus did!

Prayer: Loving Lord, how You speak to every culture in the world with this "serving others" message. We see Peter learned Your message well. He wrote in 1 Peter 3:1 that a wife can win over an unbelieving husband without a word, by just serving him. He also wrote in 1 Peter 3:7 that a husband must serve his wife so that *"nothing will hinder your prayers."* Lord, may we humbly show our love by serving others as You *"showed"* us to. In Jesus' name we pray. Amen

March 12

"The rooster crowed. The Lord turned and looked straight at Peter."
Luke 22:60b-61a

"The look" that melted Peter's heart

Peter denied Jesus three times, all while the trial that condemned Christ, was going on. Jesus had His back to Peter, yet *"the Lord turned."* All of God's divine power, mercy, and grace *"turned"* to look at His beloved disciple. Even in His own hour of trial, Jesus *"turned and looked straight at Peter."* Try imagining that forgiving, tender, and most compassionate "look" from Jesus. Songs have been written about it. Afterwards, Peter *"went outside and wept bitterly,"* Luke 22:62. Even though Peter disowned Christ, his Lord did not disown him! May this comfort us and direct us when we sin. How often our lips and actions deny our Lord, yet His eye still remains on us. How wonderful and gracious it is that Christ does not deal with us like our sins deserve.

Notice what real love does not do. Peter made a public spectacle in loudly denying Christ, three times! Yet how Christ in love, very privately exposed the sin of Peter. The "one look" privately washed Peter again, just like Jesus did earlier in the day. Oh that our rebukes to others would be like our Lord, who would not break a bruised reed or snuff out some smoking flax.

Jesus is truly the way, the truth and the life. How gracious of God to show us what His love does to others. Others have often heard our rebukes in the street to those we profess to love. A Puritan minister, Rev. Richard Steele, once said, "True love requires rebuke, but it must be given with the greatest wisdom and tenderness imaginable, not before strangers, rarely before the family, mainly for sins, seldom for anything else." May we see that just as a knife dulls with constant use, so do we dull others by our constant cutting them down. Oh, that we were more like our Savior.

Prayer: Precious Lord, how thankful we are to You for showing us the loving "look" of Jesus. What power there is in our eyes to heal or to hurt. Our eyes have said, "I want to kill you" as well as, "I love you." Out of the same eye comes blessings and cursings. May we overcome evil with good, like Jesus. In His loving and tender name we pray. Amen.

March 13

"You shall have no other gods before Me." Exodus 20:3

Identifying our idols

Last night a man came who was very depressed. He had a great job in business. He was soon to be married to a very nice Christian lady. He was involved in ministry and was studying good doctrine. He was even teaching good things to the youth. But still he was depressed. Why? What was wrong in his life? It turns out he had two idols. He had made his ministry into an idol, and he also had a pornography problem, another idol.

You can easily understand the idol of pornography. But how can ministry itself be an idol? Isn't that what we are supposed to be doing? Yes, it is! <u>But what if our doing ministry, the going here and there, is more important than our relationship with our God?</u> There is a huge difference between knowing the Word of God than knowing the God of the Word! The first commandment is, *"You shall have no other gods before Me,"* Exodus 20:3. Ministry to others, although good, is not a substitute for knowing God. <u>Our great God is more interested in what we are becoming, than what we are doing</u>.

What if you owned a big business and your son worked for you and ran that business quite well. Would you not be pleased with such a son? You would! But what if this son basically ignored you and almost never talked to you? What if your son thought more of the married lady next door and viewing her beauty, than in spending time with you? Even though your son worked hard to impress you, after working hours he secretly helped your enemy Satan, build his business. Would you not be hurt? Would your son not be a double agent, a traitor?

It is possible to know good doctrine and still not love God more than all else. Christianity is about relationships! God wants to know us and for us to know Him! After that, our life will fall into place. Jesus said, *"seek first His kingdom and His righteousness, and all these things will be given to you as well,"* Matthew 6:33.

Prayer: O holy Lord, we seek a closer walk with You. Fill us with Your presence Lord, that we may shout Your praises. Protect us from the evil one who tries to pull us away from You. In Jesus' name we pray. Amen.

March 14

"See, I have engraved you on the palms of My hands."
Isaiah 49:16a

Is your name written on Christ's hands?

How precious are the words of Jesus in our text, and they are true for every single Christian! How personal and amazing it is, that Christ wrote our name, right where He can always see it. Writing our names on the palm of His hand is not just a figure of speech! Christ actually moved an engraver to hammer nails right through both of His palms, to nail Himself to that Cross. Meditate on how Christ, not only planned it all, but the all-seeing omniscient eye of God the Father, watched His plan of salvation unfold. How great is God's love for us, His children!

After Jesus arose from the dead, the disciples saw Jesus. *"Now Thomas (called Didymus), one of the Twelve, was not with the disciples when Jesus came. So the other disciples told him, 'We have seen the Lord!' But he said to them, 'Unless I see the nail marks in His hands and put my finger where the nails were, and put my hand into His side, I will not believe it,"* John 20:24-25. A week later, *"Jesus said to Thomas, 'Put your finger here; see My hands. Reach out your hand and put it into My side. Stop doubting and believe,'"* John 20:27. Thomas saw the risen Jesus. Thomas saw the engraved hands, realizing that those nail marks were for him personally. Thomas believed, do we? What we believe about Jesus' nail prints is eternally important!

The song, "Is my name written there," has a second verse: "Lord, my sins they are many, like the sands of the sea, But Thy blood, O my Savior, is sufficient for me; For thy promise is written in bright letters that glow, 'Tho your sins be as scarlet, I will make them like snow." The chorus is, "Yes, my name's written there on the page white and fair. In the book of Thy kingdom, Yes, my name is written there!"

Prayer: Forgiving Lord, how amazing is Your grace in loving such vile sinners like us. How beautiful that even before we knew You, already You wrote our names on the palms of Your hands. You loved us while we hated You. We worship You for Your grace and for giving us such a personal and private salvation. May Your name be forever praised! In Jesus' name we pray. Amen.

March 15

"'But LORD,' Gideon asked, 'how can I save Israel? My clan is the weakest in Manasseh, and I am the least in my family.'"
Judges 6:15

God uses common people!

David was a shepherd boy; Esther was an orphan; the disciples were fishermen, and Jesus was a carpenter. Gideon was a humble country boy, very weak in the eyes of the people, yet chosen by God. Are you small and weak? God can and will use you too.

Israel had again rejected God. For seven years God *"gave them into the hands of the Midianites,"* Judges 6:1b. The Midianites ruined their crops, killed their animals, and overran the land. *"Midian so impoverished the Israelites that they cried out to the LORD for help,"* Judges 6:6. Israel's suffering was because of their disobedience. God finally brought about a deliverer named Gideon. God chose a weak man to show that the victory was His alone. If God had used a powerful or highly educated man, they could claim that the victory was because of their ability! God has not changed. God still, *"gives strength to the weary and increases the power of the weak,"* Isaiah 40:29.

Are we weak also? Have hope! *"God chose the foolish things of the world to shame the wise; God chose the weak things of the world to shame the strong. He chose the lowly things of this world and the despised things — and the things that are not — to nullify the things that are, so that no one may boast before Him,"* 1 Corinthians 1:27-29.

God will use common people to do His work. When He does, the more educated will mock and ridicule, saying we are not qualified. God says we are, through His strength. We must not think like the Pharisees who were so proud of their education that they had no room for God. That is self-righteousness. Thinking that we need Bible school or Seminary training to qualify us for a lifetime of service to God stops many. God still uses common people.

Prayer: O Lord of our co-mission, keep us near the Cross, dependent on You who said, *"My power is made perfect in weakness.'"* 2 Corinthians 12:9b. May we say, *"for Christ sake, I delight in weaknesses, in insults, in hardships, in persecutions, in difficulties. For when I am weak then I am strong"* In Christ's name we pray. Amen.

March 16

"'Leave her alone,' said Jesus, 'Why are you bothering her? She has done a beautiful thing to Me.'" Mark 14:6

People will mock you!

Our text comes from the scene in Mark 14:1-11. Here Jesus rebukes those who criticized the woman from Bethany for pouring a bottle of expensive perfume on His head.

First, in the 4th verse, some people had a better idea about what this woman could do for the Lord. Jesus did not agree. This woman likely spent her inheritance for her Lord. The question for us is, will we spend our self for Him?

Second, this woman was not concerned about what others thought! She had eyes for her Lord and Savior alone. Nothing stood in her way of serving Him. She knew others would mock her, but she worshiped Him anyway. If we give our all to Christ, we will be mocked. Do we fear to love Christ because others might mock us?

Third, it is likely that the disciples were mocking her! When we honor Christ with our lives, most of the criticism will come from within the church. When it happens, know the mind of Christ! *"'Leave her alone,' said Jesus, 'Why are you bothering her? She has done a beautiful thing to Me,'"* Mark 14:6.

Fourth, *"She did what she could,"* Mark 14:8a. People do have different gifts and abilities. She sought to bring honor to Christ. She understood Jesus' coming death. She was grateful for what Christ did for her. She was compelled to express her gratitude. She hungered to give her all to Him who gave His all for her!

Fifth, in verse 10 we see Judas, one of the 12 disciples. He sold Jesus for a small amount of money. Great was his sin of pretending to love Jesus, only to sell Him for so little. What are we willing to give for our Lord who bought us with His precious blood?

Prayer: O Lord, we are put to shame by this woman who gave her all for You! So often we hold back because we are more concerned about what others think, than what You think. Lord, forgive us. May we do "beautiful things" for You, to show our appreciation for how You poured out Your life for us! Lord accept our thanksgiving and praise for such a great salvation. In Jesus' name we pray. Amen.

March 17

"The heart is deceitful above all things and beyond cure. Who can understand it? I the LORD search the heart and examine the mind, to reward a man according to his conduct, according to what his deeds deserve." Jeremiah 17:9-10

What our hearts are really like

We learn in our text that our hearts are *"beyond cure."* The NKJV reads, *"desperately wicked."* The Bible teaches that we are born, 100% sold out to Satan. No wonder we are so *"deceived."* We are so far off, that God tells us, *"there is a way that seems right to a man, but in the end it leads to death,"* Proverbs 14:12. An example will help.

The world today teaches that man hates himself, suggesting that he needs to love himself more to come out of his problems. Jesus teaches, *"No one ever hated his own body, but he feeds and cares for it, just as Christ does the church,"* Ephesians 5:29. Who will we believe? There is such a world of difference between these two "theologies." Will we believe Jesus who says that no one hates himself and that we need to deny self? Or, will we believe man who says that our big problem in life is that we hate ourselves and need to love self more? Apart from God's Word, we have no clue as to what ails us!

God asks us concerning our hearts. *"Who can understand it?"* Only God fully knows what our hearts are like! Only by reading His Word do we begin to understand what we are like! Compared to God, the natural man in all his sin is, *"only a worm,"* in Job 25:6b; *"only a breath,"* in Psalm 62:9b; *"like grass,"* in Isaiah 40:6; *"senseless and without knowledge,"* in Jeremiah 51:17a. Even *"all the nations are... worthless and less than nothing'"* in Isaiah 40:17. James says, *"Why, you do not even know what will happen tomorrow. What is your life? You are a mist that appears for a little while and then vanishes,"* James 4:14.

Prayer: Eternally wise Lord, we thank and praise You for telling us the true condition of our hearts. Forgive us for being so proud and arrogant! We pray that we may live out Proverbs 3:5-6, that says, *"Trust in the LORD with all your heart and lean not on your own understanding; in all your ways acknowledge Him, and He will make your paths straight."* In Christ Jesus' name we pray. Amen.

March 18

"The prayer of the upright is His delight." Proverbs 15:8b NKJV

Five ways we are not *"upright"* in prayer

1. We are not praying. *"You do not have because you do not ask God,"* James 4:2. We need to ask to receive! It is true that when we work, we work. But when we pray, God works.

2. We will not let go of a certain sin. Do we keep a pet sin close to our heart? David committed adultery and did not confess it; and he grew spiritually and physically weak. David knew; *"If I had cherished sin in my heart, the LORD would not have listened,"* Psalm 66:18. It is wise to confess specific sin early on in our prayers, so God will hear us. This is exactly what Mark 11:25 also teaches.

3. We are selfish. *"When you ask, you do not receive, because you ask with wrong motives, that you may spend what you get on your pleasures,"* James 4:3. If God were to bless proud and selfish people, we would become even prouder. In Matthew 22:37-40, love for God must be first in our lives and love for others must be second. Do our prayers reflect that? How concerned are we for God's reputation?

4. We have relationship problems. *"If anyone says, 'I love God,' yet hates his brother, he is a liar. For anyone who does not love his brother, whom he has seen, cannot love God, whom he has not seen. And He has given us this command: Whoever loves God must also love his brother,"* 1 John 4:20-21. Are we fixing our relationships?

5. We have unbelief. If we are not convinced God can do something, why should He do it? *"Now faith is being sure of what we hope for and <u>certain of what we do not see,</u>"* Hebrews 11:1. Faith believes in the powerful attributes of God. *"But when he asks, he must believe and not doubt, because he who doubts is like a wave of the sea, blown and tossed by the wind. That man should not think he will receive anything from the Lord,"* James 1:6-7. Lord, help us to believe!

Prayer: O Lord, we have often said we are too busy to pray, but the truth is, we love other things more than You. Forgive us and help us to cultivate a close relationship with You and with others. We know You want this, and we want to please You. In Jesus our Savior's name, we pray. Amen.

March 19

"Therefore I tell you, whatever you ask for in prayer, believe that you have received it, and it will be yours." Mark 11:24

A prayer that moves mountains

What is a prayer of faith? Too often we hear that if we say this or that ten times in a day, God will surely give us what we want. But if this is true, then God is like a candy machine in the sky. The real power is us, putting the money into the God-machine. A prayer of faith is a confidence in the Object of our faith, namely God. A prayer of faith does not focus on our "mountain" of problems, but on the One who moves mountains.

In 1 Samuel 17, unbelieving Israel saw only Goliath. He was the biggest and meanest mountain of a man who was nine foot tall, had thick armor, and a huge spear! David saw God, the giant mover, who was much bigger and stronger. David knew that *"the battle is the LORD's"*! The big question for us is: do we have our eyes on God, the mountain mover? If in prayer, we think about God's power, wisdom and all His wonderful attributes, then we will have our minds on God!

Another prayer problem for us is that we are more interested in God's table of blessings, than in a close relationship with God Himself! In Mark 11:12-19, Jesus cleared the temple of those who wanted their "religion" just for the blessings! What is greater, God the Creator, or the things God has created? Right here is where so many of us just don't get it. *"Have faith in God,"* Mark 11:22a shouts to us!

Seeking blessings without a real relationship with God is mocking God! Why should God bless us when we pretend to worship Him just for what we can get? God blesses real heart-felt religion, not mouth religion! God blesses people who love Him for who He is!

Prayer: Lord, we confess we have not had prayers of faith because we have not had our eyes clearly on You, or on Your Word. We know that *"faith comes by hearing, and hearing by the Word of God."* Yet we have not treasured Your Word as we should. Lord, please move to us, when we are so unwilling to move to You! Strengthen our relationship with You! In Christ's name we pray. Amen.

March 20

"Sin is crouching at your door; it desires to have you, but you must master it." Genesis 4:7b

How close can I get to sin?

The title question is the thought of a person ready to fall. Fallen man wants to get close to sin, to see what it is like, to enjoy it. Sin is fun, for a very short time! The covenant youth know this! But do they see the danger? In our text, God is speaking to Cain, also a covenant youth. Cain's heart was not right. He was playing with sin, just like many are today. God is very direct in His counsel to Cain and to us also. He gives Cain and us a picture of a lion, *"crouching at your door."* More than that, the lion *"desires to have you,"* for dinner, that is to destroy you. And Cain still went out that door, to be by that lion. Cain saw how close he could get to sin even though he knew it was dangerous. Quite frankly, Cain had a real anger problem. Look at the spelling of anger. See how close it is to danger. God told Cain that he *"must master it."* Cain was obviously not concerned about it, because we read Cain's anger took another step towards evil, when *"Cain attacked his brother Abel and killed him,"* Genesis 4:8b.

See the principle concerning sin that is for us today. Sin, *"desires to have you."* If we try to see how close we can get to sin, it will grab us like a lion would a piece of fresh meat.

Think of a fly. What would happen if a fly tried to see how close it could get to a spider? Why, that spider would wrap that fly up in its web, and then suck it to death. Sin does the same to us! When God wants to really impress a truth on us, He gives us a picture, so we won't forget it! Know this fact for sure. If we pursue sin, it is addictive and *"it desires to have you."* Do we want to try alcohol? *"It desires to have you."* Do we want to try sexual sins? *"It desires to have you."* If we listen to God, it will be well with us and with our soul!

Prayer: Most loving Lord, we worship You for warning us on how sin is like a lion that *"desires to have"* us. Lord, forgive us for seeing how close we can get to sin! You have asked us in the same verse, *"If you do what is right, will you not be accepted?"* Lord, You offer us Christ and a good life. You tell us to flee evil and turn to Christ! Change our hearts to do this, Lord. In Christ's name we pray. Amen.

March 21

"Here is a trustworthy saying that deserves full acceptance: Christ Jesus came into the world to save sinners — of whom I am the worst."
1 Timothy 1:15

Are you satisfied spiritually?

A former pastor once asked me, "Are you satisfied with your spiritual walk with God?" I said, "Yes." How ignorant I was to the real truth. In the years to come I never forgot his great question and my terrible answer. If ever anyone had a reason to think that his walk was good, it would have been the Apostle Paul. At the beginning of his ministry, Paul said, *"For I am the least of the apostles and do not even deserve to be called an apostle, because I persecuted the church of God,"* 1 Corinthians 15:9. Later on Paul had a different view of himself! He said, *"I became a servant of this gospel by the gift of God's grace given me through the working of His power. Although I am less than the least of all God's people, this grace was given to me: to preach to the Gentiles the unsearchable riches of Christ,"* Ephesians 3:7-8. Then at the end of his ministry, Paul said the words of our text, *"Here is a trustworthy saying that deserves full acceptance: Christ Jesus came into the world to save sinners — of whom I am the worst,"* 1 Timothy 1:15. Paul went from the least of all the apostles, to chief of all sinners. He did not have an inflated sense of importance.

I remember meeting a pastor who was not yet like the humble Paul. He told a church full of people that he had not sinned for the past seven years! He was telling his congregation that they had to be like him if they wanted to be holy. If only he would have told the people that they had to be more like Christ! We all need a closer walk with God more than anything else in our life. If we are too blind to notice that, then God may allow us some pain, to see that we need Him. For we are all sinners who need more of God's presence.

Prayer: O holy Lord, we thank and praise You for giving us many examples in the Scriptures to see our spiritual pride. Help us to see how bankrupt we really are without Christ! Lord, help us to see our brokenness from Your eyes. Give us the righteousness and humility that You desire. In Jesus' name we pray. Amen.

March 22

"The LORD said to Moses and Aaron, 'These are the regulations for the Passover...'" Exodus 12:43a

The Passover

In idolatrous Egypt, the male sheep (ram) was their main god. This god, also called Amon, was believed to be the source of life. The ram could not be touched, eaten, or brought into their homes. At full moon in the month of Nisan, (the 14th night) the ram was believed to be at the peak of his power. God chose this exact time, to deliver His people from the slavery to the people and gods of Egypt!

The Passover week was from 14-21 of Nisan - our March to April. The Passover is the first of three major feasts for which all the males in Israel were later required to travel to Jerusalem for, Exodus 23:14-19. The Hebrew word for Passover is Pesach, which means "their flight." The original Passover was the birth of the nation of Israel. On that night, the Angel of Death (the Lord Himself) took the life of the firstborn animals and people of Egypt. The exception was where the blood of the Passover Lamb was poured or sprinkled on the door post. Only then, the Angel of Death passed over that home.

After building the temple, the people came to Jerusalem once a year for the Passover, until the temple was destroyed in the year, 70 AD. After this, there was no lamb sacrifice because there was no temple. The Law said the sacrifice must be made by a qualified priest, only at the altar, only at a place of God's choosing. When Christ became the Passover Lamb, He became the Priest, the Altar, and the Place of God's choosing! Jesus said, *"Destroy this temple, and in three days I will raise it up,"* John 2:19 NKJV.

Today, we take the bread and wine in a communion service. We do this because Jesus said, *"This is My body given for you; do this in remembrance of Me,"* Luke 22:19b. *"In the same way, after the supper He took the cup, saying, 'This cup is the new covenant in My blood, which is poured out for you,'"* Luke 22:20. The old is out. The new is in.

Prayer: Our Father in Heaven, we praise You for the blood of Christ, the Passover Lamb. How eternally wonderful it is that Jesus takes away our sin when His perfect blood is sprinkled on the door post of our hearts. What power that blood has! In Jesus' name we pray. Amen.

March 23

"On the fifteenth day of that month the LORD's Feast of Unleavened Bread begins; for seven days you must eat bread made without yeast."
Leviticus 23:6

The Feast of Unleavened Bread

The Feast of Unleavened Bread is a week-long Passover celebration of God's deliverance from Egypt. The three million Israelites were set free so quickly that the bread dough did not have time to rise. Thus, yeast (leaven) was not even put in the bread. Yeast or leaven is also symbolic of sin because sin affects our entire life as yeast does the dough. Still today, Jewish housewives do spring cleaning to rid the house of all dirt and any trace of leaven. What is collected is burned outside the city. Can you see all the symbolism of God's forgiveness of sin? Can you see how this feast points to Christ? Can you see how and why Christ, the Bread of Life, today cleanses our spiritual house of all sin/leaven? Can you see why Christ took our sin to the Cross, outside the city?

God gives a very clear command! *"On the first day hold a sacred assembly and do no regular work. For seven days present an offering made to the LORD by fire. And on the seventh day hold a sacred assembly and do no regular work,"* Leviticus 23:7-8. No work because God's deliverance from sin is His work! It is fully grace, meaning we do nothing. Neither did the Israelites do anything to free themselves.

It was God who led Israel from slavery in to Canaan! God also delivers us from sin to righteousness. No heart is changed, until this two-part daily process is in place. The apostle had this in mind when he wrote, *"Get rid of the old yeast that you may be a new batch without yeast — as you really are. For Christ, our Passover Lamb, has been sacrificed. Therefore, let us keep the Festival, not with the old yeast, the yeast of malice and wickedness, but with bread without yeast, the bread of sincerity and truth,"* 1 Corinthians 5:7-8.

Prayer: O Lord, You tell us in Numbers 33:3, *"The Israelites set out from Ramses on the fifteenth day of the first month, the day after Passover. They marched out boldly in full view of all the Egyptians."* As You sent the Israelites out, You also send us! Strengthen us so that we can walk *"boldly"* through this sinful world! In Jesus' name we pray. Amen.

March 24

*"The LORD said to Moses, 'Speak to the Israelites and say to them:
'When you enter the land I am going to give you and you reap its
harvest, bring to the priest a sheaf of the first grain you harvest. He
is to wave the sheaf before the LORD so it will be accepted on your
behalf; the priest is to wave it on the day after the Sabbath,'"*
Leviticus 23:9-11

The Feast of First Fruits

We can see Christ clearly in this Old Testament feast also. The Feast
of First Fruits could not be celebrated until after the Israelites *"enter
the land"* - a picture of Christ and us together in Heaven! A seed of
grain dies and goes into the ground, to come alive once again when
planted. At harvest time, there is a great celebration as the first fruits
are seen. So too, the body of Christ went into the ground and there
was great rejoicing at His rising! Christ's victory over death is our victory over death. Christ's resurrection on that Easter morning, is our resurrection! *"Christ has indeed been raised from the dead, the first fruits
of those who have fallen asleep,"* 1 Corinthians 15:20.

A Jewish man, Alfred Edersheim, described the life of an Old Testament Jew. "Each family, and every individual separately acknowledged, by a yearly presentation of the first-fruits, a living relationship
between them and God, in virtue of which they gratefully received at
His hands all they had or enjoyed and solemnly dedicated both it and
themselves to the Lord." We who know Jesus as Messiah, have even
more reason to wave our hands in gratitude and praise to God!

With the temple destroyed, the Jewish community has not been
allowed to celebrate this feast since 70 A.D. Now, with Christ's death,
resurrection, and ascension, He is the much looked for First Fruit! He
now tabernacles (dwells) in our hearts by giving us the needed, "living
relationship" the old Jewish man spoke of.

Prayer: Dear Lord, what a great picture of Christ's resurrection for
the redeemed You give us in the Feast of First Fruits. You clearly show
us that Christ is indeed the fulfillment of all of the old feasts. The fact
that He is our First Fruit, the proof of our resurrection, takes our breath
away! We treasure the gracious relational promise You freely gave us
through Christ's resurrection. In Jesus' name we pray. Amen.

March 25

"Count off seven weeks from the time you begin to put the sickle to the standing grain. Then celebrate the Feast of Weeks to the LORD your God by giving a freewill offering in proportion to the blessings the LORD your God has given you. And rejoice before the LORD your God at the place He will choose as a dwelling place for His Name."
Deuteronomy 16:9-11a

The Feast of Weeks or Pentecost

This is the second of three major feasts that all the males in Israel were required to go to Jerusalem for. The Feast of Pentecost, also called the Feast of Weeks, was in the month of Sivan, our May or June. It came exactly 50 days after the Passover night. There are seven weeks of seven days each. This adds up to 49 days + the Passover night = 50 days. This seven-week period was a time to meditate on God's commandments, in self-examination. God originally gave the Law at Mount Sinai at this time, with fire, to show His power. Since that time, there was a "Shavuot" service in the temple once a year, on Pentecost. In later years, Ezekiel 1 was read to remember the fire of the Lord and His holy presence.

On Pentecost, the disciples had just been to a "Shavuot" memorial service. They were gathered in the upper room. *"Suddenly a sound like the blowing of a violent wind came from Heaven and filled the whole house where they were sitting. They saw what seemed to be tongues of fire that separated and came to rest on each of them. All of them were filled with the Holy Spirit and began to speak in other tongues as the Spirit enabled them,"* Acts 2:2-4. The holy breath of God descended on the people. This is the same Holy breath that gave life to Adam, and the Ten Commandments to Moses!

Do you see why the people were so afraid of Peter's sermon on Pentecost Day? When Moses gave the Law on this day, <u>3000 died</u> for worshiping the calf. It is believed King David died on this day. There was Ezekiel's vision with God's fire on this day. The people realized that the tongues of fire they were seeing was the Christ they crucified, in Spirit-form. The result was, <u>3000 lived</u> who turned to Christ.

Prayer: Lord, You are a consuming fire. We are an unholy people! What shall we do? We need Your salvation! In Christ we pray! Amen.

March 26

"But women will be saved through childbearing - if they continue in faith, love and holiness with propriety." 1 Timothy 2:15

The high calling of motherhood

It is my mother's birthday today, and she was a godly mother. Notice that the context of 1 Timothy 2 is the worship of God. The chapter then calls women to be good mothers and to be holy, which is the daily worship of God. Today, some women feel oppressed to work in the home, and want out, to try find meaning in life. God here praises a woman that bears children and faithfully works in the home to raise them. Why do some families want to have children, but then don't want to raise them? Why do some husbands bully and frustrate their wives, tempting them to flee the home life, and furthermore, tempting them not to respect their husbands? A truly liberated and honored mother is one who respects her husband and is faithful in raising her family.

Before sin came into the world, "The LORD God said 'It is not good for the man to be alone. I will make a helper suitable for him,'" Genesis 2:18. Soon, in the fall, Eve determined to lead the man, rather than to be submissive and be led by him. Eve was greatly responsible in not only leading the world into sin, but also in pulling down the high calling of motherhood. Many of today's efforts to liberate women only further enslaves and frustrates them. The search for acceptance in business, and making a career in the place of a "home life" is not the primary role God had in mind for the woman.

God has throughout history raised up women like Jochebed, the mother of Moses; Hannah, the mother of Samuel; and Mary, Jesus mother. These stand as examples of how God uses godly, submissive wives and mothers to bring many people into salvation. Husbands, families, and the church need to recognize the sacrificial actions of wives and mothers and praise them for it. The calling of motherhood is still a God-ordained method of molding the next generation.

Prayer: Lord, forgive us for not elevating motherhood! We pray for all godly mothers to see the fruit of their labors, which is their children following the Lord. May our mothers receive the appreciation from their family with many hugs and kisses. May God bless godly mothers everywhere. In Christ Jesus' name we pray. Amen.

March 27

"A greedy man brings trouble to his family, but he who hates bribes will live." Proverbs15:27

Is our greed killing us?

A greedy man is never satisfied with what he has! The gravestone of Mr. Greedy should say, "If I only made another dollar." The Bible warns us to watch for all kinds of greed because greed breaks the tenth commandment. God said, *"You shall not covet your neighbor's wife. You shall not set your desire on your neighbor's house or land, his manservant or maidservant, his ox or donkey, or anything that belongs to your neighbor,"* Deuteronomy 5:21.

A greedy person is completely out of step with the rest of God's creation. Even vegetables and trees labor to give fruit to sustain life. A greedy person wants the fruit of other people's labor. Has God ever given us an example of a greedy person who was one of His saints? No, in fact, greed is the heartbeat of false teachers who are headed for the fires of Hell. *"Many will follow their shameful ways and will bring the way of truth into disrepute. In their greed these teachers will exploit you,"* 2 Peter 2:2-3a.

An auto-rickshaw driver in India complained to me on how high officials took bribes. I asked him if poor auto-rickshaw drivers were included in the bribe game. He admitted, "we are the worst." I then asked him if he took bribes. He admitted that at times he did. Why? Because selfish people want more! If he could only see that if a man cheats and steals to get ahead, God will surely not bless him, but instead, curse and bring *"trouble to his family."* Let us forsake all kinds of greed and be faithful in all that we do. Then we will be a blessing to many, and God will also bless us.

Prayer: O Lord, You who love truth and honesty. We are not innocent of this sin of greed. It is not only an epidemic in the world, but it has touched us also. In our greed, we have been proud and You do not bless proud people! May we humble ourselves and heed Your holy command in Matthew 6:33, *"Seek first His kingdom and His righteousness, and all these things will be given to you as well."* In Jesus' name we pray. Amen.

March 28

"I have made a covenant with my eyes not to look lustfully at a girl."
Job 31:1

Why is lust idolatry?

As a righteous man, Job exercised control over his eyes. His eyes did not control him! Job knew that lust is a fire, and once started and fed, it will keep burning. Job made a covenant with his eyes, a solemn vow that can be much clearer if I tell you two stories.

Levi was a Bible college student with a real lust problem. He told me it was impossible to get through the day because of all the beautiful girls in his class. He would imagine himself being with them. He would do things every day in private that he thought would help satisfy his cravings of lust. I told him this story to help him understand: "There was an Eskimo man in Alaska who had two beautiful sled dogs. One day a city man asked him, 'Which dog is the strongest?' The old Eskimo man wisely said, 'Depends on which dog I feed the most. The one I feed the most gets the strongest.'" I asked Levi, which dog do you feed the most? You've fed the dog of lust well, and it is the strongest. Christ is not a dog, but are you willing to work on a relationship with Him and feed that relationship?"

No one can put off a "lust problem" until it is replaced with a real relationship with Jesus and concentrated on. A habit of lust is fully idolatry because it is more important to us than our love for God.

Levi, if you think lust is mainly a physical problem, then listen to this story! An 85-year old man who lived in a rural village said to me in private, "Please help me, my lustful thoughts are driving me crazy." I said to Levi, "can you see how lust is more of a spiritual problem, than it is a physical one? Your mad pursuit of fun and fantasy are very wrong. You need to repent. Jesus said *'Deny yourself,'* not please yourself. God gives us all desires to use in a proper way. When we use them in a right way, He blesses us. When we use them wrong, He gives us guilt and that is basically, why you are so miserable. None of us can serve two masters."

Prayer: O Lord, the righteous Job was so right in making a covenant with his eyes. Lord, forgive us for our wandering eyes. Strengthen us so You are the number one love of our life. In Jesus' name we pray. Amen.

March 29

"Go to the ant, you sluggard; consider its ways and be wise! It has no commander, no overseer or ruler, yet it stores its provisions in summer and gathers its food at harvest." Proverbs 6:6-8

What is so wrong with laziness?

God is a worker! This alone should tell us that work is important. God said at the end of each day of creation, *"and God saw that it was good."* God set the pattern for work in Creation. He worked six days and rested one. Laziness is wrong! God's created world gives and works. See how the trees give fruit and nuts. Plants give vegetables. Chickens give eggs. God gives the moon to light the night and the sun to give light and energy by day. Who are we to take and not give?

A lazy person is actually a wicked thief, demanding that others provide for them. Jesus taught the Parable of the Talents, in Matthew 25. He showed us a lazy person who was *"afraid"* to work and be faithful. That *"wicked and lazy person"* (Jesus' words) was sent to the fires of Hell. It is that important to work and be faithful. The Apostle Paul *"worked night and day in order not to be a burden to anyone while we preached the Gospel of God to you,"* 1 Thessalonians 2:9b. The Proverbs have much to say about the evil of laziness. It is a disgrace to be lazy in Proverbs 10:5b. It is a lack of good judgment in Proverbs 12:11b. And it will lead to poverty in Proverbs 14:23. *"If anyone does not provide for his relatives, and especially for his immediate family, he has denied the faith and is worse than an unbeliever,"* 1 Timothy 5:8.

If a person cannot sleep, they should try honest work, and their pills may no longer be needed. *"The sleep of a laborer is sweet, whether he eats little or much, but the abundance of a rich man permits him no sleep,"* Ecclesiastes 5:12. Laziness is sin! If God tells us to work and we say "no," we are being rebellious. May God convict us of our bad attitudes!

Prayer: O majestic Lord who works, we thank You for pointing out the seriousness of laziness. You even show us how a little ant is a faithful worker, even without a boss. It is amazing how the ants and birds praise You with work and song, while we grumble and cry about our work. Forgive us and give us hearts and bodies that are willing and able to work. In Jesus' name we pray. Amen.

March 30

"A man can do nothing better than to eat and drink and find satisfaction in his work." Ecclesiastes 2:24a

Do I love and enjoy my daily work?

For years, I did not enjoy my daily work. Other pleasures were calling! The wise Solomon said, *"find satisfaction in your work."* He had more money, possessions, knowledge, influence, women, and more of everything this world could offer, yet there was no lasting satisfaction in all these other things. Why? The more I am in this "counseling" business, the more I see it is all about schedule, no matter who we are.

We say, "If I get a promotion and more money, I will finally be happy." But we're not! Then we say, "When I get married I will then have all the happiness I can manage." It doesn't happen! We think, if I could just buy a house, happiness will come. But that doesn't satisfy very long either! Surely, I will be happy when I retire. No, why not? God created us to spend our time for Him. *"Finding satisfaction"* in our work is when we are in the center of God's will in our daily schedule. The *"satisfaction,"* is a gift from God for being obedient to His call.

We spend about 10 hours a day in our place of work; and at home about 8 hours sleeping and 1 hour eating. There are only 5 hours left in the day! If we are not happy and content in the 19, we surely will not be happy in the 5. We are very selfish people, looking for contentment in what we do not have! Looking for lasting satisfaction in "things" other than God is idolatry. Our bad attitude complains to God; "I deserve better than what You are giving me." "You do not know how to satisfy me."

Convicted by God of my foolishness, I started to do my work to honor God and to be a blessing to others. Wow! I started to enjoy my work more. But then, didn't God tell us to love Him and others more than anything? No wonder I had such little joy!

Prayer: Amazing Lord, help us to live out Colossians 1:10-11, which says; *"that we may live a life worthy of the Lord and may please Him in every way: bearing fruit in every good work, growing in the knowledge of God, being strengthened with all power according to His glorious might so that you may have great endurance and patience and joy."* In Jesus' name we pray. Amen.

March 31

"It is not by sword or spear that the Lord saves; for the battle is the LORD's, and He will give all of you into our hands."
1 Samuel 17:47b

"The battle is the LORD's"

The words of our text are the final words David, the shepherd boy, spoke to the giant Goliath before killing him. The rest of the people in Israel were greatly afraid of this giant obstacle in their life. Their fear was "small faith," a complete lack of trust in God! That is the main problem with fear. Their fear paralyzed them with a lack of action or purpose in their daily living. They were lazy and not faithful to God. Is there a giant in our life? Is there some problem that seems bigger than God? If there is, then our faith is like unfaithful Israel instead of faithful David. I, too, have fearfully turned things over and over in my mind and lost sleep. The words, *"the battle is the LORD's,"* must settle our minds. Let us see more of the context of the battle we, too, are in.

"David said to the Philistine, 'You come against me with sword and spear and javelin, but I come against you in the name of the Lord Almighty, the God of the armies of Israel, whom you have defied. This day the LORD will hand you over to me, and I'll strike you down and cut off your head. Today I will give the carcasses of the Philistine army to the birds of the air and the beast of the earth, and the whole world will know that there is a God in Israel,'" 1 Samuel 17:45-46. David went out *"in the name of the LORD."* David's enemies were stronger than him, but he had God, the "Difference Maker," the One who is "All Mighty."

Jesus said, *"And surely I am with you always, to the very end of the age,"* Matthew 28:20b. The battle is still the Lord's! We need to concentrate on being faithful and then leave the results of the battle to our powerful God. If we could learn this, our faith would greatly grow. O Lord, build our confidence in You!

Prayer: Almighty Lord, in this age of many Goliaths, we need You as much as David ever did! We live in a violent world that is filled with corruption. We have good reasons to fear, but far better reasons to trust in You, our Lord. You are still bigger than life, because You are the Creator of all. Deliver us! In Jesus' name we pray! Amen.

APRIL

"The angel said to the woman,
'Do not be afraid,
for I know that you are looking for Jesus,
who was crucified. He is not here;
He has risen, just as He said.
Come and see the place where He lay.'"
Matthew 28:5-6

April 1

"They took palm branches and went out to meet Him, shouting, 'Hosanna! Blessed is He who comes in the name of the Lord! Blessed is the King of Israel!'" John 12:13

Why do we have a Palm Sunday?

We see here, the King of Heaven and Earth honored. If Jesus was honored and received on this Palm Sunday in the Old Covenant (Testament), how much more should He be honored for shedding His blood now, in the New Covenant (Testament.) *"The great crowd that had come for the Feast,"* John 12:12b. It was the Passover. All Jewish adult males were required to come to Jerusalem to observe this occasion. This all dates back to Israel's great deliverance from Egypt. Every family had to kill a lamb and put the blood on the door post. Then the Angel of Death, God Himself, would pass over their house without killing the firstborn. God rescued the people from their slavery to sin, which Egypt was a symbol of. He delivered them and still delivers us from sin today!

Jesus, as the Passover Lamb of God, did die as the Passover Lamb just a few days later! This is the Jesus that the people received on Palm Sunday. The convicting part is, they did not fully understand the whole picture like we do today, yet still they received Him. If we do not receive the same Jesus and honor Him as King, we too will see the angel of death that will snatch our life away. When the blood of the Passover Lamb is on the doorpost of our hearts, we too are saved from the wrath of God! Should we not rejoice, too?

Why did Jesus come into Jerusalem riding on a donkey? Some kings and especially judges rode on *"white donkeys, sitting on saddle blankets,"* Judges 5:10a. Jesus is the Judge of all Heaven and Earth. Why the palm branches? *"The righteous will flourish like a palm tree,"* Psalm 92:12. A palm branch is a sign of beauty and health. What beauty and health we have as God's very own sons and daughters!

Prayer: Dear Lord and Savior, You deserve our praise and worship, for You are our Passover Lamb. You are the judge. You alone make us beautiful and spare us now and in The Judgment. We adore You. In the name of Christ, the risen King, we pray. Amen.

April 2

"Father forgive them, for they do not know what they are doing."
Luke 23:34

The 1st of 7 sayings on the Cross

We can see the praying heart of our Lord and Savior in this tender saying. Jesus here prays to the Father that the rebellious people who are killing Him will be forgiven. His prayer was answered when Peter ,and John later preached to this same crowd that had shouted for His death. Such is the tender and loving heart of the Lord Jesus Christ. We can see how mission-minded Christ was. <u>Jesus was more concerned that sinners were separated from God, than He was about His own suffering</u>. May His example sink into our selfish hearts!

In our suffering, we quickly fall into self-pity, the opposite of the perfect love Christ showed to us! Loving self first is such a "poor me" martyr syndrome that is sinful. Jesus, who was a true martyr, thought constantly of the Father first and others second. This is exactly what the commandments teach about how we should love. Most often we are so concerned about our own suffering that we do not even think of others and their separation from God. If we die in Christ, we are with God instantly. Others, who do not know God, will be eternally separated from God instantly. That is a far greater problem than our temporary suffering.

On the Cross, Jesus deliberately showed us how to successfully pass one of the greatest tests in our life. So then, *"Let us throw off everything that hinders and the sin that so easily entangles, and let us run with perseverance the race marked out for us. Let us fix our eyes on Jesus, the Author and Perfecter of our faith, who for the joy set before Him endured the Cross, scorning its shame, and sat down at the right hand of the throne of God,"* Hebrews 12:1b-2.

Prayer: Precious Lord, we are humbled by Your suffering on the Cross. You prayed with Your last breath for us sinners to know the forgiving love of God. You prayed for us who are often not even praying for ourselves! You bore the shame of the Cross for us. O Lord, help us to meditate on Your sacrifice for us. May we learn to love what You love. In Jesus' humble name we pray. Amen.

April 3

"I tell you the truth, today you will be with Me in Paradise."
Luke 23:43

The 2nd saying on the Cross

There are at least two main points here. First, just prior to this verse, in the first saying, Jesus prayed for God to forgive. How quickly this prayer was answered! One of the two criminals being crucified next to Jesus said, *"Jesus, remember me when You come into Your kingdom,"* Luke 23:42. This dying man accepted Jesus as His Savior and Lord. Many of us have been instructed from our early years about the truths of Scripture. We have memorized parts of the Bible, learned songs, and heard the Gospel again and again. Yet in all of this instruction and pleadings, we have not yet come to Christ. The words from the man hanging next to Jesus do not comfort us, but accuse us of our covenant neglect! Woe to us, if we hear the Word yet refuse to come! If this is as close as we get to the Cross, it would be better in The Judgment if we had never heard of Jesus.

Secondly, in the midst of great personal agony, Jesus reached out to a penitent sinner dying next to Him. Are we reaching out to those who are dying? Do we care what they believe? After all, there really is either an immediate Paradise or an immediate Hell for everyone. Which place will they go to? They will instantly be in one or the other. There is no in-between place. There are no other options. Remember the story of the rich man! *"So it was that the beggar died, and was carried by the angels to Abraham's bosom. The rich man also died and was buried. And being in the torments in Hades, he lifted up his eyes and saw Abraham afar off, and Lazarus in his bosom,"* Luke 16:22-23 NKJV. What we believe and how we live matters, now and forever!

Prayer: Loving Lord, You show us two destinations before us in our text. How thankful we are that in Christ, there is a pardon for sin, and a place in Heaven for us. Help us by Your Spirit to live in the light of that great truth. But Lord, so many are on the wrong road! Lord help them to see that their present walk leads to a place they do not want to go, a place from which there is no escape. In Jesus' saving and loving name we pray. Amen.

April 4

"'Dear woman, here is your son,' and to the disciple, 'Here is your mother.'" John 19:26b-27a

The 3rd saying on the Cross

In the first saying, Jesus' concern was for lost sinners to be forgiven. In the second saying, one sinner already came to Him for forgiveness. Now we see that Jesus is concerned about immediate family, His mother. In the midst of great suffering, Jesus reaches out to family. Mary's husband, (Jesus' earthly father) was already gone. Jesus cared for His mom up to this point. After Jesus' death, it is reported Mary lived with the disciple John the rest of her days.

Jesus thought of others to the very end. How often, when we are sick or going through some great trial in life, we want people to feel sorry for us. Jesus as our perfect example, shows us in the first three sayings that He was more concerned for others, than for Himself. Jesus lived a selfless life the whole time He was on earth, always reaching out to others. Oh, that we would be more like Jesus!

Sad to say, many who call themselves Christian, are quicker to steal from one another rather than help them. Suddenly we too, are on our deathbed. Now family and friends are much more important. May we keep this in mind today and make the "others" God gave us a priority. If we reach out to others when times are good, we will never regret it on our deathbed! Paul wrote to Timothy, *"If anyone does not provide for his relatives, and especially for his immediate family, he has denied the faith and is worse than an unbeliever,"* 1 Timothy 5:8. God put us in families to care for each other. It is a great sin to neglect the *"immediate family,"* and the family of God!

It is also important to note that the family also was there to attend to the suffering of Jesus. His mother and the disciple John did not want Jesus to suffer alone. They were there with Him.

Prayer: Compassionate Lord, what a powerful sermon You preached on the Cross. How wonderfully You reached out to Your mother and the disciple John. Forgive us for not having that kind of dedication to our families. May we deny ourselves, take up our cross, and follow Your example. In Jesus' loving name we pray. Amen.

April 5

"My God, My God, why have You forsaken Me?" Matthew 27:46

The 4th saying on the Cross

It is difficult to imagine God the Father so completely forsaking His perfect Son. Jesus was always present with God the Father and God the Holy Spirit. There never was a single day in which the Godhead existed apart from each other. Yet here on the Cross, because our sin separates us from God, Christ had to be separated from God the Father. Christ had to completely identify Himself with us to experience the Hell that our sin deserves. He had to know our separation from God to be our sympathetic High Priest, our advocate to God. What dedication Christ has for us, personally!

Jesus was in such extreme pain here that the rocks split apart and there was darkness. Here on the Cross, Jesus' cry of pure agony is the real scream of the damned in Hell, totally separated from the love of God! There will be this kind of agony in Hell for those who are not covered by the blood of the Lamb. But with Christ here, there is a 100% total forsaking by God! Because Christ was so separated from God for us, He can fully say to us, *"I will never leave you or forsake you."* This promise can only be made because God totally forsook Christ so He could literally bring us into His holy presence forever!

What incredible misery the Father was in to hear His Son cry, *"My God, My God, why have You forsaken Me?"* Yes, *"God so loved the world that He gave His one and only Son, that whoever believes in Him shall not perish but have eternal life,"* John 3:16. What will we do with these facts? Will our eternity be filled forever with the same agony Christ is facing here? Will we be separated from the love of God like Jesus was? Will we need to pay for our own sin because we have not received Jesus perfect forgiveness? Or, did Christ suffer our Hell for us while hanging on the Cross?

Prayer: Dear forgiving Father, we can see the pain of how You and Your Son were separated for our sin! We worship You for the depths of Your love to us. If our Lord and Savior cried out with such agony from being separated from You, how can we ever stand before Your righteous wrath? How horrible is the absence of Your love! How great is Your grace to us through Christ! In Jesus' name we pray. Amen.

April 6

"I thirst." John 19:28b NKJV

The 5th saying on the Cross

This verse in the NIV version reads: *"Later, knowing that all was now completed, and so that the Scripture would be fulfilled, Jesus said, 'I am thirsty.'"* There are a number of reasons Jesus was *"thirsty."* First of all, Hell is burning hot. And when Jesus experienced our Hell, He was working hard, for there is no rest in Hell. It is Heaven that is the place of eternal rest. So Jesus is enduring hard, tormenting labor, and He is thirsty. How completely our Lord and Savior Jesus Christ died and suffered to pay the penalty that our sins deserve. The rich man, in the Lazarus parable, literally begged for a drop of water to cool his tongue. This is part of what Jesus was feeling when He cried out, *"I thirst."* We are the ones who deserved this thirst!

Secondly, Jesus was *"thirsty"* physically from His all night and next day of extreme pain and suffering. Jesus lost a lot of blood through His many lashes and a lot of water through sweating. The very God who made every single river and every single well in the world physically thirsted. He did this so we did not have to go through this! To what a great and full extent, our Lord and Savior Jesus Christ poured Himself out, yes, literally. There is no one that ever lived who suffered such extreme torture physically. Christ did this to reconcile lost sinners to a holy God.

Thirdly, *"I thirst,"* is a fitting description of the spiritual suffering of Jesus. Such was the travail of Jesus' own soul, as He thirsted to finish the work of redemption on the Cross. Jesus was most eager to go all the way to reconcile God to man, once and for all. Christ "thirsted" spiritually for the salvation of our precious souls. Every drop of Christ's blood cries out, "I thirsted for you."

Prayer: O what a Savior You are. Be merciful to us sinners who have thirsted more for the things of this world than for You. How fitting is the song: "Years I spent in vanity and pride caring not my Lord was crucified." Lord, create in us a real thirst to see that those who are lost become united to You. May we thirst for Your kingdom to come. In Jesus' precious name we pray. Amen.

April 7

"It is finished." John 19:30a

The 6th saying on the Cross

When Jesus said *"It is finished,"* *"He bowed His head and gave up His spirit,"* John 19:30b. Jesus came into the world on God's sovereign timetable. His work of redemption is now over. The Lamb of God has been slain. The perfect Son of God has given His precious and holy life for all who come to Him in true faith. God's plan of salvation is 100%, completely *"finished."* The suffering of Christ is *"finished."* The veil or curtain of the temple is *"finished."* The priest going into the old temple once a year *"is finished."* Now we can go to Him anytime. The old place of worship in the temple *"is finished."* Our perfect High Priest Jesus, completely opened the way to God through His broken body and shed blood. Our High Priest is on a throne in Heaven, welcoming us into His presence saying, *"Come to Me, all you who are weary and burdened, and I will give you rest,"* Matthew 11:28.

"It is finished," means God is now satisfied with Christ's atonement for sin once and for all. No other work to enter Heaven will ever please God! Christ did it all. There is nothing left for us to do! *"It is finished!"* When Christ cried out these last words He had totally paid our debt to God for our sin! Christ *"finished"* what Adam did not do and what we could not do. Other efforts to enter Heaven by our own work are as pathetic as Adam trying to get back to God by picking fig leaves in Genesis 3:7. The only thing left for us to do is to accept Christ's *"finished"* work on the Cross. May the truth of Leviticus 17:11 ring in our ears! *"For the life of a creature is in the blood, and I have given it to you to make atonement for yourselves on the altar; it is the blood that makes atonement for one's life."* His blood takes away every sin: past, present and even future. Today is the day of salvation!

Prayer: Beautiful Savior, there has never been so great a work of any kind in the world as Your finished work on the Cross. Please do forgive us for admiring our own works that are like filthy rags! Lord, it is hard for us to think that we need to do nothing to earn our salvation. Put to death our pride that says, "do something," and help us to focus on what Christ "has done." In Jesus' name we pray. Amen.

April 8

"Father, into Your hands I commit My spirit." Luke 23:46

The 7th saying on the Cross

The power of God did many noticeable signs and wonders in the three-hour period that Christ was on the cross. God was testifying that some big changes were taking place on the world's stage. *"It was now about the sixth hour,* (12:00 noon) *and darkness came over the whole land until the ninth hour, for the sun stopped shining. And the curtain of the temple was torn in two,"* Luke 23:44-45. The ripped curtain that separated off the holy of holies, shows us that the ceremonial laws and the sacrifices in the temple were now over. Christ opened the way for sinners to come to Himself, the perfect High Priest.

Saying, *"Father, into Your hands I commit My spirit,"* Jesus willingly placed His life into the hands of God. No one took the life of Christ! Jesus gave His life! Freely Jesus came, and freely He left! The question is: Will we accept the free gift of His perfect life and innocent blood so that we can be reconciled to God?

It was King David who first used these words, *"Into Your hands I commit my spirit,"* Psalm 31:5a. Christ used the same words for at least two reasons. First, He showed that He was the One the Old Testament prophets all pointed to. Secondly, He now totally fulfilled the Old Testament promises.

Christ also showed us the personal importance of faith in claiming the words of Scripture. To die with Scripture on our lips like this, we need to live with Scripture on our lips. In giving His life to God, Christ trusted in God for His resurrection. What a beautiful testimony of trust and faith in God's promises. Do we trust our soul to the grace and mercy of God like Christ did? Do we believe that God's power will someday raise us to newness of life in a new Heaven and earth?

Prayer: Dear Lord, we are so grateful that with the eyes of faith, we too can say, *"Father, into Your hands I commit my spirit."* With the old, faithful saint Job, we can also say, *"I know that my Redeemer lives, and that in the end He will stand upon the earth. And after my skin has been destroyed, yet in my flesh I will see God; I myself will see Him with my own eyes - I and not another. How my heart yearns within me!"* Job 19:25-27. In Christ, our Redeemer's name we pray. Amen.

April 9

"The chief priest and the whole Sanhedrin were looking for false evidence against Jesus so that they could put Him to death."
Matthew 26:59

Liars, the 1st voice by the Cross

Liars surrounded the Cross of Christ! It is so amazing, those who were the leaders in the Church, headed the list of liars by the Cross. Even today, many still use the Cross as a means to gain position, praise, and money. Liberal Christians have always attempted to remove Christ from the Church and try to make themselves the object of worship. But then, a liberal Christian is not really a Christian at all.

Lying breaks the ninth commandment and is a very selfish sin. God did command us, *"You shall not give false testimony against your neighbor,"* Deuteronomy 5:20. Spurgeon wisely said, "Show me a man who is habitually a liar, and you have a man who will have his portion in the lake that burns with fire and brimstone. I do not care which denomination of Christians he may belong. I am sure he is none of Christ's. And it is very sad to know that there are so many you cannot trust to tell the truth. God deliver us from that." Spurgeon also said that he saw all sorts of people converted but rarely had he seen a hard-hearted liar converted. Why? Lying knows very little about the conviction of the Holy Spirit. A person, who can lie so easily, has a godless heart. We see people who claim to be Christian think so little of lying often. Lying and cheating is never good business as some think. Liars believe that God cannot help them, so they must help themselves. Where is their trust in God?

In our text says, *"false evidence"* is used to pull down the Lord. Jesus knew this would also happen to those who followed Him! That's why He said, *"Blessed are you when people insult you, persecute you and falsely say all kinds of evil against you because of Me. Rejoice and be glad, because great is your reward in Heaven, for in the same way they persecuted the prophets who were before you,"* Matthew 5:11-12.

Prayer: O Lord, forgive us for saying false things. May our speech testify to the fact that You have changed our hearts. May we love truth as You do. In Christ's name we pray. Amen.

April 10

"I tell you, whoever acknowledges Me before men, the Son of Man will also acknowledge him before the angels of God. But he who disowns Me before men will be disowned before the angels of God."
Luke 12:8-9

Deniers, the 2nd voice by the Cross

There were two different kinds of people who denied Christ. The Pharisees/Sadducee's group is one kind who denied Christ. Peter also denied that he knew Christ. But there is such a big difference between the two. After Peter denied Christ, he *"went out and wept bitterly,"* Matthew 26:75b. Peter was very sorry that he denied his Lord and Savior. When the Pharisees and Sadducees denied Christ, they were blind to the truth and said He was some kind of devil. Attributing the real work of God and His Son and Spirit to demons is very dangerous ground.

We can also deny Jesus by the words we speak, or by the words we should have said to honor Him. Do we, like Peter, weep bitterly over this? Jesus said in our text, *"Whoever acknowledges Me before men, the Son of Man will also acknowledge him before the angels of God. But he who disowns Me before men will be disowned before the angels of God."* Christ will not own those who disown Him! Those who stand with Christ in this world will stand with Him in Heaven!

In our text, even angels will stand with us in eternity if we stand for Christ today. But the opposite is also true! Those who deny the Lordship of Christ will *"be tormented with burning sulfur in the presence of the holy angels and of the Lamb. And the smoke of their torment rises forever and ever,"* Revelation 14:10b-11a. It is a serious thing to deny Christ. Peter confessed his sin and repented. Have we confessed our sin and repented from our denying Christ? We can never promote the interest of Christ until we first deny our own self-centered interests. Lord, strengthen us!

Prayer: O Lord of lords, we have seen the evil of denying You. Like Peter, we have been ashamed of You. We have even cursed or spoke lightly against Your holy name, braking the third commandment. Lord, forgive us for these sins. May we lose our life for Your holy purposes. In Christ's name we pray. Amen.

April 11

"In the same way the chief priests, the teachers of the law and the elders mocked Him. 'He saved others,' they said, 'but He can't save Himself!'" Matthew 27:41-42a

Mockers, the 3rd voice by the Cross

When Jesus was on the Cross, *"those who passed by hurled insults at Him, shaking their heads,"* Matthew 27:39. One robber mocked Jesus. The people walking by mocked Jesus. Also, *"some began to spit at Him; they blindfolded Him, struck Him with their fists, and said, 'Prophesy!' And the guards took Him and beat Him,"* Mark 14:65. Christ was mocked at every turn. He was abused and made sport of in the hours He hung on the Cross. Today, many people still mock Christ day and night with their evil thoughts and actions. *"Do not be deceived: God cannot be mocked. A man reaps what he sows,"* Galatians 6:7.

Today many people mock Christ by pointing to their own dreams, experiences, healings and miracles so that the people will forget God. We also mock Jesus' death and resurrection by our refusing to die to certain sins in our life.

When we stand with and for Christ, we will be mocked. Expect it! It is good to expect it because when it happens, it is a difficult blow. It especially hurts when those closest to us, mock us. It was the temple leaders who thought they were doing a good ministry that mocked Jesus in our text. The people also mocked Jesus because He said He would destroy the temple and then rebuild it. Of course, Jesus was speaking of His death and resurrection, the cornerstone of our Christian faith.

The people mocked Jesus because He was the Son of God. We will be mocked because we are sons and daughters of God. It will do our souls so much good if we can remember the words of Asaph, *"When I tried to understand all this it was oppressive to me till I entered the sanctuary of God; then I understood their final destiny,"* Psalm 73:16-17.

Prayer: Dear Lord, it is so profane that Your Son, the perfect God-man, the Creator, was mocked by the creature. Forgive us! When we are mocked for following Your way of living, help us to have the right attitude. We pray this in our dear Redeemer's name. Amen.

April 12

"They divided My garments among them and cast lots for My clothing." John 19:24b

Gamblers, the 4th voice by the Cross

Gamblers rolled the dice, probably spattered with Christ's precious blood. They wanted to see who would get Jesus' seamless robe! Gambling is considered by many to be "harmless entertainment." But is it? Does not gambling break the tenth commandment? *"Thou shall not covet your neighbor's house, wife, manservant or maidservant...or anything that belongs to your neighbor,"* Exodus 20:17. When we "covet" we are not content with what God has given us. Gamblers try to get more! A radio program said that even churchgoers spend more on gambling than they give to the Lord! Something is really wrong! Can gamblers pray and meditate on the Creator when their hearts are set on getting more created things? Gamblers literally take their anxieties to the place of gambling, not to God who alone can give grace and mercy! Truth is, gambling is idolatry.

It is not just those who gamble that are wrong. Gambling houses and lotteries seek to extort even the pensions of the retired! One gambling place even owns a bus. The day the government checks arrive to the poor people, the bus goes out to collect these same people and bring them to the gambling house. There they give the people cheap food, and then some alcohol to help them feel a little better about being robbed of their money! Most of the people return home either broke or having little to live on for the rest of the month. If we went to these same people with a gun and took their money, we would be arrested and brought to jail!

We must work faithfully and be content with what we have. May we give out of our abundance to organizations that are promoting God's kingdom! God blesses that kind of living and giving!

Prayer: Dear Lord, like the soldiers by the Cross, we have not been content with what You have given us! We often spend more time thinking about how we are going to get more, than thanking You for what You have already given us! Forgive us for being so greedy! May we honor You with all that we have. In Christ's name we pray. Amen.

April 13

"Then one of the criminals who were hanged blasphemed Him, saying, 'If you are the Christ, save Yourself and us.'" Luke 23:39 NKJV

Blasphemers, the 5th voice by the Cross

To bring an accusation against anyone is a very serious (Jude 9). To speak lightly or carelessly of God is blasphemy. Commandment three says, *"You shall not misuse the name of the LORD your God, for the Lord will not hold anyone guiltless who misuses His name,"* Deuteronomy 5:11. The Israelites were so afraid of blasphemy they would not even mention the name of God. Blasphemy was punished with death by stoning in Leviticus 24:10-16. In our text, *"one of the criminals who were hanged blasphemed Him saying, 'If You are the Christ, save Yourself and us.'"* The other criminal rightly rebuked him saying, *"Do you not even fear God, seeing you are under the same condemnation?"* Luke 23:40 NKJV.

Many people today can hardly say a sentence without saying a cuss word. They have so little fear of God. Our holy God will not overlook such pride. Every single person will be held accountable for every word they speak. Why is that? Because our words reveal the true condition of our hearts! *"The good man brings good things out of the good stored up in his heart, and the evil man brings evil things out of the evil stored up in his heart. For out of the overflow of his heart his mouth speaks,"* Luke 6:45. Our words reveal our spiritual maturity! *"God will bring every deed into judgment, including every hidden thing, whether it is good or evil,"* Ecclesiastes 12:14.

What should we say when we hear people curse God? We could remind them of the last two verses mentioned, and that there is a judgment coming! Lovingly grab them by God's holy commandments and by how a righteous God has to punish evil because He cannot allow sin into His holy presence. May the Spirit and Word convict us all!

Prayer: Dear Lord, forgive us for uttering words that do not praise You and build up others. How our words reveal our selfish and sinful hearts! May we heed Your warning! *"Out of the same mouth come praise and cursing. My brothers, this should not be,"* James 3:10. In Christ Jesus' name we pray. Amen.

April 14

"Jesus, remember me when You come into Your kingdom."
Luke 23:42

Repenters, the 6th voice by the Cross

These sincere words of the one thief next to Jesus are the words of repentance and confession. They are words of faith that proclaims that Jesus is Lord. This thief was most likely not brought up in a Christian home! This man did not have hundreds of pleadings to come to Christ! Yet still, he became a believer! How many of our covenant children and adults too, have been encouraged, instructed, rebuked and disciplined to walk the narrow road, yet at this point still reject the Lord Jesus Christ! This repentant thief accuses their unbelief.

We say that we hate sin, but is that necessarily repentance? We may know the creeds and confessions and have even memorized them, but is that repentance? Real repentance is turning from sin and practicing that which is right. Repentance is delighting in a relationship with God. When we love sin more than we love God, we have a problem. Until we really love God more than our sin, we will not repent! When we are concerned about how much our sin hurts Christ, we will turn from it!

It is true that God gives us the power to repent when He gives us a new heart! Yet still, no one can stand before God in The Judgment and say, "God did not give me that power." Man is equally responsible to repent. God said to sinning Cain, *"If you do what is right, will you not be accepted? But if you do not do what is right, sin is crouching at your door; it desires to have you, but you must master it,"* Genesis 4:7.

Jesus said to His own disciples, *"'Who do people say the Son of Man is?' They replied, 'Some say John the Baptist; others say Elijah; and still others, Jeremiah or one of the prophets.' 'But what about you?' He asked. 'Who do you say I am?' Simon Peter answered, 'You are the Christ, the Son of the living God,'"* Matthew 16:13b-16. Who do we say Jesus is?

Prayer: Dear Lord, forgive us for not seeking a close relationship with You! We have been lazy spiritually. Lord, convict and strengthen us where we need it. One thief saw You and repented! May we not only see You, but also live for You. In Christ's name we pray. Amen.

April 15

"Two robbers were crucified with Him, one on His right and one on His left." Matthew 27:38

Robbers, the 7th voice by the Cross

There are still *"robbers"* near the Cross of Christ today! And do not think that these robbers are not in the Church! Like Judas, many use the Cross to put money in their own pocket! If the money that comes into the Church is more important than preaching "Christ Crucified," then a type of extortion is happening!

For even more than 30 pieces of silver, some ministry workers are in the ministry for the gold! The "good living" drives them. Not all pastors are for real. Holiness does not come in a title or a degree. If someone tells us that if we give him a hundred bucks, then God will give us 100 times more, beware! God commands us to give a tithe for the furtherance of His kingdom. Whose kingdom is being advanced if a pastor or church is dishonest?

If anyone wants to be blessed by their giving, then it has to go for the work of the Lord, not into the treasuries of thieves and charlatans! A true Church spends the member's tithes for the poor and downtrodden, or to share the truth of the Gospel. But if that same money is used for bigger salaries, bigger buildings, and bigger programs that are designed to look like "ministry," something is wrong. God still says in James 1:27 that pure religion is remembering the widow and orphan and keeping yourself pure!

God reminds us, *"You shall not steal,"* Deuteronomy 5:19. God wants us to know that *"wealth gained by dishonesty will be diminished, but he who gathers by labor will increase,"* Proverbs 13:11. Judas used "religion" to make an easy living but landed in Hell! We are warned to be honest in our giving and in our living! *"Do not trust in extortion or take pride in stolen goods,"* Psalm 62:10a.

Prayer: Dear Lord, we see that one thief repented and lived forever. May all those who are involved in dishonest gain come to the Cross today while there is still time! And Lord, please give each one of us discernment to see what is truly Your work! Then You and others will be honored and we will be blessed. In Christ's name we pray. Amen.

April 16

"Joseph son of David, do not be afraid to take Mary home as your wife, because what is conceived in her is from the Holy Spirit. She will give birth to a Son, and you are to give Him the name Jesus, because He will save His people from their sins." Matthew 1:20b-21

Why Jesus had to be God and man

There was great confusion in the early Church as to whether Jesus was both fully God and man. Arius was wrongly teaching that Christ is the first and highest of all created beings. Arius taught that Christ did not exist from eternity and is not the same substance or essence as the Father is. Arius thought that if Christ was only fully God, then Christianity was just like the heathens who had more than one god. The emperor Constantine called a council together in 325 AD at Nicea. There 300 bishops debated this matter according to the Scriptures, and Arius was rightly condemned as a heretic. If anyone denies the deity of Christ, that He is fully God, equal to God, they are considered part of a cult. It was the Gospel of salvation that was on trial at Nicea.

Jesus, as a man, was still fully God. He was from the Holy Spirit (God) and from Mary. Jesus as God said, *"Go therefore and make disciples of all the nations, baptizing them in the name* (one God existing in three persons) *of the Father and of the Son and of the Holy Spirit."* Jesus had to be fully God to be sinless, and to be able to bear the awful wrath of God against every Christian that ever lived. *"The Word was God,"* John 1:1b.

Jesus was also fully man, except for sin. He had to completely identify Himself with our flesh. Our Savior needed to come as a man to do what Adam did not do, to live a perfect life. God's justice does not allow for any other creature to make satisfaction to Him for our sin. Angels do not have bodies. Animals do not have souls! Neither angels nor animals qualify to provide atonement to God for our sin. Christ, as perfect Man had to die and shed His blood to become the Perfect Lamb of God that takes away sin.

Prayer: O Lord, we can see that no other man could pay the penalty of our sin. No one else could take Your holy wrath against sin. So in love, You sent Your Son to be that God-Man. In Jesus' name we pray. Amen.

April 17

"Are not all angels ministering spirits sent to serve those who will inherit salvation?" Hebrews 1:14

Angels work for God and bless believers

As Christians, God will never leave us or forsake us. God's *"angels"* are one way that God is with us. Angels in the Bible are described as created, immortal, normally invisible, wise, and powerful spiritual beings that are neither male nor female. *"For by Him* (Christ) *all things were created: things in Heaven and on earth, visible and invisible, whether thrones or powers or rulers or authorities; all things were created by Him and for Him,"* Colossians 1:16. Angels, like us, have emotions. We read that *"there is rejoicing in the presence of the angels of God over one sinner who repents,"* Luke 15:10. Angels do not fully understand spiritual things, but *"long to look into these things,"* 1 Peter 1:12b.

Angels announced the conception of Jesus in Matthew 1:20-21. Angels announced Jesus' birth in Luke 2:10-12. Angels ministered to Jesus during His temptations in Matthew 4:11. Angels also witnessed Jesus' resurrection in 1 Timothy 3:16. Angels told the disciples, *"'Men of Galilee,' they said, 'Why do you stand here looking into the sky? This same Jesus, who has been taken from you into Heaven, will come back in the same way you have seen Him go into Heaven,'"* Acts 1:11. Jesus will use angels to gather the souls of the believers in Heaven for The Judgment that is coming!

God's angels bless us in that they are *"ministering spirits sent to serve those who will inherit salvation."* Angels serve us by guiding us. Abraham said to his servant: *"He will send His angel before you so that you can get a wife for my son from there,"* Genesis 24:7b. Angels also protect us. Daniel said, *"My God sent His angel, and He shut the mouths of the lions. They have not hurt me, because I was found innocent in His sight,"* Daniel 6:22a. Angels bring worship and glory to God and bless believers everywhere.

Prayer: Lord God, our awesome provider, we praise You for creating angels. What a blessing they are for Your glory, and for our benefit! Lord, You are so good to give us such guidance, love, and protection. The angels will even carry us into Your presence. In the name of Jesus our Lord, who is also, Lord of the angels, we pray. Amen.

April 18

"Because Herod did not give praise to God, an angel of the Lord struck him down, and he was eaten by worms and died."
Acts 12:23b

Angels bring mercy as well as justice!

King Herod, *"had James, the brother of John, put to death with the sword"* in Acts 12:2. The king then *"proceeded to seize Peter"* in 12:3b. Then *"an angel of the Lord,"* was sent to give mercy and free Peter from prison in Acts 12:7. Very soon after this, in fact, *"Immediately, because Herod did not give praise to God, an angel of the Lord struck him down, and he was eaten by worms and died,"* Acts 12:23. God uses angels as His messenger, to execute His justice. It is very possible that the same angel who brought mercy to Peter also brought God's divine justice to Herod.

In the destruction of Sodom and Gomorrah, it is clear that the same angels brought mercy and judgment. *"Two angels arrived in Sodom,"* Genesis 19:1. The angel spoke these exact words to Lot, *"Get them (Lot's family) out of here because we are going to destroy this place. The outcry to the LORD against its people is so great that He has sent us to destroy it,"* Genesis 19:12b-13. God used angels to destroy evil, and at the same time, showed God's mercy by protecting His children. In the process, God is glorified and His kingdom is built.

As a missionary in India, several terrorists tried to harm me. The terrorists were caught a week later. On the witness stand one of the terrorists confessed everything when he could have lied and got off the hook. He told the judge, "I tried to harm this missionary, but his God protected him. I am more afraid of his God than you, Mr. Judge." To this day, I do not know what God did but He commands His angels to do His will.

We praise God that He still uses His angels to give mercy to His children and justice to those who are His enemies.

Prayer: O gracious Lord who loves mercy and is just, we thank You for Your angels. If You and Your angels are for us, who can harm us? You comfort us with a most precious truth in Psalm 91, *"For He shall give His angels charge over you to keep you in all your ways."* In Jesus' blessed name we pray. Amen.

April 19

"And there was war in Heaven. Michael and his angels fought against the dragon, and the dragon and his angels fought back. But he was not strong enough, and they lost their place in Heaven. The great dragon was hurled down-that ancient serpent called the devil, or Satan, who leads the whole world astray. He was hurled to the earth, and his angels with him." Revelation 12:7-9

Angels who hate God and believers

Satan and his wicked band of angels fell from Heaven. Pride was their downfall. It seems that God instantly judged these angels and then bound them so that the Gospel could go out to all the world. The good angels and their leader Michael were more powerful than the evil ones in that holy war! In our text, Satan is called the *"dragon,"* a creature that is strong and fierce. But as strong as this *"dragon"* is, he could not defeat Christ and His disciples, pictured in Revelation 12:1 as the woman with a crown of 12 stars. In Jesus Christ, we too have protection from evil angels. Three points are important.

First, in verse 10, we see that Satan is called *"the accuser."* Satan and his angels cause much trouble for the Church by accusing us, just as he accused the righteous Job in the courts of Heaven. Let us give him no fuel for his accusations!

Second, in verse 11, *"they overcame him by the blood of the Lamb."* We will only overcome Satan by that same blood! We must stop all the gimmicks and games and preach Christ crucified, for that is what defeats Satan!

Third, what God did to fallen angels, He will surely do to fallen man. *"For if God did not spare angels when they sinned, but sent them to hell,"* 2 Peter 2:4a, and in 2:6b, *"made them an example of what is going to happen to the ungodly,"* 2 Peter 2:6b.

Prayer: Most righteous Lord, we praise You that there already is an *"eternal fire prepared for the devil and his angels,"* Matthew 25:41b. How amazing it is that in Christ, You rescue us from this wicked *"devil and his angels."* How wonderful that Your own angels are stronger than Satan's angels. How blessed we are! Through our great conquer Jesus, we pray. Amen.

April 20

"We love because He first loved us." 1 John 4:19

Why can we love God and others?

Our text is an amazing truth that we must praise God for. Our God loved us when we were completely unlovable. It is both prideful and arrogant on our part to think that it was our wisdom that decided to choose Christ. That is not the case at all. Jesus said, *"You did not choose Me, but I chose you and appointed you to go and bear fruit,"* John 15:16a. The book of Romans teaches us that, *"When we were still without strength, in due time Christ died for the ungodly"* Romans 5:6. Would not the grace of God cease to be grace, if God did not in fact move to us when we were *"without strength"* to move to Him?

God lovingly revealed to us how our first father Adam tried to cover his own sin by picking some fig leaves. Adam couldn't cover one sin or move to God on his own. In love, through God's gift of grace, God killed an animal in Genesis 3:21. God covered Adam's sin for him, because Adam could do nothing! That's why Paul could say, *"When we were God's enemies, we were reconciled to Him through the death of His Son,"* Romans 5:10b.

It is God who moves in us to love others also! We don't somehow love others because of any good we stir up in ourselves. *"We love because He first loved us."* Why? God, *"appointed you to go and bear fruit — fruit that will last,"* John 15:16a. By His grace alone, *"we are God's workmanship, created in Christ Jesus to do good works, which God prepared in advance for us to do,"* Ephesians 2:10. It is wrong to say, as some do, that God saw the good we would do and then gave us the power to do it. Such thinking denies God's love, His grace, mercy, sovereignty, wisdom and power.

I cannot meditate on the love of God without thinking about the chorus of my favorite song, "The Love of God" by F. Lehman. "O love of God, how rich and pure! How measureless and strong! It shall forevermore endure — the saints' and angels' song."

Prayer: Dear Lord, we worship You for the love You put in us! It is hard to put into words our appreciation for Your love. We just worship and lift up Your most holy name. May Your loving kingdom come, for Yours is an everlasting kingdom. In Jesus' name we pray. Amen.

April 21

"But seek first His Kingdom and His righteousness, and all these things will be given to you as well." Matthew 6:33

From self-esteem to Christ-esteem

If ever there was an evil teaching today, it is that we need more self-esteem to somehow "make it" in life. This whole "self-esteem thing" is very bad doctrine, another religion! It turns the whole Bible completely upside down. We need to seek *"His Kingdom and His righteousness."* Since *"righteousness"* is found in Christ alone, more Christ-esteem is what we need. Before we can possibly love Christ more, we need to love self less! As a child of God, we find our esteem in our relationship with Christ. God gives us many difficult tests in this life to see if we will esteem Him, or esteem self. Until we can pass these kinds of tests, trials actually, we will never esteem Christ more.

Giving in to self-pity is self-esteem, and that kills us physically and spiritually, quicker than anything. How easily we can fall into self-pity when things do not go our way. Self-pity never makes good friends with God or man. Self-pity does not make us a team player in the home, school or workplace. Self-pity does not worship God or lift up others. Self-pity is pure self-esteem, and the worship of self.

If we think we have to please self first to be fulfilled in life, we have completely swallowed the world's theology. *"Seek first the Kingdom of God and His righteousness"* means self must be last. Jesus said that a Christian must, *"deny himself and take up his cross and follow Me,"* Luke 9:23. Self-pity, self-esteem, even self-exaltation, are enemies of the Cross. We must confess our self-centeredness as sin, then replace it and begin to esteem God with all of our heart. God blesses that kind of humble living!

Prayer: Holy Lord, as we study Your Word we see that the father of self-centered living is none other than Satan himself. Forgive us for being so attracted to his lies. Just as Satan fell when he said, *"I will ascend above the tops of the clouds; I will make myself like the Most High,"* Isaiah 14:14, so too, our self-esteem is too proud. Lord, help us to dump our self-first religion and esteem You with all of our hearts! In Christ's name we pray. Amen.

April 22

"Therefore, just as sin entered the world through one man, and death through sin, and in this way death came to all men, because all sinned."
Romans 5:12

Total Depravity, the T of TULIP

We will study five important points concerning the amazing grace of God. A summary of the Gospel of salvation by grace alone through Christ alone is needed to define what grace is.

We had nothing to do with our salvation. How could we? *"We were dead in our trespasses and sins,"* in Ephesians 2:1. Dead depraved people don't choose anything. Already in Genesis 6:5, *"The LORD saw how great man's wickedness on earth had become, and that every inclination of the thoughts of his heart was only evil all the time."* Adam's sin "determined us all" from being good, to being *"only evil all the time"*? Our text tells us. *"Therefore, just as sin entered the world through one man, and death through sin, and in this way death came to all men, because all sinned,"* Romans 5:12.

The truth of total depravity teaches that all persons descended from Adam are born guilty sinners and are totally corrupt, and most miserable because of it. We are all in bondage to Satan, slaves to sin as Romans 6:6-7 teaches. This does not mean that every person is equally wicked. God prevents some people from being more abase than others, yet still all are *"slaves to sin,"* and all need to be set free by God.

The truth of total depravity means, it is useless to try to get any person to change their actions before their heart is changed. A drunk cannot stop drinking until he has a new heart. It is because of total depravity then that we must do evangelism before we do discipleship. Anyone that ignores this fact is trying to affect change in someone without the power of the Father, Son and Spirit in them. Our spiritual problems need God's spiritual solutions, not man's.

Prayer: Wise and loving Lord, we thank and praise You for showing us our condition. We can only fall down before You, the great and perfect Judge, and beg for mercy. Even that is You humbling us. Set us free Lord. We praise You for Your mercy and for the power to change. In Jesus Christ's name we pray. Amen.

April 23

"Praise be to God and the Father of our Lord Jesus Christ, who has blessed us in the heavenly realms with every spiritual blessing in Christ. For He chose us in Him before the creation of the world to be holy and blameless in His sight. In love He predestined us to be adopted."
Ephesians 1:3-5a

Unconditional Election, the U of TULIP

Election teaches us that it's the grace of God that selects us. God *"adopted"* us to be His sons and daughters in Christ before the world was made. An orphan child doesn't choose a parent. They love the parent because the parent first loved them, same as John 15:16. The Holy Spirit convicts us of our sin, moving us to God. That is God choosing us, planned even before the world was made.

Adam and angels had a free will, at one time. Satan's free will was kicked out of Heaven, Adam's free will was kicked out of the Garden. Since then, *"every inclination of the thoughts of his heart was only evil all the time,"* Genesis 6:5. With salvation, we again have the will to sin or not to sin. In Heaven, we will only have a will to praise God. Damnation was the will of man. Salvation is the will of God.

One problem some have with God's election is thinking that a sinner has a right to be saved. Not true, for *"the wages of sin is death,"* Romans 6:23. A criminal with a death penalty is doomed to die unless the judge gives him a free pardon. If an earthly judge chooses to forgive some, is there something cruel in this judge? Adam was told before he sinned that he would die if he sinned.

The way God forgives us by grace is important for our relationships with others. We, too, must forgive others by grace as taught in Ephesians 4:32. If we chose God by asking for forgiveness, then we will require others to ask for our forgiveness when they hurt us. If they don't ask, we think we can remain bitter at them. Read Ephesians 4:31; Mark 11:25 and Hebrews 12:15. Our bitterness kills us.

Prayer: Most loving Lord, we thank You that You are merciful and gracious! Thank You for planning our salvation *"before the creation of the world."* We, who were dead and in bondage to Satan, were rescued by You, our God. We praise You for planting the gift of faith in us. In Jesus' name we pray. Amen.

April 24

"Blessed is the man You choose, and cause to approach You, that he may dwell in Your courts. We shall be satisfied with the goodness of Your house, of Your holy temple." Psalm 65:4 NKJV

Limited Atonement, the L of TULIP

First let us deal with the atonement part here. Even the Arminian believes this. The atonement was God's grace to Adam, after he sinned. God killed an innocent animal to cover man's sin in Genesis 3:21. God said, *"For the life of a creature is in the blood, and I have given it to you to make atonement for yourselves on the altar; it is the blood that makes atonement for one's life,"* Leviticus 17:11. This verse points to Jesus shedding His blood so that sin might forever be removed from every believer. The message of the Cross for all eternity is: Jesus Christ, in our place, bore both our sins and our punishment forever. If this true message is changed, then we are forever lost. If we go to a believer's death-bed, we will never doubt the importance of Jesus paying our sin debt.

Now the limited part. Our text says, *"Blessed is the man whom You choose."* It does not say, blessed is the man who chooses Christ. Again, we see the free will of God at work. We also see His free will is limited to those God will *"cause to approach You, that he may dwell in Your courts."* Those in Heaven will be limited to those whom God caused to approach Him! It is because of limited atonement that any believer can truly say, "I have a personal relationship with Christ." We may know salvation is personal, but this is why it is!

One example of limited atonement is God saying, *"Jacob have I loved, but Esau I hated,"* Romans 9:13b. God also said, *"I will have mercy on whom I have mercy, and I will have compassion on whom I have compassion,"* Romans 9:15b. Did not God limit the animals He did *"cause to approach"* the ark to be saved? To not believe in limited atonement says all people deserve salvation not death.

Prayer: Amazing Lord, we worship You that Jesus Christ, *"the good Shepherd laid down His life for the sheep,"* John 10:11b, and that He calls them by name. How beautiful and personal is Your grace to those You are calling to Yourself! We worship You. In Jesus' name we pray. Amen.

April 25

"I tell you the truth, a time is coming and has now come when the dead will hear the voice of the Son of God and those who hear will live."
John 5:25

Irresistible Grace, the I of TULIP

Irresistible grace is that sovereign act of Christ in a believer whereby God produces regeneration by His Spirit in giving life to that dead sinner. In our text, we see the word, *"hear"* twice. This call to dead sinners is called an effectual call. This means it is the call itself, from our Lord that wakes dead sinners so they *"hear"* His voice speaking to their spirit. The dead sinner wakes up and cannot resist the call. What a beautiful "grace truth" this is! If we do not believe this, then we will somehow think that God presents His Gospel to people, and then He is wringing His hands hoping they will love Him. What a slap in the face to the power of God's sovereign grace!

Paul was on the road to Damascus to persecute Christians. He was dead and sinning, moving against God, not to God. Paul knew and could say, *"But because of His great love for us, God, who is rich in mercy, made us alive with Christ even when we were dead in transgressions - it is by grace you have been saved,"* Ephesians 2:4-5. The bright light on the Damascus road was Jesus Himself, revealing Himself to Paul. The persecutor Paul contributed nothing! That is what grace always is: God calling us! It is also the irresistible grace of God, that makes sanctification (growing up in Christ) possible! *"My sheep listen to My voice; I know them, and they follow Me,"* John 10:27. God not only limited the animals on the ark, to two of a kind, but they could not resist His calling.

Prayer: O sovereign Lord, we worship You for calling us into a real relationship with Yourself. We are so thankful that we do not have a free will to reject Your irresistible call! For with a free will, we would reject You again and again, simply because of the truth in Genesis 6, *"every inclination of the thoughts of"* our *"heart"* is *"only evil all of the time."* Thank You for waking us from our dead spiritual condition, for pulling us to the Cross and Your forgiveness! In Jesus' name we pray. Amen.

April 26

"The Lord will rescue me from every evil attack and will bring me safely to His Heavenly kingdom. To Him be the glory for ever and ever. Amen." 2 Timothy 4:18

Perseverance of the Saints, the P of TULIP

The doctrine of the perseverance of the saints is a point of grace that says a true Christian will never lose their salvation. Why? *"For it is God who works in you to will and to act according to His good purpose,"* Philippians 2:13. It is more correct to talk about the perseverance of God in a believer's life. We fall again and again, but God convicts us by His Spirit and preserves us by rescuing us as our text teaches.

Paul said, *"being confident of this, that He who began a good work in you will carry it on to completion until the day of Christ Jesus,"* Philippians 1:6. Peter said that nothing can happen to God's Heir (Christ) and His inheritance (the Christian). Peter said, we, *"through faith are shielded by God's power until the coming of the salvation that is ready to be revealed in the last time,"* 1 Peter 1:5.

Jesus said, *"My sheep listen to My voice; I know them, and they follow Me. I give them eternal life, and <u>they shall never perish; no one can snatch them out of My hand</u>,"* John 10:27-28. If one Christian could perish, then we are without hope, have no gospel to preach, and no inheritance to look forward to. The Bible knows nothing about a temporary faith. The faith of God's elect is an abiding faith. *"Now these three remain: faith, hope and love,"* 1 Corinthians 13:13a.

It is impossible, then, to be a child of God and still go to Hell!. Can you imagine an old man or woman who lived for God their whole life, but then lost their salvation just weeks before they died? Noah's ark is a picture of our safety in Heaven. Could even one of the animals jump off the ark? Is there even one example in Scripture of a person who lost their salvation? Spurgeon said, "If anyone could convince me that a person could lose their faith I would never teach the Bible again, for I have nothing worth teaching."

Prayer: O most loving Lord, we worship You for Your protection and an inheritance that can never perish, spoil or fade, kept in Heaven for us. We are so grateful to You for rescuing us and bringing us to our heavenly home to be with You! In Jesus' name we pray. Amen!

April 27

"And Mephibosheth lived in Jerusalem, because he always ate at the king's table, and he was crippled in both feet." 2 Samuel 9:13

Am I a Mephibosheth?

The story of Mephibosheth is a picture of God working a covenant of grace with His specific and personal child. Jonathan, the father of Mephibosheth, was a very close friend of David, a type of Jesus, looking forward to what Jesus now does. Jonathan said to David, *"'Show me unfailing kindness like that of the LORD as long as I live, so that I may not be killed, and do not ever cut off your kindness from my family'... So Jonathan made a covenant with the house of David,"* 1 Samuel 20:14-16a.

Years later, in 2 Samuel 9, David remembered his covenant with Jonathan. Finding one son alive, he called the now lame Mephibosheth to come to his palace. What a beautiful picture of God calling us, His people! Do we yet have a son or daughter who is lame (spiritually speaking) and has not yet seen the face of the King? If we do, then rejoice! The King sought out the lame one who could not come on his own! How we must believe with joy. God also came to the prodigal son and caused the prodigal to come to Him. We must pray to God, for our King still makes the lame come to Him!

"'Don't be afraid,' David said to him, (Mephibosheth) *'for I will surely show you kindness for the sake of your father Jonathan. I will restore to you all the land that belonged to your grandfather Saul, and you will always eat at my table,'"* 2 Samuel 9:7. The lame man's response: *"Mephibosheth bowed down and said, 'What is your servant, that you should notice a dead dog like me?'"* 2 Samuel 9:8. Wow!

Mephibosheth knew he was lame. He came to eat at the king's table, knowing that he did not deserve to be there! What a Lord's Supper message for us! The king gave him the privileges of his own sons. We, too, are invited to come and eat at the King's table. *"Come, all you who are thirsty, come to the waters; and you who have no money, come, buy and eat!"* Isaiah 55:1.

Prayer: Amazing Lord, we can only say, "What a Friend we have in Jesus!" We worship You, the One that causes the lame to walk. In Jesus' name we pray. Amen.

April 28

"Everyone who speaks a word against the Son of Man will be forgiven, but anyone who blasphemes against the Holy Spirit will not be forgiven." Luke 12:10

The unpardonable sin

Are you worried that you may have committed the unpardonable sin? If that is anyone's concern, then certainly they have not committed this sin. A person who has really committed the unpardonable sin has a dead conscience! They are no longer convicted of their sin. They are not sensitive to the Holy Spirit. *"Anyone who blasphemes against the Holy Spirit"* has rejected God in the past and continues that in the present. The Pharisees were good examples. This rejection of God the Holy Spirit is a rejection of the One who brings a person to repentance and faith. God will not give forgiveness in the face of continued rejection and that is why it is unpardonable.

In Mark 3 there is a confrontation between Jesus and the Scribes. These *"teachers of the law who came down from Jerusalem said, 'He is possessed by Beelzebub! By the prince of demons He is driving out demons,'"* Mark 3:22. Jesus condemns these self-righteous leaders who traveled a great distance, just to accuse Jesus and try stop His ministry. They hated God that much!

God's Spirit changed various people after their demons were cast out! Attributing this work of God in a person's heart to Satan, is treason. God and all of His beautiful attributes did the work, which we are called to praise God for! They were praising Satan. *"He who blasphemes against the Holy Spirit never has forgiveness, but is subject to eternal condemnation,"* Mark 3:29 NKJV.

Prayer: O Lord of grace and truth, we praise You for showing us what the unpardonable sin is. May we always be sensitive to Your Spirit working in us! We praise You for Your work in changing lives for all eternity. How beautiful is Your amazing grace that changes us selfish people into gracious souls. May Your everlasting kingdom come, and may Satan be exposed for who he is. In Jesus' name we pray. Amen.

April 29

"Let us examine our ways and test them, and let us return to the LORD." Lamentations 3:40

When our love grows cold

At times, we become so "earthly minded," so content in life, that we will lose our hunger for God. As a result, we start walking away from God. Soon thereafter, our spiritual life will become like a spouse who longs for her absent husband to return. A long separation from her husband is a partial death to her spirit. So it is with souls that the Savior loves much. We must see His face once again! We cannot bear being away from sweet communion with Him! We are the happiest in the smile of our Savior!

When we wander from God, He will soon bless us with the rod-of-affliction. Then we will fly back to our Father's feet, crying *"Search me and know my thoughts and see if there be any wicked way in me."* Is this our situation today? Have we been too content to follow Jesus from a distance? Can we accept a suspended communion with Christ without any alarm? Can we bear to have our Beloved walking away from us, because we have walked away from Him? Have our sins separated us from our God?

It is a cold heart that can live contentedly without the present enjoyment of the Savior's face! It is then, that we need sorrow for our hardness of heart. May the Lord make us willing to kneel before the Cross, the only place our heart can be warmed. No matter how hard, how insensitive or how dead we may have become, may we flee to the Cross. May we clutch that Cross and look into those eyes filled with tears and bathe in that fountain filled with blood. Christ is the only remedy to bring back our first love. Only Christ can restore the simplicity of our faith, and the tenderness of our heart!

Prayer: Compassionate Lord, we are so thankful that we can flee to You. We worship You for Your tenderness that restores us again and again. Lord, make us burn with desire for You! We praise You that *"He who began a good work in you (us) will carry it on to completion until the day of Christ Jesus,"* Philippians 1:6. In Christ's name we pray. Amen.

April 30

"You must teach what is in accord with sound doctrine." Titus 2:1

Is my life teaching *"sound doctrine"*?

In our text Paul is writing to a young pastor called Titus. From the thirteen references to him in the Pauline epistles, we can see that Titus is one of Paul's closest, trusted companions. The letter to Titus tells us it's important to live a godly life, to teach right doctrine!

It needs to be said that Paul is not encouraging Titus here to get a higher education to learn doctrine in order to preach and teach it. He is clearly talking about living his life in such a way that good practical doctrine is taught and caught. How much this message is needed today. Even today we received a letter from a rural pastor here in South India.

"God touched my heart and encouraged me. That's why I praise God. Before I receive this message (How can I change), I pray to God for repentance. Suddenly on the next day, I receive your magazine. I have no repentance like this before 15 years. The Lord has shown me a new life. Before I repented, I was troublesome for my family. I was an ordinary pastor without changing my heart. Now I forsake the old nature and became a new man with tears before God."

This pastor of 15 years was finally convicted of the need to live a godly life himself. Maybe this surprises some of you. It shouldn't. We are all sinners. Jesus called the Pharisees *"whitewashed tombs."* They were unconverted, even though they were church leaders. How about us? Are we teaching *"sound doctrine"* by how we live? The blind cannot lead the blind, for they will both fall into the ditch. *"In everything set them an example by doing what is good. In your teaching show integrity, seriousness and soundness of speech that cannot be condemned, so that those who oppose you may be ashamed because they have nothing bad to say about us,"* Titus 2:7-8.

Prayer: O Lord, have mercy on us sinners! For there is nothing more confusing to others than giving good advice from Your Word, and then setting a bad example by how we live! We so often preach the wrong message with our lives. Help us change fully. In Jesus' name we pray. Amen.

MAY

*"I have hidden Your Word in my heart
that I might not sin against You."*
Psalm 119:11

May 1

"'Why do you look at the speck of sawdust in your brother's eye and pay no attention to the plank in your own eye? How can you say to your brother, 'Let me take the speck out of your eye,' when all the time there is a plank in your own eye? You hypocrite, first take the plank out of your own eye, and then you will see clearly to remove the speck from your brother's eye.'" Matthew 7:3-5

"Take the plank out of your own eye"

This verse is essential to understand our personal problems in life. For example, when a student is having difficulties with their parents and some classmates, we will ask them, "Why are you struggling so much?" It is common for the student to say, "My problem is what my parents or classmates did to me." Truth is, the student's wrong response is the *"plank"* (sin) in his eye (heart) that really is a bigger problem.

A parent may be very strict or a classmate may cheat us and they are wrong. Still, it is not what they do to us that is our main problem! Our wrong response to what they did is worse. Others will <u>tempt</u> us to be angry, bitter, or worried. Yet the <u>real cause</u> of our ongoing hurt is the condition in our own heart! That is what our text is teaching us.

We so quickly want to fix the other person. God here is saying, "Fix yourself first." Why? God is the only one who is responsible to convict the other person and change them, not us! If we don't agree, then we are saying that our main problems in life are others, and "things" outside of us, not what is in our hearts. The "log" or "plank" in our eye is our real problem.

The picture God gives us is a log that is long, not short. How can we take a speck of sawdust out of someone's eye if we cannot get close to them? If we have a log or plank in our eye, how can we even see the other person to fix him or her? We can't. We are responsible to fix our own problems, even if others don't change! When we get serious with God about the sin in our own heart, our life will change. God will then be glorified and we will be blessed.

Prayer: Most gracious Lord, forgive us for blaming others for our problems, when it is our own heart that needs to change. Lord may this be an "eye opener," to see our need to personally repent. Then, Your kingdom will come in us. In Christ's name we pray. Amen.

May 2

"One of them, an expert in the law, tested Him with this question: 'Teacher, which is the greatest commandment in the Law?' Jesus replied: 'Love the Lord your God with all your heart, and with all your soul, and with all your mind.' This is the first and greatest commandment. And the second is like it: 'Love your neighbor as yourself.' All the Law and the Prophets hang on these two commandments." Matthew 22:35-40

A brief summary of the Bible

The lawyer in our text represents the wisdom of the world compared to God's wisdom. Jesus shows us here, that God's order of our love is important, by summing up the Ten Commandments in Exodus 20. These are, love God first in commands 1-4, then love others second in 5-10. There are no commandments to love self. We are wrong, very wrong, if we think that we must love ourselves more before we can love God and others. Such thinking is not in the Bible. See how the Ten Commandments do not include loving self.

Commandment # 5   *"Honor your father and your mother"* - Are they not others?

Commandment # 6   *"You shall not murder"* - Is not murder what we do against others?

Commandment # 7   *"You shall not commit adultery"* - Is this not with others and against others?

Commandment # 8   *"You shall not steal"* - Obviously this belongs to others, otherwise we wouldn't take it.

Commandment # 9   *"You shall not give false testimony against your neighbor"* - Is this not ruining another's name?

Commandment #10   *"You shall not covet"* - Is this not wanting what God gave to others?

Prayer: O holy Lord, like the lawyer in the Bible, we often doubt the order of Your Commandments by how we live out our lives. Truly our problem is we are selfish, and live to please self first, before You and others. How quickly we ignore the Bible's pattern of love. Lord forgive us. In Jesus' name we pray. Amen.

May 3

"After all, no one ever hated his own body, but he feeds and cares for it, just as Christ does the church." Ephesians 5:29

Can you hate yourself?

The thought that man has problems because he hates himself is such a huge lie! If that were true, then we would need to love ourselves more to come out of our problems. The Biblical fact is, we are all born 100% selfish, totally in love with self. Our sinful nature knows well, how to love self. We don't need a command for what we already know and practice. In fact, we have a necessary command from Jesus to do the opposite, *"deny ourselves,"* in Luke 9:23. The wisdom of our Lord has not changed over the years. Jesus clearly agreed with the Ten Commandments that teach God must be loved first, others second, making self last of all.

It is so important to understand that, *"No one ever hated his own body."* For if we listen to the opposite, to those who teach that a depressed and suicidal person hates himself or herself, we will never understand anyone's problem, including our own. We already love self, *"just as Christ does the church,"* Ephesians 5:29b. Christ loved the church so much that He willingly died for it. Those who think a suicidal person hates himself or herself should examine how such a person thinks.

"I don't care what anyone thinks." "I've had enough." "I'm going to get out of here." "No one understands me." "No one loves me." "Even my family hates me." This very self-centered person is full of "I, I, I, me, me, me." They love self too much, not too little. Self-exaltation, self-pity, and self-confidence are all selfish.

To correct their problems and ours, we must first agree with God that, *"No one ever hated his own flesh,"* Ephesians 5:29a. Then, by correcting the many ways we are being so selfish, we will climb out of our depression. And this is just one example.

Prayer: Dear loving Lord, we praise and thank You for telling us the truth about ourselves. Forgive us for accepting the world's theology that is the opposite of Your holy Word. Help us to deny our self so we can love You and others more! May Your kingdom come, not ours. We pray in the name of Jesus,' the One who denied Himself. Amen.

May 4

"But in your hearts set apart Christ as Lord. Always be prepared to give an answer to everyone who asks you to give the reason for the hope that you have. But do this with gentleness and respect."
1 Peter 3:15

The reason for our hope

When we lose hope in life, we are in serious trouble, mentally, physically, spiritually and even financially. We believers are commanded here in our text to give hope to others. But to give hope, we need to be filled with hope ourselves. We are not talking about the world's kind of hope, as that is merely a wish. The world has hope as long as people, possessions, and circumstances in their life are just right. When things change, their hope quickly flees. Biblical hope is different. Here is a definition of Biblical hope that is worth memorizing.

"Biblical hope is the application of your faith that supplies a confident expectation in God's fulfillment of His promises, which are grounded in God's character, not dependent on people, possessions or circumstances for it to be real."

In our text, we need to *"set apart Christ as Lord"* in our heats, to have real hope. Think too, of the definition of the faith in Hebrews 11:1 NKJV. *"Faith is the substance of things hoped for, the evidence of things not seen."* A Christian's hope is in God, in His Word, in His Son, and in His Spirit, knowing that nothing, *"in all creation, will be able to separate us from the love of God that is in Christ Jesus our Lord,"* Romans 8:39b. We will be separated from people, possessions, and circumstances. But if our hope is in our Creator, then we know that no one and nothing can separate us from God's love. In later devotions, we will discuss those who are experiencing anger, fear, worry and depression issues. They are putting their hope in the created things, including people, not in God. They will then struggle, without real hope.

Prayer: God of all hope, thank You for giving us real hope through a relationship with You. Forgive us for putting our hope in good health, more money, and a good education, instead of putting our hope in You and Your ability to care for us. Bless us as we study Your Word, to clearly see that through the Cross, You give us hope! In Jesus' name we pray. Amen.

May 5

"Blessed be the God and Father of our Lord Jesus Christ, the Father of mercies and the God of all comfort, who comforts us in all our tribulation, that we may be able to comfort those who are in any trouble, with the comfort with which we ourselves are comforted by God." 2 Corinthians 1:3-4 NKJV

Testimonies

These two verses are the very heart of evangelism. God saves us and then ministers to us so mercifully. A faith response, on our part, is to give a reason for the hope that is now in us. Others need the same hope and comfort that we have, that only God can give. The question is: What does our testimony sound like?

We hear testimonies about how, "I did this, and then that," in their trials. The I, me, my, in the testimony goes on and on. Then in the very last breath, there is a "praise be to God." Who is the author of such a faith? Should the praise for God's mercy, go to us or to God?

If we want to give real Biblical hope and comfort to others, then we need to point to the source of our faith, that is God, not us. He is, *"the Father of mercies and the God of all comfort, who comforts us in all our tribulation, that we may be able to comfort those who are in any trouble."* The words *"all"* and *"any"* point to God's never-ending supply of "mercy" and "comfort." May we point people to God who is the Father of all mercy!

Christians, *"are God's workmanship, created in Christ Jesus to do good works, which God prepared in advance for us to do,"* Ephesians 2:10. With this in mind, can any of us claim praise for any good work of *"mercy"* or *"comfort"* to others? Perhaps we were faithful, but even our faithfulness is the love of God at work in us. God alone is the "source" of what we are in Christ. Let us all give a clear testimony to what God has done, and will keep doing!

Prayer: O Healer of our spirits, forgive us for being too proud of even our spiritual accomplishments. We have acted as if Your wisdom and strength originated in us. You are the One who rescues us and others from every kind of trouble. May Your grace and peace abide in us and others for Your glory alone. You, are our loving God in Trinity who is worthy of praise. In Jesus' name we pray. Amen.

May 6

"For we know that our old self was crucified with Him so that the body of sin might be done away with, that we should no longer be slaves to sin." Romans 6:6

"Slaves to sin"

A 15-year-old Hindu boy came in yesterday who was on drugs. He was rebellious to the core, constantly in trouble, an embarrassment to his family. What can you tell a sad, proud, and self-centered young boy? You cannot just tell him to quit his drugs, drinking and that he needs to respect his parents. He has no power to change! He was much aware of all this as he nodded his head when we discussed this verse. I told him that life has two roads, a wide road and a narrow road. He was on the wide road that leads to total destruction. By nature, it is easy to travel this road. He agreed. But he didn't know that he was on this road because he was literally, a *"slave to sin,"* and that Satan was his father who wanted to steal his soul for all eternity.

Anyone working with this boy really needs to know that he can't just change his living habits until his heart changes first. It is Jesus alone who changes any heart, never a counselor. We can only point a person to Christ. When a person's heart is changed by God, it is then that their thoughts, words, and actions would start to change also. Now, after their thoughts, words, and actions are changed, would they know peace, which also comes from God.

God Himself, then through the working of His Holy Spirit, convicts us all of our guilt (John 16:7-8) and shame caused by our sinful living. It is only God can set us free who are *"slaves to sin."*

We cannot do evangelism if we do not see the "many" who have a *"slaves to sin"* problem. Some of these *"slaves"* go to church, but that never freed anyone in itself. Freedom from slavery to sin is not in a program either. It is in a Person, Christ alone!

Prayer: O Lord who sets us free, we pray for those who are sons and daughters of Satan, totally, *"slaves to sin."* Lord, open their hearts to the need of a Savior so that they can become *"slaves to righteousness."* Lord, do this for Your name's sake and for the building of Your kingdom. In Christ's name we pray. Amen.

May 7

"But thanks be to God that, though you used to be slaves to sin, you wholeheartedly obeyed the form of teaching to which you were entrusted. You have been set free from sin and have become slaves to righteousness." Romans 6:17-18

"Slaves to righteousness"

We just saw that without Christ we are *"slaves to sin,"* and that is what we must put off. Now, becoming a "slave to righteousness," is the PUT-ON part that completes the Biblical change or repentance process. The word *"slave"* is an important word, for whatever we are *"slaves to,"* that is what controls us.

True, we still sin after becoming a Christian. But there will be a big change in our attitude towards sin. The reason is, *"For it is God who works in you both to will and to do for His good pleasure,"* Philippians 2:13 NKJV. If our salvation is real, it is now our new desire to not only be righteous, but to be a *"slave to righteousness."* Like Apostle Paul, we must and will sin less and less, but we will be more and more sensitive to that sin which remains in us. Why? Because God the Holy Spirit is in us, making us a slave to do what is right. *"You have been set free from sin and have become slaves to righteousness,"* Romans 6:18.

In Christ, we are all saved from both the power as well as the penalty of sin. That is the reality of the Christian life. We now look to Christ in gratitude, giving God glory for working obedience in us.

Think of what being *"slaves to righteousness"* means for drunkards, sex addicts, the angry, and the unforgiving. Christ alone breaks the power of sin that holds them. Forgiven, we now cling to Christ, not to the sin. *"Therefore, do not let sin reign in your mortal body so that you obey its evil desires,"* Romans 6:12. A big secret to real Biblical change is concentrating on a relationship with Christ. Our Christian obedience happens because of our love relationship with Christ.

Prayer: O Lord, we thank You for changing our hearts, for sending Your Spirit to convict us of our sin and pull us to the Cross. Now as Your servants You pour more and more of Your grace in us, making us obedient. This world has no hope to offer. You are the Way, the Truth and the Life! Thank-You for making us *"slaves to righteousness."* In Jesus' name we pray. Amen.

May 8

"No temptation has overtaken you except such as is common to man; but God is faithful, who will not allow you to be tempted beyond what you are able, but with the temptation will also make the way of escape, that you may be able to bear it." 1 Corinthians 10:13 NKJV

"God is faithful"

We have four bold points that give hope to a struggling believer. First of all, every problem every believer will ever have is a *"common"* problem to God. There are no new problems in this world. There is no new trial, no new testing, no new temptation that will ever come upon any believer that is beyond our ability to handle, if, that is, we keep our eyes on Him and His Word!

"God is faithful" is a promise to us, built on the very faithfulness of God. If God's faithfulness can fail us, then so can this promise! But it cannot fail, if we are in Christ. God can no more leave us, than He could ever leave His own Son. God has a covenant with every single Christian that He will always keep. He will never disappoint the love and hope of His children. He is a faithful, covenant-keeping God!

"The way of escape" is God's sovereign ability to lead us through any trial without sinning. This does not mean we will immediately be out of every trial. After all, God allows trials to help us grow, and to test our faith. Jesus was not spared any of His trials, but He did go through them without sinning. *"The way of escape"* is God's covenant promise to all believers. Every true Christian can say; *"the Lord will rescue me from every evil attack and will bring me safely to His heavenly kingdom,"* 2 Timothy 4:18a.

In Christ, we are *"able to bear it"* because God is all-powerful, has all wisdom, and sees everything. He knows just how much we can take. Our trials as a Christian will always be in proportion to our strength. Our loving Father here promises never to give us more than we can bear. We can now handle life because our God is always in us and for us. Our God is so good!

Prayer: Caring Lord, You teach us that there is no affliction so grievous that You can't prevent, remove, or enable us to accept it. In the end, You work all things in our life for Your glory and for our good. What great promises we have in Christ! In His name we pray. Amen.

May 9

"For we do not have a high priest who is unable to sympathize with our weaknesses, but we have One who has been tempted in every way, just as we are - yet was without sin. Let us then approach the throne of grace with confidence, so that we may receive mercy and find grace to help us in our time of need." Hebrews 4:15-16

Mercy *"in our time of need"*

Jesus knows how heavy of a "misery load" we can handle. Our High Priest hears our cries for mercy. He understands our weakness and every temptation we will ever have! If this is not true, then this verse is a lie. Jesus was tempted by Satan in all the ways we are, yet He did not sin. When we are about to lose strength and hope, Jesus reaches down and gives us more grace so we won't fail. What Jesus said to Peter is true of us. *"Satan has asked to sift you as wheat."* *"But I have prayed for you, Simon, that your faith may not fail,"* Luke 22:31b-32a.

"Approach the throne of grace with confidence." Jesus, our High Priest, is alive, sitting on a throne at the right hand of God. Jesus is holding out the scepter to us. He invites us to come. Jesus not only understands our pain, but can also do something about it, which is to give us mercy. The *"mercy"* of Jesus never comes too soon. Neither will it come too late! God allows our trials and even designs them. Why would He remove them before the very reason for the trial has been accomplished? That reason, is more Christ-likeness in us or perhaps in others near us.

Notice that, Jesus gives grace, *"in our time of need,"* not in our time of "want." This is essential to understand if we are now without hope. God's grace will never be so late that we could ever sink. Our Savior gives us grace, exactly *"in our time of need."* We must believe in God's "timing of mercy" with the eyes of faith today, so that we can learn to keep our eyes on our Lord, instead of focusing so intently on the trial we are in.

Prayer: Lord of love, we are grateful that You constantly have Your eyes on us, delighting to give us grace *"in our time of need."* We praise You for building our faith and for working a spiritual life in all those You call to Yourself. May Your name be praised and may Your kingdom be built up. In Christ's name we pray. Amen.

May 10

"My brethren, count it all joy when you fall into various trials, knowing that the testing of your faith produces patience. But let patience have its perfect work, that you may be perfect and complete, lacking nothing." James 1:2-4 NKJV

"Count it all joy"

James writes his letter to hurting Christians, forced from their homes by the cruel Nero, and the will of God. Yes, the will of God because they were not going out into the world to preach and teach the Gospel, so God forced them out by using Nero. To these scattered people James writes: *"count it all joy"* when you have these trials. James knew that when we as believers have a serious trial, we need to have the right attitude in them. This is not something we normally want to do. Most often, we just want out of the pain and out of the trial quickly. This is how the world thinks.

Chuck Swindoll said, "The older I get, the more I realize that life is 10% what happens to us and 90% how we respond to what happens!" That is great theology and exactly why James said, "Count it all joy when you fall into various trials." But why?

James answers the question. *"Knowing that the testing of your faith develops patience."* The attitude of *"patience,"* is listed first in the love chapter. *"Love is patient,"* 1 Corinthians 13:4a. Until we are *"patient"* Christians, we cannot be kind, stop envying, stop being proud, stop boasting, stop being rude, stop our self-seeking, and stop our easily angered responses. You see, grace needs to replace. God will make us more like Christ. God's *"patience"* in us, sets us up to be faithful in so many ways. God's purpose in sending us trials is, *"patience has its perfect work, that you may be perfect and complete, lacking nothing."*

Prayer: O wise and all-knowing Lord, we confess, we have complained about our trials as if You hate us! Then we learn that just the opposite is true. Forgive us, because we can see that You are developing a Christ-like heart in us through our trials. We know by faith that looking like Christ is more important than anything else in life. Help us to have a right attitude so we not only persevere in our trials but also worship You for them. In Christ's name we pray. Amen.

May 11

"Let us fix our eyes on Jesus, the Author and Perfecter of our faith, who for the joy set before Him endured the Cross, scorning its shame, and sat down at the right hand of the throne of God." Hebrews 12:2

How to endure trials

Our text commands us to look to Jesus, because as God and perfect man, He is *"the Author and Perfecter of our faith."* When we see just how our Lord *"endured"* suffering, we will have the secret to follow His example. Jesus did not *"endure the Cross,"* by looking at the Cross. We often fail in our trials, because we stare so intently at the trial. Jesus kept His eye on God the Father, knowing why He was suffering. He knew the "big picture" of God's plan for His life. Jesus was able to fit his temporary suffering into the larger picture of life and eternity. When we focus so much on our present trial, we quickly fail to see what God is doing in us, for His kingdom. Jesus knew the Cross itself was not the problem but was the solution to redeem man.

Jesus *"endured"* by thinking of *"the joy that was set before Him."* That joy was to be with God, with the angels, and with all of God's children. While on the Cross, Jesus thought about fulfilling His Father's perfect design for His life while remaining faithful as we must also do. Jesus knew His trials were for the making of peace between God and man, sealing the covenant of grace as its Mediator.

Jesus did not give into self-pity while on the Cross. How often we are filled with such self-love in our trials. Then we wonder why we are in them so long and are even depressed! We too, can get through any trial in complete peace if we *"keep our eyes on Jesus."* Jesus lived perfect love. God was first. Others were second. Self was last. Even in death, Jesus lived for the will of God and held His hands out to sinners. The *"Perfecter of our faith,"* showed us how to live the Christian life.

Prayer: O Lord, You call us Christian because we follow Christ. Help us poor wandering sheep to follow in His steps. Help us to remember Jesus' perfect love the next time someone treats us like dirt. Help us to see how You use our trials to mature our faith. May we not give in to the temptation to wallow in self-pity, but *"count it all joy,"* as You tell us to do. In Jesus' name we pray. Amen.

May 12

"You intended to harm me, but God intended it for good, to accomplish what is now being done, the saving of many lives." Genesis 50:20

Trials are for our good

Joseph understood the theology of difficult trials. Joseph's brothers hated him so much that they sold him. He ended up a slave in Egypt. Joseph worked seven years, moving from the position of slave to overseer of his master's house. One day his master's wife tried to catch him and pull him into bed. He refused, but she accused him anyway. He went to jail. For seven more years, Joseph had to start all over again. For seven years, Joseph was faithful in his daily responsibilities and relationships even in great trials. May this shout to us in our trials. It is not recorded that Joseph did anything wrong.

Why do we have the life of Joseph's life? God tells us: *"Everything that was written in the past was written to teach us,"* Romans 15:4. Why? *"So that through endurance and the encouragement of the Scriptures we might have hope,"* Romans 15:4b. We do not endure much, because we do not hope much. A lack of hope is a faith issue, for it is a lack of trusting in God! Joseph's life is written to help us to trust in God.

With a great famine in the land, Joseph's brothers came to Egypt for food. In our distress, we come to Jesus begging for spiritual food. Joseph recognized his brothers. Jesus recognizes us as His brothers when we come to Him. Joseph's brothers begged for their lives. Do we beg Christ for our spiritual life?

After the death of Joseph's father, the brothers thought Joseph would take revenge. Joseph calmed them saying, *"You meant evil against me but God meant it for good,"* Genesis 50:20a NKJV. Why? *"In order to bring it about as it is this day, to save many people alive."* Understand this! God gives trials to help us look more like Christ. Why? So that He can use our lives to work with Him, helping, *"to save many people."*

Prayer: O wise Lord, may we learn to trust in You during all our trials. Help us when we can't see Your hand, to trust Your heart. Forgive us for our doubts and fears about Your sovereign ability to work out all things for our good. In Christ's name we pray. Amen.

May 13

"Great peace have they who love Your law, and nothing can make them stumble." Psalm 119:165

The secret to peace

We may say and even sing that we love God's law, but do we? When we ask how many Commandments there are in the Bible, many cannot even say ten. Fewer yet know that the first four commandments are to love God and the next six are to love others. It is rare people know that there is no commandment to love self. Is it any wonder then, that so many people lack peace, with their "love" life so messed up?

I once met a professor from a normally solid denomination. He said millions of young people are very depressed because they hate themselves. His suggestion was that if they would love themselves more, they would not be depressed. God tells us, *"No man hates his own flesh,"* Ephesians 5:29a. This professor turned the Bible upside down! How can such a person help people with their spiritual problems? God promises peace when we *"love His law,"* which is, loving God and then others, in that order. The world's self-first idea of peace is only when circumstances, possessions, or people are momentarily just right.

The reason we lack peace is because, in reality, God is not the most important relationship in our lives. Others are not second. When such selfish love happens, the Holy Spirit gives frustration, not peace. Prisons all over the world would be empty, and churches would be full, if the Biblical order of love was lived out. The letters J.O.Y. spell joy. The "J" stands for Jesus, the "O" for others, and the "Y" stands for yourself. To truly experience joy and "peace" in our life, the order must remain, 1. Jesus 2. Others 3. You. Only then will we have peace. If we put the O or the Y before the J, there will be no joy and no peace. A small step away from selfishness is a big step towards God.

Prayer: O Lord of peace and joy, we have blamed a lack of money, a difficult circumstance, an unloving spouse, or a wayward child, for our lack of peace. Forgive us for looking to You, who are perfect Love. We praise You for giving us a peace the world cannot give it. In Jesus' name we pray. Amen.

May 14

"I will give you a new heart and put a new spirit within you; I will take the heart of stone out of your flesh and give you a heart of flesh."
Ezekiel 36:26 NKJV

Are we responsible to change others?

There is a real temptation to think we are responsible to change others. After all, the Great Commission tells us *"to go into all the world."* But does this mean we are responsible to change them? No, we are responsible to tell them the truth about God. Then it is God's responsibility to change them. Only God can change a human heart, as our text teaches. If we think we are responsible to change others, we will easily be defeated when a person does not change. An example will help us see this.

A new Christian wanted his wife to come back to him. I suggested he follow the love chapter, 1 Corinthians 13:4-8. I asked him to start doing the things for his wife and family that he neglected while he was a drunk. After two weeks, he cried out, "She won't come back!" What was the problem? What should have been made clearer? This man was doing these loving deeds first and foremost to change her, so she would come back. Wrong, he needed to do these things for God first, as worship. Then, importantly, he needed to wait for God to change her. Yes, all this, while he continued to love her! How wonderful that when we love people God's way, God changes us, and sometimes others too!

What a blessing it is that we are not responsible for changing even one heart, other than our own. God shows us that we are to be faithful and accountable to Him for our own thoughts, words, and actions. We are to be an example of a believer. It is when we live the Christian life and teach God's way of living, that God keeps His promises. Then His Word does not return void. He will definitely change some hearts!

Prayer: Faithful Lord, forgive us for thinking we need to change others. We are grateful the Christian life begins with You, continues with You, then ends with You. We are thankful that in The Judgment, You will never say to us, "Why didn't you change this or that heart?" Help us to be faithful in ministering the love of Christ to others. In Jesus' name we pray. Amen.

May 15

"He lifted up His hands and blessed them. While He was blessing them, He left them and was taken up into Heaven." Luke 24:50b-51

The benefits of Christ's ascension

The ascension of Jesus Christ going back to Heaven is the fulfillment of the transfiguration, with Jesus on the mountain with Moses and Elijah. This transfiguration event took place before Christ died and arose. Had Christ ascended earlier with Moses and Elijah, He would not have ascended as the Son of Man, but only as the Son of God. But now ascended, Christ has full authority as our representative in Heaven. He has full power as the King of kings and the Lord of lords with three benefits for us.

First, the ascended Christ is our Advocate to God. Like a lawyer, He pleads our case to God the righteous Judge. As our High Priest Jesus is able to obtain the grace and mercy that we need, instead of the wrath of God we deserve! *"Therefore He is able to save completely those who come to God through Him, because He always lives to intercede for them,"* Hebrews 7:25.

Second, the ascended Christ now sends His Spirit to gather in His elect and to fill them with His presence. Why, because *"the man without the Spirit does not accept the things that come from the Spirit of God, for they are foolishness to him, and he cannot understand them, because they are spiritually discerned,"* 1 Corinthians 2:14. Without Christ sending His Spirit we could not be either justified or sanctified.

Third, Christ's ascension is the guarantee of our own ascension. Jesus said, *"In My Father's house are many rooms; if it were not so, I would have told you. I am going there to prepare a place for you. And if I go to prepare a place for you, I will come back and take you to be with Me that you also may be where I am,"* John 14:2-3. Because of Christ's ascension, we will someday be with Christ, both in body and in soul!

Prayer: O Lord how beautiful is Your ascension. How worthy You are to sit on the throne as both the perfect Son of God and the one and only perfect Man. Because of Your mercy and grace, we too can be rescued from this body of death and obtain life forever. We worship You, our ascended Prophet, Priest and King. In Your beautiful name we pray. Amen.

May 16

"Now when He saw the crowds, He went up on a mountainside and sat down. His disciples came to Him, and He began to teach them."
Matthew 5:1-2

Why "The Beatitudes"?

In Jesus' day many people were discontent, lacking happiness. Jesus wanted to assure His new disciples that if they followed Him they would be happy and blessed. Today, so many of us are still searching! Churches try to give happiness, often without much success. The reason is, we are not using Jesus' methods.

Jesus makes a shocking point in The Beatitudes. It is not what happens around us that makes us either happy or unhappy. It is what happens in us. Jesus is not teaching commands to His disciples, but "character qualities" that result in happiness and blessedness. Jesus wanted His disciples to follow Him, to have a relationship with Him. Blessedness and happiness comes from following the person Jesus!

Why did Jesus teach like this to new disciples? If fallen man is given many rules and regulations to follow while we are still totally unregenerate, how can we keep them? This was exactly the Pharisee's problem. There was no power in them to keep the rules! This is still a big problem yet today. The answer is not in creeds, commands, or liturgies, but in loving the person, Jesus! For example, *"Blessed are you when people insult you, persecute you and falsely say all kinds of evil against you <u>because of Me</u>,"* Matthew 5:11. The Christian is not blessed simply because he or she is persecuted. Only because of our love for Christ will we be blessed.

When we try to keep God's commands without first loving God, we are headed for frustration, not for lots of blessings. I am not antinomian (against the law God). Paul called the law a schoolmaster that led him to Christ, because where Paul couldn't keep the law, Christ kept it for him. Jesus came into the world to fulfill the demands of the law perfectly. Thus, happiness is found in knowing the person of Christ, the one the Old Testament law pointed to.

Prayer: O Lord help us! We cannot be satisfied unless we know Jesus as our Friend, our Brother, our Savior, our all. Give us Jesus, every day and every hour. In His name we pray. Amen.

May 17

"Blessed are the poor in spirit, for theirs is the kingdom of Heaven."
Matthew 5:3

"Poor in spirit"

The Amplified Bible reads, *"Blessed-happy, to be envied, and spiritually prosperous that is, with life-joy and satisfaction in God's favor and salvation, regardless of their outward conditions,"* Matthew 5:3a. Contrast this verse, to the world's idea of happiness, which is centered on the externals, like wealth, looks, position in society, etc... What happens when these are gone? Only sad hopelessness.

"Poor in spirit" does not mean financial poverty will somehow make us happy! Many people over the years have taken vows of poverty to seek happiness. It does not work. *"Poor in spirit"* is the opposite of being proud. *"Poor in spirit"* is humility that comes from a correct evaluation of who we are, spiritually speaking. There is a song that says, *"Nothing in my hand I bring, simply to Thy Cross I cling."* This realization of spiritual poverty leads to an eternal blessed happiness that so transcends daily happenings. When Jesus told parables of the lame, the blind, and the lepers, He was painting a picture of our spiritual condition without Him. This understanding of our spiritual condition is absolutely necessary to be *"poor in spirit."*

We are unworthy to have Christ pay for our sins! Those who are *"poor in spirit,"* understand we are "totally depraved," lost, unable to move to God. Until we realize we are lost, there is no perceived need to be found by Christ. A common problem is that we think we are ready for Heaven because we are "pretty good." Such thoughts are far from being, *"poor in spirit."* Being *"poor in spirit"* then, flies right in the face of the world's theology that says, we need to assert ourselves to have fulfillment or a blessed happiness!

Prayer: O holy Lord, we thank You for teaching us that we need more of You, not the things of the world, in order to have eternal happiness. O Lord, Your wisdom is so radically different than the wisdom of the world. Compared to Your eternal truth, *"There is a way that seems right to a man, but the end leads to death."* Lord, thank You for opening Your spiritual treasury of blessings to those of us who are *"poor in spirit"* by Your amazing grace. In Jesus' name we pray. Amen.

May 18

"Blessed are they who mourn, for they will be comforted."
Matthew 5:4

"Mourn"

If we are *"poor in spirit,"* we understand our spiritual bankruptcy and "mourn" over how our sins hurt God. The "mourning" spoken of here is a sorrow for our sin and for the sin of others, which leads us to do the work of evangelism.

We are *"blessed"* if we *"mourn"* for our own sin. One of our biggest shocks should be the uncaring attitude in the Christian community over the topic of personal sin. Psychology has made such significant inroads in the Church that people rarely *"mourn"* over their own sin anymore. How can we *"mourn"* over our sin if we do not specifically acknowledge it in our lives? We will never *"mourn"* for our personal sin if we blame society or our parents for the problems we have. Can we be forgiven and *"blessed"* if we confess their sins and not our own?

We also do not *"mourn"* for our personal sin because we call sin something it is not. One good example is anger. We call our anger "tension" or "stress" and then claim this is how God made us. We call our anger "righteous," when God says it is *"not righteous"* in James 1:20. God also calls 7 kinds of anger, deeds of the flesh in Galatians 5:19-21. If we do not confess it, and put it off, we *"will not inherit the kingdom of Heaven."* Another example is, we justify our bitterness, while God calls it *"demonic"* in James 3:14-16. We quickly call our many sins: diseases, disorders, stresses, personal problems, chemical imbalances, anything but sin! Our blessings begin, only after such blame-shifting ends! We have to agree with God about what is sin!

How can we, in the spirit of evangelism, grieve over the sin of others, if we do not first grieve over our own sin?

Prayer: Dear Lord, forgive us for not mourning over our sin. *"Have mercy on me, O God, according to Your unfailing love: according to Your great compassion blot out my transgressions. Wash away all my iniquity and cleanse me from my sin. For I know my transgressions, and my sin is always before me,"* Psalm 51:1-3. Lord, truly *"blessed is the man whose sin the LORD does not count against him,"* Psalm 32:2. Thank You for Your mercy Lord! In Christ's name we pray. Amen.

May 19

"Blessed are the meek, for they will inherit the earth."
Matthew 5:5

"Meek"

"Blessed are the meek for they will inherit the earth!" We most often use the word "humble" today, instead of the word *"meek."* Proud is the opposite of *"meek."* To be *"meek"* is to be spiritually mature. This means that we are so fully satisfied with God, that we are not dependent on outward conditions changing to have peace and joy.

The *"meek,"* are those who willingly submit to God's Word, His Son, His discipline, even His blessings. "Meekness" means that we are willing to put to death our passions and desires for sinning. To be *"meek"* is to have compassion for stubborn people. *"Meek"* people are able to teach simple Gospel truths to those who need Christ. Jesus said, *"Take My yoke upon you, and learn of Me; for I am meek and lowly in heart: and ye shall find rest unto your souls,"* Matthew 11:29 ASV. *"Meek"* people are not stressed out.

Meekness is a beauty secret that puts a shine on the face of a believer. *"Now Moses was a very humble man, more humble than anyone else on the face of the earth,"* Numbers 12:3. The older King James Version says, *"Moses was very meek."* *"When Aaron and all the Israelites saw Moses, his face was radiant,"* Exodus 34:30a. God gives this beauty when we spend much time with Him. Deacon Stephen, was also a *"meek"* man. The people who put him to death noticed, *"his face was like the face of an angel,"* Acts 6:15b. Christians almost always have a brighter countenance than non-believers. I really noticed this in India. When God cleans up the inside of a person, it moves to the outside face also.

Those who are not *"meek"* are still too full of themselves. It is not safe for God to bless people who are not *"meek"* because they will become even more proud of His blessings.

Prayer: O holy Lord, we are so often angry and bitter instead of meek and humble. Forgive us! We thank You for Your grace of meekness, the fruit of walking closely with You, our God. You tell us, *"The meek will inherit the land and enjoy great peace,"* Psalm 37:11. We praise You for such blessings Lord. In Christ our Savior's name we pray. Amen.

May 20

"Blessed are those who hunger and thirst for righteousness,
for they will be filled." Matthew 5:6

"Hunger and thirst for righteousness"

Our *"righteousness"* is in Christ alone. There is no *"righteousness"* apart from the Righteous One. *"Hunger and thirst"* are intense feelings of desire. When we are extremely hungry or thirsty, we will give anything for just a little food or drink. With this very same passion, if we hunger for Christ and His righteousness, we *"will be filled"* spiritually. If we are not *"filled,"* it stands to reason we have not hungered for it. It was Spurgeon who said: "Never does the Lord work in any man a firm resolution to find the Savior and yet allow him to perish."

What is it, we hunger for in life? What do we want more than anything? Whatever that is, that is where our heart is. We have an invitation here to come and be filled by the Lord of Heaven and Earth! What more could we want than real, solid, spiritual food to feed the spiritual nature that God gave each of us? Seek or starve is just as true spiritually as it is physically! *"Seek ye the LORD while He may be found, call on Him while He is near,"* Isaiah 55:6a. We have a personal responsibility to seek the Lord!

At the same time, our hungering and thirsting is a gift from God! Jesus said, *"No one can come to Me unless the Father who sent Me draws him,"* John 6:44a. If we do not hunger for God, pray for God to give us an appetite for Himself! Then, when God puts that hunger in us, we need to act on it! Know that hungering and thirsting are very temporary passions, both physically and spiritually! We do not stay in this condition very long. We are either filled, or we soon start dying.

Prayer: O Lord of our spiritual blessings, we thank and praise You that if we *"hunger and thirst after righteousness,"* You will fill and bless us. We thank You for helping us better understand the process of Biblical change here. We can see that it is not enough just to realize we are sinners and to confess our sin. You also show us that our old way of living needs to be replaced! In the same way, may we exchange our sinning for *"hungering and thirsting after righteousness."* May we treasure this secret to real change and concentrate on living for You! In Christ's name we pray. Amen.

May 21

"Blessed are the merciful, for they will be shown mercy." Matthew 5:7

"Merciful"

Being *"merciful"* is the first example Jesus gives, to show us what it means to *"hunger and thirst for righteousness."* Mercy is a judicial word. Mercy is what God gives to us instead of His justice and wrath against sin. With God's gift of mercy in our hearts, He expects us to give it to others. He will bless us when we do. In the Greek, mercy means "pity plus action to relieve misery." I have noticed in my life that the times I am feeling the most down, God often shows me others who need mercy. The more God gives us the gift of mercy, the more it must overflow to others! Interesting, that by helping others, we forget about ourselves.

God's mercy in Luke 1:78 is *"tender"* and is intended to create tenderness in us. If we break the word apart, we see that God tends to us dearly. Tenderness is also what makes a man a gentleman and what makes a woman dear to others. It is mercy in us, that makes us charitable people. A heart of mercy gives to others especially when they do not deserve it. When a judge is merciful to a lawbreaker, they give a lighter sentence than what is deserved. Mercy, like forgiveness, is only given to those who do not deserve it. Otherwise it really isn't mercy at all. In fact, mercy often shows that we have lovingly granted forgiveness to someone. Mercy and forgiveness are the opposite of anger and bitterness, and this is why the merciful are happy. They do not have a bad "attitude" towards others. Being merciful is the opposite of being selfish. Merciful people genuinely care about and pray for others. A merciful person makes a great spouse or friend. A person with a critical spirit is far from being merciful and will not be happy or blessed! In fact, they will be down and depressed!

Prayer: Most loving Lord, You show great mercy in saving us. You continue to give us mercy in so many forms every day. With Your mercy in our hearts, may we plan acts of mercy to others, then follow up on our plan. Lord, give us a servant heart to show mercy. Give us the financial and physical strength to carry it out. In Jesus' name we pray. Amen.

May 22

"Blessed are the pure in heart, for they will see God." Matthew 5:8

"Pure in heart"

The *"blessed,"* are those who understand and experience God's amazing grace. They are the ones that are spiritually prosperous. They not only know God personally now, but they will *"see God"* forever.

It needs to be said that being a true Christian is much more than head knowledge or good doctrine. It also involves a pureness of character. If we claim to be a Christian based on knowledge alone, we still could be more like Satan than Christ. The faith of a father, mother or grandparents, does not automatically pass on to the children. If we go to church on Sunday, but don't really want to, that is not a good sign. If Christ and His holiness are just thoughts that roll around in our heads and then are quickly overruled by the passion of our hearts, we have a "religion" that does not fool God! We need to be *"pure in heart."*

To be inwardly pure, we all need a heart transformation. That process consists of Christ coming in, and wickedness going out. Wickedness cannot dwell long in a heart where Christ lives. With a new heart from God, we will live differently and seek pureness. Before salvation we are literally, a *"slave to sin,"* Romans 6:6. With a new pure heart, we now become *"slaves to righteousness,"* Romans 6:18. The heart change is very noticeable.

I am convinced from the Word of God and from my own personal experience, that many in our churches will miss Heaven by 18 inches. We must make sure that God is in our heart as well as in our head! We must not rest until we find our rest in Him. Let us then, desire His holiness and a closer walk with Him. We all need our heart to be pure from being washed in Jesus' blood and then we *"will see God"*!

Prayer: Dear Holy Lord, You tell us that none but the *"pure in heart"* are able to see You. Lord, we must admit, too often we see how close we can get to sin, instead of how close we can get to You. Lord be merciful to us! We need You more than anything. Help us because we are weak. We pray as unworthy sinners who need the worthy One, Jesus Christ. In His name we pray. Amen.

May 23

"Blessed are the peacemakers, for they will be called sons of God."
Matthew 5:9

"Peacemakers"

If we have peace with God, we will soon be peaceful towards man also. If we love the Creator, then we will love the creature that was created in His image. When we have peace with God, we will love sinners but like Jesus, will hate the sin in their lives. Make no mistake, pride divides. Peace unites. God has given every Christian the ministry of reconciliation. Sad to say, it often takes many years for us to be interested in making peace with others. In fact, we can't even do the work of evangelism until we are a peacemaker! The first concern of a peacemaker is the lost souls of others. Everyone's greatest need is to have peace with God and then to have peace with man. The Ten Commandments teach this clearly.

"Peacemakers" have beautiful feet. *"How beautiful are the feet of those who bring good news,"* Romans 10:15. Jesus Christ Himself is called the *"prince of peace."* Christ came here to earth to reunite God to man, and man to man. The fall in the Garden of Eden separated both God and man, and also man to man. Sin separates us all. Peace then, is a beautiful fruit of grace! We lack peace, because we lacking in grace! If the grace of God is in our heart, grace will come out of our mouth, even more and more. *"For out of the overflow of his heart his mouth speaks,"* Luke 6:45b. Why then, are there so many people (in the church) who claim to know so much about the grace of God, yet are far from being gracious in how they treat others? God clearly tells us, *"If you harbor bitter envy and selfish ambition in your hearts, do not boast about it or deny the truth. Such wisdom does not come down from Heaven but is earthly, unspiritual, of the devil,"* James 3:14-15.

Prayer: Dear Lord, You are the One who makes peace with us, through Jesus Christ. Your Wisdom is awesome. The book of James says that *"the wisdom that comes from Heaven is first of all pure; then peaceful, considerate, submissive, full of mercy and good fruit, impartial and sin-cere. You make us wise. You make us "peacemakers," fit for this world and the next. Thank You Lord. We pray this in the name of the Prince of peace, Jesus Christ. Amen.

May 24

"Blessed are you when people insult you, persecute you and falsely say all kinds of evil against you because of Me. Rejoice and be glad, because great is your reward in Heaven, for in the same way they persecuted the prophets who were before you."
Matthew 5:11-12

Persecuted and falsely accused

"Blessed-happy, to be envied, and spiritually prosperous (that is, with life-joy and satisfaction in God's favor and salvation, regardless of your outward conditions) are you when people revile you and persecute you and say all kinds of evil things falsely on My account. Be glad and supremely joyful, for your reward in Heaven is great (strong and intense) for in the same way people persecuted the prophets who were before you," Matthew 5:11-12 the Amplified Bible.

First, our text says, *"when people insult you,"* not *"if."* Christians will be persecuted. Jesus wanted us to know this, so we will not be surprised by it. Expect it and have the right attitude when it happens. The more we are on the cutting edge for Christ, the more Satan will devise schemes to cut us up.

Second, bear persecution patiently for, *"Great is your reward in Heaven."* The word *"is,"* again means today also. Jesus is currently, today, storing up rewards for His children who receive evil slander and persecution. *"Because of Me,"* are key words. Many people are persecuted because they are a little different. But it is those who are different because of Jesus Christ that are spoken of here. *"Great is your reward in Heaven."*

Third, the Church of Jesus Christ prospers the most when she is the most persecuted. His-story teaches this. Jesus said, *"in the same way they persecuted the prophets who were before you."* Winning the world for Christ still involves suffering.

Prayer: O Lord of truth, we thank You for filling us with love, hope and direction. Too often we complain about our sufferings and persecutions instead of being thankful for them. May we have the mind of Christ and the mind of Paul who said, *"I consider that my present sufferings are not worth comparing with the glory that will be revealed in us,"* Romans 8:18. In Jesus' name we pray. Amen.

May 25

"You are the salt of the earth. But if the salt loses its saltiness, how can it be made salty again? It is no longer good for anything, except to be thrown out and trampled by men." Matthew 5:13

"The salt of the earth"

Charles Spurgeon tells a helpful story that puts our text into a proper perspective. "The teacher said, 'Boys, here's a watch. What is it for?' The children answered, 'to tell the time.' 'Well,' said he, 'suppose my watch does not tell the time. What is it good for?' 'Good for nothing, sir.' Then he took a pencil. 'What is this pencil for?' 'It is to write with sir.' 'Suppose the pencil will not make a mark. What is it good for?' 'Good for nothing, sir.' Then the teacher asked, 'What is the chief end of man?' and they replied, 'To glorify God.' 'But suppose a man does not glorify God. What is he good for?' 'Good for nothing, sir!'"

Jesus wanted His disciples to know that they were good for something! They were, *"the salt of the earth."* Jesus wanted His disciples to fully understand that their personal Great Commission, to go into the world, was a co-mission, Christ with them. Just as Jesus was *"salt,"* He also wants us, His disciples, to be *"salt"* also.

"Salt" purifies and preserves. Without *"salt,"* meat will soon stink. *"Salt"* makes things good to eat. If the salt is not salty, it is good for nothing and should be thrown away. So too, God calls Christians to be salt. The Gospel itself is *"salt"* that purifies to the very core of our being. An unsalty Christian is an unprofitable, pretending churchgoer who is not concerned about evangelism and discipleship! An unsalty minister of the Gospel is worse than that. They, who are supposed to be salt but are not, will be thrown out by God. May God fill us with His grace and Spirit and cause us to be salty for Him and for the benefit of many others!

Prayer: Holy and loving Lord, You use such common words to get us to see simple but important truths. We praise You for that! We praise You that *"created in Christ,"* we are salt and light by Your grace alone. We are acceptable to You, preserved for all eternity. And thank You for protecting us from the evil one who tries to take our salt away. In Jesus' name we pray. Amen.

May 26

"For the love of money is a root of all kinds of evil. Some people, eager for money, have wandered from the faith and pierced themselves with many griefs." 1 Timothy 6:10

The deceitfulness of riches

Money is not evil! We all need money. We can't live without it. It is the *"love of money"* that is the root of all kinds of evil. One problem with the *"love of money"* is, if we have too much, we can easily become proud. If we love money more than our God, then money becomes a god and becomes a *"grief"* to us. Money is good if it is our slave, but bad, if it becomes our master. *"Some people, eager for money, have wandered from the faith."* All we need to do is turn on the TV to see evangelists who are acting just like the Pharisees who sold birds in the temple. There was no prayer and proper worship because to them; ministry was all about money.

If making more money is our obsession, we have *"wandered from the faith."* We do not lose our salvation, but we are like the wanderer who *"pierced themselves with many griefs."* We bring these *"griefs"* on ourselves because we love money more than God.

Riches are deceitful if we think we have money, only because our good work practices have earned it. According to Ephesians 2:10, God planned our good works. Honest wealth is actually a gift of God! We know that God gives different gifts to many in His Church, all for the purpose of building "God's business." Most Christians that are wealthy understand that the gifts God gave them have a higher purpose: to promote God's kingdom.

"Do not wear yourself out to get rich; have the wisdom to show restraint," Proverbs 23:4. The story goes that a man was on a ship that was starting to sink. He found a pile of gold coins and quickly stuffed his pockets and jumped overboard. He sank like a rock, forever dead! The love of money will sink us all.

Prayer: Righteous Lord, forgive us for loving money more than You! You told us to love You, not money, with all of our heart! Help us to have a passion for You in all of Your beauty. May we use Your money to bless Your kingdom, to lift You up. In Christ's name we pray. Amen.

May 27

"Will a man rob God? Yet you rob Me. But you ask, 'How do we rob you?' In tithes and in offerings." Malachi 3:8

God's blessings if we tithe

In Malachi 3:6-12, God tells His people that they have turned from Him and have forfeited many blessings. God pleads, *"Return to Me and I will return to you, says the LORD Almighty,"* Malachi 3:7b. When we rob God, He is concerned about our hearts, not our money. When we rob Him *"in tithes and in offerings,"* we give up four big blessings. Our giving the 10% tithe, is the only place in the Bible where God says to us, *"Test me in this."*

God promises us **abundance** in verse 10 if we tithe. *"'Bring the whole tithe into the storehouse, that there may be food in My house. Test Me in this,' says the LORD Almighty, 'and see if I will not throw open the floodgates of Heaven and pour out so much blessings that you will not have room enough for it,'"* Malachi 3:10.

God promises us **protection** in verse 11. *"'I will prevent pests from devouring your crops, and the vines in your fields will not cast their fruit,' says the LORD Almighty,"* Malachi 3:11.

God promises us a good **reputation** in verse 12. *"'Then all the nations will call you blessed, for yours will be a delightful land,' says the LORD Almighty,"* Malachi 3:12.

God promises the **certainty** of blessings in verse 10 if we will give the tithe. God also says, *"test Me in this."* God will, *"throw open the floodgates of Heaven and pour out so much blessings."*

"Whoever sows sparingly will also reap sparingly, and whoever sows generously will also reap generously," 2 Corinthians 9:6. Also, no one can tell you how you must give for the building of God's kingdom. It is written, *"Each man should give what he has decided in his heart to give, not reluctantly or under compulsion, for God loves a cheerful giver,"* 2 Corinthians 9:7.

Prayer: Promise keeping Lord, we see Your command to give back 10% of what we earn. Lord, we can see how You want our precious hearts to be right with You. How much You want to bless us but require an obedient heart so You can. May we worship You with all of our heart! In Jesus' name we pray. Amen.

May 28

"Then God said, 'Let us make man in Our image, in Our likeness...' So God created man in His Own image, in the image of God He created him; male and female He created them." Genesis 1:26a & 27

Am I normal?

You may think our title is kind of weird. But, it is not! Really, this is not a crazy question. After all, what is "normal"? From God's eyes, the only normal man and woman that ever existed were Adam and Eve, before they sinned. After sin came into the world, the only "normal" man was Jesus Christ.

We were made by God, perfect, in the image of God, sinless and yes, normal. God gave our first father, the sinless and normal Adam, a free will. Adam exercised his free will to sin. When Adam chose to sin he chose for all of us, as Romans 5:12 teaches. When Adam and Eve fell in the Garden of Eden, they were no longer normal! Soon after they sinned, *"The LORD saw how great man's wickedness on the earth had become, and that every inclination of the thoughts of his heart was* **only evil all of the time,**" Genesis 6:5. Today, many people somehow think man still has a free will like Adam once had. How wrong they are! Man has "*only*" a will to sin, "*all of the time*"!

When we ask the question, "Am I normal" and if we think "Yes," then we are saying that we are a true Christian, restored by God! "Normal," is when Christ has covered our abnormal sin. Every true Christian has the Lord Jesus Christ, as the Lord and Master of their life! Is He our Lord? Or, do we still want to set the rules for how we live? Jesus cannot be our Savior if He is not also the Lord of our life.

A big question today, and for all eternity is, "Am I normal?" If not, *"Ask and it will be given to you; seek and you will find; knock and the door will be opened to you. For everyone who asks receives; he who seeks finds; and to him who knocks, the door will be opened,"* Matthew 7:7-8.

Prayer: Dear Lord, take our hearts that are bent on evil, "*all of the time.*" Deliver us from Satan so that we can be set free and normal once again. We thank and praise You. What an act of grace on Your part to remake us like we originally were: Your sinless children. In Christ's name we pray. Amen.

May 29

"Cast all your anxiety on Him because He cares for you."
1 Peter 5:7

How big is our God?

Do we often walk around with a sad face with all the cares in our world just swirling in our head? How quickly we can feel crushed and not able to bear our burdens! Why don't we trust Christ to help us? Don't we yet know that the heavy load we carry is just a small particle of dust on God's scale of things? God invites us, *"Cast all your anxiety on Him because He cares for you."*

Did not God keep David safe when King Saul sent his best men to kill him? Did not God provide for His servant Elijah in time of famine? Did not God give King Hezekiah 15 more years to live to honor Him? Did not God allow Joseph to suffer for 14 years only to bless him more! Did not God deliver the prostitute Rahab? Does not our God keep even the sparrow fed? Then why do we cling to our own cares so tightly when He is able and willing to carry them?

Is not our God, a God of providence? Does He not give all living things their next breath? Let us then look to Him with the eyes of faith and cast our cares onto His everlasting arms. Our Jesus is sitting on a throne in total control! He is our powerful King, our perfect High Priest, our Brother and Friend. God's Holy Spirit is walking with us wherever we go. He, who promised never to leave or forsake us, wants our cares. Will we give them up to Him who "cares"?

The eye of our Trinitarian God is always upon us! May we believe fully then. For He who has taken pity on our soul for all eternity will also care for our body and mind today! He has a storehouse of mercy and He wants to give it to us in our time of need! But we must also humble self to, *"cast all your anxiety on Him."* He who is able and willing to help, *"cares for you."* Don't doubt it! Faith goes to Him!

Prayer: Lord, forgive us for not trusting You to carry our burdens. What a beautiful and practical God You are by inviting us to cast all our cares upon You! We praise You that You not only can carry our burdens but can also pour out Your mercy exactly when we need it! We worship You for this! In Christ's name we pray. Amen.

May 30

"If I had cherished sin in my heart, the Lord would not have listened."
Psalm 66:18

When God doesn't hear prayer

This verse explains why God sometimes does not answer our prayers. The word *"cherished"* is not a word we use often anymore. It means to think highly of, or to admire. A still older version of the Bible, uses the words, *"if I harbored sin in my heart."* If a ship is in a harbor, it is in safe water. So God is telling us, that if certain sins are safe in our hearts, if we will not confess them, He will not listen to our other prayers.

Serious Christians dread sinning, and after they sin they cannot wait to get to their prayer room to pour out their heart to God. A loving son or daughter does not want to offend their caring father. So too, a loving adopted son or daughter of God cannot rest knowing that their sin separates them from their God.

Another verse that carries the same message as our text is: *"And when you stand praying, if you hold anything against anyone, forgive him, so that your Father in Heaven may forgive your sins,"* Mark 11:25. Here we see that if we keep bitterness in our hearts, we should not be surprised that God seems silent to our prayers and petitions. The problem is not that God moved away from us, but that we moved away from Him with our uncaring attitude. Confessing our sin and then asking for forgiveness is what we desperately need.

Sometimes God just says "no" in answer to our prayer request. We then may say, God is not answering our prayer. What we really mean is God is saying "no," not "yes." God's "no" is an answer to a prayer! If we pray that things should happen according to God's will, then we need to listen to God's will. God's "no" will always serve to protect His kingdom and us!

Prayer: Dear Lord, we have offended You by holding tightly to some sins. In our pride, we have often loved sin more than You! Lord, forgive us! We pray that sin may never be safe in our hearts! Lord, search our hearts and expose our sin so that we might confess it fully. We need You every hour and want to be in Your will and grace. We pray this in the holy name of Jesus Christ. Amen.

May 31

"So we fix our eyes not on what is seen, but on what is unseen. For what is seen is temporary, but what is unseen is eternal."
2 Corinthians 4:18

Everything in this world is temporary

Everything in this world is temporary. Beauty and strength are very temporary. Every beautiful woman that ever lived lost her beauty. Every strong man lost his great strength. We must thank God for both beauty and strength, but because they are temporary, we must not fix our eyes on them. God's Word is clear. *"The world and its desires pass away,"* 1 John 2:17a. Even our trials are temporary! They will soon be at an end. It's okay to keep our trials in our side vision, but we must *"fix"* our eyes on *"what is unseen,"* on the eternal. God's reasoning is that someday soon, we will all be eternal in one state or another, in Heaven or in Hell. This *"temporary"* world will soon be gone.

Everything in the coming world is eternal. *"The things that are not seen are eternal."* The coming world is different from the world that is now. *"Set your minds on things above, not on earthly things. For you died, and your life is now hidden with Christ in God,"* Colossians 3:2-3. The Bible tells us that the new Heavens and earth will go on forever and ever. In Heaven there is *"an inheritance that can never perish, spoil or fade — kept in Heaven for you,"* 1 Peter 1:4b. Hell is an *"unquench-able fire"* in Matthew 3:12. In Hell, people and devils are *"tormented day and night forever and ever,"* Revelation 20:10. Everything in the coming world is eternal.

Our place in eternity depends on what we are now. *"God will give to each person according to what he has done. To those who by persistence in doing good seek glory, honor and immortality, He will give eternal life. But for those who are self-seeking and who reject the truth and follow evil, there will be wrath and anger,"* Romans 2:6-8.

Prayer: Lord, we all have the sinful habit of living for that which is temporary, more than for that which is eternal. You lovingly tell us, *"The one who sows to please his sinful nature, from that nature will reap destruction; the one who sows to please the Spirit, from the Spirit will reap eternal life,"* Galatians 6:8. O Lord help us! Help us to live in the light of eternity! In Christ's name we pray. Amen.

JUNE

"If we claim to be without sin,
we deceive ourselves and the truth is not in us.
If we confess our sins,
He is faithful and just and will forgive us
our sins and purify us from all unrighteousness."
1 John 1:8-9

June 1

"Wives, in the same way be submissive to your husbands so that, if any of them do not believe the Word, they may be won over without words by the behavior of their wives, when they see the purity and reverence of your lives." 1 Peter 3:1-2

Good conduct wins over others!

A Christian wife here is called to submit, even to an ungodly husband. What an important principle for all relationships here. Why? Because good conduct, more than speech, encourages people to change their life. The saying, "actions speak louder than words," is Biblical. By putting on a gentle, quiet spirit, a woman and all of us, are pleasing to God and to others. A gentle quiet spirit is irresistible to others. Real beauty begins with a beautiful heart and then radiates to the face and the rest of the body. God knows about real beauty and wants to open, not only our eyes, but the eyes of others who do not know the Savior. We all need respect. We also need to give respect, first in our family, then to our neighbors and then to a lost world. An example of no respect or submission will help us see what is broken.

A 45-year-old lady had a husband who was a drunk. He worked late 6 days a week. She was miserable, alone with the children, bitter, lonely, and discouraged. This lady saw her husband's mistakes, but not her own. Finally, her husband came to our counseling class. After class she angrily introduced him to me. With a finger in his face, she shouted, "This is the problem in my life!" He pulled her finger down five times, as she loudly repeated that he was the problem in the home. With her finger still in his face, the husband said to me, "Do you see my problem?" And this woman wondered why her husband would not come home from work, or go to church with her?

She began to change her own life, instead of his. Her husband started coming home. She was now happy as she learned the truth of this text! She learned that it was her bitter heart that was making her miserable, not so much her husband's bad habits! Her husband also wanted to be loved and respected as much as she did.

Prayer: Lord, how we all need Your wisdom to be successful in our difficult relationships! Forgive us for expecting others to change and not working on self first. In Christ's name we pray. Amen.

June 2

"If we say we have no sin, we deceive ourselves, and the truth is not in us." 1 John 1:8 NKJV

Agreeing with God about our sin

The Apostle John wrote this letter with two main purposes in mind. He wanted to expose false teachers, and he wanted to give assurance of salvation. Immediately, John begins with the subject of confession, for it is true religion and it gives assurance. Nothing is more basic to Christianity than a Biblical confession of sin. The purpose of confession is to obtain forgiveness. We need peace and reconciliation with God and man. Satan works hard to destroy the basics of Christianity, like confession. *"When the foundations are being destroyed, what can the righteous do?"* Psalm 11:3. Over the next nine lessons, we will study issues important to confession.

Before we can ever confess anything we need to see our sin as God does! A big problem we have is that we do not call certain behaviors sinful. For example, we may see our anger as righteous. God says, *"man's anger does not bring about the righteous life that God desires,"* James 1:20. Satan sees abortion as family planning. God sees it as murder. Satan sees cheating as a shrewd business practice. God sees it as stealing. Satan calls drinking too much, alcoholism, like it is a disease. God calls it the sin of drunkenness. Satan calls some sexual behaviors an alternative lifestyle. God calls it an abominable sin. Satan calls gambling a form of harmless recreation. God calls it a sinful waste of our time and resources. Satan calls lust a harmless natural desire. God sees it as adultery. Satan calls pornography free speech. God says it breaks the seventh commandment. Satan calls the love of money a good work ethic. God calls it the root of all evil.

If we agree with Satan, we have nothing sinful to confess! *"If we say we have no sin, we deceive ourselves, and the truth is not in us,* 1 John 1:8 NKJV. We will not move on to the next step of confessing our sin, if we do not first agree with God about what is sin!

Prayer: Holy Lord, we do not want to be deceived. We need Your "truth" in us. Thank You for teaching us about confession. We do need Your forgiveness, the goal of confession. Help us to see our sin from Your holy eyes. In Christ's name we pray. Amen.

June 3

"If we confess our sins, He is faithful and just and will forgive us our sins and purify us from all unrighteousness." 1 John 1:9

"If we confess our sins"

We not only need to see our sin as God does in verse eight, now we need to confess it in verse nine. Only then will we be forgiven of the guilt of our sin. Amazingly, even after we know our sin is wrong, we so often still refuse to confess it. To be unwilling to confess our sin and establish a right relationship with God and others is rebellion on our part.

A Biblical confession is when I agree with God about the sins that I have committed against Him and against others, with a commitment to forsake that sin. With this definition in mind, we will look at various points covering several Bible studies. Memorize the definition. It will help to see some of the errors concerning confession. Agreeing with God concerning confession is essential to salvation and the assurance of salvation.

The word *"if"* in our text is important. *"If we confess,"* we are cleansed. Too often we talk much about how we are right, little about how we are wrong. In some churches, the Law is read every Sunday, which is good. But then the worship service goes right into giving an assurance of God's pardon. Great, but where is the "confess our sin" part in our private and corporate worship? *"If we confess our sins"* we are forgiven.

God even gives us a personal incentive to confess our sin: healing. *"The prayer offered in faith will make the sick person well; the Lord will raise him up. If he has sinned, he will be forgiven. Therefore confess your sins,"* James 5:15-16a. God tells us to get on our knees, to meet with Him, and to confess our sin. We will then see either physical or spiritual healing, or both.

Prayer: Beautiful forgiving Lord, the song is so correct: "My guilt, my shame, I all confess, I have no hope nor plea, but Jesus blood and righteousness, be merciful to me." Lord, we are so foolish not to pour out our hearts to You with a sincere confession. Lord, impress on us the necessity to confess our personal sins. In Jesus' name we pray. Amen

June 4

"Your sorrow lead you to repentance. For you became sorrowful as God intended… Godly sorrow brings repentance that leads to salvation and leaves no regret, but worldly sorrow brings death."
2 Corinthians 7:9b-10

Confessions are more than saying "I'm sorry"

Our text says, *"Godly sorrow brings repentance."* There is a *"worldly sorrow"* that is worthless! *"Worldly sorrow"* is ungodly because even if someone does confess the sin, their life does not change. For example, if we simply say, "I'm sorry" to God and others, without mentioning anything else, that's not really a Biblical confession. "I'm sorry," speaks about how we feel about what we have done wrong. A Biblical confession may begin with how we feel, but must also include the wrong words and actions that we did.

"Sorry" by itself: 1. Doesn't ask for forgiveness; 2. Doesn't forsake the sin; 3. Doesn't express an interest in establishing new, loving *actions* to the one we have hurt. God did much more than "feel sorry" for our broken condition. Jesus entered into our world. He lived among us. He suffered for us. He died for us, all to establish an eternal relationship with us. What do we intend to do differently when we say, "I'm sorry"? So, saying, "I'm sorry, I was really mad at you yesterday," did not ask for forgiveness, the main purpose of confession. Will we seriously commit to repent of our particular sin? We must do more than "feel" differently. We must think, speak, and act differently also.

We could use "sorry" correctly if we said, "My dear friend, I was wrong when I gossiped to the neighbor about how you fought with your husband. Sorry, I was wrong to hurt you. I never want to do this again as long as I live. Instead, I will say things that bless you in front of others. Will you forgive me for what I have done?" In this example, our use of the word "sorry" did not omit an actual confession of the wrong. Forgiveness was asked for and repentance was promised.

Prayer: Gracious Lord, forgive us for our lazy confessions. Help us to have a *"godly sorrow that leads to repentance."* We want all of our relationships to be what pleases You and builds up Your kingdom. In Christ's name we pray. Amen.

June 5

"If we confess our sins, He is faithful and just and will forgive us our sins and purify us from all unrighteousness." 1 John 1:9

Don't stop your confessions

After we were upset about being stuck in traffic, we treated our best friend rudely. We were very wrong in the words that we angrily spoke. When we went to our friend to confess our sin and ask for forgiveness, she told us that she was not really hurt by what we did. What must we do? What a great opportunity to witness to our friend. We can say that all sin is serious, and God tells us to confess it. We might say, "I hurt God and you too. I have asked God to forgive me. Will you forgive me also?" We all need forgiveness from God and others, not their sympathy.

A Biblical confession shows the holiness of God and His hatred for sin. An honest confession sets the stage for real repentance and change. By not confessing, the temptation is to basically bribe others and God with some "good actions" to gain their approval. "Good works" in the place of confession is Satan's crazy idea. We must not allow anyone to stop our confession of sin. How important this is, even for basic evangelism alone.

Let us not forget the last part of our text where God will *"purify us from all unrighteousness."* If and when we openly admit our sin in confession, God makes us clean, just as if we never even sinned. God is honored; others, and we too are blessed. We want God's blessings, but so often we do not want to follow God's methods to receive them. One of those ways is confessing sin. God promises us, *"If we confess our sins, He is faithful and just and will forgive our sins and purify us from all unrighteousness,"* 1 John 1:9.

Prayer: Forgiving Lord, we are so foolish. We have been far more interested in wanting our friends to feel good, than for You to be honored. We so often shut our ears to Your words in the Bible. Gracious Lord, forgive us, and *"purify us from all unrighteousness."* This is what You want and what we need! We thank You for making us just as white as snow through Christ's perfect blood. In His holy and loving name we pray. Amen.

June 6

*"Then I acknowledged my sin to You and did not cover up my iniquity.
I said, 'I will confess my transgressions to the LORD' and You forgave
the guilt of my sin." Psalm 32:5*

Saying, "forgive my sin," confesses nothing!

When David no longer covered up his sin, he was finally specific on
what he did wrong. He confessed his *"transgressions."* Our confessions
also need to be specific. Why? Imagine this scene. By the end of the
day, I had sinned against my wife in the five ways. First, my wife did
a beautiful job of cooking a special Saturday dinner for her mother's
birthday and I was two hours late without calling her. Second, my wife
asked where I was and I shouted at her, "It is none of your business."
Third, my wife cleaned the house well, yet I complained about one
window that was a little dirty. Fourth, I watched a sports match for two
hours, and I did not help her with the children. Fifth, I complained that
the children needed more study time and she should help them more.
I did not pray with my wife or family all day either!

With these personal sins in mind, I simply say to my wife at the end
of the day, "Please, forgive my sin." How unusual it would be if I only
said that! But still, are these words really a confession? No, not at all.
My wife's response to such a statement should be, "Which sin?" Simply
saying, "Please forgive my sin," confesses nothing in particular.

Worse yet, how often do we go to God in prayer without much
thought, and simply say, "Please forgive my sin"? We need to pray
more specifically about what we have done wrong! If we are not very
specific in prayer, what exactly will we commit to change in the future.
If we confess nothing, we are forgiven of nothing and then we repent
of nothing. That is a main reason we repeat our sin again and again!
When we get SPECIFIC about what we have done wrong, then we are
finally serious about changing! We never change in generalities, only
in specifics!

Prayer: O Lord, David clearly said, *"I will confess my transgressions to
the LORD."* May we worship You with sincere, specific confessions that
humble us and lift up Your holiness. May we agree with You about all
that is sinful. In Christ's name we pray. Amen.

June 7

*"I will confess **my** transgressions to the LORD."* Psalm 32:5b

Confess your own sins

When we kneel to pray, it is a great temptation to bring up what others did wrong to us, not what we did wrong! When we meet with friends, we confess what others have done wrong to us. Little children learn this at a young age. We say to our young son or daughter, "Why is the little neighbor boy crying?" Our child will say, "He called me names, so I hit him with a stick." We must instruct our child that even if someone calls you names, it does not give you the right to hit them with a stick. "Now, go and confess your sin to this boy and ask for his forgiveness." The child obediently goes and gives this confession, "Forgive me for hitting you with a stick, when you called me names." The confession started good, but as soon as the neighbor boy's wrong was added in, your child was really saying, "I had a good reason to do what I did." That is not really a confession! That is blame-shifting. It sounds more like Adam and Eve in the Garden of Eden.

Our motive for confessing sin must be that we are convicted that we are 100% guilty, and we cannot ever make up for our wrong. With this in mind, we are now asking for another person (or God) to forgive us from the guilt of what we have done wrong. True confession only begins when we quit trying to justify our sin. Confession begins when we finally judge the log in our own eye and stop acting the part of the hypocrite. Biblical change begins with judging our own life.

What about saying; "If I hurt you, I'm sorry"? Is that a confession? No. Often such a question is tempting the other person to lie, just so that we don't have to admit that we were wrong. How wicked it is to tempt someone else to sin! If we have offended God, it matters not what others think. *"I will confess my transgressions to the LORD,"* Psalm 32:5b.

Prayer: O holy Lord, we have often confessed other people's sins more than our own. Lord, forgive us. Help us to confess our own wrong ways of living. May we listen to David who said, *"I will confess my transgressions to the LORD."* May we praise Your holiness with our confessions. In Jesus' name we pray. Amen.

June 8

"For it is by grace you have been saved, through faith, and this not from yourselves, it is the gift of God, not by works, so that no one can boast." Ephesians 2:8-9

Can we make up for our sin?

A certain woman sinned by committing adultery and also by saying bad things about her husband. This husband and wife are now in a counseling session with their pastor. Caught, and expected to say something, she says to her husband, "I know I have hurt you, I will make up for what I have done wrong." What should this pastor say? He must kindly say to her, "Even if you are perfect for the next 50 years, you can never make up for what you did wrong. You need to ask God and your husband for forgiveness!"

If this wife could "make up" for her wrong living by doing good things, she does not believe in either confession or forgiveness. To promise some good work to earn her husband's favor is bribery, not good theology. Can a guilty sinner ever get God's favor by bribing Him with some good works? Never! To do so is to ignore what Christ did to pay for our sins. This wife thought she was sincere, but she was self-righteous, manipulative, and arrogant. She was mocking God's sacrifice of Christ on the Cross for her sin.

Works righteousness is a worldwide problem, and it is not just people outside the church who are guilty. Some get baptized to earn God's favor. Some take mass to be forgiven. Some even go to church twice on Sunday to earn God's favor. Some do "ministry" so God will like them. All such works are in vain. A Biblical confession is God's way to be forgiven. God's forgiveness and favor are available, after confession!

Prayer: Merciful Lord, forgive us for thinking: "Our blood, our sweat, or our tears can make up for our sin." We are so often just like Adam who tried to do some good work by picking some fig leaves to cover his sin. A perfect blood sacrifice was needed then, and it is needed now. We need You to clothe us, just as You clothed Adam. Lord, forgive and cleanse us with Christ's precious blood. In His name we pray. Amen.

June 9

"Nothing in all creation is hidden from God's sight. Everything is uncovered and laid bare before the eyes of Him to whom we must give account." Hebrews 4:13

Our confessions finally agree with God

This is somewhat of a review lesson because of its importance. In our text we can see that God as the divine Judge has perfect eyesight. He saw *"everything"* that ever happened in the past, *"everything"* in the present, *"everything"* that will happen in the future. *"Everything is uncovered and laid bare before the eyes of Him to whom we must give account."* With this truth in mind, let us go back to our definition of confession to see the importance of our text. A Biblical confession is when I agree with God about the sins that I have committed against Him and against others, with a commitment to forsake that sin. We must take personal responsibility for sinning by openly admitting what we have done wrong. We must not go man's way in life, but instead ask for God's forgiveness and power to live His way.

In the end, we must not think the quality of our confession will somehow save us! It is the perfect, blood sacrifice of Jesus Christ on the Cross that alone forgives us. He is the spotless Lamb and the only sacrifice for our sin. Even the weakest plea to Him for forgiveness will be heard. Biblical confessions ask for forgiveness, are specific about sin, serious about repentance, and always look for reconciliation. When we do confess our sin, God is worshiped and honored, others are receiving our love, and we too are blessed!

Prayer: Forgiving Lord, we praise You for teaching us the truth about confession. It is so simple, yet we fail miserably in this area. Forgive us for not openly confessing our sin to You. Help us Lord to remember that we do not need to be "good" to go to Heaven, but perfect. What a blessing it is to be to made perfect through the blood of Christ. How blessed we are that we have a faithful and caring High Priest in Jesus Christ our Lord. We praise You that our Savior is alive and sitting on a throne at Your right hand, delighting to hear our prayers. In His precious name we pray. Amen.

June 10

"To Him all the prophets bear witness that, through His name, whoever believes in Him will receive remission of sins." Acts 10:43 NKJV

There is only one Mediator for sin

Some say there are many ways to God. They say that other priests and prophets can be a channel to get to God. Even in the church, some believe we can go through a holy saint who is either dead or alive to get to Jesus or God. Others believe that we can even go through Jesus' mother to get to Jesus. The Bible, even Jesus Himself, does not support any of this.

How do we get back to God? Isaiah tells us, *"Your iniquities have separated you from your God; and your sins have hidden His face from you; so that He will not hear,"* Isaiah 59:2 NKJV. God also provides the answer for our sin problem. *"He saw that there was no man, and wondered that there was no intercessor; therefore His own arm brought salvation for Him; and His own righteousness, it sustained Him,"* Isaiah 59:16 NKJV. No mere man could be the perfect Mediator (intercessor), so God in grace provided one.

In the New Testament, Jesus said, *"I tell you the truth, I am the gate for the sheep,"* John 10:7. And, *"I am the door. If anyone enters by Me, he will be saved, and will go in and out and find pasture,"* John 10:9 NKJV. Those seeking God other than through Christ will be frustrated, defeated, and worse yet, still separated from the One who created us. It is God alone who determines how we can approach Him and have a relationship with Him.

The church cannot forgive sin. Jesus forgives. The church cannot save. Jesus saves. As great as the Apostle Peter was, he was still the "little rock," and cannot forgive sin. Jesus is "The Rock." Peter himself testified about Jesus, *"To Him all the prophets bear witness that, through His name, whoever believes in Him will receive remission of sins,"* Acts 10:43 NKJV. That's why we end our prayers, *"In Jesus' name we pray."*

Prayer: O Lord God, the words of this song is true. "On Christ, the solid Rock, I stand, all other ground is sinking sand." We thank You that You are the Way, the Truth, and the Life. We praise You that Jesus is our Advocate to settle our sin problem with You! In His name we pray. Amen.

June 11

"You were taught, with regard to your former way of life, to put off your old self, which is being corrupted by its deceitful desires; to be made new in the attitude of your minds; and to put on the new self, created to be like God in true righteousness and holiness."
Ephesians 4:22-24

The Biblical process of change

There are six chapters in Ephesians. The first three show us how the grace of God comes into us. Chapters four to six show us what now must change in our lives. Grace in, Grace out!

God's process of change here is so little understood. As a result, a cycle of anger, bitterness, fear, and worry continues. This repentance process starts when we first *"put off"* the old habits and then *"put on"* the new ones. Note the old *"put-off"* must come before the new *"put-on,"* yet both are necessary. The next verse is a practical example. *"Therefore each of you must put off falsehood and speak truthfully to his neighbor,"* Ephesians 4:25a. The put-off is lying or falsehood. The put-on is to *"speak truthfully."* If we have not replaced the lying with *"speak truthfully,"* we haven't changed.

In verse 28 is another example, *"He who has been stealing must steal no longer, but must work, doing something useful with his own hands, that he may have something to share with those in need."* Again, the put-off is listed first. There are two put-ons. A thief is not changed until he/she gets a job and begins to give. That is when a heart is changed. We do not just quit sinful habits. We must replace them! To finish the process of change, we must now concentrate on new Biblical *"put-ons"* with all of our heart. Then we will change.

Another Biblical example is: *"Let no corrupt word proceed out of your mouth* (the put-off), *but what is good for necessary edification, that it may impart grace to the hearers* (the put-on),*"* Ephesians 4:29 NKJV. Our hearts change when we replace the old with new loving thought, word, or action.

Prayer: Holy and powerful Lord, we have so many sins in our life that need to be put off. Convict us, so that we are serious about changing our sin habits. Lord, we so need Your Biblical ways of living to please You and to bless others! In Christ's name we pray. Amen.

June 12

"Consider it pure joy, my brothers, whenever you face trials of many kinds, because you know that the testing of your faith develops perseverance. Perseverance must finish its work so that you may be mature and complete, not lacking anything." James 1:2-4

Tests and Temptations - Part 1

We have opportunities to change every day that come in the form of trials big and small. These trials, at the same time, are both tests and temptations. If we are going to pass these trials God's way, we must know the difference between a test and a temptation. Three things are important. Two are in this lesson.

1. What is a test? A test is an opportunity to practice Christ-like behavior. God tests us in our relationships and in our responsibilities. His testing gives us a chance to prove the reality of our faith. God in His mercy gives us many chances to "prove" our faith to see if it is real or not. Peter tells us that our faith is tested, just like gold is tested and refined over a fire, making it pure, improving its value.

A goldsmith was once asked, "How do you know when the gold is pure?" He replied, "When I can look into the pot of gold and see a clear reflection of my face!" That is exactly what God is doing in our trials. God is looking to see a clear reflection of Christ in us. It is through the passing of tests that our faith is refined and matured.

2. What is a temptation? *"Let no one say when he is tempted, 'I am tempted by God;' for God cannot be tempted by evil, nor does He Himself tempt anyone. But each one is tempted when he is drawn away by his own desires and enticed,"* James 1:13-14 NKJV. We often blame Satan for the evil desires and thoughts we have. Our human nature has evil desires, Satan appeals to those desires that are basically selfish. Some people try to get rid of Satan instead of changing their behavior. *"Each one is tempted when he is drawn away by his own desires."*

Prayer: O holy Lord, thank You for giving us many tests to prove the reality of our faith. Protect us from Satan who appeals to our evil desires. Help us to, *"Consider it pure joy, whenever we face trials of many kinds, because we know that the testing of our faith develops perseverance."* Lord, we want to be *"mature and complete, not lacking anything."* In Christ Jesus' name we pray. Amen.

June 13

"In this you greatly rejoice, though now for a little while you may have had to suffer grief in all kinds of trials. These have come so that your faith - of greater worth than gold, which perishes even though refined by fire — may be proved genuine and may result in praise, glory and honor when Jesus Christ is revealed." 1 Peter 1:6-7

Tests and Temptations - Part 2

3. Every trial is both a test and a temptation. John was a drunkard. Every Saturday for twenty years, John received $500.00 for his weekly work. He would buy a few bottles and get drunk and then stagger home. He gave his dear wife just $300.00 for the weekly expenses. This family had big problems! After twenty years, by the grace of God, John became a Christian. Now the bigger trial begins: Once again it is Saturday night. John is paid $500.00. John has a great test from God to prove the reality of his new faith. At the same time a great temptation floods his whole body and spirit. Satan whispers to his self-centered feelings, "John, just one bottle will feel so good!" "John, you have worked so hard all week and you deserve a drink." John gives into his feelings and fails the test. After the initial high, John is filled with guilt as the Holy Spirit convicts him (John 16:7-8). If John had gone home to be a blessing to his family, the Holy Spirit would have filled him with joy instead of all that guilt.

We also have many trials every day that are both tests and temptations. We have relationship problems, health problems, money problems and more. Right here is the real spiritual battle we are all in. Right here is where we either pass or fail the tests of life. This point is so critical! Will we respond by giving in to the temptation to please self by lying, cheating, stealing, lusting, getting angry, or worrying? Or, will we trust in God, and pass the test by acting like Christ? There are blessings for being faithful, curses for being unfaithful. May God help us to be faithful!

Prayer: Holy Lord, like sheep, we are weak. We need You the Shepherd of our souls to put Your Word and Spirit in our hearts. Protect us from the evil one. May we pass Your tests in life as worship to You. We pray these things in Jesus' name. Amen.

June 14

"For man's anger does not bring about the righteous life God desires."
James 1:20

Why is my anger so wrong?

We often insist that our anger is righteous. We say, "My anger is okay because I am angry for a short time." Or we say, "God made me an angry person." These are excuses to not change. They are lies. We also claim that, "others make me angry," another lie! God says: *"The good man brings good things out of the good stored up in his heart, and the evil man brings evil things out of the evil stored up in his heart. For out of the overflow of his heart his mouth speaks,"* Luke 6:45. Our anger "issues" are inside us, not outside of us. They are in our hearts.

From God's eyes, others tempt us to become angry. The cause of anger is in our own "heart." Yes, there is such a thing as righteous anger. But 99 times out of 100, ours is not righteous. God did say, *"man's anger does not bring about the righteous life God desires,"* James 1:20. Some people still say, "Jesus was angry in the temple, so I can be angry too." Does it really say that? Read Matthew 21:12-15. See who was angry in the temple. It was the self-righteous Pharisees, not Jesus. There are other verses that show us God's view of man's anger.

"A wise man fears the LORD and shuns evil, but a fool is hot headed and reckless," Proverbs 14:16.
"A fool gives full vent to his anger," Proverbs 29:11.
"An angry man stirs up dissension," Proverbs 29:22.
"Better to live in a desert than with a quarrelsome and ill-tempered wife," Proverbs 21:19.

Prayer: Righteous Lord, You give us many verses to show us that our anger is not righteous. You make it clear that it is our own evil hearts that need to change. May we believe You today and quit making so many excuses for our anger. Instead, may we confess our evil anger quickly, forsake it completely, and then act lovingly! Help us to have the right response to people and situations that we face each and every day. In Christ Jesus' name we pray. Amen.

June 15

"The acts of the sinful nature are obvious: sexual immorality, impurity and debauchery; idolatry and witchcraft; hatred, discord, jealously, fits of rage, selfish ambition, dissensions, factions, and envy... and the like. I warn you, as I did before, that those who live like this will not inherit the kingdom of God." Galatians 5:19-21

The practice of anger ends in Hell

Our text here shows how serious the sin of anger really is. God tells us that if we are known as an angry person, we won't be in Heaven. God tells us the truth so we can clearly see that we need a change of heart to be with Him. Our text lists eight various kinds of anger in the same sentence, along with the big sins of murder, idolatry, adultery and drunkenness. These are the commonly called, *"the acts of the sinful nature,"* not the works of righteousness. God's righteous conclusion is, *"those who live like this will not inherit the kingdom of God."*

We look again at the seriousness of anger because from man's eyes, anger is not so bad. In the final judgment, man's view will not matter! We will all be judged according to God's holy standard of right and wrong. We are wise to see things from God's eyes today, while there is time to change.

What is so wrong with our anger is that when God saves us, He puts His changing grace in our hearts. God's grace in us, is not some invisible doctrinal belief. If a heart change is not visible, it is because we are not yet changed. Matthew 15:18-19 shows us that anger comes from our heart, never from another person. When others treat us wrong, our response will come from the condition of our heart. If grace is there, then a gracious response will come out of us. *"The good man brings good things out of the good stored up in his heart, and the evil man brings evil things out of the evil stored up in his heart. For out of the overflow of his heart his mouth speaks,"* Luke 6:45.

Prayer: Holy and beautiful Savior, Your Word cuts us deeply, as it should. You clearly show us that Your grace must flow out of us! Our anger and bitterness are the complete opposite of grace. We are so grateful that You warn us today, before The Judgment. Forgive us Lord. Help us to practice a right response to those who hurt us. In Jesus' name we pray. Amen.

June 16

"My dear brothers, take note of this: Everyone should be quick to listen, slow to speak and slow to become angry." James 1:19

Replacing the sin of anger

Remember how Biblical change involves put-offs and put-ons. We need to put off the sin of anger, before we can put on forgiveness and love. Simply concentrating on the fact that we need to get over our anger, actually prevents change. We need to replace it, and then concentrate intently on our new behavior! That is essential to lasting Biblical change. We must concentrate on three things.

A. *"Be quick to listen."* *"Listen,"* is awesome theology in just one word! *"Listen,"* focuses on the other person, the key to change. Until we shut our angry mouths, we cannot possibly *"listen."* We might say, "I love you" to another person, but if we fail to "listen" to them, we do not really love them. *"In humility consider others better than yourselves,"* Philippians 2:3b. Can we *"consider others better,"* if we refuse to *"listen"* to them?

B. Be *"slow to speak."* We *"slow"* down the vehicle we are driving when danger is nearby. Do we *"slow"* down our mouth when anger is nearby? If we are interested in loving others, we will be *"slow to speak."* One good way to put *"listen"* and *"slow to speak"* into practice, is by trying to summarize what someone has just said to us. That would force us to listen to them.

C. Be *"slow to become angry."* Don't attack the person. Instead, work on the problem. Ask questions. Respond softly and gently to the one that we disagree with. *"A soft answer turns away wrath, but a harsh word stirs up anger,"* Proverbs 15:1 NKJV. *"Restore him gently"* is a command in Galatians 6:1.

We need to face the truth. Anger is wrong. Love manages relationships God's way. God never said that our anger does not work to move others. It does, and that is why we do it! What God tells us is that our anger is not His way for us to manage our relationships.

Prayer: Lord help us to use our mouth, not to blaspheme You, not to tear up others, not even to destroy ourselves, but to love You and to love others. In Christ Jesus' name we pray. Amen.

June 17

"But if you harbor bitter envy and selfish ambition in your hearts, do not boast about it or deny the truth. Such 'wisdom' does not come down from Heaven but is earthly, unspiritual, of the devil."
James 3:14-15

Why bitterness is evil

The NKJV calls bitterness *"demonic."* The NIV calls bitterness *"unspiritual"* and *"of the devil."* Devils do not make good friends! Devils are interested in breaking relationships, not making them. Jesus showed relationships were essential when He summarized the Bible as first loving God and then loving others. Bitterness hates God and others. It is a fact that others will hurt us often. We have two options when this happens. We can get bitter and act like a demon. Or, we can follow Christ by forgiving others. God holds us responsible today and in The Judgment for our Biblical reaction to when people wrong us!

One verse that is helpful to overcoming bitterness is: *"And when you stand praying, if you hold **anything against anyone, forgive him,** so that your Father in Heaven may forgive you your sins,"* Mark 11:25. In our prayer life, God requires us to give up bitterness and forgive others, or He will not forgive us, meaning He will not hear our prayer, as Psalm 66:18 also teaches. Refusing to forgive is a lack of grace to others.

Bitterness dies, only when the root of it is dead. *"See to it that no one misses the grace of God and that no bitter root grows up to cause trouble and defile many,"* Hebrews 12:15. If the wrong words and actions of others keep coming back to us, then the *"root"* of bitterness is not very dead. *"Roots"* are powerful. A living tree root can tip over a wall, raise a sidewalk, and destroy a foundation. We can't just cut down the tree of bitterness, we need to dig out the *"root,"* or it will grow back! God's process of change to overcome bitterness is to: *"Overcome evil with good,"* Romans 12:21. The *"good"* begins when we agree with God that bitterness is sin and confess it as such.

Prayer: Perfectly holy Lord, thank You for telling us the truth about our *"demonic"* bitterness. We do not want the *"root"* of this in our hearts any longer. Help us to replace the sin of bitterness and have Your grace flow out of us. In Jesus' name we pray. Amen.

June 18

"Rebellion is like the sin of divination, and arrogance like the evil of idolatry. Because you have rejected the Word of the LORD, He has rejected you as king." 1 Samuel 15:23

King Saul's path away from God

Today, King Saul would surely be labeled a schizophrenic. He had a lot of different faces. Saul's real problem was that he became proud, rebelled, and went his own way. Saul very quickly went from bad to worse. His downward spiral was filled with fear, worry, bitterness, anger, jealousy, murder, even witchcraft. He became more depressed as his behavior became more bizarre. As we look at Saul's fall away from God, we see a lesson for us today. God presents these events so that we might understand them and be warned.

In 1 Samuel 13:6, Saul saw that the enemy was large. In 13:7, instead of trusting God, he gave in to fear. In 13:11, he would not wait for God, which led to wrong worship practices in 13:12. In 13:13, Saul refused to listen to God. In 15:9, he was unwilling to obey God. In 15:15, he blamed the people for his bad decisions. In 18:25, he tried to kill a man. In 18:28-29, he became jealous and afraid. In 22:18, he had a priest of the Lord killed. In 28:7, he went to a witch for advice. In 28:15, he spoke to the dead. In 28:20, he was again filled with fear and refused to trust in God. In 31:4, he took his own life.

Here is an important counseling question. Did the various hard or difficult circumstances in life **cause** Saul to sink? No, Saul had many **temptations** to lose focus that he gave in to! But the real cause of Saul's downfall was the condition of his heart! Remember Matthew 15:19, *"Out of the heart come evil thoughts..."* We could sort out so many of our personal problems if we understood that the difficult circumstances we face are temptations, not causes to be depressed! There is so much bad theology that says the cause of our problems are outside of us. God says the problems are inside of us, in our heart, causing a wrong response in our daily trials!

Prayer: Loving Father, like Saul, we also rebel against You. We follow our own way instead of living Your way. Forgive us Lord for our wanderings! May we overcome temptations, not give in to them. May we trust in You, our great God. In Christ's name we pray. Amen.

June 19

"Does the LORD delight in burnt offerings and sacrifices as much as in obeying the voice of the LORD? To obey is better than sacrifice, and to heed is better than the fat of rams. For rebellion is like the sin of divination, and arrogance like the evil of idolatry."
1 Samuel 15:22-23a

Partial obedience is still disobedience

The wrong way of living in King Saul's life is summed up in our text. God wants us to know His will for our lives.

First, Saul was given a very clear command! *"Now go, attack the Amalekites and totally destroy everything that belongs to them. Do not spare them; put to death men and women, children and infants, cattle and sheep, camels and donkeys,"* 1 Samuel 15:3. Is that clear or what? God also gave us ten really clear commandments.

Second, Saul's partial obedience was still disobedience! *"But Saul and the army spared Agag and the best of the sheep and cattle..."* 1 Samuel 15:9a. He destroyed the rest. By not completely listening to the Lord, Saul (in our text) committed both *"idolatry"* and *"rebellion."* He thought God didn't know what was best for them! God hated Saul's partial obedience, nor is He impressed with ours!

Third, Saul blamed others, for his wrong response! This is our problem too! God sent a prophet to confront Saul's selfish response. *"But Samuel said, 'What then is this bleating of sheep in my ears,'"* 1 Samuel 15:14a. *"Saul answered, 'The soldiers...they spared the best of the sheep and cattle to sacrifice to the LORD your God, but we totally destroyed the rest,"* 1 Samuel 15:15. Saul blamed others for that which was wrong. He patted himself on the back for that which was right. When hurt, we blame others for our wrong response. We say others make us angry? Our hearts are the real problem.

Fourth, Saul's sin had consequences! God was finally fed up with Saul's unwillingness to be loyal to Him! The kingdom was ripped away from Saul because his heart was not right!

Prayer: Holy Lord, we can plainly see the sin of Saul and point a finger at him, and not see that our own partial obedience is so offensive to You! Lord, forgive us and move us to the Cross for a closer walk with You! In Christ's name we pray. Amen.

June 20

"Although he did not remove the high places from Israel, Asa's heart was fully committed to the LORD all his life." 2 Chronicles 15:17

What are *"the high places"*?

"The high places," are groves of trees where many different gods were worshiped. Good kings like Asa removed the false gods from these *"high places,"* but did not do the next step, get rid of these false places of worship! God commanded His people: *"You must not worship the LORD your God in their way. But you are to seek **the place** the LORD your God will choose from among all your tribes to put His Name there for His dwelling. To that **place** you must go; there bring your burnt offerings and sacrifices, your tithes and special gifts, what you have vowed to give and your freewill offerings, and the first born of your herds and flocks. There in the presence of the LORD your God, you and your families shall eat and shall rejoice in everything you have put your hand to, because the LORD your God has blessed you,"* Deuteronomy 12:4-7. God commanded, *"Be careful not to sacrifice your burnt offerings **anywhere** you please,"* Deuteronomy 12:13. Israel had a temple and altar of God's choosing, but they were not going there! What about us?

With the Old Testament temple destroyed, we must give sacrifices to God only at His place and altar! Where is that? Christ is now both the place and the altar of God's choosing! God is a jealous God! If we give our worship and tithe to *"high places"* of our own choosing, like the bar, movies, gambling etc... but not at God's altar, Jesus Christ, we should not expect God to bless us. God only accepts Christ-centered worship! That is His choosing, and it must be ours!

"Asa's heart was fully committed to the LORD all his life." God is still a God of grace and mercy. Even though some duties were missing, King Asa's heart was one with God.

Prayer: Righteous Lord, like good King Asa, may we love, worship and praise You as commanded. May we find our number one joy in You, Your Son, Your Spirit and in Your Word. You destroyed the old temple and the altar for a very good reason. You replaced it with a better Altar, Jesus Christ. May we worship Him alone. In Christ's name we pray. Amen.

June 21

*"Can a man scoop fire into his lap without his clothes being burned?
Can a man walk on hot coals without his feet being scorched? So is he
who sleeps with another man's wife; no one who touches her will
go unpunished."* Proverbs 6:27-29

Why do people cheat on each other?

A man cheated on his wife. In a counseling session, he told me that he
did not have those special "feelings" for his wife anymore, so he found
them elsewhere. Such a statement needs to be challenged Biblically!
"Sir, true love in marriage is far more about love and commitment,
than "feelings." The "good feelings" come after loving commitment is
practiced. To say that we are in love with our spouse one day and not
the next, is more like lust than love. Lust is never satisfied! Real love in
marriage is an ongoing investment into the relationship because we
are committed to each other by covenant. If you are so concerned
about your bad feelings, consider the bad feelings God gives to
cheaters in our text, feelings of guilt, shame and depression.

*"Out of the heart come evil thoughts, murder, adultery and sexual
immorality,"* Matthew 15:19a. A cheater has a selfish heart that wants
others to make him feel better. If a marriage is weak and hurting, a
cheater "feels" that others value me more than my spouse does. The
cheater does not yet realize that love is about giving, not getting!
Cheating is 100% self-centered.

What about "flirting" with others? Is that cheating on a spouse? A
cheater argues, "I simply enjoy being with this or that person. I am not
physically involved." Not yet! Just as anger leads to murder, loose talk
leads to loose living. Flirting talk can quickly lead to actions.

What are the success rates for relationships after cheating, when
an attitude of hurt and distrust remains? Without Biblical forgiveness,
a loving home will not be reestablished. Along with forgiveness, a new
commitment to fidelity is able to rebuild a trusting "love relationship."

Prayer: Lord of loving relationships, we thank You for being so open
to the problem of cheating in a relationship. Help us to always see
that if we have a lack of respect for You, we will also have a lack of
respect for our spouse. May our marriages be like the relationship of
Christ and the church, totally in love! In Jesus' name we pray. Amen.

June 22

"Yet I hold this against you: You have forsaken your first love. Remember the height from which you have fallen! Repent and do the things you did at first." Revelation 2:4-5a

"Remember," "Repent," and "Do"

These are three powerful words of Jesus. The love of the Ephesian church had grown cold, and it needed to be warmed up. Their love had not always been so cold! Once it was on fire. What was wrong needed to be fixed! These words of Jesus also apply directly to a marriage that was great for years and now is a mess. Jesus' three step outline here will warm up a church and a marriage!

First, *"Remember"* the good years. Don't go back further and start blaming your parents or your childhood! *"Remember"* what you did when the marriage was going well. *"Remember"* how you spent time together. *"Remember"* how you looked at your spouse, and how you touched your spouse, and how you did things for your spouse. Don't look at your spouse and think they are the problem! *"First remove the plank from your own eye,"* Matthew 7:5a. Jesus pointedly says here, *"You have forsaken your first love."*

Second, *"Repent."* Confess your own sins, your failure to love the Lord and your spouse. Confess how you have moved away from your spouse and God after those good years! Get rid of all bitterness you have against your spouse. Plan how you will again love them in spite of all of their weaknesses. Life isn't about finding many men or women to like you; it is finding the right one that God prepared for you and never letting go.

Third, *"Do the things you did at first."* Love is still a sacrificial action for another! Get busy. You will change when you concentrate on your good behavior with all of your heart. Be humble, for such people are easy companions. Humility keeps a husband from being a tyrant, and makes a wife have a sweet and gentle spirit.

Prayer: Wise and holy Lord, You say, *"He who has an ear, let him hear what the Spirit says to the churches. To him who overcomes, I will give the right to eat from the tree of life, which is in the paradise of God,"* Revelation 2:7. Lord, forgive us for not being concerned about leaving our first love! Strengthen us, and in Christ's name we pray. Amen.

June 23

"So he got up and went to his father. But while he was still a long way off, his father saw him and was filled with compassion for him; he ran to his son, threw his arms around him and kissed him." Luke 15:20

The Prodigal Son

In Luke 15, Jesus tells one parable, three different ways. All deal with salvation issues. We know it is one parable because in verse three it says, *"Then Jesus told them this parable."*

1. Something was lost and something was gained. The first way of telling the parable is with a story about "The Lost Sheep." Then we have another story about "The Lost Coin." Then finally we have our text, "The Lost Son." A sheep is lost and the Shepherd Jesus finds it. A woman lost a coin and then finds it. A son leaves the father and is lost. Father God welcomes him back.

2. The lost was sought for. The shepherd searched for the sheep! The woman searched for the coin! The father's eyes searched the road for the lost son. All are a picture of Jesus seeking us. We did not seek Him! He sought and found us.

3. The lost was rejoiced over. The shepherd, the woman, and the father all call their "friends and neighbors" to rejoice. Yet in the parable of the lost son, we have a so-called *"brother"* who is unwilling to *"rejoice."* Well, guess who this *"brother"* is? It is none other than the self-righteous scribes and Pharisees who *"muttered"* (grumbled) about the *"tax collectors and sinners,"* that *"were all gathering around to hear"* Jesus. The quotes are from Luke 15:1-2. Are we *"rejoicing"* when people of every tongue are being added to God's kingdom? So many people are not interested when missionaries report that lost souls are coming to Christ. The lost are rejoiced over by those in Heaven! Should we not also rejoice on earth? So then, we saw that the lost were found, and the lost were rejoiced over!

Prayer: Seeking Lord, how graciously You searched for us when we were completely lost! Unable to find our way, You, *"made us alive with Christ even when we were dead in transgressions — it is by grace you have been saved,"* Ephesians 2:5. We just want to thank You and live for You! In Christ's most holy and precious name we pray. Amen.

June 24

"These things I have spoken to you, that in Me you may have peace. In the world you will have tribulation; but be of good cheer, I have overcome the world." John 16:33 NKJV

A picture of peace

By nature we quickly look for peace first in created things, and then wonder why we lose our peace so quickly! For example, to have peace we look for others to treat us right. We look for peace in having many possessions and good health. There is a temporary peace in these things, however, this is the world's idea of peace. When we look for peace in created things more than in our God, we actually have an idolatry problem!

Real lasting peace is in Christ alone! In fact, He is *"the Prince of Peace."* See the two facts in our text that are true for every believer. First, *"In the world you will have tribulation."* And second, *"in Me you may have peace."* Christ then, gives a peace that the world cannot give. Christ can give us peace in the midst of difficult circumstances.

A story may help you understand our text of John 16:33. "There was once a contest to see who could paint the best picture of peace. The winning artist painted a cyclone on the Bay of Bengal. The wind was blowing and the waves were high. Wedged in the big rocks along the shoreline was a bird's nest. In the nest was a baby bird fast asleep, right in the middle of the big storm." Now, that's peace! But even more than that, the little bird is us in the hands of Jesus, safe in the storms of life. This *"peace"* of Jesus is not some mystical thing. Jesus said, *"If you love Me, keep My commandments. And I will pray to the Father, and He will give you another Helper, that He may abide with you forever, - the Spirit of truth,"* John 14:15-16a NKJV. The Holy Spirit sent from Christ Himself, fills us with eternal peace.

Prayer: God of all peace and joy, we are so grateful that You, the *"Prince of peace,"* are able to give us eternal peace. The world does not have a relationship with You and will not know Your peace until they do. We pray that Your Word will go out in all of its power to change many hearts, giving them peace. Equip us to tell the message of the Gospel clearly. In Christ's name we pray. Amen.

June 25

"Do not merely listen to the Word, and so deceive yourselves. Do what it says." James 1:22

The importance of obedience

Our text shows us that reading or hearing God's Word is not enough. We also need to be obedient to what the message says. *"Anyone who listens to the Word but does not do what it says is like a man who looks at his face in the mirror and, after looking at himself, goes away and immediately forgets what he looks like,"* James 1:23-24. A person walks up to a mirror to see if his face is clean and his hair is combed. He sees he must make an adjustment, but does not do it. Is not such a person rather foolish? Why did they even go to the mirror?

What about us? Do we read the Bible to find out how to have a better relationship with God and others, so we can live differently? Are we making the changes God demands? Are we not foolish if we do not make the adjustments that God asks us to make? Some of us are in college working towards a degree, but will that in itself, make us wise? Others have a PhD, but are still angry, stealing, drinking and committing adultery? Is not such living, the life of a fool? Can we see that there is a big difference between head knowledge and heart knowledge? *"The heart of the wicked is of little value,"* Proverbs 10:20b. *"I, wisdom, dwell together with prudence; I possess knowledge and discretion,"* Proverbs 8:12.

We sometimes act as if God will bless us just for opening the Bible. The truth is, we have a greater condemnation if we read the Bible, but do not listen to it. *"But the man who looks intently into the perfect law that gives freedom, and continues to do this, not forgetting what he has heard, but doing it — he will be blessed in what he does,"* James 1:25.

God clearly tells us what changes we need to make. *"Get rid of all moral filth and the evil that is so prevalent and humbly accept the Word planted in you, which can save you,"* James 1:21.

Prayer: *"Search me, O God, and know my heart; test me and know my anxious thoughts. See if there be any offensive way in me, and lead me in the way everlasting,"* Psalm 139:23-24. In Christ's name we pray. Amen.

June 26

"When they saw the courage of Peter and John and realized that they were unschooled, ordinary men, they were astonished and they took note that these men had been with Jesus." Acts 4:13

Is it clear we have been *"with Jesus"*?

There are three points in our text. First, we have *"the courage,"* of Peter and John. Too often today, some leaders in ministry can be so denominationally attached, that they fear to bring up anything that is wrong in that body, for fear of reprisal. Also, if someone is too attached to the world, they will be unwilling to speak openly about what is wrong. When something was wrong, Jesus and His disciples spoke with *"courage"* about it. God commands His followers to do so also. We must be careful about "how" we speak, yet we must speak.

Secondly, Peter and John *"were unschooled, ordinary men."* Concerning spiritual gifts, the Holy Spirit still distributes *"to each one individually as He wills,"* 1 Corinthians 12:11b NKJV. God has not changed in how He relates to people. When Christ "calls" someone to be His mouthpiece, He will also "equip" them. Too often there is a wrong attitude towards those who do not have an extensive "formal" education, as if seven years of higher education qualifies them. This self-righteous attitude does more to stop the work of the Lord than to promote it. The mantra today is often, "by their degree you will know them." Christ said, *"by their fruit you will know them."* Peter and John were common people, *"unschooled,"* who bore much fruit for the Lord.

Thirdly, Peter and John were *"with Jesus."* Jesus was also *"with"* them. When we are *"with"* Christ, the way Jesus acts rubs off on us. We meet with Jesus through prayer, through time in the Word and through following His will. In the same way, children need to spend much time *"with"* their Christian parents as Deuteronomy 6 teaches. We learn to imitate whom we associate *"with."* If we are too busy to spend time *"with Jesus,"* we are too busy.

Prayer: Personal and loving Lord, we praise You that You still take common, *"unschooled, ordinary men"* to do Your work. No one has an excuse to not be active in evangelism and discipleship. We pray that we will be imitators of Christ so others can imitate You also. Lord, equip us to shine like stars for You. In Christ's name we pray. Amen.

June 27

"The men said to her, (Rahab) 'This oath you made us swear will not be binding on us unless, when we enter the land, you have tied the scarlet cord in the window through which you let us down."
Joshua 2:17-18a

The *"scarlet cord"* of redemption

The story of Rahab is a good example of how the Bible is a book about redemption - God rescuing people like Rahab and us from sin and death. God's grace selected Rahab to be included as His child when all the others were destroyed. That is exactly what grace is. God as the Judge never intended to pardon all who are guilty. What judge does that? The *"scarlet cord"* of redemption is the Bible's history about the few who are saved by the grace of God and placed on the narrow road that leads to Heaven.

Redemption is basically two things. It is about deliverance, which we have seen. But it is also the price paid for that deliverance. Jesus shed His blood to redeem His chosen children from the penalty and the power that sin holds on a soul. Not only was Rahab's life spared, but her house was the only structure left standing! God chose to save the city prostitute to make sure we could clearly see that it was not her "decision" to choose God, but His decision to choose her. And then, because of a covenant of grace, God also saved her family!

Rahab's salvation was also a freedom from her sinful lifestyle! God broke Satan's hold on her. To showcase His grace even more, God made sure that Rahab was the great-grandmother of David (Matthew 1:5) who was also Christ's ancestor. Rahab is also included in the heroes of the faith in Hebrews 11:31. In redeeming Rahab (and us), God forgave her sins and restored her position as His child. God also delivered her in the judgment against Jericho when it was destroyed. Do we have this grace? How will we fare in The Judgment?

Prayer: Lord, what can we say, but worship You for the depths of Your grace. Like Rahab of old, You sought us out to deliver us, while we were still Your enemies. Now, we can also climb down through the scarlet thread (Christ's shed blood) to be given life forever with You and Your people. In Christ's name we pray. Amen.

June 28

"Therefore, just as sin entered the world through one man, and death through sin, and in this way death came to all men, because all sinned." Romans 5:12

Why evolution is not true!

Evolution is a lie that pretends to be real science. But real science only deals with what can be tested in the present. Evolution cannot be tested or proven! For evolution to be true, in-between forms of life must be found. There are none. Evolution attacks God and the book of Genesis. Evolution rejects God and His authority as the Creator. Make no mistake, evolution is a religion.

Genesis is foundational to all life and Christianity. Most of the important doctrines of the church are in Genesis. Christ Himself defended the accuracy of Genesis. Jesus told the unbelieving Jews, *"Do not think I will accuse you before the Father. Your accuser is Moses, on whom your hopes are set. If you believed Moses, you would believe Me, for he wrote about Me. But since You do not believe what he wrote, how are you going to believe what I say?"* John 5:45-47. The reason the evolutionist attacks Genesis is that *"when the foundations are being destroyed, what can the righteous do?"* Psalm 11:3. Without Genesis, the Gospel message is incomplete. If the fall into sin by Adam and Eve is not true, then why do we need a Savior to be born, to die, and then to be resurrected?

The Gospel is clear in Genesis. Adam sinned and then tried to do some work by picking fig leaves to cover his sin. God in grace saw the inability of man to redeem himself and took pity! God killed an animal in Genesis 3:21, shedding its innocent blood to cover Adam's sin. This was the first death in the world! Evolution requires death after death for millions of years. The truth remains, the first death came after sin, to cover sin, Romans 5:12. Our world is about 6,020 years old, not millions, according to Bible genealogies and world history.

Prayer: Creator God, Father, Son and Spirit, how evil are the lies of those who teach evolution as truth. The arrogant evolutionist sets himself up as knowing more about our beginnings, who was there! By faith we believe what You say about our beginnings. In Jesus' name we pray. Amen.

June 29

"But we see Jesus, who was made a little lower than the angels, now crowned with glory and honor because He suffered death, so that by the grace of God He might taste death for everyone."
Hebrews 2:9

Should we fear death?

The book of Hebrews was written so that we may know Jesus is the best High Priest. All who trust in this Priest will live with Christ forever. Our bodies will temporarily sleep until the resurrection when the body is reunited with the soul.

"Since the children (believers) have flesh and blood, He too shared in their humanity so that by His death He might destroy him who holds the power of death, that is, the devil - and free those who all their lives were held in slavery by their fear of death. For surely it is not angels He helps, but Abraham's descendants. For this reason He had to be made like His brothers in every way, in order that He might become a merciful and faithful high priest in service to God, and that He might make atonement for the sins of the people," Hebrews 2:14-17. Our Lord, by His death, resurrection, and ascension, crushed Satan's head as He said He would do in Genesis 3:15. Christ broke the power of death. The big question is: Are we in Christ?

"Precious in the sight of the LORD is the death of His saints," Psalm 116:15. What a beautiful future is in store for those who love Christ! But what a horrible future is in store for those who do not love Him. Even though our physical bodies are wasting away, our spiritual souls are maturing in Christ. *"Now we know that if the earthly tent we live in is destroyed, we have a building from God, an eternal house in Heaven." "Therefore we are always confident and know that as long as we are at home in the body we are away from the Lord,"* 2 Corinthians 5:1 & 6.

Prayer: Lord, by faith we can say with Job, *"I know that my Redeemer lives, and that in the end He will stand upon the earth. And after my skin has been destroyed, yet in my flesh I will see God; I myself will see Him with my own eyes — I, and not another. How my heart yearns within me!"* Job 19:25-26. Lord, what a beautiful future we have because of Your gracious pardon in Christ! In Jesus' name we pray. Amen.

June 30

"Anyone who does not carry his cross and follow Me cannot be My disciple." Luke 14:27

The cost of following Christ

Jesus wants us to know that the cost of following Him will not be easy! Before this verse, Jesus explained what the cost of true discipleship involved. He said, *"If anyone comes to Me and does not hate his father and mother, his wife and children, his brothers and sisters — yes, even his own life — he cannot be My disciple,"* Luke 14:26. We know we are not to hate our father and mother and all others, for this is what commandments 5 to 10 cover. So, what does Jesus mean?

The love and adoration for our God must be so far out in first place that it must "seem like" we hate all others. There must be no question as to whom we love and are loyal to the most. And then we read the shocking words that we must hate, *"even our own life."* Again, it is not even possible for anyone to hate his or her own life! *"After all, no one ever hated his own body, but he feeds and cares for it, just as Christ does the church,"* Ephesians 5:29. So, the love, devotion and affection that we have for Christ must be so great that it seems that we hate ourselves.

Jesus' message is: Be a faithful Christian. Carry your cross and don't be a coward concerning your love and duty to your Savior. God hates cowards with a passion. A faithful soldier is expected to spend himself single-mindedly for his country. Our King Jesus expects no less. Jesus said, *"Go out to the roads and country lanes and make them come in, so that My house may be full,"* Luke 14:23b. Will you suffer and spend your all for Him who gave His all for you? This is a hard but good question!

Prayer: Lord, You have asked us to leave some of the comforts in life to work for You. Lord, we are weak and often lazy. We don't like the stone You had for a pillow. We don't take rejection well. We would rather hang on to our money than spend it for Your kingdom. We want to count the comforts we have, not the cost of following You. Help us to keep our eyes on You, who left the comforts of Heaven for sinners like us. May Your name be praised. In Christ's name we pray. Amen.

JULY

"Be kind and compassionate to one another,
forgiving each other,
just as in Christ God forgave you."
Ephesians 4:32

July 1

"For if you forgive men when they sin against you, your Heavenly Father will also forgive you. But if you do not forgive men their sins, your Father will not forgive your sins." Matthew 6:14-15

Why must we forgive others?

Anger and bitterness is a lack of graceful living coming out of God's children. We will never change from these sins until we replace them with forgiveness. The word, replace, is critical. We will need to go against our feelings to forgive. But praise God, He outlines the process in how we must forgive, and then God gives us the power to forgive.

We will quickly see that how we must forgive others is an exact copy of how God, in Christ, forgives us. Our forgiveness to others is a "spirit-filled" response by which Christians can graciously solve their relationship problems, instead of living as the world does. God is very serious in His command for us to forgive. In fact, it is a major test from God to see if we will obey Him. To see how important forgiveness is, we need to view it from the overall theme of the Bible.

Jesus summed up the whole Bible in Matthew 22:35-40 as <u>love God first</u> and <u>love others second</u>. Then, in 1 John 4:20-21, we learn that *"If someone says, 'I love God', and hates his brother, he is a liar."* We cannot love someone if we refuse to forgive them.

In our text, the necessity to forgive others, immediately follows the Lord's Prayer. Think about what we pray in verse 12, the heart of the Lord's Prayer. *"Forgive us our debts (sins) as we have also forgiven our debtors (those who sin against us)."* We are pleading with God to forgive us in the same way we forgive others. What if we are angry and bitter; not willing to forgive some people in our lives? If this is so, then in praying the Lord's Prayer, we are asking God not to forgive us. God will not forgive us if we do not forgive others.

Prayer: O Lord of our hearts, we can see that our need to forgive others is really serious. How You demand compassion in Your children! Lord, forgive our rebellion in not forgiving others, for we need Your daily forgiveness to live close to You! Help us to understand that You are only commanding us to do what You have already done in forgiving all of our sins. In Jesus' name we pray. Amen.

July 2

"Be kind and compassionate to one another, forgiving each other, just as in Christ God forgave you." Ephesians 4:32

How must we forgive others?

We must forgive others exactly how God in Christ forgave us! Right doctrine matters! One Christian will say: "I chose Christ" in the salvation process. Others will say: "Christ chooses us." Those who say they chose Christ are somewhat right. Don't argue. Just ask them, "Why did you choose Christ?" All Christians choose Christ because the Holy Spirit who is God, convicts them of their sin, (John 16:7-8). That is God persuading us, because He chose us. After the Spirit convicts, we move to Christ. We now confess our sins, asking for forgiveness. Jesus said, *"No one can come to Me unless the Father who sent Me draws him,"* John 6:44a. The truth is: God *"chose us in Him before the foundation of the world, that we should be holy and without blame before Him in love, having predestined us to adoption as sons by Jesus Christ to Himself, according to the good pleasure of His will,"* Ephesians 1:4-5 NKJV.

This all really matters because: If someone thinks that they chose Christ (asked for forgiveness) on their own, then they could believe that those who hurt them must ask for forgiveness before they are required to forgive them. This would mean that we have a right to hang on to bitterness until others choose to ask us for forgiveness.

The truth is that if the one who hurt us is either dead or unwilling to ask us to forgive them, we must still forgive. That eliminates our anger and bitterness that God requires us to do. Jesus did say in Matthew 6:14-15, if you won't forgive others, He won't forgive us.

God's forgiveness to us is a gracious pardon to us who have hurt Him! *"For by grace you have been saved through faith, and this not from yourselves, **it is the gift of God**,"* Ephesians 2:8a. Grace is 100% God rescuing us. We cannot understand grace until we see that we are sinners, deserving death. Grace then is a gift where God, by His own choice, gives us Christ.

Prayer: Dear loving Lord, You give us a clear picture of Your grace so that we might be gracious to others, following Your example. Forgive us for not paying attention to Your command to forgive others as You have forgiven us. In Jesus' name we pray. Amen.

July 3

"You have put all my sins behind Your back." Isaiah 38:17b

Does God forget sin?

We are required to forgive *"just as God in Christ also forgave us,"* Ephesians 4:32b. So how did God forgive us? Our text says *"You have put all my sins behind Your back."* But does this mean God forgets our sins? Many think, "Yes." The answer is an important "No." Some think "Yes" because Hebrews 10:17 reads, *"Their sins and lawless acts I will remember no more."* Psalm 103:12 teaches, *"as far as the East is from the West, so far has He removed our transgressions from us."* Yes, our sins are removed from us. But they were not removed from Jesus.

A verse that shows more of how God forgives is, *"None of the offenses he has committed will be remembered **against him**,"* Ezekiel 18:22a. The "he" and "him" refers to a Christian. The word *"against"* is key! David also wrote *"Blessed is the man whose sin the LORD does not count against him,"* Psalm 32:2a. *"Against"* is an accounting term. Before we were Christians, our sins were against us, on our account. We were responsible to pay for them, but we couldn't! So, God took our debt and placed it on Christ, to pay it. As Christians, our debt is totally paid, transferred, *"against"* Christ.

God does not forget our sin, but does not remember it *"against"* us anymore. In The Judgment, every sinful thought, word, or action will be remembered. It will not be a blank book. Every secret thought will come up according to Ecclesiastes 12:14. Like a financial store receipt, our list of sins will be "paid in full," stamped in Jesus' blood.

God does not forget our sin and neither do we need to forget the sin of others. If you still think God forgets sin, answer this: "Why is your Bible so thick?" God tells us much about the sins of Biblical characters. He didn't forget their sins. Forgiven, their sin was no longer against them. We now must, forgive *"just as God in Christ also forgave us,"* Ephesians 4:32b. We will see what else that means tomorrow.

Prayer: Forgiving Lord, how grateful we are that every page of the catalog of our sins is stamped, PAID IN FULL BY JESUS' BLOOD. We praise You for Your amazing grace. May we follow Your example and be just like You, and not hold anyone's sin against them anymore. In Jesus' name we pray. Amen.

July 4

"Love... keeps no record of wrongs." 1 Corinthians 13:5b

The 3 promises of God's forgiveness

Our forgiveness of others concludes an inner struggle, heals our past hurts and allows us to move on. Forgiveness is very hard to do if we do not understand it. Since God does not hold our sins *"against"* us anymore, this means three things for every believer.

1. Forgiveness is God's promise to never bring a believer's sin against them in person again. God never brings our sin against us in person again as He has *"covered"* it, Psalm 32:1. *"You have put all my sins behind Your back,"* Isaiah 38:17b. *"Love... keeps no record of wrongs,"* 1 Corinthians 13:5b. If we forgive our spouse and then bring their sin *"against"* them in person again later, we really did not forgive them. God never brings our sin *"against"* us in person again. We must forgive others *"just as in Christ, God forgave us."*

2. Forgiveness is a promise by God, not to tell another person. We may not bring up someone's sin *"against"* them in person again. But, we tell others about how our husband, wife or friend has sinned against us. When we gossip and tell others about those who have hurt us, we have just held it against them. God never holds our sin *"against"* us by telling others about it. May we forgive each other *"just as in Christ, God forgave"* us.

3. Forgiveness is God's promise not to dwell on a believer's sin anymore. We may not bring someone's sin against them in person or tell anyone else. But, instead of sleeping at night, in great bitterness, we remember over and over again, what that someone did to us. We just held their sin *"against"* them. It is not wrong to remember what someone did to us, but it is wrong for us to dwell on it. *"Love... keeps no record of wrongs,"* 1 Corinthians 13:5. God is not in Heaven dwelling on the sins of Christians. He has forgiven us. Does God dwell on Christ's sin? He doesn't have any! Neither do we, in Christ.

Prayer: O Lord, we have been prisoners to our past, slaves to the one who hurt us. We blame them for our pain yet it's mainly our bitterness, Help us to forgive like You do. In Jesus' name we pray. Amen.

July 5

"Then I acknowledged my sin to You and did not cover up my iniquity. I said, 'I will confess my transgressions to the LORD' and You forgave the guilt of my sin." Psalm 32:5

Physical consequences

Are there consequences from a person's sin once it is forgiven? YES, sin always has consequences. Even though God forgives, and always removes the guilt completely, physical and material consequences may remain. When David finally confessed his sin of adultery and murder, God forgave him from the *"guilt"* as our text shows. However, God made sure there were tragic consequences to King David's sin of adultery and murder. Why? So, all Israel, along with us today know that sin has consequences. Why? So, we will stop sinning.

There were physical consequences of David's adultery. The baby died. Furthermore, the sword did not depart from the house of David (2 Samuel 12:10-11). As a physical consequence today, a person may get HIV and then AIDS. Sin has consequences, even *"to the third and fourth generations,"* Deuteronomy 5:9. Guilt from our sin is different. Ezekiel 18:1-20 is clear about how guilt is removed in a righteous person. To see how physical consequences of our sin may remain, let me give a family example.

Our son gets into a fight at school. When daddy comes home from work, the little boy says, "Daddy, I was wrong, please forgive me!" Good. Daddy must forgive. But, a spanking is still needed. Why? When the child feels some pain as a consequence of his sin, it serves as a reminder to not sin again. If Daddy does not discipline, the child would learn to say, "I'm sorry" as a false confession, without changing his heart. Then, a father would be making a Pharisee out of his child by not working to change the heart. Of course, the father must discipline in love, not in anger, and then comfort the child afterwards, as God does to us. God gives us consequences, usually painful, always as a blessing, so we will stop sinning!

Prayer: Holy and loving Lord, it is good for us to see that sin has consequences, so that we stop sinning. Help us to appreciate how much You love us when You discipline us. In Jesus' name we pray. Amen.

July 6

"I, the LORD your God, am a jealous God, punishing the children for the sin of the fathers to the third and fourth generation of those who hate Me." Deuteronomy 5:9b

Material consequences

There are consequences in how a parent's sin affects their children. This is not the guilt of sin that is passed on to the next generation! *"The son will not share the guilt of the father, nor will the father share the guilt of the son. The righteousness of the righteous man will be credited to him, and the wickedness of the wicked will be charged against him,"* Ezekiel 18:20b. But there are physical, material, and even emotional consequences that may remain.

A drunkard father is instantly forgiven of the guilt, when his sin is finally confessed and forsaken. However, available food, clothing, and an inheritance to the third or fourth generation may not be a reality. Why? The past sinful lifestyle did not build up any wealth.

A man steals from a bank and is caught. He confesses his sin to God, the bank, his family, and church. He is forgiven of the guilt of it. But, he has a huge fine as a "material consequence." In the Bible, restitution was a material consequence for those who were guilty of sinning against God and man. A thief has consequences like restitution, a responsibility to restore the property to the rightful owner, and to restore sinners to each other.

Through Nathan the prophet, God told David, an amazing point about how God works in a believer's life. *"I gave you the house of Israel and Judah. And if this had been too little, I would have given you even more."* 2 Samuel 12:8b. David gave up material blessings when he sinned and so do we. God doesn't bless proud people or we would be even more proud. He disciplines us to walk the righteous road by giving us material consequences for sinning, all because He loves us.

Prayer: Righteous Lord, thank You for giving material consequences. We need the constant reminder of how much our sin hurts You, others, and even ourselves. Lord, we can see that You bless obedience but curse disobedience. Thank You for the necessary reminder that it is humble, obedient children that You choose to bless. In Jesus' name we pray. Amen.

July 7

"Be kind and compassionate to one another, forgiving each other, just as in Christ God forgave you." Ephesians 4:32

Putting forgiveness into practice

Our verse means at least four things. First, we must forgive any sin that is confessed to us. Why? Because God does! *"If we confess our sins, He is faithful and just to forgive us our sins and to purify us from all unrighteousness,"* 1 John 1:9. Since God is willing to forgive any and all sin, we must forgive any and all sin. If we do not obey, God will not forgive us as taught in Matthew 6:14-15.

Second, anyone who says, "I will not forgive until you prove to me that you deserve to be forgiven," is wrong. Did we prove to God that we deserved to be forgiven? If we say, "yes," then we believe salvation is by works, not grace. How can we prove that we deserved forgiveness when we were dead as Ephesians 2:1 teaches? According to Romans 5:10, did we, as an enemy of God deserve forgiveness? No. We must forgive others, *"just as in Christ, God forgave"* us, on the basis of grace.

Third, God's forgiveness gave us what we needed, not the death we deserved! Now, we must give others what they need, not what they deserve. When God gave us what we needed, we were changed. When we give others what they need, even though they don't deserve it, they too may have a better relationship with us. We must forgive, *"just as in Christ, God forgave"* us.

Fourth, it was very costly and painful for God to forgive us. It will be costly and painful for us to forgive others. The next time we need to forgive someone who has really hurt us, it would be most helpful to meditate on how hard it was for God to forgive us.

Prayer: Gracious Lord, You came to wicked Earth to forgive people who were cruel, unloving, and hated You! To forgive us, You were, *"wounded for our transgressions and bruised for our iniquities,"* Isaiah 53:5a NKJV. It cost You so much to forgive us! How wrong we are to think it will cost us nothing to forgive others. Lord, help us to see that it will cost us our pride, time, and money to forgive. It is hard to forgive others, but we praise You that the rewards of forgiving are literally out of this world! In Jesus' name we pray. Amen.

July 8

"If you bring your gift to the altar, and there remember that your brother has something against you, leave your gift there before the altar, and go your way. First be reconciled to your brother, and then come and offer your gift." Matthew 5:23-24 NKJV

Must I forgive if I did no wrong?

Our giving of a tithe for God's kingdom is an act of worship, a right response to God's gracious care of us. The only place in Scripture where we are even permitted to test God is when it concerns the giving of the 10% tithe, Malachi 3:10-12. God does not tell us to give because He needs our money, but to test our hearts. God wants to see if we really love Him more than the things of this world.

In our text, we are actually on the way to the altar with our tithe gift in our hand. Jesus tells us not to give it yet. Why? Since we are *"on the way to the altar,"* we have already decided in our hearts to give and have passed the "giving test." Jesus now has a bigger test for us. *"Your brother has something against you."* Be reconciled to him or to her.

Perhaps we did nothing wrong, but our brother "has something against us." Our Lord requires us to do something about it. Jesus here commands us to leave the worship of Him in the sanctuary and pursue the worship of Him in the world. When we go to reconcile with others, this extended "worship time" is part of the Great Commission. We must not only "go," but must watch how we go! It is possible to say the right things, but yet be wrong in how we say it. *"A gentle answer turns away wrath but a harsh word stirs up anger."* Also, to *"be reconciled,"* is to make sure that the one who has something against us knows that we want nothing between us.

Prayer: Dear caring Lord, You ask us to examine our hearts to see if there is a reconciliation matter in our life that is unresolved. We have often pretended that our hearts are right with You in giving gifts, while there are relationships that need our attention. You convict us that we need to do something. We thank You that in these difficult relationship times, You promised that *"Where two or three come together in My name, there am I with them."* Lord, thank You for blessing our needed relationships. In Jesus' name we pray. Amen.

July 9

"Therefore I tell you, whatever you ask for in prayer, believe that you have received it, and it will be yours. And when you stand praying, if you hold anything against anyone, forgive him, so that your Father in heaven may forgive you your sins." Mark 11:24-25

"Anything against anyone"

The word *"and,"* is that part of speech called a conjunction, a word joining two sentences. *"And"* here, connects *"believing"* and *"forgiving"* to an intimate prayer life. *"And"* connects *"believing"* in God to, *"if you hold anything against anyone, forgive him."* The principle here is: if we say we *"believe"* in God, in His Son, and in His Spirit, but fail to forgive *"anything against anyone,"* we do not really *"believe"* in God's Word. If God says, *"forgive,"* and we say, "no," we have unbelief, not big faith. Can we expect God to answer our prayers if we are so rebellious to His command to forgive *"anything against anyone"*?

We don't want to forgive because someone hurt us deeply and they do not deserve to be forgiven. The question is: <u>Did we deserve God's forgiveness</u>? No, the wages of sin is death. That is exactly what we deserved. God wants us to forgive others, to heal us of our pain. Forgiveness is letting go of the past hurt, allowing us to move on in the future. Others do not deserve our forgiveness. That's true. But then, we only need to forgive those who do not deserve it!

Every excuse we have for not forgiving others, we have done to Christ. We continue to hurt Him and still He forgives, *"anything."* We say so many things against Jesus, and He forgives, *"anything."* We deny Him and He forgives, *"anything."* We worship other things more than Him and He forgives, *"anything."* *"Believe"* and *"forgive"* go hand in hand. The two cannot be separated. It is our serious responsibility to *"believe"* and *"forgive."*

Prayer: Forgiving Lord, have mercy on us! We have held things against others and then expected You to hear our prayers and forgive us. How often we have been hearers of the Word only, not doers. We pretend to be righteous but are still so wicked. Lord, help us to forgive others this day, just as You have forgiven us, on the basis of grace. Just as we did nothing to earn Your forgiveness, may we expect nothing from others before we will forgive them. In Jesus' name we pray. Amen.

July 10

"If he sins against you seven times in a day, and seven times comes back to you and says, 'I repent,' forgive him." Luke 17:4

We must forgive again, and again!

First, *"If your brother sins, rebuke him, and if he repents, forgive him,"* Luke 17:3. If any Christian sins against us, we are required to rebuke him, but *"in a spirit of gentleness,"* according to Galatians 6:1 NKJV. *"If he repents,"* we are required to forgive him. But be careful here! This verse does not teach that if our brother does not repent, we do not have to forgive him. In the next verse we will see why. Verse three is one of God's rules we need to follow in forgiveness.

Second, *"If he sins against you seven times in a day, and seven times comes back to you and says, 'I repent,' forgive him,"* Luke 17:4. This *"seven times in a day"* in Luke, is recorded as 70 times 7 in Matthew 18:22. Jesus is saying we must forgive someone an endless amount of times in one day, even if they only say they will repent. If someone sins against us this many times in a day, there is not sufficient time for them to prove their repentance! When God forgives us, do we always repent?

In verse 3, we saw that if someone repents we must forgive them. In verse four if they even say they plan to repent, we need to forgive them. Romans 12, goes even further, saying we have to forgive our enemies. Our enemies do not even say they are going to repent! Mark 11:25 goes still further. If we have *"anything against anyone forgive them."* And if we don't obey, God will not hear our prayers as taught in Matthew 6:14-15. Forgiveness is the very oil that runs our spiritual engines! Forgiveness lets go of our past hurts and finally ends our inner struggle and bitterness.

Prayer: O Lord, how often You forgive all our sins! Yet we have not forgiven others in the same way. We have even demanded that those who hurt us, prove their repentance before we will forgive them. Lord, how we continue to mock Christ's forgiveness and grace to us. O Lord, help us to see that our loving others is not gracious unless we are willing to forgive all the ways they have hurt us. May we forgive all others, *"just as in Christ God forgave us."* In Jesus' precious name we pray. Amen.

July 11

"He replied, If you have faith as small as a mustard seed, you can say to this mulberry tree, 'Be uprooted and planted in the sea,' and it will obey you." Luke 17:6

Do we need "Big Faith" to forgive?

After Jesus told His disciples they had to forgive an endless amount of times in a day, their response to the Lord was: *"Increase our faith!,"* Luke 17:5. Jesus' answer revealed that it did not take a lot of faith, but simple obedience was required. Jesus actually rebuked His disciples lovingly, when they asked for more faith to forgive. He showed His disciples a little mustard seed between His fingers. He then explained that faith, even "as small as a mustard seed," you could move a tree. Jesus said that we do not need more faith to forgive, but more obedience! Jesus tells the following story to show that forgiveness is merely a matter of our Christian *"duty."*

> *And which of you, having a servant plowing or tending sheep, will say to him when he has come in from the field, 'Come at once and sit down to eat'? But will he not rather say to him, 'Prepare something for my supper, and gird yourself and serve me till I have eaten and drunk, and afterward you will eat and drink'? Does he thank that servant because he did the things that were commanded him? I think not. So likewise you, when you have done all those things which you are commanded, say 'We are unprofitable servants.* **We have done what was our duty to do,**'" Luke 17:7-10 NKJV.

Like Jesus' disciples, we have a difficult time forgiving others. We even say that we can't forgive someone. But the real reason is a very stubborn "won't!" The problem is that we don't feel like forgiving them, so we don't do it. Biblical forgiveness requires going against our feelings and practicing obedience, as does all of the Christian life. It is our Christian *"duty"* to forgive.

Prayer: O Lord, we stand guilty before You once again! Forgive our rebellious spirits. Strengthen us to replace our bitter grudges with very gracious forgiveness. In Jesus' name we pray. Amen.

July 12

"He will not quarrel or cry out; no one will hear His voice in the streets. A bruised reed He will not break, and a smoldering wick He will not snuff out, till He leads justice to victory." Matthew 12:19-20

Are we bruising reeds?

There are at least three main points in our text. We first see the sin. Second, we see the correction. Third, we see the victory.

The sin, is plain to see. *"He (Jesus) will not quarrel or cry out; no one will hear His voice in the streets."* That begs the question: "Is our voice heard in the streets?" Make no excuses. This is a simple "yes" or "no" answer. Our son or daughter did something wrong and our habit is to have our voice go way up. Why? If we try to justify our loud, angry tone, God's Word accuses us here and also in James 1:20, Galatians 5:19-21, Proverbs 29:20; Proverbs 21:9; Proverbs 26:21 and Matthew 15:18-19. Our loud and proud is not allowed. We must confess our sin and turn from it.

The correction, *"A bruised reed He (Jesus) will not break, and a smoldering wick He will not snuff out."* A reed is the most delicate of all of the grasses in the marsh. It is easily bruised, and then it breaks quickly. There are many bruised reeds walking around in this world. It is the job of all Christians in the church to help them, not break them!

Our text about perfect Jesus is to correct our error of being too harsh. The sin of *"quarreling"* must first be put off for us to change. Gentle Jesus, commands us to be gentle. Gentleness is evidence that the grace of God is in us because it is coming out of us. Do we have this necessary grace of God coming out of us?

The victory, is certain if we address spiritual problems with God's spiritual solution, that is Jesus Himself. We will not *"quarrel or cry out"* when our spirit gets more of Christ's Spirit. May we too, help heal many people gently with God's Word. God's will is that a spiritual and a physical healing will happen in many people as they obtain the sure victory that is in Christ alone.

Prayer: Tender Lord, forgive us for our quickness to hurt rather than to heal. Give us soft hearts and gentle spirits so Your kingdom may be advanced. In Jesus' name we pray. Amen.

July 13

"For since the creation of the world God's invisible qualities — His eternal power and divine nature - have been clearly seen, being understood from what has been made, so that men are without excuse." Romans 1:20

What can we tell an atheist?

The atheist loudly shouts out, "We do not have a soul." "Everything is just matter!" "There is no God." What can we say to an Atheist who rejects the Bible? Ask them gentle questions! "Who sprinkled the stars in the sky? Who gave us the sun, a bright light by day? Who gave us the moon, a smaller light at night? Was it chance? Was it a blind force of nature that put these objects there? If we were invited to some great feast, would we doubt there was a great cook who prepared the fine dishes? Would we say the possibility of a cook is nonsense? What do we see in the market? Do we not see onions, carrots, potatoes, cauliflower, tomatoes, milk, eggs and chickens, along with oranges, apples, bananas, pineapples and coconuts? Is it possible that there was a Creator of these good things?"

"Dear atheist, your view of no life after death is like a child in the womb thinking, 'I will never need the fingers and toes growing on my body." Like that little baby, is it not possible that our life here now, is important to prepare us for something in the future, even if we can't see it today? You say everything is just matter. If I throw a glass bottle down, it breaks without feeling anything. It truly is only matter. If you are only matter, would you permit me to push you down? I would not do that, but if I did, you would be mad, proving that you have feelings, thoughts, and even a soul that can be hurt. Can you not see the truth of life, even without a Bible?"

It is a fact that there will be no atheists in Heaven. More than that, there will be no atheists in Hell either! Everyone in Hell will know and fully experience God in all of His holy wrath. A "no God" belief is limited to this earth! Today, even the *"demons believe there is one God... and 'tremble,'"* James 2:19b.

Prayer: O Holy Lord, we thank You that we are important to You! We worship You that even Your creation tells us about the greatness of You, our Creator. In Jesus' name we pray. Amen.

July 14

"All Scripture is given by inspiration of God, and is profitable for doctrine, for reproof, for correction, for instruction in righteousness, that the man of God may be complete, thoroughly equipped for every good work." 2 Timothy 3:16-17 NKJV

Four main purposes of Scripture

<u>First</u>, the Bible shows us the proper *"doctrine,"* to get on the correct path of life. God has a right to teach us because we are His created creatures. Even more than that, as Christians, we are members of His family and must obey His Fatherly will. If God has given us the right *"doctrine"* to equip us fully, how dare we use other competing sources for the mind/soul of man.

<u>Second</u>, the Bible *"reproves"* or rebukes us when we go off the path of life. God's *"<u>reproof</u>"* is meant to convict us so that we might have a real heart change. Without conviction by the Holy Spirit, we would never confess any sin. Many people do not want to use the Word of God to reprove, rebuke, or convict. Therefore, our sin is not confessed, and there is no repentance. Such a neglect of God's Word stops the process of evangelism and discipleship. The problem is that some people just don't want to hear God's will for their life or that they have a sin problem. If they only knew that both spiritual and physical healing come from seeing sin as God does. God reproves us because He loves us!

<u>Third</u>, the Bible *"corrects"* us, putting us back on the path of life. We need to listen to God's directive will, not just His decreed will. God does not just cleanse us from sin, but to righteousness. God's corrections are forever right because God's wisdom never changes.

<u>Fourth</u>, the Word of God is, for *"<u>instruction in righteousness</u>,"* so that we can stay on the path that leads to Heaven. *"All Scripture is given by inspiration of God... that the man of God may be complete, thoroughly equipped for every good work."*

Prayer: O holy Lord, Your *"divine power has given us everything we need for life and godliness."* Thank You for writing things down in Your Word, the Bible, so we can know You and Your will for our lives. We truly are blessed! Accept our praise and worship. In Jesus' name we pray. Amen.

July 15

"Those controlled by the sinful nature cannot please God."
Romans 8:8

Addictions are never satisfied!

If you pursue any addictive vice, misery, not pleasure, will be yours. No one can pursue sin and find peace! Why? The various lust of the flesh, just like a fire, are never satisfied! Addictive lust are marriage spoilers, like nothing else. What spouse could ever please you if you have an addiction problem? Are you ready to pursue the love life of a loser? Do you really want to walk away from God to a Christ-less eternity? Did you know that the worst sexual pervert started out by looking at a simple nude picture; the biggest drunk started with just one drink; the addict hooked on the hard drugs started out with just a little "harmless marijuana"? All addictions cry, "more, more, more"! The previous high is never enough!

You may be thinking that you just want to check it out for yourself and that you can stop at any time. You do not understand! Can a fire stop burning at any time? Once started it cannot stop until the burning is done. A *"slave to sin"* in Romans 6:6, cannot free self! Meditate on the word *"slave"* because that is where lust will bring you! If you are so willing to give your soul to the devil, he will gladly have it! He wants you to serve him alone. Once your soul is his, you will fall deeper and deeper. Those who you hoped would love you, will loathe you!

Only God can help us all. Every addicted person needs to get into the river of grief over their selfish sin and to follow God's life giving stream of grace and forgiveness that He has prepared for a complete healing. Jesus is the way, the truth, and the life. Permanent peace comes from Christ alone. Flee to Christ who still says, *"My peace I leave with you; My peace I give you. I do not give to you as the world gives. Do not let your hearts be troubled and do not be afraid,"* John 14:27. When Christ forgives, He gives a new heart, and then we become *"slaves to righteousness,"* Romans 6:18.

Prayer: O Lord, help us all to see how this world offers enslavement, not peace! We want to be *"slaves to righteousness."* So work in us Lord. We are weak and like sheep that wander. Protect us and guide us we pray. Make us trophies of Your grace! In Christ's name we pray. Amen.

July 16

"Many are the victims she has brought down; her slain are a mighty throng." Proverbs 7:26

How a strong man is made weak

Samson was set aside by the Lord, for Himself. However, Satan wants Samson also. Samson was enticed by evil Delilah, meaning dainty one. There are strong demonic powers moving intensely at Samson through the "compromised Delilah," all to pull down Samson. *"The rulers of the Philistines,"* also work with the demonic, to destroy the strength of Christ's church. They employ this "good looking" woman to help them, Judges 16:4-21. Delilah pleads with Samson to give her the secret of his strength. In verse 15, she questions him saying, *"How can you say, 'I love you' when you won't confide in me?"* Delilah seduced Samson until he gave God's strength away. Samson was betrayed by kisses from the one who pretended to love him.

After Delilah questions his love, Samson now sees the need to prove it, to his own destruction. Samson gives her the secret of his strength and falls *"asleep,"* (spiritually speaking also). She cuts the seven braids of his hair. Seven, a sign of godly completeness is now gone. Without the strength of the Lord, Samson was a common man.

We, too, are vulnerable and incomplete, without the strength and protection of the Lord! The enemy burned Samson's eyes out. Lust does that to us. Why didn't Samson run? The answer is, He was more captivated by his love for her (lust really) than his love for the Lord.

Words of loyalty to our Lord are a lie when they are overruled by the passions of our heart! May we learn from the life of Samson that we should never see how close we can get to sin! Paul warns young Timothy, *"flee youthful lust"* 2 Timothy 2:22. If we think we stand, take heed lest we fall.

Prayer: Most holy Lord, like Samson, our eyes wander. Your righteous justice should put out our eyes too. We cry for Your forgiveness. We need Your mercy and strength. May our spirits grow stronger and our sinful flesh weaker. May we not only flee evil, but diligently pursue righteousness, the secret to change. Thank You for the righteousness of Christ and the power of Your Spirit. In Jesus' name we pray. Amen.

July 17

"God has said, 'Never will I leave you; never will I forsake you.'"
Hebrews 13:5b

Why are people lonely?

Loneliness is a feeling that hurts. Elisabeth Elliot wrote, "Loneliness can be a <u>wilderness</u>, or it can be a <u>pathway to God</u>." Loneliness is like a wilderness when we think too much about ourselves! Some say we need to think more about ourselves to get over loneliness. The Bible does not agree. When almost every thought is centered intensely on "I, my, and me," that is too much of self. The various ways in which we are selfish need to seriously go away to get over loneliness.

When we feel loneliness coming at us, we must be careful, It is at this very point, we will either give in to self-pity, which will increase the loneliness, or we will turn to God and others, and come out of it. If our life is hid in Christ, we will identify with Him. For Jesus is not just alive in Heaven, He is also alive in hearts all over the world. The number one cure for loneliness then is not more self-love, but loving God and others more. Loneliness is a warning that we need more of something, and that is God first of all.

Those who have lost a loved one to death have an empty place in their life that is not easily filled. Others who have been rejected, may have an even bigger void, since the one who has rejected them is still alive. But be careful. These kind of troubles do not <u>cause</u> loneliness! It is our <u>wrong reaction</u> to trouble that causes the loneliness. Even if we lose a loved one, giving in to self-pity will make it worse. It is far better to be thankful to God for giving us loved ones, than to feel pity because they are gone. That is a huge difference in perspective!

Being alone then, is not the same as being lonely. At times it is good to be alone. Jesus *"left the house and went off to a solitary place, where He prayed,"* Mark 1:35b. After a difficult day, we, too, can take a walk or just get away to relax or pray.

Prayer: Lord, we thank You that through Your Word we can see that Your loving character is our main cure for loneliness. Lord, we thank You for Your presence and Your promise, *"Never will I leave you; never will I forsake you."* Hebrews 13:5b. Teach us also to bear one another's burdens. In Christ's name we pray. Amen.

July 18

"Now Dinah, the daughter Leah had borne to Jacob, went out to visit the women of the land. When Shechem, son of Hamar the Hivite, the ruler of that area, saw her, he took her and violated her."
Genesis 34:1-2

When the party gets too hot!

At about 15 years of age, Dinah wanted out of the house to see the town. She saw far more than she wanted! She was not prepared for the consequences. Our text is similar to our recreational dating or dating for fun. The young man who *"saw her,"* didn't fully realize that his "love" for this girl was really lust. Quite frankly, he wanted Dinah's body, and he took it most likely against her will. Today you might call this situation, date rape.

Girls need to learn something about boys. A young man does not need a relationship to "get physical." The sight of a beautiful girl is enough to get his engine started. And, if the boy is used to getting what he wants, the girl's "no," will surely not stop him. Thinking you are safe from this great evil is very foolish.

Apart from "date rape," one of the greatest dangers of the whole dating scene is a young man or woman can fall in love quickly. God's process is not first love, and then consider if they are the right one! God's way is, to <u>consider the godly qualifications, and then love</u>. Why? Because a man and woman are called to love both a spouse's body and soul. Granted a person should be physically attractive. But the soul of the man or woman must be the main concern, not the appearance, skin color, education, or money. If you are mainly in love with the physical beauty, what will you do when the "appearance" changes? Find out what he or she is really like before you are married. Think! If lust gets you a spouse now, it will likely get you a divorce later.

Prayer: O Lord who protects, help us. We live in dangerous times. Take away our eyes from that which is evil, and replace it with the mind to stay where it is safe. Help us appreciate our families instead of running from them like Dinah did. Help the church to do a better job with safe, supervised social group encounters. In Jesus' name we pray. Amen.

July 19

"Like a gold ring in a pig's snout is a beautiful woman who shows no discretion." Proverbs 11:22

A pretty face with an ugly heart, is ugly!

Who would like to marry a pig? The answer is another pig. Not that a pig ever marries, but God has a way with words to get our attention! Having *"discretion,"* is to continually make good decisions. Right knowledge is not the same as right *"discretion."* Knowledge knows what to do. *"Discretion"* does it. A person who *"shows no discretion"* is rebelliously unwilling to make good decisions.

On the farm, we put a ring in a pig's nose so they wouldn't use their nose to dig out of their pen. We see many people who need a ring in their nose, to keep their face on the right side of the marriage fence. God went through much effort to put a Bible in our hands so we could feed on His Holy will. God wants us to look like His Son, not a pig. To look like His Son, we need a new heart, willing to do what is right.

Real beauty starts in the heart. If God gives anyone a beautiful face, and then they persist in their heart being ugly, He will make their face match their heart. God promised, and He will do just that.

"The LORD says, 'The women of Zion (in the church) *are haughty, walking around with outstretched necks, flirting with their eyes, tripping along with mincing steps, with ornaments jingling on their ankles. Therefore the LORD will bring sores on the heads of the women of Zion; the LORD will make their scalps bald.' In that day the LORD will snatch away their finery: the bangles and headbands and crescent necklaces, the earrings and bracelets and veils,"* Isaiah 3:16-19.

God goes on yet for seven more verses and ends up saying *"The gates of Zion will lament and mourn; destitute, she will sit on the ground,"* Isaiah 3:26. A beautiful face with an ugly heart, becomes ugly.

Prayer: Amazing Lord, how Your love in us makes us not just spiritually beautiful, but physically also. O Lord, may we all go to Your beauty parlor and get a new heart. We pray in the name of Christ, who makes all of His children beautiful. Amen.

July 20

"For I have told him (Eli) that I will judge his house forever for the iniquity which he knows, because his sons made themselves vile, and he did not restrain them. And therefore I have sworn to the house of Eli that the iniquity of Eli's house shall not be atoned for by sacrifice or offering forever." 1 Samuel 3:13-14 NKJV

How Eli spoiled his boys

Priest Eli seriously failed at discipleship both as a parent and as a ministry worker. Eli was actually a double failure! A church leader *"must manage his own family well and see that his children obey him with proper respect,"* 1 Timothy 3:4. This must happen before he is even eligible to be in ministry. Paul argues in 1 Timothy 3:3, *"If anyone does not know how to manage his own family, how can he take care of God's church?"* Why does God say this to us? The exact same discipleship relationship between a pastor and congregation exists between a parent and a child. Additionally, the same discipleship relationship also exists between a teacher and a student and a boss and a worker!

Leadership in the home must lovingly tell the children to do what is right, then enforce that with love also. That is what discipleship is. Priest Eli did not *"restrain"* or try to correct his sons evil living habits. His sons were privileged and spoiled. They grew up doing what they wanted and ended up not responsible as adults. God tells us, *"Train a child in the way he should go, and when he is old he will not turn from it,"* Proverbs 22:6.

God not only rebukes Eli for his poor parenting habits, but He warns us at the same time! Don't repeat Eli's failures by how we managed our own house and ministry. All children, even every disciple, belongs to God. *"Children are a heritage of the LORD."* God gives us His children to raise and disciple in His way. We have no right to disciple or guide anyone by the world's standards, especially children.

Prayer: Wise and holy Lord, Your Word is precious and enlightening to us. You tell us that, *"Folly is bound up in the heart of a child."* How we too live in a day that hates Your truth. Yet it is Your truth that sets us free! We praise Your wisdom about the importance in having correct discipleship relationships. Forgive us Lord for our failure. We want to follow You. In Jesus' name we pray. Amen.

July 21

"Do not be misled: 'Bad company corrupts good character.'"
1 Corinthians 15:33

Watch who you hang around with!

If there is ever a warning that our covenant young people need, it is this verse. So many promising young people, who are brought up in the church, were taught right from wrong, then go to school and hang out with the wrong crowd. They quickly go backwards in their spiritual walk to match the level of those they are "hanging out" with. Young people, this warning is for you. You know, there are many different groups of kids in your school. Who will you seek out for your friends? There are the rowdies, those who love music, those interested in sports, and then there is the "party" crowd. But there are also those who are genuinely interested in studying and preparing themselves for what is ahead of them in life. Your parents will try to guide you, but the decision on whom you will hang out with is also your responsibility. You do need to think about these things. Look before you leap!

Guard yourself from the party group especially. If partying is your goal from early on in life, do not expect it to change when you are older. Sin, of all kinds, is very addictive! Sex leads the list and is probably even more addictive than drugs and alcohol. You naturally are attracted to these things because you too are born a sinner. Don't touch! You will not know that the addiction messes with your mind until you are horribly hooked. Like a fish, you will not so easily get off that hook.

Satan wants to have you, and have you he will, if you cooperate with him. Bad habits developed when young and become an obsession sooner and later, according to Proverbs 22:6b. Know for certain, "*As a dog returns to its vomit, so a fool repeats his folly,*" Proverbs 26:11. One of the most important decisions of your life is: "Who will be your friends in your school years!"

Prayer: O Lord our protector, we thank You that You give us Your truth to warn us. Sad to say, there will be so many in the fires of Hell, that will eternally regret not following Your advice. Put Your Holy Spirit of discernment in us. In Jesus' name we pray. Amen.

July 22

"With persuasive words she led him astray; she seduced him with her smooth talk. All at once he followed her like an ox going to the slaughter." Proverbs 7:21-22a

A man in lust can't lead a home!

By God's created design, a married man is commanded to lead the home. This is a very important part of a man's covenant responsibility in marriage. A man with a lust or pornography problem cannot lead a home in a Biblical way. The reason is, lust is leading him! *"She led him."* *"She seduced him."* *"He followed her."* With three strikes against him, this man is out!

How did such a man come to be a follower instead of a leader? Lust is a burning fire that is never satisfied. Lust hotly pursues a bigger thrill continually. In Romans 6:6, we can see that a man who pursues a lust habit soon becomes a *"slave"* to it. We are all slaves to what controls us.

Becoming a slave to all the addictive sins usually starts very young in life. How does it happen? *"I noticed among the young men, a youth who lacked judgment,"* Proverbs 7:7b. It was because of this lack of good judgment that the man took the next step. *"He was going down the street near her corner,"* Proverbs 7:8a. When we see how close we can get to sin, we are already in trouble! Sin is selfish. Job was called a righteous man in Job 1:1 because, *"He feared God and shunned evil."* We have to deny self and instead fear or love God before we can shun evil. May God help us to shun evil.

Although he was warned, the young man got closer and became hooked on a woman *"dressed like a prostitute with crafty intent,"* Proverbs 7:10b. And then our text, *"She led him."* *"She seduced him."* *"He followed her."* Unless God changes this man's heart, *"her house is a highway to the grave,"* Proverbs 7:27a.

Prayer: O Lord, our great protector who loves us, we thank You for showing us the danger that is in the world to lure us to an eternal death. Forgive us, Lord, for seeing how close we can get to what is evil and profane. Fill us with Your love, and help us by Your Spirit to become *"slaves to righteousness.* In Jesus' name we pray. Amen.

July 23

"What do you people mean by quoting this proverb about the land of Israel: 'The fathers eat sour grapes, and the children's teeth are set on edge'? 'As surely as I live,' declares the Sovereign LORD, 'you will no longer quote this proverb in Israel.'" Ezekiel 18:2-3

What is a child's problem?

God hates the belief that parents or society are the cause of a child's personal problems. The "world" and even our fathers, will tempt us to sin, but the cause is in our own heart, per Matthew 15:18-19. In contrast, this evil saying or proverb in our text wrongly suggests that a child's problem is outside of himself. The evil saying is: If a father is a drunk the child will be no good. Worse yet, do not expect the child to be good because they are a hopeless victim.

The problem with anyone having a "victim mentality" is that their wrong response from "hurts" is their fault. Do not limit this discussion to a child! We blame others for our bad attitude when we say, "You make me angry." Truth is, others tempt us, but the cause of our anger comes from our own heart. God requires us all to act right, regardless of what others do to us. If we think our problems are outside of us, we are not listening to God who says that our problems are inside of us! Herein lies a big reason so many people do not change. They think, "Everyone else is the problem. Don't look at me because I am a victim." God gives us three examples in Ezekiel 18, to show us the truth.

In verses 5-9, a righteous man lives a good life, but he has an ungodly son. The ungodly son then has a good son. Three different lives to show us that we are personally responsible for the way we live. God concludes this discussion saying, *"The soul who sins is the one who will die. The son will not share the guilt of the father, nor will the father share the guilt of the son. The righteousness of the righteous man will be credited to him, and the wickedness of the wicked shall be charged against him,"* Ezekiel 18:20.

Prayer: O Loving Father in Heaven, we need Your wisdom to stop blaming others for our problems and instead need to take personal responsibility for our own sins. Our personal sin has separated us from You! Send Your Holy Spirit to convict us where we need conviction. Impress upon us our need of a Savior. In Jesus' name we pray. Amen.

July 24

"God disciplines us for our good, that we may share in His holiness. No discipline seems pleasant at the time, but painful. Later on, however, it produces a harvest of righteousness and peace for those who have been trained by it." Hebrews 12:10b-11

Why does God discipline us?

God disciplines us because He loves us and wants to restore us. Love and restore are key words. See God's love, *"And you have forgotten that word of encouragement that addresses you as sons: 'My son, do not make light of the Lord's discipline, and do not lose heart when He rebukes you, because the Lord disciplines those He loves, and He punishes everyone He accepts as a son.' Endure hardship as discipline; God is treating you as sons. For what son is not disciplined by his father? If you are not disciplined (and everyone undergoes discipline), then you are illegitimate children and not true sons. Moreover, we have all had human fathers who disciplined us and we respected them for it. How much more should we submit to the Father of our spirits and live! Our fathers disciplined us for a little while as they thought best; but..."* Hebrews 12:5-10a. God shows us clearly here and in our text, the how and why that He disciplines us.

Discipline from God may be the fruit of His displeasure, but it is also the proof of His love. We are spiritual beings who must learn right from wrong. Punishment is different than discipline. Discipline is correction for the purpose of restoration and reconciliation. Punishment is more of a word for judgment. God punishes people in Hell. Many well-meaning Christian parents have said that they would never spank their small children because of some of the abuses they have seen. True, abuse is wrong because that is over discipline. But little discipline or no discipline is wrong also. God, who especially knows the heart of a child, says a child must be disciplined in Proverbs 13:24, and 22:15, for the purpose of correction. We are all children of God.

Prayer: Dear Father in Heaven, we praise and thank You that You discipline us for our good because You love us, and *"that we may share in His holiness."* May we remember that You lovingly discipline us *"for our good"* and that we must not give in to Satan, who tempts us to doubt Your goodness. In Christ's beloved name we pray. Amen.

July 25

"Folly is bound up in the heart of a child, but the rod of discipline will drive it far from him." Proverbs 22:15

When is discipline needed?

Babies may be born cute, but they are not innocent. Children are born with Adam's original sin and are foolish. Biblical discipline drives out the foolishness. But what exactly is the *"folly"* that requires discipline? Things like spilling water are not foolish, that's a type of accident. It is when a child questions a parent's or God's authority that they are foolish and rebellious. *"A fool's talk brings a rod to his back,"* Proverbs 14:3a.

Without discipline, foolish children continue to get worse, not better. A child will soon disrespect all authority if not disciplined. The battle is: children want to be in control of a parent, and the home! If you let them, they will most willingly take control, even at age one. A little baby will soon wail with a fake cry. If a parent consistently rushes to pick up a baby when nothing is really wrong, that little child will begin to establish control. It won't hurt if they cry once in a little. Just know that a child is born selfish, and will try to manipulate the parent very early in life. Expect it.

By the time a child is old enough to crawl and grab what they should not have, discipline must carefully begin. Say "NO," and slightly slap the child's hand when they reach for an item they cannot have. They never heard the "NO" word before, so they will not understand at first. They will reach for it once more. Again say "NO" and slap their hand a little bit harder. If the child cries, it's okay. If again they reach for the object, the "NO" and slap must be still harder. This time they cry, but they are starting to understand there are rules in life. In time, children will thank their parents for disciplining them. It is actually abuse not to discipline a child. But it is also abuse if the parent disciplines a child and leaves bruises or injuries. We must discipline Biblically.

Prayer: Lord of all wisdom, when we see that foolishness is bound up in the heart of a child, we can see why they act so foolish. Lord give us the courage to discipline as You say we must. We do not want our children to end up being bigger fools! In Jesus' name we pray. Amen.

July 26

"Train a child in the way he should go, and when he is old he will not turn from it." Proverbs 22:6

Permissiveness is not Biblical strategy

Since *"folly is bound up in the heart of a child,"* letting them do what they naturally want to do, will be their destruction. The verse, *"Train a child in the way he should go, and when he is old he will not turn from it,"* is seen by many people as a promise in a very wrong way. Bruce A. Ray in his excellent book, "Withhold Not Correction" says: "In its proper context, Proverbs 22:6 is not a promise so much as it is a warning to Christian parents. In the Hebrew text, *'in the way he should go'* is entirely lacking. Rather the Hebrew says, *'If you train up a child in his way when he is old he will not depart from it.'*"

Jay Adams comments on Proverbs 22:6: "This verse stands not as a promise but as a warning to parents that if they allow a child to train himself after his own wishes (permissively) they should not expect him to want to change these patterns when he matures. Children are born selfish sinners and when allowed to follow their own wishes, they will naturally develop sinful responses. Such habit patterns become deep seated when they have been ingrained in the child from their earliest days."

A little tree is easily bent to change its growing direction. If we try to straighten a tree when it is full grown, it cannot be done, even with a team of oxen. So too, the longer bad habits are practiced, the longer it will take to implement new Biblical ones. If we see a problem and ignore it, the situation will get worse not better. "If it isn't broke don't fix it," is not a Biblical proverb! Our children are born broken sinners, not innocent but selfish. Along with all of us, they too need a Savior.

Prayer: Loving Lord, You gave the wayward Cain and us a picture of a lion waiting to attack us. You said, *"sin is crouching at your door; it desires to have you, but you must master it,"* Genesis 4:7b. We see that Paul also counseled Timothy, *"flee youthful lust"* in 2 Timothy 2:22, showing all of us to quickly leave our pattern of sin. May we get it into our heads that waiting to stop sinning is the devil's plan, not Yours! In Christ Jesus' name we pray. Amen.

July 27

"You shall beat him with a rod, and deliver his soul from hell."
Proverbs 23:14 NKJV

Why discipline children?

God knows, children will quickly question their parent's authority, and that they are foolish when they do. By ten months or so, children will begin to test their parent's "NO." Their actions will be a challenge to see if the parent really means it. The child is starting to think, "What are you going to do if I do what I want?" "Do you really mean your no?" This is a bigger test than most parents realize. It is essential that the parent is faithful to God right here. If the child refuses to listen, slap their hand a little. They must feel some pain. *"You shall beat him with a rod, and deliver his soul from hell,"* Proverbs 23:14 NKJV. Be careful with the word beat. The word "strike" is a better word in our western context. Discipline faithfully and lovingly and later on, the child will understand. First, they need to learn obedience. Don't shout. Discipline from the parent should be immediate, and without anger.

First, we discipline because God tells us to. *"He who spares the rod hates his son, but he who loves him is careful to discipline him,"* Proverbs 13:24.

Second, we discipline because children belong to God. Children are on loan to parents, but they are His. God says, *"every living soul belongs to Me,"* Ezekiel 18:4a. *"The earth is the LORD's and everything in it, the world, and all who live in it,"* Psalm 24:1.

Third, we discipline children because God says, our children are sinful and corrupt, intent on doing evil. *"Folly is bound up in the heart of a child but the rod of correction will drive it far from him,"* Proverbs 22:15. David said, *"Surely I was sinful at birth, sinful from the time my mother conceived me,"* Psalm 51:5.

Fourth, Christian parents are a God-ordained discipline tool to direct children towards Heaven instead of Hell.

Prayer: O Lord our God, we can see from our text that Biblical discipline is very loving and part of the discipleship process. We can see that to withhold discipline is the world's way of living, not Yours. Forgive us for not disciplining when we should. We want our children to love and obey You. In Jesus' name we pray. Amen.

July 28

"For if you forgive men when they sin against you, your Heavenly Father will also forgive you. But if you do not forgive men their sins, your Father will not forgive your sins." Matthew 6:14-15

How God disciplines us

God disciplines us when we sinfully rebel against His authority. God is looking for us to confess our sin and turn from doing wrong. With this in mind, we have three points.

1. Is confession of sin part of our discipline process? We try to teach confession in church, but the home is better. If we are going to separate the sin from the sinner, then confession is essential. What is true for us is true for our child. *"If we confess our sin, He is faithful and just and will forgive us our sins and purify us from all unrighteousness,"* 1 John 1:9. If a child has not sinned, they should not be disciplined.

2. Do we forgive our children after we discipline them? What better place is there to teach forgiveness than when a child has done wrong and both God and the parent forgive them? It is not wrong to discipline a child we have forgiven. God still disciplines us after we are forgiven! God's discipline is a consequence of sin, but also proof of His love for our soul. If the parent or child have a bitter attitude after the discipline process, it's wrong! That is the direct opposite of forgiveness and repentance. Jesus said, *"If you do not forgive men their sins, your Father will not forgive your sins,"* Matthew 6:15.

3. Do we discipline in anger? *"For man's anger does not bring about the righteous life that God desires,"* James 1:20. This is especially true in the discipline process. If we are angry, how can we comfort the child after the discipline? That is what God does to us. One lady said, "How do I get my child to listen if I don't get angry?" Ah, but you trained him like that. The child knows you will not use discipline when you speak softly, so he does not listen. Tell him that from now on, you will say something once, softly, and then discipline immediately if he does not listen!

Prayer: Lord our Comforter, we are grateful that after we confess our sins, You forgive us and then comfort us. Lord forgive us for not doing the same to our children. How Your Biblical truths are so needed. Help us, O Lord to do what is right. In Jesus' name we pray. Amen.

July 29

*"A whip for the horse, a halter for the donkey, and a rod
for the backs of fools."* Proverbs 26:3

Does discipline have to be painful?

You too have heard someone say, "I don't believe in spanking my child." God has a good answer for that. *"No discipline seems pleasant at the time, but painful. Later on, however, it produces a harvest of righteousness and peace for those who have been trained by it,"* Hebrews 12:11. God, who knows the heart of all, way better than us said, *"Do not withhold correction from a child, for if you beat him with a rod, he will not die. You shall beat him with a rod, and deliver his soul from Hell,"* Proverbs 23:13-14 NKJV. When we see that the pain of discipline acts to save a child from the fires of Hell, it is very loving! Would we want our children to cry in Hell for all eternity? If we refuse to discipline, with pain at times, we think lightly of our child's eternal soul! God said, *"Those I love I rebuke and discipline,"* Revelation 3:19a.

But why pain? Is pain by itself a blessing? No. Some people cut themselves and beat themselves for no gain. Yet as Christians we know that Jesus' pain on the Cross was a great gain for us. *"Although He was a Son, He learned obedience from what He suffered,"* Hebrews 5:8. If Jesus *"learned obedience from what He suffered,"* how much more do we need the same. God uses human trials and all the pain that goes with them, as heavenly tools to train our hearts to follow Him. The Apostle Paul speaks about this pain in his own life. In 2 Corinthians 12:7, he was given "a thorn in the flesh" to keep him humble. In fact, God never wastes pain. "No pain no gain," is Biblical.

"A whip for the horse, a halter for the donkey, and a rod for the backs of fools," Proverbs 26:3. Some people pick up rebellious children and just rub their back and speak softly to them. Those actions, after discipline are great, but used in the place of painful discipline, will not train a child to stop acting like a fool.

Prayer: Lord of all wisdom, forgive us for creating our own ways to train children. We ignore Your methods and end up with a rebellious child, who is self-centered, and then we wonder why. Fill us with more of Your wisdom so that we can change and live Your way. In Jesus' name we pray. Amen.

July 30

"Show him his fault, just between the two of you." Matthew 18:15b

Do you discipline privately?

1. Do you discipline in private? How would you like it if God told others about your sins? Would you like it if you did something wrong, and then your family went all over broadcasting what you did wrong? A family does not act like this! We would surely say, "Why didn't you come to me and tell me my fault?" God is saying the same thing. *"Show him his fault, just between the two of you,"* Matthew 18:15b. This is always the first rule of loving Biblical discipline for the business, the church, the school, or the home. Love goes alone to show a fault.

    2. Do you threaten or use harsh words instead of discipline? It is very common, yet wrong, to use loud threats without discipline. For example, when a father, employer, teacher or pastor threatens a young disciple in the presence of others, rebellion and resentment is built up. God says, *"A servant cannot be corrected by mere words; though he understands, he will not respond,"* Proverbs 29:19. A private, serious word with loving discipline if needed is effective in producing change. Any type of leader who has to raise their voice to try to gain control, is out of control. That is basically a fear-based management practice (the opposite of love) that disciplines in public.

    Loving management methods in discipline promote respect and loyalty. Reconciliation is what is needed to fix our relationships and responsibilities in every part of our lives. The fear based method of management does work. That's why we do it. But it doesn't work as well as God's loving method! True love is kind, not cruel. If we gossip (say things that are true to those who do not need to know) the one we are talking about will be tempted to become bitter. Then we wonder why our relationships are not very good. May we see our faults in our discipline practices and change!

Prayer: Loving Lord, forgive us for using the world's fear-based living model. May we use Your loving ways and experience Your beautiful results, changed hearts. We know that if You change a person's heart, the thoughts, words, and actions will also change. Thank You for teaching us how to live Your way. In Jesus' name we pray. Amen.

July 31

"We have all had human fathers who disciplined us and we respected them for it. How much more should we submit to the Father of our spirits and live!" Hebrews 12:9

Learning to *"submit"* to God's discipline

Submission protects us in a big way. Imagine a boy or girl that is 18 years old and now they have their first job. Up to this point in life, they never learned to submit to their parents, meaning they basically got their own way whenever they wanted it. Will they now suddenly listen to their new boss? What will they do when their new boss rebukes them and disciplines them for any wrong behavior? They will follow the pattern they have firmly established, and then fail miserably!

Temper tantrums and pouting that are allowed early in life will set us all up for many failures later in life. A main issue is that children from the age of 6 months to 2 years need to learn to obediently respect their parent! Submission must happen before a child can understand why it is important! If you have to chase your child to discipline them, that is not even close to submission! A child that is allowed to reject any form of discipline promotes bitterness, brooding, and revenge, all the opposite of restoration, which is the main goal of discipline. The parent must explain to the older child the necessity and the reason for submission. If we fail to submit to parents and authority in general, we will fail to submit to God!

Can you see why teaching a child to submit to discipline now, helps to protect them later from problems like anger, bitterness, fear, worry, eating disorders, depression and even suicide? Submission is having a right attitude in life! We, in authority, encourage submission when our discipline is private, quiet, short, and finished when it is done. In the end, may we all learn to submit to God and live eternally!

Prayer: Forever loving Lord, forgive us for not submitting to Your good discipline and to those in authority over us. Help us to model a submissive spirit as parents and leaders. May we all be able to say, *"Before I was afflicted I went astray, but now I obey Your Word,"* Psalm 119:67. Lord, thank You for disciplining us personally, for our good! In Jesus' name we pray. Amen.

AUGUST

" 'Haven't you read,' He replied,
'that at the beginning the Creator
made them male and female, and said,
"'For this reason a man will leave his father and
mother and be united to his wife,
and the two will become one flesh'"?*
So they are no longer two, but one.' "
Matthew 19:4-6a

August 1

"The LORD God took the man and put him in the Garden of Eden to work it and take care of it." Genesis 2:15

What is a bridegroom and husband?

The words bridegroom and husband are God's words, packed with meaning. Bridegroom is the name first given to a new husband. As the name suggests, it is the responsibility of the man to groom the bride. The Bible teaches that a married man is called a husband. The word comes from the word "husbandry," the care of a vineyard, trees, plants, or animals. Grooming and husbandry were foundational tasks for Adam and are for farmers yet today. Those faithful in husbandry will have healthy crops and animals. Farmers know that neglected crops and animals suffer from a lack of care, as do brides and wives! Just as wilted and diseased plants are the result in poor growing conditions, so are wives. Neglect in husbandry produces sad looking fruit.

Good marriages do not "just happen," any more than good gardens "just happen." God's primary command is, *"Husbands, love your wives, just as Christ loved the church and gave Himself up for her to make her holy, cleansing her by the <u>washing with water through the Word</u>,"* Ephesians 5:25-26. This means that a husband is to read the Bible in the home. When a wife's heart is transformed by the Spirit of God and softened by the love of her husband, her countenance will glow so that she is beautiful. A wife with a soft, gentle heart on the inside will reflect and radiate that love on the outside. The two go together, and the bridegroom or husband is greatly responsible for this. He is the husbandman. If the wife is not more beautiful after years of marriage, the husband must not complain! After all, he is the groom.

Prayer: Dear Lord who loves us, we thank You for giving us simple words to see the responsibility of a husband. How praiseworthy that Christ did not find the Church lovely but made it lovely, as He <u>gave</u> Himself graciously for it! May we, as husbands, so graciously care for our brides. Forgive us Lord for not following Your example in caring for our marriages. Help us to change. We pray in the name of Jesus, the Bridegroom of the Church. Amen.

August 2

"The LORD God said, 'It is not good for the man to be alone. I will make a helper suitable for him.'" Genesis 2:18

What is a bride and wife?

A bride is described in Revelation 19:7b as one who, *"has made herself ready"* for the bridegroom. Quite simply, a married woman is a wife. In Scripture a wife is described as *"a helper,"* Genesis 2:18, 20b, *"the crown of her husband,"* Proverbs 12:4, *"a good thing,"* Proverbs 18:22 NKJV and *"your partner,"* Malachi 2:14. These words are instructive. The Church itself is the bride of Christ, reflecting the relationship of the bride to the bridegroom.

A Biblical wife is described in Proverbs 31 NKJV as one who *"her husband safely trusts"* (vs.11), *"does him good and not evil all the days of her life"* (vs.12), *"willingly works"* (vs.13). She, *"brings food"* (vs. 14), has a small business outside the home (vs. 16), gives to the poor (vs. 20), manages the household (vs. 27), is praised by her children and husband (vs. 28), *"a woman who fears the LORD"* (vs. 30) and is praised for her work by many (vs. 31). A Biblical wife is a woman of great value, has much virtue, delights in her work, and finds fulfillment as a loving wife and mother. She is, in turn, deeply appreciated by her family.

A wife came into the picture soon after creation because man was lonely and without a suitable companion. For a good reason, a wife is lovingly referred to as a man's better half. A Biblical wife truly does complete a man yet is submissive to him. Sad to say, many "liberated" women are leaving their husband and family to find fulfillment in "the world." But the approval, peace, and satisfaction they are looking for will not be found. Only God gives fulfillment in the role He provides for all of us. Unless a woman has the gift of singleness, she finds her main fulfillment by being a godly wife and mother. A godly marriage is a covenant of companionship.

Prayer: Dear Lord, we thank You for giving us wisdom about what a Biblical wife is. What a blessing a godly wife is to marriage and to the building of Your kingdom. Lord bless our marriages! Bless our Biblical wives. In Jesus' name we pray. Amen.

August 3

"Then the LORD God made a woman from the rib He had taken out of the man, and He brought her to the man." Genesis 2:22

Why did God make a wife from a rib?

We read that the Triune God created the world in six days. On the sixth day, God first created male and female animals so that they could be fruitful and multiply. Then God created Adam. *"But for Adam no suitable helper was found,"* Genesis 2:20b. The point is, an animal was not *"suitable"* to be man's lifetime helper. So, God then formed (not created) the woman because man needed her help. *"Then the LORD God made a woman from the rib He had taken out of the man, and He brought her to the man,"* Genesis 2:22. Man slept when his wife was being formed, showing man had nothing to do the process. Man has nothing to do with a new life in Christ either. God forms us while we are still sleeping spiritually.

Matthew Henry has a beautiful quote concerning the reason God took the woman from the rib of her husband: "The woman was 'made out of a rib out of the side of Adam.' She was not made out of his head to rule over him, nor out of his feet to be trampled on by him, but out of his side to be equal with him, under the arm to be protected, and near his heart to be beloved."

God did not make "women" (plural) for man, but He made a woman for a man, ruling out polygamy. Today, we need to know that these rules are God's design for all time. The very first Christian marriage was made in Heaven by God, as Christian marriages still are. May we look to God to arrange our marriages.

Prayer: Covenant Lord, we praise You for giving us clear principles to understand how You designed marriage. You know us intimately. May we trust Your wisdom while living in a world that wants to do things a different way. We also see that just as You put a hole in Adam's side to make his bride and a new life. So too, You put a hole in Christ's side to purchase us, His Bride, and give us new everlasting life! How grateful we are that You made this marriage between Christ and the Church. In Jesus' name we pray. Amen.

August 4

"The LORD God took the man and put him in the Garden of Eden to work it and take care of it." Genesis 2:15

How is a man created different?

There is a God-designed difference between a man and a woman. When God created man, <u>He gave Adam a task or work to do</u>. We can see this in our text. In Genesis 2:19-20, God gave Adam the task of naming the animals and managing God's creation. After sin entered the world, God reduced man from a manager to a laborer, saying; *"Cursed is the ground because of you; through painful toil you will eat of it all the days of your life. It will produce thorns and thistles for you, and you will eat the plants of the field. By the sweat of your brow you will eat the food,"* Genesis 3:17b-19a. Man's task or job just became much harder.

The woman was created by God to be <u>interested in relationships, more than the man</u>. We will see more of the womans role in tomorrows devotion, but we need to bring it up here to see how man's role in marriage is different. If we don't understand these God-given roles of men and women, it will cause problems in the marriage.

A problem for the man begins when he becomes <u>too focused on the task</u>. When the man seeks a wife, he may spend much time winning her confidence and love. She interprets all this attention thinking, "he is interested in relationships, just like me." She doesn't quite understand that getting a wife is his current "task or job." Soon after they are married, she finds him mostly working, leaving little time for her. Since she is very interested in relationships, she is upset and confused. If the husband does not meet his wife's deep relational needs, she will be more easily tempted to be unfaithful to her marriage responsibilities.

Prayer: Loving Lord, some of us are guilty. We often talk more to the family dog or to the cows, than with our wife. Your Word reminds us as husbands to take care of our primary relationship, our wife. You remind us, *"She is your partner, the wife of your marriage covenant."* Lord, strengthen us to keep our covenant marriage vows to You, and to our spouse. In Jesus' name we pray. Amen.

August 5

"So the man gave names to all the livestock, the birds of the air and all the beasts of the field. But for Adam no suitable helper was found," Genesis 2:20. *"Your desire will be for your husband."* Genesis 3:16b

How is a woman created different?

After the animals were created and named, God said there was *"no suitable helper"* for the man. Some do not like these words thinking; "This is Old Testament theology and no longer relevant." Paul brings it up again in the New Testament. *"For man did not come from the woman, but woman from man; neither was man created for woman, but woman for man,"* 1 Corinthians 11:8-9. The woman was made to be a helper and a companion to the man.

After sin came into the world, the woman's difficulties in being a companion increased. Because the woman fell into sin first, God said to her, *"your desire will be for your husband,"* Genesis 3:16b. By God's created design, and as part of the results of the fall, a woman desires and craves a close relationship with her husband. This makes a woman very relationship-oriented.

When the woman is first interested in a man, she may polish his motor bike, talk about football, and ask many questions about his work. The man interprets this attention thinking the woman is really interested in his various tasks. But soon after marriage, the husband cannot understand why his wife is more interested in spending time with her family than having anything to do with his God-given task. It is wrong for a wife to spend so much time pursuing other relationships, to the neglect of her husband. God created her out of man, to be part of a man, *"a helper comparable to him,"* Genesis 2:18 NKJV. A bride must be adorned for her husband first.

Prayer: O Lord of all wisdom, we see Your created design for both the husband and wife. Forgive us for not living as we should. Help us as spouses to meet the other's God-given needs. May we do this for Your glory and for the building up of Your church. In Christ's name we pray. Amen.

August 6

"Make the price for the bride and the gift I am to bring as great as you like, and I'll pay whatever you ask me. Only give me the girl as my wife." Genesis 34:12

What about paying a dowry?

In the Bible, a dowry was a sum of money or goods a man paid as proof that he was able to support a wife, and insurance in case he didn't. In the Old Testament, a dowry price secured a woman as a wife. The money was paid to her parents to be held as a guaranteed protection package in case of desertion or divorce. If a man did not pay the bride price (dowry), the woman was a concubine or a mistress. Paying the dowry was honorable.

If a man caused a woman to lose her virginity, he had to pay the highest bride price of 50 shekels of silver, as a penalty. A shekel today would cost about $150. Fifty shekels would cost about $7,500. The dowry price was negotiable in most cases. Saul required David to pay as dowry, 100 lives from Saul's enemies. But then, Saul really wanted David dead.

In our text, Shechem wanted Jacob's daughter Dinah as his wife. There are other examples of dowry in Exodus 22:16-17, and also in Exodus 21:7-11. There is one case, in Joshua 15:16-19, where the father of the bride (Caleb) paid a gift to his daughter.

Note that the money did not go to either of the parents for their use or living expenses. A dowry was required because of cheating and stealing. Thus, a dowry protected a girl. An unbiblical dowry leaves a woman in a serious position if the man finds no pleasure in her as it is recorded in Deuteronomy 24:1. We do not find any example of dowry in the New Testament. Sad to say, today dowries look more like an old age pension plan for either the parents of a boy or girl, depending on the country where the practice is used.

Prayer: Lord our protector, we can see that You are concerned that a girl is treated with respect and is cared for. We can see how a Biblical dowry helped care for possible widowhood. We also see that to buy the Bride of Christ, the Church, it cost You a lot, even Your Son's precious blood. We praise You for Your love. In Jesus' name we pray. Amen.

August 7

"Miriam and Aaron spoke against Moses because of the Ethiopian woman whom he had married; for he had married an Ethiopian woman." Numbers 12:1 NKJV

What about crossing race or caste to marry?

The subject of caste is such a big deal. The Bible is clear. Twice in one verse God points out that Moses married out of caste. Both Miriam and Aaron were working with Moses. Aaron was priest and Miriam a prophetess. They thought they knew better than Moses on whom he should marry. God agreed with Moses. When Aaron and Miriam became critical *"because of the Ethiopian woman,"* *"suddenly Miriam became leprous, as white as snow,"* Numbers 12:1b &10b NKJV. God severely and quickly disciplined the sister of Moses for criticizing her brother's marriage from a different cast or race.

Others marrying out of caste were: Abraham in Genesis 16:1, Joseph in Genesis 41:45, Ruth and Boaz, Salmon and Rahab, David in 1 Samuel 18:27, and many others. In fact, Jesus' physical heritage is a result of crossing castes often. The Bible nowhere prohibits marrying out of caste when the partner is a Christian. God looks at the hearts of people, and so must we!

Jesus is the King of Heaven and was a perfect Man! He crossed all castes by touching lepers, prostitutes, the blind, and the lame. Christ, as the bridegroom, married the bride (redeemed sinners) *"from every tribe and language and people and nation,"* Revelation 5:9. More than that, God adopted all nations as sons and daughters in Christ. The rule that we must marry in caste only is partly an invention of man to keep the power and wealth in the hands of a few. Jesus said, *"How hard it is for the rich to enter the kingdom of God,"* Mark 10:23. Each must marry in the Lord, according to the will of the Lord.

Prayer: O wise and loving Lord, we praise You that in Christ, we are all Your sons and daughters. What comfort it is, that you take Your children from every tribe and nation on earth. What a great picture this is for us to go into all the world with the Gospel also. We thank You that You teach us, so that we might know Your will in marriage. We praise You that there is neither slave nor free, for we are all one in Christ. In Jesus' name we pray. Amen.

August 8

"Do not be yoked together with unbelievers. For what do righteousness and wickedness have in common? Or what fellowship can light have with darkness?" 2 Corinthians 6:14

How to determine a marriage match

A Biblical marriage is one in which the man and the woman are both Christians, committed to Christ and each other. Only then can they be *"yoked together,"* like a team of oxen, pulling for the Master. God not only gives us clear words, He also gives us a clear picture of a Biblical marriage. In the picture, we can also see different levels of spiritual maturity.

A nominal Christian is a man or woman who goes to church, but is not committed to Christ. They pretend to be for Jesus on Sunday, but are all for themselves the rest of the week. A nominal Christian looks good on the outside, but the heart is basically unchanged by the Word and Spirit of God. Jesus called nominal Christians, lukewarm, neither hot nor cold. Jesus said in Revelation 3:16 that He was about to spit them out of His mouth. A nominal Christian is self-righteous, angry, bitter, unforgiving, uninterested in personal Bible study, prayer, or listening to the Word of God. Such a "pretending Christian," is repulsive to God, even more than an unbelieving pagan is. A "nominal Christian," is not a potential marriage partner, for they are not in God's will.

A baby Christian has a changed heart and is beginning to work on repentance or Biblical change. A baby Christian will change, all because God has called him or her into an eternal relationship. *"Being confident of this, that He who began a good work in you will carry it on to completion,"* Philippians 1:6a. In fact, baby Christians are eager to change! The easiest way to tell the difference between a nominal Christian and a baby Christian is not how they live on Sunday, but how they live the other six days of the week. The only difference between a baby Christian and a more mature Christian is that God has been at work, changing the mature Christian for a longer period of time.

Prayer: Righteous Lord, we appreciate Your wise warning in our text. Give us the spiritual eyes to see the difference between a nominal Christian and a baby Christian. May our marriages be a picture of Christ and the Church. In Jesus' name we pray. Amen.

August 9

"What harmony is there between Christ and Belial? What does a believer have in common with an unbeliever? What agreement is there between the temple of God and idols? For we are the temple of the living God." 2 Corinthians 6:15-16b

Why not a marriage to an unbeliever?

Yesterday we looked at a nominal Christian and a baby Christian. Now we turn to the impossibility of being *"yoked"* to an unbeliever. Our text shows a match between a child of Satan and a child of God is completely outside the will of God. The unbeliever will not submit to God, and anyone else either. Yesterday's text gives the picture. Can a wild ox (unbeliever) be yoked to a trained one (Christian)? The wild ox will never lower its head so that we can put the yoke on it. Even if we managed to get a wild ox in a yoke, how can two oxen pull a plow when they want to go in different directions? A wild ox as a marriage partner, is a candidate for a yoke, only after they are tamed by God. We cannot tame anyone!

Marriage partners need a desire and ability to solve problems as described in the Bible. Christians are committed to resolving "issues" God's way. A committed Christian prays to solve problems. It's true, a family who prays together stays together. Solving problems requires humility, empathy, or sensitivity to the needs, hurts, and desires of others. Unless we want a life of constant tension, stay away from a marriage partner who is not willing to solve problems Biblically.

Possible marriage partners come with a big, huge, enormous and giant warning: A beautiful face with an ugly heart will not pull the plow in the direction the Master demands. A beautiful ox with a wild spirit is still wild!

Prayer: Holy and loving Lord, when we need to understand something clearly, You so often give us a clear picture. Help us to get rid of the nonsense of the world, which is looking for exterior beauty before thinking about inner beauty. Impress Your message on us that beauty starts in the heart, inside of us, and then works outward. Thank You for the graces You put in us to make us beautiful to You, and then to others also. In Jesus' name we pray. Amen.

August 10

"A certain man...was very wealthy...His name was Nabal and his wife's name was Abigail. She was an intelligent and beautiful woman, but her husband, a Calebite, was surly and mean in his dealings."
1 Samuel 25:2-3

Can we change him or her?

Our text is an example of a marriage mismatch. Abigail was a very beautiful woman, married to Nabal, who was *"surly and mean,"* a real jerk. There are still countless marriages today that are filled with heartache. Many couples do not heed God's advice to be equally yoked. We have seen the Biblical requirements for a good marriage. Like many before, we may be thinking, "I know, but I will change him or her." That kind of thinking is so wrong and is idolatry also! God, through His Son and Spirit, alone changes hearts, Ezekiel 36: 26-38. We can't change anybody. Thinking "I will change him or her," will pave the road to disappointment.

One woman who came seeking counsel thought she could change her wild husband. She openly admitted, "When I got married I was looking for an ideal, but I got an ordeal, and now I want a new deal." She was in love with the exterior and thought she could change the interior. She was one sorry woman!

Often people persist in marrying an unbeliever because they are nominal Christians themselves! A committed Christian follows Christ command, *"Do not be yoked together with unbelievers."*

Another important point in the selection of a spouse is that both spouses must be willing to work. A good team of oxen pulls together. If one spouse is lazy and the other has a good work ethic, they are not equally yoked. One ox cannot pull the plow if the other is lying down. A person who is lazy physically is often lazy spiritually. A good work ethic is primarily a spiritual issue, essential to a good marriage.

Prayer: O Lord our eternal matchmaker, we are grateful that You willingly guide us to the right spouse. Left to ourselves, we go our own way and fail, then wonder why You didn't help us. Forgive us for being so worldly. May all of our marriages be made by You, in You, for Your kingdom. In Jesus' name we pray. Amen.

August 11

"God blessed them and said to them, 'Be fruitful and increase in number; fill the earth and subdue it.'" Genesis 1:28a

Biblical reasons to get married

<u>A Biblical marriage fulfills the need to produce godly children</u>. God most often extends His kingdom by parents in covenant with Him.

First, the Lord must build the family. God said, *"Be fruitful and increase."* God never took this rule away. *"Unless the LORD builds the house, its builders labor in vain. Children are a reward from Him... Blessed is the man whose quiver is full of them,"* Psalm 127:1, 3b, 5a.

Second, it is God who opens and shuts the womb.

Third, blessed is the family who has godly children! Not blessed is the family who has children. A quiver full of crooked or broken arrows is not a blessing. The best way to produce godly children is when the husband and wife are first committed to God, then to each other, and then to the children. Only real Christians have this kind of commitment.

<u>A Biblical marriage was given to avoid sexual immorality.</u> Dear Christians, *"Do you not know that your bodies are members of Christ Himself?"* 1 Corinthians 6:15a. *"He who unites himself with the Lord is one with Him in spirit,"* 1 Corinthians 6:17. Christians belong to Christ, in body and in spirit. Our bodies must be pure, for our spirits to be one with God. Our God gives us rules to keep our bodies pure. *"Since there is so much immorality, each man should have his own wife, and each woman her own husband,"* 1 Corinthians 7:2. We are told to "flee from sexual immorality," 1 Corinthians 6:18a. We don't get married just to flee sexual immorality. But it is one of the reasons God gives for marriage. A person who has the gift of singleness does not have a burning desire for the opposite sex. God gives a desire for sexual relations to be used, not abused.

Prayer: O Lord, we want children who love You to grace our homes. We know that such a home will be a blessing to Your church, and to society also. Lord, we also thank You for the desires we have for You and for each other. This is indeed, a gift from You. May we use our passions as You direct us. Forgive us where we have sinned. In Jesus' name we pray. Amen.

August 12

"It is not good for the man to be alone." Genesis 2:18a

Preparing for marriage or singleness

Marriage is God's common design for man. Singleness is a special gift. If God calls a Christian to singleness, He will do two things. He will equip us with a special service for the church, and He will give us the peace and grace to accept it. Jesus said, *"Not everyone can accept this word but only those to whom it has been given. For some are eunuchs because they were born that way; others were made that way by men; and others have renounced marriage because of the kingdom of Heaven. The one who can accept this should accept it,'"* Matthew 19:11b-12. Preparation for marriage or singleness is the same process:

1. Praying is not enough: God gives us daily bread, but we still need to go to work. *"If a man will not work, he shall not eat,"* 2 Thessalonians 3:10b. If we seek a spouse, work at it. Many do not have the delights of marriage because they are not working towards it.

2. Discover your gifts: God gives each true Christian at least one gift. Why? *"To prepare God's people for works of service,"* Ephesians 4:12a. Our gifts are, *"to serve others,"* 1 Peter 4:10. We must die to self, first. Then start serving others with our life and discover our gifts.

3. Develop your gifts: Schedule your time to help others whether it is teaching, serving, contributing, leadership, administrative, etc...

4. Demonstrate your gifts: As we lovingly serve God and others with our lives, people will see our readiness for marriage. *"Therefore, I urge you, brothers, in view of God's mercy, to offer your bodies as living sacrifices, holy and pleasing to God – this is your spiritual act of worship,"* Romans 12:1.

5. Let God decide: *"For we are God's workmanship, created in Christ Jesus to do good works, which God prepared in advance for us to do,"* Ephesians 2:10. God knows if we need a helper to the task.

Prayer: O Great Provider, forgive us for our impatience concerning marriage. We expect You to lead us, but we are often not willing to follow You. You have told us to seek first Your righteousness and the other things will be added unto us, including marriage. May we listen to You. In Jesus' name we pray. Amen.

August 13

"When a young woman still living in her father's house makes a vow to the LORD or obligates herself by a pledge and her father hears about her vow or pledge but says nothing to her, then all her vows and every pledge by which she obligated herself will stand. But if her father forbids her when he hears about it, none of her vows or the pledges by which she obligated herself will stand; the LORD will release her because her father has forbidden her." Numbers 30:3-5

Decisions in the home

What an amazing text! As a missionary in India, I get asked often about "taking a decision." Two principles are in our text for making decisions in the home before and after marriage. These verses show that the father or husband is the head of the home, bearing the final responsibility before God for decisions. Even in the selection of a spouse, the final decision, really is the father's. This is why historically, a groom asks the girl's father for his daughter's hand. But, if father keeps quiet after having knowledge of any agreement or vow the daughter makes, he has agreed to them. The father cannot come back later and say he did not approve. However, the father is a foolish man if he does not listen to and consider the wisdom of his wife and daughter. *"Where there is no counsel, the people fall; but in the multitude of counselors there is safety,"* Proverbs 11:14 NKJV. This verse surely includes decisions in the home.

After marriage, if a husband fails to question and even reverse a decision his wife has made, including a child's marriage, her decision stands. *"If she marries after she makes a vow or after her lips utter a rash promise by which she obligates herself and her husband hears about it but says nothing to her, then her vows or the pledges by which she obligated herself will stand. But if her husband forbids her when he hears about it, he nullifies the vow that obligates her or the rash promise by which she obligates herself, and the LORD will release her,"* Numbers 30:6-8. Read all of Numbers 30 for a fuller explanation.

Prayer: O Lord, we thank You for giving us Your wisdom on decisions in the home. How often we run into trouble because we do not listen to You. Forgive us and continue to guide us into all truth. In Christ's name we pray. Amen.

August 14

"Where there is no counsel, the people fall; but in the multitude of counselors there is safety." Proverbs 11:14 NKJV

Seeking help to find a spouse

This is written in India, where the parents basically choose the person their child marries. Here in the west, most often the children choose. A balance between the two is wise, as our text teaches.

Part of the parents letting go of the children is working with them in the selection of a marriage partner. If children are old enough to marry, they are old enough to help decide whom they should marry. After all, they must live with the person until death. Too often the kids are left to work out the marriage possibilities alone. This is as bad as the parents making the decision alone. Mature Christian parents know the joys and difficulties in marriage and can help the younger ones. Whom to marry should become clear after much prayer and counsel. God does work through people as our text teaches.

In India I often get this question: "What if a girl or boy is in love with a particular person and the parents want her to marry a different person?" First, a hurried marriage should not occur. Too often either the parent or the child looks at money, appearance, status in society, or education before looking at the heart like God does. Neither the parent nor child should be quick to look at these things. For example, God says, *"The love of money is a root of all kinds of evil. Some people, eager for money, have wandered from the faith and pierced themselves with many griefs,"* 1 Timothy 6:10. A marriage based on these things is headed for the rocks even before it begins! *"The LORD does not look at the things man looks at. Man looks at the outward appearance, but the LORD looks at the heart,"* 1 Samuel 16:7b. If we would look at the heart of a possible spouse first, the final decision will be in line with God's thoughts.

Prayer: O wise Lord, we have seen many marriages condemned before they began because we were not willing to follow You. Forgive us, Lord. It was You who put the first marriage together, and it is You who still makes marriage matches. Help us to wait for You while we pray and work on changing our own lives. In Jesus' name we pray. Amen.

August 15

"Therefore shall a man leave his father and his mother, and shall cleave unto his wife: and they shall be one flesh." Genesis 2:24 KJV

"Leaving" to establish a new covenant

God gave this "leaving and cleaving" rule in the Old Testament. Jesus reconfirmed it in the New. The verse begins with a command for the man to *"leave"* his family. Why does "covenant" require a man to *"leave"* home?

In the Old Testament, all male children were circumcised on the 8th day with the sign of the covenant. This was an initiation rite into the covenant family. The parents, in covenant with God, promised to bring up the child in the ways of the Lord. After the boy becomes a man, he is now in our text commanded to *"leave"* the covenant protection and blessings of his father and begin his own covenant family. The leaving has to happen before the cleaving can begin. The word *"cleave"* is a KJV word for the important process of the bride and groom being joined together spiritually, mentally, emotionally and physically.

The woman or new bride in the Bible did not really *"leave"* home when she got married. Instead, her father (and mother) gave her to this man. Thus, the bride was never without covenant protection. She transferred from God's covenant covering of her father and family, to a new covenant union with her husband and God. This is why in many marriage ceremonies today the pastor correctly asks the parents of the bride: "Who gives this woman to this man?" This is asked because of the covenant!

It is totally a man-made rule that expects the new couple to live with the groom's or bride's parents. This puts a huge strain on both marriages! Our text is clear. The newlyweds should not live with their parents.

Prayer: O Lord, help us to follow Your righteous rules that build new relationships instead of man-made rules that make things difficult. May we also marry in covenant to true believers who are baptized – the replacement for the Old Testament circumcision. In Jesus' name we pray. Amen.

August 16

"Therefore shall a man leave his father and his mother, and shall cleave unto his wife: and they shall be one flesh." Genesis 2:24 KJV

"Leaving," a command to parents

We remind the reader that we wrote these marriage pieces as missionaries in India. However, they have a much wider use. Part of the command to *"leave"* the father and mother means a new adult relationship must be established between the parents and their child, replacing the former parent–child relationship. In the Old and the New Testament, God commanded the new spouse to become the new number one relationship.

When children are little, parents are supposed to protect and care for them. However, when it is time for the children to *"leave,"* the parents need to grant liberty. Even birds with a brain the size of a pea, push a young bird out of the nest when it is time for them to fly on their own. God knows a little child that has turned into a man or a woman will always be a piece of his or her mother and father. But a husband or wife must be much closer than a piece of a parent - she is him and he is her. She is his own flesh, made from his own flesh. That is essentially why a man must *"leave"* and *"cleave."* This is also why adultery is so wrong.

If we as parents hang on to our kids after marriage, God is against us. What are the real reasons parents won't let go? Why don't we parents just openly tell the truth? It is usually because we have built our lives around our children. If we parents have a closer relationship with our children than with each other, shame on us. That situation must change. What a poor example we have set over the years to our children and to the world. God does not want us to ruin our children's relationship with their new spouse by trying to hang on to them! God says let the children leave to set up their own covenant home. Let us not try to be wiser than God in this.

Prayer: Lord, we praise You for Your thoughts on a proper relationship in marriage. Forgive us as parents for being selfish and stubborn in not letting go of our children. Help us to *"cleave"* to our own spouses to glorify You, to bless each other, and to love our children. May Your kingdom come and not ours. In Jesus' name we pray. Amen.

August 17

"Therefore shall a man leave his father and his mother, and shall cleave unto his wife: and they shall be one flesh." Genesis 2:24 KJV

"Leaving," a command to newlyweds

As a missionary, this is what I see. The parents are pulling on one arm of their child. The new spouse is pulling on the other. Both want possession. The son or daughter is being torn apart mentally and spiritually and it is affecting them physically. Whom should he or she love? God's command to *"leave"* the parents, makes so much sense. This does not mean the children are to forsake their parents. In 1 Timothy 5:4-8, the command is to care for them, especially if the parent is alone. However, the number one relationship for the new husband or wife must be their new spouse. The new couple must start their own covenant home as part of their new-shared identity in being joined together as one. The new *"cleaving"* of a husband and wife is necessary in two ways.

Physical *"cleaving"* is necessary. A married couple that refuses to be joined as one physically after marriage is against God and their spouse. *"The wife does not have authority over her own body, but the husband does. And likewise the husband does not have authority over his own body, but the wife does,"* 1 Corinthians 7:4 NKJV. God created the man and woman to be more intimate than the rest of creation. Animals were created only to procreate (make new life). God intended for man and woman to recreate (have fun) as well as reproduce little ones. There must be much private and public affection in the marriage. *"Let the husband render to his wife the affection due her, and likewise also the wife to the husband,"* 1 Corinthians 7:3 NKJV.

A mental or spiritual *"cleaving"* is necessary. A man and woman need to be *"one flesh"* and *"cleave"* mentally, emotionally, and spiritually. The Lord wants a marriage to be in agreement with Him. The way we think, speak, and act must bring, *"every thought into captivity to the obedience of Christ,"* 2 Corinthians 10:5b NKJV.

Prayer: Wise Lord, thank You for showing us sinners what a one-flesh relationship is. We want our marriages to be like the relationship of Christ and the Church, close and intimate. May our marriages be characterized by true love and respect! In Jesus' name we pray. Amen.

August 18

"A man will leave his father and mother and be united to his wife, and they will become one flesh." Genesis 2:24b

Newlyweds not *"leaving"* spiritually

It is common for a newly married person to "leave" home physically, but not spiritually. A wife has not left her father spiritually when she nags to her husband, saying, "My father helped my mother buy food and cook." "My father helped with the children." "My father helps my mother clean." My father this, my father that. This new wife is still living mentally/spiritually with her father!

The new husband has not left his mother when he says, "My mother buys good food and is a great cook!" "My mother washes clothes much better than you." "My mother always has her house clean." This husband is still living with his mother! God's command is clear. *"A man will leave his father and mother and be united to his wife, and they will become one flesh,"* Genesis 2:24b.

A man I recently counseled, did not "cleave" mentally or spiritually with his wife. He constantly pointed out her bad behavior and neglected any compliments for work she did well. The result was a very bitter wife in response to this very arrogant man. This man refused to see and work on his own personal problems. He was clearly the *"hypocrite"* in Matthew 7:3-5. He didn't leave his bad habits behind.

Any adult child who is bitter towards a parent cannot leave home spiritually either. Such a bitter spirit carries the parent to dinner, to work, and even to bed. When we continue to hate the one we are bitter towards, they continue to control us! Even if that person died, they would still control us, that is, until we finally learn to forgive them! God says about bitterness, *"Such 'wisdom' does not come down from heaven but is earthly, unspiritual, of the devil,"* James 3:15. When we harbor bitterness in our hearts, our happiness will dock elsewhere.

Prayer: All seeing Lord, You wisely test each of us to see if we will cling spiritually to our spouse. You even allow our spouse, parents and others to do wrong things to us, just to see if we will respond like Christ. Help us to model all of our relationships with grace, kindness and compassion. May we be trophies of Your grace and mercy. In Jesus' name we pray. Amen.

August 19

"Wives, submit to your husbands as to the Lord. For the husband is the head of the wife as Christ is the head of the church, His body, of which He is the Savior. Now as the church submits to Christ, so also wives should submit to their husbands in everything."
Ephesians 5:22-24

Why is headship necessary?

A body needs a head. Biblical headship in a marriage relationship protects the wife, just as Christ protects the Church as her head. Our text does not say the husband should be the head of the wife, but that *"the husband is the head of the wife."* A husband can be a poor head, but still he is the head. A husband is a "bad" head when he physically beats his wife instead of saving and protecting her. A husband who beats his wife, beats his own body! Second, a husband may appear to be a really "nice" guy, but the truth is, he runs from his headship responsibilities, leaving the wife to run the home. This is also abuse! What head ever leaves its own body? Sad to say this condition is common in the Christian camp.

A domineering wife thinks "headship" does not apply to her when she tries to play the role that God has given her husband. In 1 Peter 3:1, a Biblical wife must *"submit"* even to an unbiblical husband. Our text says she must submit *"in everything,"* just as the Church is to submit to Christ in everything. A wife or church who fails to *"submit"* is selfishly more interested in living for themselves.

A bold and domineering wife who fails to submit, complains to others that her man is not a good leader in the home. The truth is, she wants the position. In Colossians 3:18 it says, *"wives submit."* In verse 19 it says *"husbands love."* In verse 20 it says, *"children obey."* If the wife submits and the husband loves, both obedience and love is taught in the home. Why should the kids be loving and obedient if they are not taught by example to do so?

Prayer: O Lord, forgive us for not following Your loving commands. As wives, we have too often neglected our responsibility to encourage and respect our husbands. Lord, convict us by Your Spirit so we can have good marriages. In Jesus' name we pray. Amen.

August 20

"Husbands, love your wives, just as Christ loved the church and gave Himself up for her to make her holy, cleansing her by the washing with water through the Word, and to present her to Himself as a radiant church, without stain or wrinkle or any other blemish, but holy and blameless." Ephesians 5:25-27

A husband must love like Christ

"Christ loved the church" by serving it, cleansing it, protecting it, and grooming it to perfection. Some husbands find their wives lovely, and then provoke them to be ugly, and then blame the wife for her ugliness. Issues like anger, bitterness, fear, worry and depression are good examples of how a wife's beauty is not right. And yes, it is the husband who is greatly responsible, just as our head is responsible to protect the body from these danger. Christ, on the other hand, finds us as ugly sinners, and with a great action makes us sinners beautiful and rejoices in our beauty! Christ lives for His Church. Many husbands selfishly live for themselves.

Our text shows that Christ, as the head of the Church, washed us by placing the Word of God in our hearts. This means, a husband's primary responsibility is to *"wash with water through the Word,"* or, read the Bible in the home. How many of us are doing this regularly? It is the Word of God that changes all hearts.

Christ as Head, never ran away from His responsibility to save and serve the Church (sinners). Christ humbled Himself before God and us. Jesus came, He suffered, He died, and He secured the salvation of the Church. The husband has been given his headship position to protect the body and soul of his wife and family. God's law, His holy standards must guide our homes, but His grace must govern it. We need to follow His perfect example.

Prayer: Loving Lord, as husbands, we have often failed to lead our homes Your way. When we look at our own bodies, we see that our eyes, nose, ears, and tongue are all part of our head for a good reason, to protect and care for our body. Yet we have not cared for the wife and family as a good head should. Lord, help us to be more loving and caring. In Jesus' name we pray. Amen.

August 21

"Wives, in the same way be submissive to your husbands so that, if any of them do not believe the Word, they may be won over without words by the behavior of their wives." 1 Peter 3:1

The importance of submission

"Submission" applies to both men and women. Our text directs a wife how to live with a problem husband. The same words *"in the same way,"* in verse 7, shows us that these words are also for husbands. The *"Finally, all of you"* in verse 8, makes submission universal for all people. There are at least three points of instruction here.

Harsh and critical speech and actions drive husbands, wives and all others apart! God knows when others are cruel to us. He sees the abandonment of a husband, the drunkenness, and the beatings. If a wife reacts to all this with *"demonic"* bitterness (James 3:15), is she any better? A bitter wife who points an accusing finger at a sinning husband and demands that he change, without changing her own life, is far from being Biblically submissive.

Harsh and critical provokes others to flee their God-given responsibilities. *"Better to live on a corner of the roof than share a house with a quarrelsome wife,"* Proverbs 21:9. This is not just a "wife" problem. The point is a quarrelsome person drives or "provokes" others to flee their presence. All people need love and respect, even children. If someone is not strong spiritually, they may look in the wrong crowd to get respect. A submissive spirit is a willingness to give others the needed loving respect.

Win over family and friends who have issues, "without words." The world's way to respond to a sinner is to shout and scream at them in fearful anger or have a case of "lock-jaw bitterness." All anger and bitterness needs to go away as much as a drug habit does. *"If any of them do not believe the Word, they may be won over without words."* God gives us the wisdom and strength to be obedient, submissive, and respectful.

Prayer: Loving Lord, we see that when we provoke or tempt others to sin is some way, we are wrong. Forgive us for expecting others to change but to not do so ourselves. Strengthen us. In Christ's name we pray. Amen.

August 22

"Wives, in the same way be submissive to your husbands."
1 Peter 3:1a

"In the same way"

This text is so important that we need to examine it further. **"In the same way,"** is a universal principle. We often hear the excuse, "I cannot be submissive to this or that person." The words, *"in the same way,"* rule out any excuse to not be submissive. In 1 Peter 2, we have the example of a servant, then of Christ, then of a wife. Then, since 1 Peter 3:7 starts with the words, *"in the same way,"* the argument continues for husbands. A basic and so important relationship principle is this:

"Servants, be submissive to your masters with all fear, not only to the good and gentle, but also to the harsh. For this is commendable, if because of conscience toward God one endures grief, suffering wrongfully. For what credit is it if, when you are beaten for your faults, you take it patiently? But when you do good and suffer, if you take it patiently, this is commendable before God," 1 Peter 2:18-20 NKJV.

A *"submissive"* spirit is *"patient,"* and *"is commendable to God."* *"Submissive"* is not being a doormat, but willing to serve others. *"Serve"* is part of the word "servant." A servant is required to always be obedient, whether they feel like it or not. Think of how real customer service is lacking in businesses, churches, and homes. The reason is, we want to be kings or queens, not servants! We may not feel like serving in our daily work, but it is our Christian duty. Why? *"For to this you were called, because Christ also suffered for us, leaving us an example, that you should follow His steps: 'Who committed no sin, nor was deceit found in His mouth,' who, when He was reviled, did not revile in return; when He suffered, He did not threaten, but committed Himself to Him who judges righteously,"* 1 Peter 2:21-22 NKJV.

Prayer: O Lord who changes hearts, we can see that it's Your job to change people. It is our job to serve them. Forgive us for trying to do Your job. No wonder we are so frustrated. We want to be kings and queens instead of servants. Forgive us. In our daily living, may we live *"in the same way"* as Christ did. In Jesus' name we pray. Amen.

August 23

"Husbands, in the same way be considerate as you live with your wives, and treat them with respect as the weaker partner and as heirs with you of the gracious gift of life, so that nothing will hinder your prayers."
1 Peter 3:7

Are you a *"considerate"* husband?

Again, we see the words, *"in the same way." These words* show that the husband is to be like the servant, like Jesus, and like the wife, as discussed in 1 Peter 2:18 through 3:6.

"Be considerate as you live with your wives." A common complaint we hear from wives is: *"My husband doesn't listen to me."* That is not being very *"considerate."* To listen, the TV needs to be turned off and the phone set aside. Christ is not preoccupied with other things while we are coming to Him in our prayers. He delights to hear our prayers, and our problems too! Do we as husbands delight to hear our wife's problems and petitions? Jesus said, *"Come to Me, all you who are weary and burdened, and I will give you rest,"* Matthew 11:28. Are we willing to give our wife rest, or are we more willing to give her a headache? Being *"considerate"* of each other is foundational to having a God honoring marriage.

"Treat them with respect as the weaker partner." Some versions say treat her as a *"precious vase."* A 2000-year-old vase from China is a *"weaker vessel,"* fragile, a *"precious vase."* We would handle a very precious vase with respect and honor, even place it on a shelf for all to see and admire. A bride is designed by God with the need for her husband to respect and admire her. After marriage, a wife still needs to be respected and admired! A proud and self-centered husband cannot elevate his wife to a position of honor and respect until he first lowers himself.

Prayer: Most Holy Lord, how we need Your wisdom in our troubled world. As husbands, we must admit that we have been too selfish and not very *"considerate."* Forgive us and continue to guide us into Your kind of living patterns. May Your kingdom be built instead of our selfish ones. In Christ's name we pray. Amen.

August 24

"Heirs with you of the gracious gift of life." 1 Peter 3:7b

When husbands are sledge hammers

Our text reminds the husband that his precious wife is going through the same problems and trials that he is. What hurts you, hurts her. She is your own body, and you need to protect her.

It is the world that tells a man to assert himself, not God. The world says to threaten her to keep her in line. God says that the gentle approach works best. And if a "Christian" husband is unwilling to be gracious, he has a serious spiritual problem. *"Pride only breeds quarrels, but wisdom is found in those who take advice,"* Proverbs 13:10. A proud husband could not show compassion to an angel of a wife. A humble husband can honor, love, and respect any wife.

A non-caring husband is like a ten-pound sledge hammer. What happens when a hammer husband gets into a disagreement with a *"precious vase"* wife? Hammer smashes vase and leaves home to tell his friends how he put his wife in her place. Meanwhile, the broken wife is crying to God, severely depressed. Such a wife is without honor, not very beautiful, and the husband is greatly responsible for her miserable condition. God wants husbands to know that wives come packaged with a warning, "Caution, easily broken if not handled with care."

A husband is told to love and respect his wife, *"so that nothing will hinder your prayers,"* 1 Peter 3:7b. If any man treats his wife like dirt and keeps sin locked up in his heart, God will not hear his prayers! With this in mind, can you see why God requires a man to be a servant in the home, before he is qualified to serve or lead in the church? Hindered prayers by those in church leadership does not advance the kingdom of God. If a husband is a sledge hammer in the home, he is also one in the church.

Prayer: All-seeing Lord, you see everything. You know us inside and out. You tell us that You are *"acting as the witness between you and the wife of your youth, because you have broken faith with her, though she is your partner, the wife of your marriage covenant."* Forgive us for not keeping covenant with You and with our wives. In Jesus' name we pray. Amen.

August 25

"The wife must respect her husband." Ephesians 5:33b

"Respect," a one-word summary

The chapter in the Bible that says the most about marriage, ends with, *"the wife must respect her husband."* The dictionary defines respect as *"an attitude of admiration or esteem."* The Bible shows that *"respect,"* is basically a loving attitude that works out by how we act. Biblical *"respect"* involves feelings, but also results in godly actions in how a wife treats her husband.

First, a wife who gossips about her husband does not *"respect"* him. *"A gossip separates close friends,"* Proverbs 16:28b. A wife is disrespectful to her husband when she tells of his mistakes to those who cannot help and have no reason to know. When we use complaining words about others, we try to gain respect for ourself, not seriously interested in giving it to others. Such selfishness is evil. Gossip by anyone is traveling on the world's path, not God's narrow path.

Second, gentleness shows respect. *"If someone is caught in a sin, you who are spiritual should restore him gently. But watch yourself, or you may also be tempted. Carry each other's burdens, and in this way you will fulfill the law of Christ,"* Galatians 6:1-2. Rough and tough words do not show *"respect."* God has so designed husbands, even unbelieving husbands in 1 Peter 3:1, to be respected, and the wife must be the number one source of that *"respect."* One troubled wife said she couldn't respect her husband. The real reason was not can't but won't. She won't lower herself to lift up her husband.

Third, a wife who moans and groans about her husband's lack of leadership is partially responsible for it. Encouraged to lead in even the smallest areas of life, the husband may lead in other areas of life also. Amazingly, when God and the husband are honored, a wife's bitterness, fears, worries and times of depression will be history.

Prayer: O Lord, we thank You for keeping it simple. Too often we do not want to hear that we need to change anything. We expect others to change and to show respect before we are willing to do so. Help us to follow Your standard of obedience. In Jesus' blessed name we pray. Amen.

August 26

"For, as I have often told you before and now say again even with tears, many live as enemies of the Cross of Christ. Their destiny is destruction, their god is their stomach, and their glory is in their shame. Their mind is on earthly things." Philippians 3:18-19

The sin of gluttony

It is a spiritual and physical problem when we are overweight. We know it is not good for our health to eat too much, but still we do it. Perhaps, we think so little about how much it offends God. Once a rather wide pastor walked out of church and saw a couple of men smoking. The big man pointed out to the smokers that they were sinning! The smokers said, "Your big belly is also a sin." Both were right. It is self-righteous to see another person's sin and not be concerned about our own.

Overeating is a spiritual problem as much as it is a physical one. To overcome any eating problem, we first need to understand that it is not a disorder. It really is a sin. That is good news actually! Sin can be confessed, forgiven and forsaken, if the heart changes. Gluttony is even idolatry. Our text says, *"Their god is their stomach."* Knowing that overeating is another "god," is the best diet pill in the world! Unless we are convicted that overeating is wrong, we will not quickly change what or how much we eat.

Those with high stress levels often stuff themselves with food instead of working on their relationships and responsibilities. The glutton eats to feel good; just like the drunkard, the smoker, and the drug addict does. Are these not all "gods," when satisfying these desires consumes us? Finding our comfort in food more than in God is the idolatry. Solomon said, *"When you sit to dine with a ruler, note well what is before you, and put a knife to your throat if you are given to gluttony. Do not crave his delicacies, for that food is deceptive,"* Proverbs 23:1-3.

Prayer: Holy and loving Lord, Your Word cuts us! We have condemned sin in others, while we in turn eat wrong. Forgive us! May we listen to Your advice in Romans 12:1, *"I urge you, brothers, in view of God's mercy, to offer your bodies as living sacrifices, holy and pleasing to God – this is your spiritual act of worship."* Thank You for Your Godly counsel. In Jesus' name we pray. Amen.

August 27

"Everything that lives and moves will be food for you. Just as I gave you the green plants, I now give you everything." Genesis 9:3

Eat meat or be vegetarian?

What are we allowed to eat? In the beginning, man and animals were both completely vegetarian. God told man what to eat.

"God said, 'I give you every seed-bearing plant on the face of the whole earth and every tree that has fruit with seed on it. They will be yours for food. And to all the beasts of the earth and all the birds of the air and all the creatures that move on the ground - everything that has the breath of life in it — I give every green plant for food.' And it was so," Genesis 1:29-30.

To eat meat right after creation was impossible. There was no death of any kind yet, none. Death came only after Adam and Eve sinned according to Romans 5:12. If there were somehow, death after death before sin, then evolution could be true, but it is not.

It was after the flood that God now changed the rules for eating: *"Everything that lives and moves will be food for you. Just as I gave you the green plants, I now give you everything,"* Genesis 9:3. God gave man dominion over the animals and now that includes eating them. In the 14th chapter of Romans, Paul speaks very plainly about the rules for eating. *"The man who eats everything must not look down on him who does not, and the man who does not eat everything must not condemn the man who does, for God has accepted him,"* Romans 14:3. Paul reasons in verse 6, *"He who eats meat, eats to the Lord, for he gives thanks to God; and he who abstains, does so to the Lord and gives thanks to God."* Paul said, *"As one who is in the Lord Jesus, I am fully convinced that no food is unclean in itself. But if anyone regards something as unclean, then for him it is unclean,"* Romans 14:14. Let us not argue about these things, but serve God together.

Prayer: Dear Lord our provider, You give us all things, but in moderation. May we not look down on those who don't eat meat, nor condemn those who do. Forgive us, Lord, when we have done this. In Jesus' name we pray. Amen.

August 28

"A righteous man cares for the needs of his animal, but the kindest acts of the wicked are cruel." Proverbs 12:10

Are you "kind" to animals?

You may think this is a silly question in a devotional! After all, what does caring for animals have to do with living a holy life? Our text is pointed. *"A righteous man cares for the needs of his animal."* The question that begs us is: What's in a righteous man that is lacking in one who is not? The answer is one word of our text — "kindness."

Are we kind to animals? This is really a test of our hearts, for that is where kindness comes from. If God has changed the heart of a person, then he or she will be kind to animals as well as to man. *"The kindest acts of the wicked are cruel."* The reason is, they do not have the love of God in their hearts. Spurgeon wisely said, "I give you nothing for that man's religion that his animal is not the better because of it."

If we are cruel to animals, it is because we have a cruel heart! When we have a "bad day" at work, we keep the frustrations in check, there! In the workplace, we know it is not "professional" to kick people. But when we get home, we may take out our frustrations on the dog. If we say, "My animal made me mad," we're lying. Anger comes from our heart, not from an animal, not from another person! The "cause" of our anger is inside of us, in our heart!

God plainly said to us, *"Get rid of all bitterness, rage and anger, brawling and slander, along with every form of malice,"* Ephesians 4:31. This means towards animals, too! It is God's hope that even animals benefit from the grace He puts in our hearts. The same "kindness" that is able to train an animal, is the same "kindness" that is required to train a child. Carry this further. Those who have the kindness to train a child, have the kindness to train a church member. Truth is, those who lack kindness still need to be trained.

Prayer: O Holy Lord, sometimes Your Word hits us right between the eyes. It is our hope and prayer that every person and animal benefits from our increasing righteousness! Help us, Lord, to have the mind of Christ who was so meek and mild. In Jesus' name we pray. Amen.

August 29

*"You shall not misuse the name of the LORD your God, for the LORD
will not hold anyone guiltless who misuses His name."*
Deuteronomy 5:11

What is swearing?

Our text is the fourth commandment that God gave to Moses and
the church of all ages. The important question is how do we swear or
"misuse the name of the LORD"? Our great God who made us, totally
sustains us, redeems us, sanctifies us, and glorifies us. He deserves our
honor and respect! A grave warning is this: *"The LORD will not hold
anyone guiltless who misuses His name,"* Deuteronomy 5:11b.

Many Christians think that they do not swear because they do not
say "God damn it" or many of the other really nasty swear words
that non-Christians easily use. However, there are many words today
that are either abbreviations or variations of words we would not use.
"Gosh" and "golly" are words that are used in the place of saying
the word God. "Gee" is a form of Jesus. "Dang" is another word for
Damn. We would not say, "damn you," but we easily say, "dang you."
It is the same thing.

Jesus said, *"Do not swear at all: either by Heaven, for it is God's
throne; or by the earth, for it is His footstool...Simply let your 'Yes' be
'Yes' and your 'No,' 'No;' anything beyond this comes from the evil one,"*
Matthew 5:34-37. Swearing is music to the devil's ears! Don't play his
song. We do not want to glorify Satan in any way. Respect God, and
also, those who are created in the image of God.

You may think that it is not a big deal as long as we do not say
the "seriously wrong words." But our Lord cautions us, *"I tell you that
men will have to give account on the Day of Judgment for every careless
word they have spoken. For by your words you will be acquitted, and by
your words you will be condemned,"* Matthew 12:36-37.

Our words show the condition of our hearts. Jesus gives us a good
reason to clean up our mouth and to honor God and others with our
words. In eternity, we will never be sorry!

Prayer: Dear Lord, *"May the words of my mouth and the meditation of
my heart be pleasing in Your sight, O Lord, my Rock and my Redeemer,"*
Psalm 19:14. In our Redeemer's name we pray. Amen.

August 30

"Then the LORD said to Cain, 'Why are you angry? Why is your face downcast? If you do what is right, will you not be accepted? But if you do not do what is right, sin is crouching at your door; it desires to have you, but you must master it.'" Genesis 4:6-7

How jealousy destroys us

Some of the girls are very jealous of Karen, who is a very good looking girl. God gave her a sharp mind and cute body. Even though her parents do their best not to show partiality, out in public she gets more attention. What is the other girl's jealousy all about? Is it not mostly bitterness against God for not giving them, in their opinion, more? They think that they deserve better looks, a lighter or darker skin color, a better shaped body, a sharper brain and more. Truth is, if all of these jealous girls would grow in grace, they too would be more beautiful. Jealousy is ugly. A soft, gentle heart is beautiful.

Cain was jealous of his brother Abel. *"Then the LORD said to Cain, "Why are you angry? Why is your face downcast? If you do what is right, will you not be accepted? But if you do not do what is right, sin is crouching at your door, it desires to have you, but you must master it,"* Genesis 4:6-7. Cain's jealousy included a fear factor. Cain feared that he would not be blessed, tempting him to become angry. *"God has not given us a spirit of fear, but of power and of love and of a sound mind,"* 2 Timothy 1:7. Cain was a real mess!

Do you understand the mind of God here? If we change our hearts, we will be more "accepted" by God and by others. Cain did not listen to God, and he became a social wanderer. Are some of us "social wanderers," because we are too much like the jealous Cain?

It is our responsibility to change our jealous attitude. We were not put here on earth to be popular, but to worship God and to be a blessing to others. Jealousy does neither! We need to pray for soft hearts, knowing that a smiling heart becomes a smiling face. The girls and boys that smile, and are gentle and sweet, are the most attractive.

Prayer: Wise and loving Lord, we are thankful that You give each of us different looks and abilities. Lord, help us to grow in contentment, for we know that is great gain. Use us, Lord, to be a blessing to You and others. In Christ's name we pray. Amen.

August 31

"And that is what some of you <u>were</u>. But you were washed, you were sanctified, you were justified in the name of the Lord Jesus Christ and by the Spirit of our God." 1 Corinthians 6:11

People with addictions can change!

God shows us that addicts can change. The use of the word *"were"* is past tense, and is filled with so much hope. In verses 9-10, there were the sexually immoral, thieves, and drunkards. Some of these people changed because God's Spirit convicted them that they had a sin problem! When people see their "behavioral issues" as diseases or disorders, there is no hope, no confession, no power to change! All behavior changes when a heart changes. Then the pattern of living changes. This message of hope is so needed today!

The ability to change comes through a person, not a program. Our freedom from "addictions" comes through God, not some man-made idea or principle. The Great Reformation had the right idea. Their cry was "sola scriptura," Latin for "Scripture alone." Today, many people do not change because they are eclectic - they add other thoughts (belief systems) to the knowledge of God, resulting in, complicated confusion.

"His divine power has given us everything we need for life and god-liness through our knowledge of Him," 2 Peter 1:3a. Nothing more is needed. How we think, speak, or act is a spiritual problem that needs a spiritual solution! The 12 steps of Alcoholics Anonymous may be the best human program for addictions, but still, it has limitations. Imagine starting out a worship service saying, "I'm an alcoholic and I'll always be an alcoholic"? What hope is there in that? A. A. talks about coping in life. The cope of A. A. cannot match the hope of the Bible. Paul was clear in saying, *"that is what some of you were."* Praise God who gives a new heart, a new hope and a new power to change!

Prayer: Dear loving Lord, we thank You for doing what the world can never do, change a human heart. It is a miracle really! We are all born slaves to sin and Your mercy alone changes us to become slaves of righteousness. Forgive us for looking in all the wrong places for deliverance from evil. In Jesus' name we pray. Amen.

SEPTEMBER

"There is no fear in love.
But perfect love drives out fear,
because fear has to do with punishment.
The one who fears is not made perfect in love."
1 John 4:18

September 1

"Jonah ran away from the LORD." Jonah 1:3

Are we running away?

In the orphanage today, we were having devotions with the children. We were in the process of discussing being *"Kind and compassionate"* from Ephesians 4:32a. I asked an orphan boy, "Would you be willing to someday bring tea to your wife as an act of kindness?" He said: "No." The house mother asked, "What would you do if your wife beats you for not bringing her a tea?" He said, "I would run away." We all had a good laugh. But this is a common problem! How many of us today are running away from our God-given relationships and responsibilities, just like Jonah in our text?

Have you ever considered why "running away" is so wrong? Look at a common family problem. A man has a difficult situation at home and he first fights, then runs to grab a bottle of alcohol. A woman in the same house also fights, then flees to her pillow and cries. The right answer is not fight or flight, but to be faithful and responsible. Most of our hurts come through our relationships, but then, so does our healing!

"Running away" from relationships and responsibilities is not something we suddenly learn as adults. We learn this young and then practice it until we are in serious trouble. A 4th grade girl was staring into space as we were teaching this very lesson. She just, "ran away from the LORD." I know this is serious because I did this many years ago. When the teacher asked me to read something, I was very busy daydreaming! I had no idea where the class was at in the book. Truth is, I didn't care. Was my problem ADD, attention deficit disorder? No, my daydreaming was laziness and rebellion. It was sinful. I was in love with what I wanted to do, not what the teacher or God wanted me to do. I was practicing to be a Jonah. Did I need some medicine to be able to concentrate better? No, I needed a kick in the pants. A right focus is the need of every minute, which is the need of the hour. May we all run to God, not away from Him.

Prayer: Loving Lord, forgive us for our rebellion in running away from Your will in our relationships and responsibilities. Lord, if necessary, send a big fish to get our attention. In Christ's name we pray. Amen.

September 2

"Do everything without complaining or arguing, so that you may become blameless and pure, children of God without fault in a crooked and depraved generation, in which you shine like stars in the universe." Philippians 2:14-15

Beware of self-pity!

What is "*complaining and arguing*"? It is quite simply self-pity, a "Poor me, I have it so bad" attitude. Self-pity causes more problems for us spiritually, mentally and physically than most any other issue. Self-pity is perhaps the juiciest worm Satan uses on his fishhook to keep us in the sea of sin and misery. Self-pity is the fire that lights the fuse of anger and bitterness. Self-pity pushes us to do drugs and alcohol to excess. Self-pity is behind the eating disorders (is it really a disorder or sin?) Self-pity fuels lust and adultery. Self-pity brings on fear, worry and depression. In our self-pity, we are hopelessly starved for respect, yet we respect neither God nor man.

Self-pity is a lack of contentment or peace. If we really want peace, we need to get the order of our love right! "*Great peace have they who love God's law and nothing can make them stumble,*" Psalm 119:165. God's law tells us to love God first, and others second. Self-pity puts self-first, and then we wonder why we are struggling. We think we have some complicated problem when all we need is to just get the order of our love right.

Filled with self-pity, we are in a self-imposed prison, in solitary confinement. In our self-pity we say, "What so and so did to me is killing me." God has this to say: "Get over it." "Replace it." "Forgive them." Get on with life! This is the mind of God in our text. "*Become blameless and pure, children of God without fault in a crooked and depraved generation.*" People will hurt and cheat us! May we respond in a "*blameless*" way. That is, "*Do everything without complaining or arguing,*" just like Jesus did.

Prayer: Most wise and loving Lord, forgive our selfish attitudes. Help us to manage those down periods in life when we are most tempted to fall into self-pity. Help us to quickly get our eyes off from self, and back on You and on others. In Jesus' name we pray. Amen.

September 3

"There is no fear in love. But perfect love drives out fear, because fear has to do with punishment. The one who fears is not made perfect in love." 1 John 4:18

The perfect love that *"drives out fear"*

Perfect love is defined by Jesus in Matthew 22:37-40 as loving God first, then others second. That puts self-last. Loving God is in the first four commandments. Loving others is the instruction in the next six. Our trials in life will test us to see who will be first, second, or third. Two examples show us how *"perfect love"* drives out fear.

Margaret was 90 years old and was in a bad accident. She lay in the hospital, paralyzed. Her mind is sharp! She clearly understands that she will never walk again. Her response is a very real test to see if she will now put God first. At the same time, Satan will tempt her to give in to self-pity. She fearfully starts to think, "What is going to happen to me?" "I will never hold the grandchildren again." "I will never leave this bed." "I don't deserve this." "What's going to happen to me?" Filled with self-pity, she panics. Our text says, *"fear has to do with punishment,"* which she is fully experiencing. It is common for us to go into a self-pity thought process, but so wrong when we stay there! She did stay there and was most miserable because of it.

Margaret's twin sister Monica was in the very same accident. She was also paralyzed. Her response was, "Dear God, You have been my God for 90 years." "You have given me Christian parents and a good life." "I praise Your Most Holy Name." For three hours she prayed. She lifted up the Name of the Lord in thanksgiving and praise. She prayed for the well-being of her children, grandchildren, great grandchildren, neighbors, church family, and friends. Day after day she kept her eyes on God and others. She had a great faith, a great hope, and a great attitude. Monica knew how *"Perfect love drives out fear."*

Prayer: Lord, we are often paralyzed from the neck up, by how we respond to situations in life. We know perfect love is loving You first and others second. But, we have a problem. We are selfish. Lord, help us to trust You and keep our eyes on You in true faith. In Christ's name we pray. Amen.

September 4

"'I was afraid and went out and hid your talent in the ground. See, here is what belongs to You.' His master replied, 'You wicked, lazy servant!'" Matthew 25:25-26a

Fear doesn't build relationships

Fear and worry problems cripple our relationships. Why? Our text, which is part of the parable of the talents, shows us the ugliness of fear. Three servants were given talents (a sum of money). They were given time (our lives). Then these men had to stand before Jesus in The Judgment, to give an account of how they lived. The first man was faithful and gained *"five more talents."* Jesus said to him, *"Well done, good and faithful servant,"* Matthew 25:21a. The second servant was faithful! He *"gained two more"* talents. Jesus said, *"Well done, good and faithful servant."* The third servant said to Jesus, *"I was afraid and went out and hid your talent in the ground,"* 25:25a. Jesus' responded, *"You wicked, lazy servant,"* 25:26a. He then sent this man to Hell saying, *"Throw that worthless servant outside, into the darkness, where there will be weeping and gnashing of teeth,"* 25:30. Fear is concerned with self-first, not God, not others.

Why is fear *"wicked"* and *"lazy"*? When we are too focused on the past and on what will happen in the future, we are doing NOTHING in the present. A fearful person is selfishly preoccupied with what is happening to them. That is why *"fear has to do with punishment,"* or *"torment"* in 1 John 4:18.

Biblical love is concerned about God and others. Godly living *"drives out fear."* *"Fear"* is quite the opposite of faith because it is not trusting in God. A trusting faith can say, *"We know that in all things God works for the good of those who love Him, who have been called according to His purpose,"* Romans 8:28. Faith knows that even though we cannot understand some things, somehow God will work it out for our good. Our responsibility is to remain faithful every day, especially when we do not see our way.

Prayer: Lord, thank You for telling us the plain truth. We need to hear these words, before The Judgment. We praise You for giving us the time and the ability to change. In Christ's name we pray. Amen.

September 5

"Who of you by worrying can add a single hour to his life? And why do you worry about clothes? See how the lilies of the field grow. They do not labor or spin. Yet I tell you that not even Solomon in all his splendor was dressed like one of these. If that is how God clothes the grass of the field, which is here today and tomorrow is thrown into the fire, will He not much more clothe you, O you of little faith."
Matthew 6:27-30

Why is our *"worry"* so wrong?

Worry is extremely self-centered as our minds spin around and around thinking about how we will solve a particular problem. Today's worry will never solve tomorrow's problems. Worry steals today's joy. Fear and worry both block out our trust in God, as we try to solve things we cannot control. The message of our text is that worry is not profitable.

When I first read how worry was *"little faith,"* I was shocked! I thought I had big faith. Worry is *"little faith,"* because it fails to trust in God's ability to care for us, even with all of His divine attributes.

You may argue, "But I have such great trials." "It's only natural for me to fear and worry." Worry is natural in that we are naturally sinners, born that way. If we read James 1:2-4, 1 Peter 1:6-7 and 1 Peter 4:12-19, we see that our trials are huge tests from God, to build our faith. God wants to see if we will worry or if we will put our eyes on Him and trust Him. Worry fails a serious test in life, and that's why it is called *"little faith."*

There will be diseases, family problems, a lack of money, difficult job situations, persecution and even death. We will all experience rejection. We will be too fat, too thin, too white, too black, not have the right clothes, car, motorbike, looks, or the grades that we want. These things are not causes of our worries! They are temptations to worry! Knowing the difference is a main spiritual issue! May God help us to see all of life from His point of view and to be thankful.

Prayer: O Lord, how we need Your truthful evaluations of our faith. We have worried! We have not looked to You to be our help and strength. Forgive us and help our *"little faith"* to grow into a mature faith. In Christ's name we pray. Amen.

September 6

"O LORD, do not rebuke me in Your wrath, nor chasten me in Your hot displeasure! For Your arrows pierce me deeply, and Your hand presses me down." Psalm 38:1-2 NKJV

David's depression

There is a main question we wonder about. "Is depression sin?" In Psalm 38, David wisely shows us the connection of his sinful actions, to his depressed reaction. He says, *"There is no health in my bones,"* (vs. 3c). Here David speaks about the pain and feelings of depression which are not sinful in any way. However, David's next statement, *"because of my sin"* shows a real connection. David committed adultery and murder and then failed to confess them. The hand of God was now upon him. David admits, *"My guilt has overwhelmed me"* in verse 4a. Guilt is a feeling, not the sin itself, but comes from sin. Excessive guilt causes depression. Look closely at the first part of verse 5, *"My wounds fester and are loathsome."* These wounds are not sinful, but then David finishes the verse, *"because of my sinful folly"* (vs. 5b).

Also, in Psalm 32, David admits his sinful actions led to his feelings of depression. *"When I kept silent, (no confession) my bones wasted away through my groaning all the day long. For day and night Your hand was heavy upon me; my strength was sapped as in the heat of summer,"* Psalm 32:3-4. David's silence about his sin led to his depression. David tells us confession and repentance was his cure. It was his road to recovery. *"Then I acknowledged my sin to You, and did not cover up my iniquity. I said, 'I will confess my transgressions to the LORD' and You forgave the guilt of my sin,"* Psalm 32:5.

Prayer: Dear Lord, we thank You for teaching us about the depression David is going through. We can plainly see David's failure to confess his sin. Do we do the same? You tell us, *"If we claim to be without sin, we deceive ourselves and the truth is not in us. If we confess our sins, He is faithful and just and will forgive us our sins and purify us from all unrighteousness. If we claim we have not sinned, we make Him out to be a liar and His Word has no place in our lives,"* 1 John 1:8-10. Search our hearts Lord. Convict us of our sin, so that You might be worshiped and we might be healed and blessed. In Christ's name we pray. Amen.

September 7

"When I kept silent, my bones wasted away through my groaning all the day long. For day and night Your hand was heavy upon me; my strength was sapped as in the heat of summer." Psalm 32:3-4

How does God see depression?

Depression can best be defined as the word suggests, pressed down with feelings of dejection, guilt, and hopelessness. Like David we are not always faithful in our relationships and responsibilities and suffer for it. The Bible uses various words to describe depression: like *"face downcast"* in Genesis 4:6, *"a burden too heavy to bear"* in Psalm 38:4, *"weary with sorrow"* in Psalm 119:28, a *"crushed spirit"* in Proverbs 17:22, 18:14 and *"grow weary and lose heart"* in Hebrews 12:3.

College students, business workers, housewives, even people in ministry are often depressed. Why? The Bible is ready to teach us, if we are willing to listen! One problem we have is that psychology focuses too much on fixing the feelings of depression. God counsels us more concerning our thoughts, words, and actions that lead up to depressed feelings. According to God, every thought, word, or action is a "religious" issue. We must not be silent about what God has written for our edification.

It is so sad that many people in the church today get a little angry with the suggestion that depression is linked to personal sin. Do we really think we are more spiritually mature than Peter, Elijah, and David, who were depressed because of their sin? Do we not believe James 5:17 that says, *"Elijah was a man just like us"*?

The events in the Bible were *"written to teach us, so that through endurance and the encouragement of the Scriptures we might have hope,"* Romans 15:4b. Depressed people lack hope. God's Biblical examples are for our benefit! God speaks to us through them. Some Bible characters listened to God and He healed them! They got over their depression and so can we. The question is: "Will we handle life's problems God's way or man's way?"

Prayer: Lord, like David, we keep silent about certain sinful habits. In love, You "press us down," so we will change. Lord, we seek Your forgiveness, righteousness and healing through the blood of Christ. In His name we pray. Amen.

September 8

"I will instruct you and teach you in the way you should go; I will counsel you and watch over you. Do not be like the horse or mule, which have no understanding but must be controlled by bit and bridle."
Psalm 32:8-9

A recipe for depression

In His great love for us, God made David write using clear words, so that we would see depression as He does. David, tenderly urges us not to be stubborn (like he was) concerning these things. God gave David some pain to get him to come to his "spiritual senses" concerning the error of his ways. God, totally in love, still uses pain to train our brain, to move us closer to Him.

The recipe for a depression cake is simple. Begin with four cups of unrealistic expectations that are doomed to fail sooner or later. Add in a difficult situation that threatens our lofty expectations. Mix in half a cup of fear and marinate for a day or two. Throw in a liberal amount of anger and bring to a long boil. Add a dash or two of ugly bitterness. Do not add the spice of forgiveness or our depression cake will not rise. Garnish liberally with self-pity and an absolute refusal to confess anything. Make sure to neglect our daily responsibilities, and we have an nasty depression cake. This is accurate in describing how most depression commonly develops.

An unrealistic expectation can be thinking we will have perfect health, a perfect spouse, perfect children, a perfect church, and a perfect job. Then, a difficult situation comes along to test our unrealistic expectations. And if we are a bit of a "control freak," our reaction is a fear that part of our life will collapse. In response, we are now angry. Self-pity soon sets in when our expectations are not met. We complain to others about how someone has treated us (it's called the martyr syndrome). If the pattern continues, depression is sure to come along, all because we are following the recipe.

Prayer: Lord, forgive us. We have had many unrealistic expectations in our daily work, in our responsibilities, and in our relationships. Lord help us to see that people will treat us poorly, even cheat us. Help us to have a response of grace so that we might honor You and bless others by how we live. In Christ's blessed name we pray. Amen.

September 9

"So Cain was very angry, and his face was downcast. Then the LORD said to Cain, 'Why are you angry? Why is your face downcast? If you do what is right, will you not be accepted? But if you do not do what is right, sin is crouching at your door; it desires to have you, but you must master it." Genesis 4:5b-7

Why was Cain depressed?

Already people in the first family were depressed. This is partly God's design to teach us. So God counsels the depressed Cain, whose heart was not right with God. In response to a hard heart, *"Cain was very angry."* As a result of his sinful anger, *"his face was downcast,"* (the look of depression). See these three failing steps of Cain. The condition of (1) Cain's heart, then led to what (2) he did, which then led to how (3) he felt. The Lord not only questioned Cain's sinful anger, but also Cain's feelings. God asked him, *"Why is your face downcast?"*

Cain was not doing very well in life. He was selfish in following the sinful desires in his heart. As a result, he was ashamed and guilty. His negative attitude prevented him from having a close fellowship with God, and with his brother also. Cain did not come to worship God by repenting and confessing his sin. If he had, God would have forgiven him and then accepted his offering. Cain remained guilty, with his head hanging down. He was depressed.

Guilt from Cain's failure to confess his sin, did to him what it did to King David, and also does to us. Depression really is a spiritual issue. God pointed out to Cain that the sinful act of anger was a deeper problem to deal with first, to fix the lesser problem of how he felt. How we need to learn this lesson! So once again, we point out this all-important theology: The condition of our heart, leads to what we do, which in turn leads to how we feel.

Prayer: Loving Lord, for our benefit, You used the word *"you"* in the text, eight times. You clearly showed Cain and us too, that serious repenting needed to be done for his depression to be a thing of the past! Lord, so often we wait for You to fix our down feelings, while You are waiting for us to change how we are living. We can only say, thank You for the pain You give us, so that we see the necessity to live differently. In Christ's holy name we pray. Amen.

September 10

"For everything that was written in the past was written to teach us, so that through endurance and the encouragement of the Scriptures we might have hope." Romans 15:4

Follow Elijah's eyes to see his problem

There was a time when Elijah was depressed. To see the change in Elijah's emotions, follow his eyes in 1 Kings 18. He was not depressed in this chapter. The people had left the worship of God. Some were trying to worship both God and idols. Elijah gave them a challenge. Which God or god can send fire from Heaven to light the sacrifice?

"At the time of the sacrifice, the prophet Elijah stepped forward and prayed: 'O LORD, God of Abraham, Isaac and Israel, let it be known today that You are God in Israel and that I am Your servant and have done all these things at Your command. Answer me, O LORD, answer me, so these people will know that You, O LORD, are God, and that You are turning their hearts back again,'" 1 Kings 18:36-37. Elijah's eyes were on God first, others secondly, not on himself! God sent the fire, burning up the sacrifice. The people shouted, *"The LORD, He is God,"* 1 Kings 18:39b. Elijah was faithful and not depressed in this situation.

Now follow Elijah's eyes when he was depressed! *"Now Ahab told Jezebel everything Elijah had done and how he had killed the prophets with the sword. So Jezebel sent a messenger to Elijah to say, 'May the gods deal with me, be it ever so severely, if by this time tomorrow I do not make your life like one of them.' Elijah was afraid and ran for his life. When he came to Beersheba in Judah, he left his servant there, while he himself went a day's journey into the desert. He came to a broom tree, sat down under it and prayed that he might die. 'I have had enough, LORD,' he said. 'Take my life; I am no better than my ancestors.' Then he laid down under the tree and fell asleep,"* 1 Kings 19:1-5.

When Elijah's eyes were obediently focused on God and his daily responsibilities for God, he could face 850 false prophets, all alone. But when his eyes focused selfishly on self and running, he could not even face one woman, the wicked Jezebel.

Prayer: O Lord, like Elijah, we so quickly take our eyes off you and then lose our trust in Your ability to care for us. Help us to be faithful in our relationships and responsibilities. In Christ's name we pray. Amen.

September 11

"I mused, and my spirit grew faint. You kept my eyes from closing; I was too troubled to speak." Psalm 77:3b-4

Asaph, Peter, and Job depressed

Christians are depressed at times as the godly Asaph was. In Psalm 77, we can see Asaph's depressed thinking process. Asaph, by his own admission, *"mused."* He was overwhelmed and very self-focused early in the chapter. In the first 10 verses, the personal pronouns of "I" or "my," are used 20 times. In the last 10 verses, Asaph begins to come out of his selfish thoughts as "I" and "my" are used just three times. When Asaph switched his thoughts from being intent on his problems to being intent on God (the solution), his problem of depression was solved. As we read Psalm 77, see how the benefit of God-centered thinking, really worships God, and quickly improves our mental and spiritual outlook on life.

Peter was also a man of faith. Yet in Matthew 26:69-75, he fell in a time of weakness. He denied that he even knew the Lord when he lied three times! Suddenly, without hope, Peter quickly failed a major test in his life. After this, Peter wept bitterly. His depressed feelings were a direct result of his sinful action of denying Christ. Peter was a sinner, made of flesh and bone just like us. His depression was also a result of his sinful and fearful self-focus.

God said Job was *"blameless and upright,"* Job 1:1b. Yet still, Job was somewhat depressed after a great trial in his life. Job struggled with the question, *"Why do the righteous suffer if God is loving and all powerful?"* It is recorded that Job was wrong when he was, *"righteous in his own eyes,"* Job 32:1b. God finally questioned him, *"Would you discredit My justice? Would you condemn Me to justify yourself?"* Job 40:8. What powerful questions! Do you see how incredibly wicked and self-centered we are. If one of the godliest men in the Bible needed to change his self-focus, how much more do we need to change!

Prayer: Dear Lord, we praise You for giving us many examples about Biblical people who were depressed at various points in their lives. Help us to understand the principles You teach us through their lives. Forgive us for not clearly professing our love for You like Peter did. May we learn to trust in You fully. In Jesus' name we pray. Amen.

September 12

"Anxiety in the heart of a man <u>causes</u> depression, but a good word makes it glad." Proverbs 12:25 NKJV

Is a chemical imbalance the cause?

God knows people have chemical imbalances. But what's the reason for the imbalance? Is the *"anxiety"* in our text caused by a chemical imbalance? Or, is a chemical imbalance caused by our *"anxiety"*?

It is popular to just adjust the chemicals to try fix depression. That is not totally wrong, but a serious issue remains. Matthew 15:18-19 teaches that the cause of our problems are *"in the heart"* just like our text does. It's not wise to tell God that He does not know what He is talking about. It's not recorded in Scripture that anyone had a chemical imbalance as a cause for depression. A key word here is cause.

When we are angry or worried, we get a chemical imbalance. But did a chemical imbalance cause our anger and worry? Or, did our anger and worry cause our chemical imbalance? Fear, worry, anger, bitterness, lust, and adultery, all result in guilt, tension, and a chemical change in our body. This is especially true for those of us who know that these things are wrong. God actually wants us miserable, guilty, uncomfortable, upset, including a chemical imbalance, all so we do not continue to live like this. We are physical and spiritual beings. When we sin in our spiritual mind or heart, our body reacts.

Sin is not just what we do wrong, but also what we don't do right. If a chemical imbalance really is the cause of our depression, then we are not responsible for it. Because of our selfish excuses for how we live, David writes, *"Do not be like the horse or mule, which have no understanding but must be controlled by bit and bridle,"* Psalm 32:9a.

Depression is mostly a behavioral issue, a wrong response to whats going on, not a disease. The medication David took to overcome his depression was the pill of confession and the vitamin of repentance. God knows, *"anxiety in the heart of a man causes depression."*

Prayer: Dear Lord, we are stubborn people. We say our problems are outside of us. You show us our big problems are inside of us, in our hearts. Lord, forgive us for our selfish unwillingness to live out Jesus' humble lifestyle. Change us that we might walk closer to You and others, trusting in Your wisdom. In Jesus' name we pray. Amen.

September 13

"Train yourself to be godly." 1 Timothy 4:7b

Getting serious with our daily schedule

Overcoming depression, fear, and worry, without dealing with our daily schedule, is as silly as trying to gain weight without eating. A big problem among the depressed is a poor schedule. This may not be what depressed people want to hear, but it is the truth. When we observe most depressed people, we notice they commonly are students, housewives, pastors, salespeople, and retirees. What does this group have in common? They set their own schedule. Or, they fail to set their own schedule. A laborer, a bank worker, and a teacher all have their schedule set for them. They must be on time, working faithfully. If they fail to timely perform, they could lose their job. Some are depressed because of a lazy schedule. Others have schedules filled with the wrong priorities. Our daily schedule is our life, and it matters!

It is good to plan a godly schedule for our week by listing our duties and responsibilities. Of course things change, but are we working on the right things or just doing what we feel like doing? We, depressed people, commonly live too much by our feelings, not doing what we should do. Our text says, *"Train yourself to be godly."* The Bible gives the picture of an athlete pushing his or her body to train it for competition, regardless of how they feel about it.

Regarding our schedule, are we really doing what God wants us to do? Are we doing it with a good attitude? Do we schedule time for prayer and the study of God's Word? Do we as husbands, schedule time to be with our wife and family, building relationships? Wife, do you schedule time to help and encourage your husband in his work? You still are *"a helper suitable"* for him, Genesis 2:18b. Student, are you seriously studying, for that is your present job?

We may think we have a good schedule and still be depressed if we are angry and bitter. If we are unwilling to forgive some people, that is a bad schedule and God would want us depressed. Working faithfully, is important but how we work is also God's concern.

Prayer: Lord, You tell us, *"Train yourself to be godly,"* 1 Timothy 4:7b. Fill us with Your Spirit to plan our day and then live according to that plan. In Christ's precious name we pray. Amen.

September 14

"If you do what is right, will you not be accepted? But if you do not do what is right, sin is crouching at your door; it desires to have you, but you must master it." Genesis 4:7

A depressed ministry worker

To see more clearly how important a Biblical schedule is, we will first give an example of a ministry worker who has eight things he should do today. 1. Pray and have devotions; 2. Visit a sick man; 3. See a widow; 4. Prepare for a meeting; 5. Spend time with his own family; 6. Begin preparing a message; 7. Write a note of encouragement to a hurting person. 8. Visit parents in the evening.

Instead of getting up early to pray, he sleeps until 8:30. His two children have already left for school. His guilt begins! He goes to the corner cafe for breakfast and ends up talking about problems in the church. His guilt builds! Returning home at 10:00, he does not FEEL like doing his work yet, so he watches sports until past noon. His guilt grows! After an hour nap, he leaves home to see a widow lady he really doesn't want to see. Ah, bad attitude. He shows very little compassion and gives no hope to this lady. His guilt grows some more! He complains to many people about his busy schedule, yet at the same time, does not really FEEL like doing his responsibilities. God presses him to be more faithful with his time, so he starts his God-given duties.

Minutes later, the children come home from school and one is crying. Daddy yells loudly, "Be quiet, I have a lot of important work to do." His wife asks for his help in doing something and he angrily reacts by telling her to leave him alone. The man does not even have a clear mind to do his duties now! FEELING trapped, he runs to the church praying for God to deliver him from all his troubles. We see his, "schedule mistakes." Can we see our own?

Prayer: O Lord who directs us, thank You for telling the depressed Cain and us in Genesis 4:5-7, *"If you do what is right, will you not be accepted?"* Lord, we want acceptance from You and from others, too. We realize that we need to *"do what is right."* Lord, strengthen us to pursue righteousness with all of our hearts, following Your directions. In Jesus' name we pray. Amen.

September 15

"Do not merely listen to the Word, and so deceive yourselves. Do what it says." James 1:22

A depressed student or housewife

The lives of a depressed student and housewife are really the same as the example of anyone else. In self-pity, the student or housewife talks to others and complains. After getting off the phone, the wife broods about how her husband and kids are treating her. The student grumbles and complains about how students and teachers are treating him. In response, both the housewife and student watch T.V., go to the movies, or read unprofitable books. Almost anything but their daily responsibilities is their main focus. Then, surprise, an unexpected test comes to the student in science. The wife has her own test when her husband comes home early and the house is quite the mess. The wife yells, "You expect me to keep this place clean by myself? I can't do it." Can't, is the language of the depressed. This kind of person comes to us in pain, with little hope. How will we help her? There are three ways we could quite unprofitably counsel them.

First, we could offer them a pill to make them feel better. It works, temporarily. A pill to help someone feel better can be a starting point. But a pill in the place of changing wrong thoughts, words, or actions, is horrible theology.

Second, we could put our arm around them and tell them everything will be all right. But that is a lie. Everything is not all right if they have a pattern of sin they are ignoring.

Third, we could bring the housewife or student to a pastor who could cast out the demon of depression. (Don't laugh, for I have seen this often in India). This pastor is really saying, "It's all a demon's fault, no other change necessary." Hopefully, we can see that merely trying to change a person's feelings is not the deeper counsel that they need and that God gives. God wants wrong thoughts, words and actions replaced, which will result in us feeling better.

Prayer: Wise and holy God, how You desire us to be wise and holy by how we live. We are thankful that You, the Great Physician, openly tell us about our physical and spiritual issues. Lord make us more like Christ, the perfect Man. In His name we pray. Amen.

September 16

"Rejoice in the Lord always. I will say it again: Rejoice!"
Philippians 4:4

"Rejoice in the Lord always"

A true Christian will learn to "rejoice in the Lord," eventually. But how many hard knocks will it take? Our problem is, we rejoice in other things, like, our abilities, our looks, other relationships, our strength, before rejoicing in God. To test our love for Him, God will allow very difficult situations. An adulterer who turned to Christ will soon have a tempting situation. They must now decide if they are going to rejoice in the sin as before, or "rejoice in the Lord." The thief who turned to Christ will soon be tempted with something easy to steal. Will they rejoice in the easy money, or *"in the Lord"*? We rejoice in that which is our heart's desire.

It should be very obvious, we can't *"rejoice in the Lord,"* who is the Creator, if we rejoice in created things first. There is nothing wrong with more money, better health, being popular, a better vehicle, a nicer house, or a good marriage. But, if we look for our number one joy in them, we cannot *"rejoice in the Lord."*

See how *"rejoice in the Lord,"* fits into the change process. We must first put off (Ephesians 4:22-24) the old sin habits before we can put on the new ones. But that is not enough. Now, we must concentrate on God's new way of living with all of our heart. This is the secret to lasting change and to *"rejoicing in the Lord."*

God examines our life to see how we spend our time. If we are a student, worker in the house, field, or office, then we must do our work for the Lord first! Do it with all our heart, and with all integrity. Do it even as worship to the Lord. This means, we must *"rejoice"* in the Lord's approval before anyone else's. Rejoice in the fact that God is pleased with our best, even if others are not. Continue our daily schedule and don't forget whom we are doing it for first. This is a main part of our worship to God each and every day.

Prayer: We praise You Lord for Your simple but sweet advice. Forgive us sinners for looking for our number one joy in other things. Lord, we want You to be the love of our life. Strengthen us because we are weak. In Christ Jesus' name we pray. Amen.

September 17

"Let your gentleness be evident to all. The Lord is near."
Philippians 4:5

"Gentleness... to all"

Verse four focused our attention on the Lord, and the keeping of the first four commandments. The fifth verse puts our focus on others in commandments five to ten. Remember that loving self is a distant third. Self-first or our selfishness is exactly why we do not *"rejoice in the Lord."* Our super selfishness is not *"gentle"* to others as we act like graceless control freaks. Gentleness is a spirit that is full of grace. There is nothing to fear or worry about when we love someone gently, and then, leave the results of how they respond up to God! "Gentle" is the opposite of treating people with anger and bitterness. Becoming gentler to all is basically what it means to grow in the grace of God.

If we want to cut the stress out of our life, show some *"gentleness."* Why? Because in our pride, we try to gain respect by being loud and bossy in the home, school, church or business. Then, somebody gets in the way and threatens our desire for greatness. We now fear that our lofty goals will never be met. The quick response to our fear now pushes us to anger or bitterness.

Keep in mind the put-off and put-on process of Biblical change here. To be "gentle" means that our anger and bitterness needs to be put off before our forgiveness and *"gentleness"* can be put on. Pray about being gentle. Plan opportunities to show our *"gentleness."* Confess our sins to God and others when we fail to be gentle. When we concentrate on being gentle, change happens. Being gentle, makes a man a gentleman and a woman caring and loving. God knows we need more *"gentleness."*

Prayer: Gracious Lord, forgive us for the times we have blown up in anger. You tell us in James 1:20, *"man's anger does not bring about the righteous life that God desires."* You tell us that our bitterness is *"earthly, unspiritual, of the devil,"* James 3:15b. Lord, we have not shown *"gentleness."* Create in us clean and new hearts so we can be gentle to all. In Christ, our gentle Shepherd's name we pray. Amen.

September 18

"Do not be anxious about anything, but in everything, by prayer and petition, with thanksgiving, present your requests to God."
Philippians 4:6

Pray "with thanksgiving"

This word "anxious" is really worry - a sinful, self-centered concern that is paralyzing. A problem with anxiety is that many do not think it is sinful. Often, we are even proud of our worry as if it is righteous. If we do not think worry is sin, we will not confess it or try to overcome it. Jesus called worry, *"little faith"* in Matthew 6 to get our attention. Worry is also idolatry because our thought process says, "I can handle this problem without God's help." Anxiety steals today's joy and robs our daily productivity. *"Do not be anxious about anything"* is a command that must be put off before we can replace it with God's prescribed *"prayer"* and *"petition."*

Not just *"prayer"* but fervent and specific prayer is needed. *"Prayer with thanksgiving"* is especially called for. James says that we should count our trials as *"all joy."* Satan wants us anxious, not trusting in God. The following song, "Count Your Many Blessings" is great theology for us to overcome anxiety, fear, worry and even depression.

1. "When upon life's billows you are tempest tossed, when you are discouraged, thinking all is lost, count your many blessings, name them one by one, and it will surprise you what the Lord hath done."

2. "Are you ever burdened with a load of care? Does the cross seem heavy you are called to bear? Count your many blessings, every doubt will fly. And you will be singing as the days go by."

3. "When you look at others with their lands and gold, think that Christ has promised you His wealth untold, count your many blessings, money cannot buy, your reward in Heaven, nor your home on high."

4. "So, amid the conflict, whether great or small, do not be discouraged, God is over all. Count your many blessings, angels will attend, help and comfort give you to your journey's end."

Prayer: Gracious Lord, we praise You for Your help in overcoming fear, worry, and even depression. In Christ's name we pray. Amen.

September 19

"And the peace of God, which transcends all understanding, will guard your hearts and your minds in Christ Jesus." Philippians 4:7

God's "peace" will guard us!

Let us review the prior three verses to see God's road to peace. First, *"Rejoice in the Lord."* Second, *"Let your gentleness be evident to all."* After that, *"Do not be anxious about anything."* Put on much *"prayer,"* and *"petition,"* (specific prayer requests), *"with thanksgiving."* Now *"the peace of God, which transcends all understanding, will guard your hearts and your minds in Christ Jesus."* God will keep His covenant "peace promise," if we are faithful in the prior three verses.

Do not strive for the "world's peace," which is the absence of problems. The world says that as long as our family, friends, possessions, health and jobs are fine, then we will have peace. Such "peace" comes and goes quickly! As Christians, even in the midst of great problems we have peace because we are in the Lord. In John 16, Jesus promises the Holy Spirit will come to His disciples after He leaves this world. He tells them they will be scattered and miserable. Then He shows them the secret to peace. *"I have told you these things, so that in Me you may have peace. In this world you will have trouble. But take heart! I have overcome the world,"* John 16:33. Real *"peace"* is in a Person, Jesus Christ!

Here we have it! Jesus has *"overcome the world."* He put us here to love Him and others and after we do that, the results are up to God. Our part to just be faithful is small, as we keep loving God and others! The prophet Isaiah summarized God's peace: *"But those who hope in the LORD will renew their strength. They will soar on wings like eagles; they will run and not grow weary, they will walk and not faint,"* Isaiah 40:31.

Prayer: Dear most loving Lord, You know that we face temptations every day to see if we will put our hope in the things of this world, or in You. Help us to keep our eyes on You, trusting in You. We want to soar like eagles. We praise You for giving us Your peace that passes all understanding. In Christ's name we pray. Amen.

September 20

"Finally, brothers, whatever is true, whatever is noble, whatever is right, whatever is pure, whatever is lovely, whatever is admirable-if anything is excellent or praiseworthy-think about such things." Philippians 4:8

Learning to "*think*" God's way

As selfish people, it is so easy for us to dwell on the negative. We cry because some event or relationship is over in our life. We selfishly mediate on the mistakes of others. We dwell intensely on how people have hurt us. We were not created to be so selfish. God has everything under control. *"Beloved, do not think it strange concerning the fiery trial which is to try you, as though some strange thing happened to you,"* 1 Peter 4:12. God is making good adjustments in our lives. God wants us to change by replacing our old behavior. God graciously lists new ways in our text that we must focus on to be at peace.

What is "*noble*" in our life? God loves us and comes to us, who are literally, dead sinners, totally unable to come to Him on our own. It is God's amazing grace freely given to us who believe.

What is "*right*" in our life? It is right for the family of God to praise and to thank Him for His love and eternal covenant with us.

What is "*pure*" in our life? God's Word and Spirit are pure. How praiseworthy it is that we have the written Word of God made plain to us. Through His Word and Spirit, we come to faith and life.

What is "*lovely*" in our life? What a privilege we have to work for the King of kings. God says, *"How beautiful are the feet of those who bring the good news."* May we never tire of being His servant!

What is "*admirable*" in our life? It is most admirable to lift up the name of God and to disciple others to know God's truth!

What is "*excellent or praiseworthy*" in our life? God will never leave us or forsake us, His children. Our God even prays for us when we are unwilling or unable to pray for ourselves.

Prayer: Dearest Lord, united to Christ we are so blessed! May we lean on Your everlasting and loving arms more and more. Help us to see that You allow trials in our lives to teach us to trust in You more, and not give in to fear, worry and even depression. We praise You for teaching us to think properly. In Jesus' name we pray. Amen.

September 21

"Whatever you have learned or received or heard from me, or seen in me — put it into practice. And the God of peace will be with you."
Philippians 4:9

Are we practicing Christians?

The difference between a mature Christian and one who is not yet mature, is that one acts on what he or she believes. Many in the church think it's the knowledge we stuff into our head that makes us mature. Christianity involves knowledge, but without putting God's truth *"into practice,"* we are actually in rebellion to God's truth. There are four main parts to the Christian life set before us in the fourth chapter of Philippians. A review is helpful.

First, it is necessary see the world through God's eyes. We learned to *"rejoice in the Lord."* We saw the need to be *"gentle to all men."* Both are what the commandments teach.

Second, as believers, we must be filled with hope in God, because hope in God is a trusting faith. *"Do not be anxious about anything."* God rewards true faith with: *"The peace of God, which transcends all understanding."*

Third, by the Spirit's leading we understand what changes need to be made in our life to act like God's child. Paul said, *"Whatever you have learned or received or heard from me, or seen in me,"* that is what we must change into. God in love, tells us what must change.

Fourth in our text is, *"Put it into practice."* Right knowledge must equal right practice. Here is where we fail so often. It is not enough to do the first three points! It is possible to see life from God's eyes; see the hope in God that is available; see what our Biblical change needs to be, and then not *"put it into practice."* Without the *"practice"* we are foolish, deceived, not yet very mature as Christians!

Prayer: O Lord of life, we praise and worship You for encouraging us to live the Christian life, not just learn about it. In so many ways You have told us, *"Do not merely listen to the Word, and so deceive yourselves. Do what it says,"* James 1:22-23. Lord, by nature we are lazy and rebel against You and Your Word. Have mercy on us and change our hearts so that we become mature Christians, practicing Your Word! In Jesus' name we pray. Amen.

September 22

"For I have learned to be content whatever the circumstances."
Philippians 4:11b

How Paul *"learned to be content"*

Contentment is a very necessary virtue to have so we can peacefully live for God and be a blessing to His kingdom. *"Contentment"* is not natural to man. Discontentment, complaining, and arguing are! The Apostle Paul admits, he *"learned to be content."* If Paul learned contentment, then it stands to reason that we can also learn, if we follow Paul's God-given method.

"Contentment" is found in a relationship! The Proverb, *"the fear of the LORD is the beginning of wisdom,"* is foundational. No one will have *"contentment"* without a close relationship with God. Are we praying? Are we in the Word? Are we learning to live by faith in God? Are we reaching out to others, to be loving to them? Do we do this? Or are we waiting for others to reach out to us? We will never find contentment if we're waiting for others to give it to us!

Paul was in prison and in chains when he said, *"I have learned to be content."* Paul had the best education money could buy. He did not find contentment there. He had money, and he had a high position with the Pharisees. He had all these without contentment. Paul counted these things as dung! What did Paul "learn"?

Paul *"learned to be content whatever the circumstances."* Many of us think contentment will come if our circumstances change. Not so. Contentment is what happens in us, not outside of us! Paul learned that *"contentment"* is a grace from God, a fruit of His Spirit in us. God gave Paul a new heart, with new graces. Paul's anger was traded in for compassion. Paul's bitterness was exchanged for forgiveness. His worry was replaced with trust in God. Paul's former fears were cast out by the *"perfect love"* that was now in him. God's grace in Paul was visible. With God's grace filling us, contentment is on the way.

Prayer: Dear gracious Lord, we have not been content because we have not been satisfied with You! We have envied, coveted and lusted to have more, to please and elevate ourselves. Lord, how much we need a closer relationship with You, Your Son, and with Your Spirit. In Jesus' name we pray. Amen.

September 23

"I know how to abound." Philippians 4:12b NKJV

A true test of God's blessings

This is one of the greatest statements of God's abundant grace to Paul! Not many of us can honestly say, *"I know how to abound,"* but Paul could! What did Paul experience? He had gone through many very difficult trials without any bitterness, and he ended up stronger spiritually because of it.

Perhaps the biggest trial or testing that God could put us through personally would be to give us abundant possessions. Would we love God with all of our heart if we had a wonderful marriage, lots of good food, a big and beautiful house, expensive clothes, a new vehicle, the very best education and money in the bank? Growing rich in the things of this world may be the greatest temptation of all because it is the one temptation we do not dread! There are millions of people who are destroyed by prosperity. Perhaps, the greatest trial in life is having no trials at all.

There are even "preachers" who teach the prosperity gospel, "Come to Christ and He will give you many possessions." When did Jesus ever say, "Come to Me and I will make you rich in material things"? Jesus said, *"Follow Me and I will make you fishers of men,"* not fishers of money. Jesus had a stone for a pillow. The streets of gold Jesus talks about are in Heaven! After Paul was converted, he had much more than he did before. He had nothing in his hands, but he had Jesus in his heart!

Our peace in life is always a thing of the heart, not in a multitude of possessions! Having peace is a spiritual issue, not a material one! A most useful passage is Psalm 37. We need to put off envying what others have in verse 1, before we can trust in the Lord in verse 3. We must trust in the Lord before we can delight in the Lord in verse 4. Then we can commit our ways to the Lord in verse 5. Now, we can rest in the Lord in verse 7, filled with His peace.

Prayer: O Lord of all peace and joy, we are ashamed of our lack of contentment. We love idols and want more. We have not yet learned *"how to abound."* We cannot hide our wickedness from You who can see everything. Help us to change. In Jesus' name we pray. Amen.

September 24

"On the first day of the seventh month you are to have a day of rest,
a sacred assembly commemorated with trumpet blast. Do no regular
work, but present an offering made to the LORD by fire."
Leviticus 23: 24b-25

The Feast of Trumpets

God established a yearly cycle of holidays on the Jewish calendar for reflection and worship. They were designed by God to be a break from the normal busyness of life, to think about the holiness, the power, and the love of God. The first fall event is the Feast of Trumpets, also called Rosh Hashanah. It is the first two days of the month of Tishri, our September or October.

The harvest is now in and the people walk to Jerusalem to worship God. The trumpet's sound reminds the people that God brought the harvest, not their own efforts. Like evangelism, the people planted, watered, and waited, but God gave the increase! The Historian Maimonides said, "Rouse ye, rouse ye from your sleep, you who mind vanity, for slumber most heavy has fallen upon you. Take it to heart, before whom you are to give an account in the judgment." The Feast of Trumpets also looked back to father Abraham sacrificing Isaac on the altar in Genesis 22. God spared Isaac at the last moment, and instead provided a ram for the sacrifice. That is why the blowing a ram's horn as the trumpet is in the name of the feast.

Today we have both Testaments and can see how God the Father sacrificed Christ on the Cross. We can see the connection of old covenant Isaac and new covenant Christ. Both were sons of promise. Their births were heralded by angels. Both had a miraculous birth. Both had to carry the wood for the sacrifice. Both went willingly to the place of slaughter without a word. However, God did not spare His only Son!

Jesus is coming again! Ten days after the Feast of Trumpets came the Day of Atonement. So too, the end of the world will come soon. Once again, we will hear the trumpet sound.

Prayer: Lord of life, we can see the importance of confession, forgiveness, and repentance to prepare for the coming judgment that we will all face. Open our hearts to Your schedule for the end of our life on this earth. In Jesus' name we pray. Amen.

September 25

"Only the high priest entered the inner room, and that only once a year, and never without blood, which he offered for himself and for the sins the people had committed in ignorance. The Holy Spirit was showing by this that the way into the Most Holy Place had not yet been disclosed as long as the first tabernacle was still standing."
Hebrews 9: 7-8

The Day of Atonement

The Day of Atonement, also called Yom Kippur, is on the 10th day of the month of Tishri, our September or October. This celebration is so beautifully described for us in Leviticus 23:26-32. Note that this is a DAY, a specific 24-hour day. It is recorded three times in these few verses, *"Do no work on that day, because it is the Day of Atonement, when atonement is made for you before the LORD your God,"* Leviticus 23:28. If the people worked on that day, God said they must be *"cut off from His people,"* vs. 29b. How completely true this is yet today. Christ's work, not our work, is the only atonement so that we are not *"cut off"* from God!

In our text, we can see that the old covenant, which is called the Old Testament, was incomplete. The High Priest had to offer sacrifices for himself also. Christ did not need to do that. The text shows that the old tabernacle had to come down for our good and also for God's glory. *"The Holy Spirit was showing by this, that the way; into the Most Holy Place had not yet been disclosed as long as the first tabernacle was still standing. This is an illustration for the present time, indicating that the gifts and sacrifices being offered were not able to clear the conscience of the worshiper,"* Hebrews 9:8-9.

Prayer: Forgiving Lord, how privileged we are today! Formerly, there was just one day set aside where You impressed Your people with Your willingness to forgive their sins. Today, we can come to Christ anytime! What a beautiful picture of You, our merciful God, being concerned about taking away even our smallest sin. We worship You, Lord Jesus, for willingly taking our sins to the wilderness of Hell so we can be pure and clean. In the name of Jesus, our only atonement, we pray. Amen.

September 26

"The LORD said to Moses, 'Say to the Israelites: On the fifteenth day of the seventh month the LORD's Feast of Tabernacles begins, and it lasts for seven days.'" Leviticus 23:33-34

The Feast of Tabernacles

The Feast of Tabernacles is also called the Feast of Booths or In-gathering. It was in the month of Tishri from the 15th to the 22nd, our September or October. This is the third of the three major feasts that required all males to go to Jerusalem. This feast celebrated the providence of God in leading them in the wilderness for 40 years. This feast is a picture of how God not only provided for His people in the past but will do so in the present and in the future.

During these seven days the priests were to sacrifice 70 bulls. The Rabbis say this number represents the 70 nations that came from Noah's bloodlines, from which the Gentiles had their beginnings. The hope and prayer was that these 70 nations would someday accept the God of Abraham, Isaac, and Jacob. These hopes and prayers were answered when the Gentiles were grafted into the Christian faith at the time of Pentecost.

The Feast of Tabernacles honored God as the provider of life, who promised us, *"never will I leave you; never will I forsake you,"* Hebrews 13:5b. Our weak faith needs more hope in God. For we also wander in the wilderness of sin and desperately need the Good Shepherd to lead us out to the Promised Land.

By the time of Christ, the people came to the temple, on the last day of the feast, waving palm, willow and myrtle branches, praying for God to bring in the new rainy season, seeking His blessings. And what did Jesus do? *"On the last and greatest day of the Feast, Jesus stood and said in a loud voice, 'If anyone is thirsty, let him come to Me and drink. Whoever believes in Me, as the Scripture has said, streams of living water will flow from within him,'"* John 7:37-38.

Prayer: Most loving Lord, we praise Your for Your faithfulness in delivering us from sin and Your wrath against sin. Forgiven, we forever have Your living water in streams. How wonderful You are to send spiritual water in a dry land. In Jesus' name we pray. Amen.

September 27

"Blessed is the man who always fears the LORD, but he who hardens his heart falls into trouble." Proverbs 28:14

Jesus, the solution to a right attitude

What does it mean to harden our heart? One way is when we look for happiness or blessedness in all the wrong places. A lack of happiness drives some to a life of drinking, pills, greed, fame, fortune, sex, etc. It is a lack of happiness that drives others to go in for counseling. It should be obvious then, there is a big difference in people's minds in where and how to obtain true happiness and blessedness. If we could just experience the truth of out text! Being *"blessed"* by God is very connected to those who fear and reverence Him.

The first question and answer of the Heidelberg Catechism is so good. "What is your only comfort in life and in death? That I am not my own, but belong - body and soul, in life and in death - to my faithful Savior Jesus Christ." Again, we see that happiness is in the heart. It is not dependent on other people, not dependent on possessions, not dependent on circumstances! The happiness of the world is very dependent on people, possessions, and circumstances to be just right. That is why the world constantly loses their happiness!

With Christ in our hearts, we are *"blessed"* because our happiness is in us. His Spirit in us, gives us an attitude of gratitude, regardless of what happens. This is what makes us thankful and worshipful, as God created us to be. These are the kinds of disciples Jesus desires. As disciples, we first need to believe in Christ and His promises, like in our text. Then, we will become new people with new living habits.

In summary, real happiness is a direct result of the condition of the heart, which in turn leads to what we do, which then leads to how we feel. Thus, a happy or sad feeling is a direct result of our thoughts, words, or actions.

Prayer: O Lord, we worship and praise You for teaching us from Your Word on how to be blessed. We have seen that the happiness the world gives will fly away like a bird. We want a relationship with Jesus that is eternal. We want to learn from His life what produces real happiness. We thank You for sending Your Son and making this possible! In Jesus' name we pray. Amen.

September 28

"Not that we are competent in ourselves to claim anything for ourselves, but our competence comes from God. He has made us competent as ministers of a new covenant — not of the letter but of the Spirit; for the letter kills, but the Spirit gives life." 2 Corinthians 3:5-6

God's sufficiency

One of the hardest lessons we need to learn as children of God is that we really have no strength and wisdom, except that which God gives us. We are not self-sufficient! We can see this truth in the lives of many Biblical characters. *"One day, after Moses had grown up, he went out to where his own people were and watched them,"* Exodus 2:11a. Moses saw the people being mistreated and thought, "I am the man to fix this problem." He killed the Egyptian who was beating them. Moses had to learn, he was not *"competent"* for this task yet! Because of his rash actions, he fell into great discouragement. Don't think this is so strange! God allowed this event to show Moses that *"we are not competent in ourselves."* Moses needed to learn God's way of living, even with all of his privileged education! This is still so true today. Moses fled to the wilderness, to learn from God. For forty years Moses learned that the *"I Am that I Am, had sent him"* into the world.

Who are the ministers of the new covenant in our text? Who is the *"we," "us"* and *"our"*? Is it pastors alone? What does chapters 3-6 in 2 Corinthians teach that is so important? It's about missions. It is about the Great Commission. We must all learn from God who makes us sufficient or complete to do His work. Like Moses, we need to spend time with Christ and to learn Him! We are then *"competent as ministers of a new covenant."* If we don't believe it, why would we do evangelism and discipleship? Yes, *"we are competent."* Jesus Christ still says to His followers, *"Go and I will be with you."*

Prayer: All sufficient Lord, we are only *"competent in ourselves"* through You, in trinity. You are our loving Father. Your Son is our Savior, Teacher, and Brother. Your Spirit is our Guide, Comforter and personal Friend. If You are for us, no one can be against us. Your everlasting kingdom is our commission. You equip us to "go" for you. In Your strength and wisdom, we press on, fully competent. Thank You Lord. In Jesus' name we pray. Amen.

September 29

"Like an apple tree among the trees of the forest is my lover among young men. I delight to sit in his shade." Song of Songs 2:3a

Is your husband an *"apple tree"*?

This "Song" of King Solomon describes the loving relationship of a wife to a husband. The same words show a relationship of a repentant sinner to Jesus Christ. An important truth in our text is that Christ is not "a god" to the believer. Christ is "the God" as John 1:1 teaches. The passion here in the Song is that through the eyes of true love we will see Christ as the Apple Tree surrounded by just plain trees. Do we "*delight*" to sit in His shade? We worship what we "*delight*" in. "*Delight,*" shows the real condition of our hearts. In our daily schedule, do we "*delight*" to open the Word of God and pray? The question is not, do we do it, but do we "*delight*" in it? Or would we rather sit in the shade of the gods of this age?

A second issue is critical for our marriages. A wife who sees her husband as "*an apple tree among the trees*" will have a beautiful marriage. The question that begs to be answered is: "Ladies, are you more comfortable seeing the other trees of the forest, like on television, rather than being close by your husband?" How many hours per day do you spend admiring the TV personalities as compared to your husband? The answer to this question really does determine if you are really in love with your husband or not.

The issue of our text is not, "do you love what Christ or your husband does for you?" It is quite possible to be in love with the blessings that Christ and a husband can give, and still not really love them! The difference is life changing in a relationship. Adultery starts when the "*delights*" of our heart wanders. The rest of the act of adultery comes later.

Prayer: Holy and loving Lord, we do not always like what we see when You expose the condition of our hearts. We desperately need Your forgiveness and cleansing so much. Thank You for using such a clear pictures to show us what our relationship to Christ and what our marriage must look like. In Jesus' name we pray. Amen.

September 30

"Like a lily among thorns is my darling among the maidens."
Song of Songs 2:2

Is your wife a *"lily among thorns"*?

Jesus sees each individual believer as special, set apart, like a pure white lily. White because He is pure, without the blemish of sin. Every believer is purified, just like Christ. To God, every single believer is *"a lily among thorns."* Do we see God's loving grace here that is so personal for every believer? Saved by our perfect and pure Savior, we have a new status with God. He is our Father forever, no longer our Judge. In Christ, we are a new creation. Jesus in His High Priestly prayer said this about believers, *"I have given them* (lilies only) *the glory that You gave Me, that they may be one as We are one,"* John 17:22. This, by the grace of God, is our privileged position.

Since the Song of Songs is an allegory, there is a second meaning to the words of our text. A husband who is truly in love with his wife will see her as *"a lily among thorns."* However, if the husband has a lust problem, he will see his wife as a thorn, and the other ladies as lilies! Which is true for us? Our answer reveals the true condition of our heart.

We can now see the problem with pornography. Sad to say, boys as young as 12 years, to aged men are hooked on porn which leads to their spiritual, mental, and physical destruction. If the porn addict only knew how the thorns (affairs outside of marriage) have pierced many hearts for all eternity. How our young people need to know that if they want to see life through eyes of lust, even at their early age, it will do much to prevent them from seeing their future spouse as a lily!

Prayer: Gracious Lord, how precious and beautiful is the fact that Christ sees each believer as, *"a lily among thorns."* We do not deserve Your sweet love! It is so amazing how Christ took us from the garbage dump of sin and placed us in His heavenly garden. As *"lilies,"* we are now, pure, white, totally cleansed. Forgive us for even glancing at the gods in this world! Forgive us also, when we see our wives as thorns and other women as lilies. How we can hurt You and our wives. Give us the eyes of love. In Jesus' name we pray. Amen.

OCTOBER

"Do not be amazed at this, for a time is coming when all who are in their graves will hear His voice and come out — those who have done good will rise to live, and those who have done evil will rise to be condemned." John 5:28-29

October 1

"In the beginning God created the Heavens and the Earth."
Genesis 1:1

How did the present world begin?

This month we will look at the subject of eternity. We tried to put the questions about eternity in the best order for an easier study. We will start *"in the beginning"* of the created Heavens and Earth. However, it is not the beginning of God Himself! God always existed in Trinity. It only stands to reason that the very One who created everything, our Creator, had to exist before the creation of anything.

The word "create" means to make something out of nothing. We loosely use the word when we say: "She created a beautiful cake." The cake was made from something: ingredients. Whereas God spoke into existence all that is, simply by the breath of His mouth.

God in Trinity, (Father, Son & Spirit) created everything. In Genesis 1:2, we can see that the Holy Spirit was present. Jesus was also present. *"In the beginning was the Word and the Word was with God and the Word was God. He was with God in the beginning,"* John 1:1-2. Genesis 1:26 also says, *"Let Us make man in Our likeness."* The plural words show more than one person in the Godhead was involved.

The 1st day God created *"light,"* Genesis 1:3.

The 2nd day God created water and the Heavens, Genesis 1:6-8.

The 3rd day God created, *"dry land,"* the *"seas,"* *"grass,"* and the *"trees,"* Genesis 1:9-13.

The 4th day God created the sun, moon and stars, Gen. 1:14-19.

The 5th day God said, *"Let the water teem with living creatures."*

On the 6th day, God created the *"animals,"* and *"God created man in His own image…male and female He created them,"* Genesis 1:24-27.

God created the world by speaking it into existence. So too, the world will end when God speaks it out of existence!

Prayer: Creator God, we thank and praise You, our God in Trinity. You created and now continue to hold the world completely in Your almighty hand. May we always worship You, the Creator, more than any created thing. In Christ's name we pray. Amen.

October 2

"The LORD God formed the man from the dust of the ground and breathed into his nostrils the breath of life, and the man became a living being." Genesis 2:7

What is every person made of?

We see in our text that man was made of two parts in creation, and two parts we are yet today. The *"dust"* was the physical part of our bodies. The *"breath of life"* was the soul/spiritual part. Thus, we all have a physical nature, and we all have a spiritual nature. From this teaching that man is made of two parts, we get the word - dichotomy. Some people say that we are made of three parts, trichotomy. This ploy of Satan splits the soul and the spirit as being two separate entities. This belief is what psychology clings to for existence. Their implication is that the physical part of us is the doctor's responsibility. Our spirit is the church's responsibility. Our soul is the responsibility of the psychologist. Be aware, this is another religion!

We are made of two parts in the book of Ecclesiastes. At death, the two parts of man: body and spirit, separate. *"Then the dust will return to the earth as it was, and the spirit will return to God who gave it,"* Ecclesiastes 12:7 NKJV. Our physical bodies go back to what they were originally made of: dust. God told Adam this would happen as a consequence of his sin. *"By the sweat of your brow you will eat your food until you return to the ground, since from it you were taken; for dust you are and to dust you will return,"* Genesis 3:19. Our physical bodies will return to dust.

One advantage man has is that we know we will die. Yet some live as if they will never die. Some even try to stop their appointment with death, but all have failed. *"What man can live and not see death, or save himself from the power of the grave?"* Psalm 89:48. *"Altogether Methuselah lived 969 years, and <u>then he died</u>,"* Genesis 5:27.

Prayer: Holy and eternal Lord may the two words *"he died,"* ring in our ears. Even though Methuselah lived for 969 years, *"then he died."* So too, we must also die. May we be properly prepared for our time of death! Bless our study of eternity so that we can live in the light of eternity. In Christ's name we pray. Amen.

October 3

"Blessed is the one who reads the words of this prophesy, and blessed are those who hear it and take to heart what is written in it, because the time is near." Revelation 1:3

"Because the time is near"

Do we hear the clock ticking? The time passes by; Tick, tick, tick, is the pulse of eternity beating. The clock is racing to our death! Yes racing, very fast! Time is that dash on a tombstone. We read William, born April 2, 1998 – died May 5, 2018. Who was the young man who lived just 20 years? Like many others, we focus on the dates, but the dash that is in between is what was important! How is our own "dash" through life doing? Someday, many will ask how did we die. But how did we live, is the question that will echo in all eternity!

The Bible gives us many warnings concerning the subject of time. One of the most popular is: *"Remember your Creator in the days of your youth, before the days of trouble come and the years approach when you will say, 'I find no pleasure in them,'"* Ecclesiastes 12:1. The author knew that a young person has a lot of energy. The verse encourages the young person to use that energy in the light of eternity. Are we? Tick, tick, tick, the footsteps of death are pursuing us. We cannot pull away from the sound.

Ask a young person about the passing of time and they will often say, "I have the rest of my life to get serious." If you think like that, then visit a cemetery. There are young people buried there, many who thought they had more time! Hell is filled with people who hoped to one day use their time for God. Many intended to come to Christ at a later date. But then their "dash" through life was over. Remember that God has set our time here. *"From one man He made every nation of men, that they should inhabit the whole earth; and He determined the times set for them and the exact places where they should live,"* Acts 17:26. Are we using our *"times"* to seek God and live for Him?

Prayer: Beautiful Savior help us! We waste so much of Your precious time. May we not rest until we find our rest in You. Lord, create in us new hearts that see time as a temporary gift from You! May we always remember You, *"before the silver cord is severed."* In Christ's name we pray. Amen.

October 4

"The LORD God took the man and put him in the Garden of Eden to work it and take care of it. And the LORD God commanded the man, 'You are free to eat from any tree in the garden; but you must not eat from the tree of the knowledge of good and evil, for when you eat of it you will surely die.'" Genesis 2:15-17

Why must we all die?

God gave one single command to the yet perfect man, *"You must not eat from the tree of the knowledge of good and evil."* God warned man that he would die if he was not obedient. Man disobeyed. Man died. The one simple command made the offense all the greater. The man and woman sinned by doing what God forbade. Adam was our representative. *"Therefore, just as sin entered the world through one man, and death through sin, and in this way death came to all men, because all sinned,"* Romans 5:12. The fact that we are all born sinners is the doctrine of "Total Depravity." Look around, what do we see? Do we need to teach a child to sin? No, the sin gene is already in them. God said if man sinned he would *"surely die."* We're dying.

It is important to believe in the truth that we are a born sinner, for just *"as in Adam all die, so in Christ all will be made alive,"* 1 Corinthians 15:22. If we refuse to believe that Adam was our representative in giving us sin, how can we believe that Christ is our representative to take our sin away? Not only did all of us inherit the sinful nature of Adam, but also, we all have our own sins we commit every day. *"As it is written: 'There is no one righteous, not even one; there is no one who understands, no one who seeks God. All have turned away, they have together become worthless; there is no one who does good, not even one,'"* Romans 3:10-12. We are all children of Adam, born to die. In Christ, we are reborn to live.

Prayer: Just and perfect Lord, we understand that we all have an appointment with death that we will all keep, right on time. And Lord, You give us this "limited resource" called time. You tell us that *"man is destined to die once, and after that to face judgment,"* Hebrews 9:27. We have already wasted too much time, Your time. Lord, have mercy on us! Forgive us, Lord. May we live for You and for Your kingdom that will never pass away. In Christ Jesus' name we pray. Amen.

October 5

"There Abraham and his wife Sarah were buried, there Isaac and his wife Rebekah were buried, and there I buried Leah." Genesis 49:31

Should we bury or burn?

Burial plots are filling-up. What should we do? Look to the Bible, to see what God says! There are many references of God's people who died, and then, they *"were buried."* Burial is the respectful way to deal with the dead. We do not discard a body like non-human rubbish. We bury it with solemn ceremony. Jacob said, *"There Abraham and his wife Sarah were buried, there Isaac and his wife Rebekah were buried, and there I buried Leah,"* Genesis 49:31.

Even though a body returns to dust, we do not bury dust. A body is being buried. We view that body in the coffin. We take that body to the cemetery. We pray and meditate on how that body will someday be raised. We lower a body into the ground. With respect, a good-by is said to a body. We thank God for what that somebody meant to us.

Scripture rejects the pagan thought that a human is merely a soul that exists in the body for a little while. They do not understand. A body is coming back out of that grave! In fact, *"the dead in Christ will rise first,"* 1 Thessalonians 4:16b. This rising is a dead body, not a soul. The Scriptures teach about body-sleep, not soul-sleep! A sleeping body is put in bed, thus burial in a grave. Just as Jesus' body was put in a grave and then came out, so too, a Christian's body must be put in a grave and will come out again in the resurrection.

Cremation surely lacks the hope of our resurrection. In the Bible, the few references to bodies being burned is one of judgment. *"If a priest's daughter defiles herself by becoming a prostitute, she disgraces her father; she must be burned in the fire,"* Leviticus 21:9. Another example is Leviticus 20:14.

Prayer: Wise and good Lord, we thank You for giving us events of how You *"buried"* Your Son and the saints. How we need to see Your will, to live Your way. We thank You that like Christ, our bodies will come out of the ground again and live forever. What hope we have! United to Christ, we are buried in His "resurrection garden." In His name we pray. Amen.

October 6

"So it was that the beggar died, and was carried by the angels to Abraham's bosom. The rich man also died and was buried. And being in the torments in Hades, he lifted up his eyes and saw Abraham afar off, and Lazarus in his bosom." Luke 16:22-23

Where do our souls go at death?

The poor beggar died first. He was a Christian, made to enjoy God forever. The words he *"was carried by the angels to Abraham's bosom,"* show us that his soul was immediately in Heaven. The soul of the unbelieving rich man, went immediately to Hades or Hell. We can see that when it comes to man's spirit or soul, death is either a friend or a foe. When we die, "in the Lord," covered by Christ's blood, like "Lazarus," our spirits will immediately go to Heaven to be with our God.

Consider also, the two thieves who were crucified with Jesus. *"One of the criminals who hung there hurled insults at Him,"* Luke 23:39a. The other criminal rebuked his partner in crime saying, *"We are punished justly, for we are getting what our deeds deserve. But this man has done nothing wrong,"* Luke 23:41. The repentant criminal said, *"Jesus, remember me when You come into Your kingdom,"* Luke 23:42. Jesus said to the repentant thief, *"I tell you the truth, today you will be with Me in paradise,"* Luke 23:43. This great sinner was saved in practically his last breath. He uttered a prayer of confession, acknowledged Christ as Lord, and believed in His coming kingdom. That is true faith.

Jesus' own Jewish people, especially the leaders, rejected Him! Yet this great sinning thief was preferred over them, for all eternity. Like the spirits of the two thieves on the cross, our spirits will never sleep but will live on eternally. The only question is: Where will our spirits be, in Heaven or in Hell?

Prayer: Father in Heaven, it is a blessing that our physical death stops our pattern of sin, pain, and misery. We thank You for giving us souls that live and immediately return to You. We thank You that Jesus assured His sheep, *"I give them eternal life, and they shall never perish; neither shall anyone snatch them out of My hand,"* John 10:28 NKJV. In Jesus' beautiful name we pray. Amen.

October 7

"You will not surely die." Genesis 3:4a

Reincarnation is a lie

Our text is one of the three lies Satan told Eve in the Garden of Eden. This lie has been popular ever since! The Eastern religions almost all believe in a form of reincarnation. Hinduism and Buddhism teach the concept of karma, which means a work or action. According to karma every action has an inevitable consequence that requires either a reward or punishment in a cycle of rebirth. If we were "good" in this life, the next life will be better. But then, they do not accept God's standard of "good." How then would anyone know if they got it right? Who would remember all this in the next life, where they could be either as a fly or as a priest?

Belief in reincarnation denies everything Jesus did on the Cross. Jesus frees us from the curse of the law. He takes our penalty and pays our price for redemption. God is satisfied with this sacrifice, and we are now "good to go," no longer under the wrath of God. Our debt is forgiven by Christ.

Reincarnation denies one death and then one judgment. For, "*It is appointed for men to die once, but after this the judgment,*" Hebrews 9:27 NKJV. The word "*once*" and the word "*the*" do not allow for us coming back to this world again, or for being judged again later.

Perhaps some think that they can escape the reality of Hell if they believe in reincarnation. Sad to say, those who believe in reincarnation will find out the truth too late. We can only hope and pray that God opens their hearts to the truth that we only live and are judged once. May those who believe in reincarnation, see that the tragedy is not in dying! It is in dying without the Lord. There is an eternity of something better than this life, if God is our Father!

Prayer: Lord, we see this lie of Satan, "*you will not surely die.*" We weep and pray for those who believe it and are lost forever. We who do believe, thank You that we will die, and only need to live in this sinful body once. We praise You that "in Christ," we are Yours already today! May our beloved Lord and Savior who lived and died once, be praised for coming to save us from eternal death. In His name we pray. Amen.

October 8

*"Instead, they were longing for a better country — a Heavenly one.
Therefore God is not ashamed to be called their God, for He has
prepared a city for them."* Hebrews 11:16

There are many names for Heaven

I am writing this because in India as a missionary, I was surprised to
find that there are so many people who think that "Paradise" and
"Heaven" are two different places. Some believe that when we die
we go to "Paradise." Then, after the resurrection and final judgment,
the soul finally goes to Heaven. But when we search the Scriptures, we
see more than one word for Heaven. For example, we say someone is
"with the Lord," or "promoted to glory," or is now, "with the angels," "in
Paradise" or "in Heaven." These are all the same place. The Heaven
that exists now is of course different from the "New Heavens" that will
be created after the resurrection. Examine the book of Revelation and
we see how Jesus is presently in Heaven with the souls of Christians
who have died.

In the following Scriptures, "Paradise" and "Heaven" are indeed
the same place. In 2 Corinthians 12:2, "A man (Paul) in Christ... was
caught up to the third Heaven." Again, in verse 4, the same man "was
caught up to Paradise." Hebrews 4 also uses the same kind of language when it talks of Jesus *"passing through the Heavens."* The first
Heaven is in the clouds. The second Heaven is the sun, moon, and stars.
The third Heaven is with the Lord, or where Paradise is.

In our text, God uses words in the present tense and past tense
about a current Heaven, and those who are presently there. *"Instead,
they were longing for a better country — a Heavenly one. Therefore God
is not ashamed to be called their God, for He has prepared a city for
them,"* Hebrews 11:16. Paradise and Heaven are two names for the
same place where believers presently go when they die.

Prayer: Lord, we see the lie of the devil to try convince us that Heaven
and Hell are not immediate, so we will not be so concerned about our
souls. We praise You that when we die in Christ, we will immediately
be with You in Heaven. In Christ's name we pray. Amen.

October 9

"If his sons are honored, he does not know it; if they are brought low, he does not see it." Job 14:21

Can the dead see the living?

Often when someone gives a great performance in sports, music, or in life, they hope a deceased mother or father can see and understand. But can the dead really hear or see what is happening on Earth? The information in the Bible is what is true, not our hopes or imaginations! Job tells us what happens after someone dies: *"If his sons are honored, he does not know it; if they are brought low, he does not see it."* Job was convinced that someone who died will no longer see what is happening on earth. God also tells us that in Heaven: *"The Sovereign LORD will wipe away the tears from all faces; He will remove the disgrace of His people from all the earth,"* Isaiah 25:8b. If God takes our tears away in Heaven, then how can we see the *"disgrace"* of anyone on earth?

In the story of the Rich Man and Lazarus, neither of these men were able to address each other directly from Heaven or from Hell. Neither were they allowed to communicate with anyone on earth. Solomon also wrote, *"In the grave where you are going, there is neither working nor planning nor knowledge nor wisdom,"* Ecclesiastes 9:10.

Why then are some praying to Mother Mary and other deceased saints? Can they hear? Can they see who is praying to them? The Bible says, *"There is one God and one Mediator between God and men, the Man Christ Jesus,"* 1 Timothy 2:5. Jesus said, *"I am the Way and the Truth and the Life. No one comes to the Father except through Me,"* John 14:6. Even Peter (whom many wrongly see as the first pope) said, *"All the prophets testify about Him that everyone who believes in Him receives forgiveness of sins through His name,"* Acts 10:43. Our God, Father, Son and Spirit alone see us! May we live for Him and for His approval!

Prayer: Almighty Lord, we praise You for giving us Your Word so that we can think and act Biblically. We thank You for giving us One Way, our Mediator, Jesus. We look forward to being with You and with our loved ones someday, who are already with You. Together, we will praise You for all eternity. In Jesus' name we pray. Amen.

October 10

"'I am the God of Abraham, the God of Isaac, and the God of Jacob.'
He is not the God of the dead but of the living." Matthew 22:32

Our soul never goes out of existence

In the words of our text, the words *"I am"* are in the present tense. To make sure that we understand this, Jesus also adds, God *"is* (present tense) *not the God of the dead but of the living."* Jesus assured Martha and us too, about what would happen to those who lived and believed in Him. *"Whoever lives and believes in Me will never die,"* John 11:26a. Our soul does not go out of existence, not even for a second!

God also said to Moses, *"I am the God of... Abraham, the God of Isaac, and the God of Jacob,"* Exodus 3:6. In Hebrews 11, the heroes of the faith *"were longing for a better country — a Heavenly one. There-fore God is not ashamed* (present tense) *to be called their God, for He has prepared* (already done) *a city for them,"* Hebrews 11:16. Keep in mind that all those presently in Heaven are there in soul form and are not yet fully glorified. All who are presently in Heaven will receive new glorified bodies at the end of this present world.

Spurgeon tells a great story of a man who was an agnostic - a belief that there is no Heaven, because God doesn't exist. Spurgeon asked him, "The word 'agnostic' is a Greek word, is it not?" The man said, "It is." Spurgeon then asked him if he knew that the Latin word for agnostic was, "ignoramus." How fitting when God can be known just from looking at His creation. Many will say that we can know nothing for sure about God or the future, and then glory in such ignorance. Make no mistake, salvation is by faith. Damnation comes by doubt or unbelief every time!

There are so many who do not believe in Jesus and a real life with Him forever. Is their real problem that some sin is strongly attached to them? May we all live in the light of eternity, and like the prophets, lovingly call unbelievers to repentance!

Prayer: Saving Lord, help us to give hope and direction to those who are without the hope of Heaven. May we all see our sins and repent, trusting in the blood of the Lamb who alone saves us from Your righ-teous wrath. In Christ's name we pray. Amen.

October 11

"Man is destined to die once, and after that to face judgment."
Hebrews 9:27

The doctrine of Purgatory

The Catholic Church by the Council of Trent, declared the doctrine of Purgatory into existence saying: "There is a Purgatory, and souls there detained are helped by the prayers of the faithful, and especially by the acceptable Sacrifice of the Altar." And, "This holy council commands all bishops diligently to endeavor that the wholesome doctrine concerning Purgatory be believed, held, taught and everywhere preached by Christ's faithful," (Session XXV).

The Church of Rome still officially believes Purgatory is the place where the souls of deceased "church members" go to suffer, in order to purify them. The length of time in Purgatory depends on the amount of their bad deeds on earth, and on the prayers and gifts of the saints on their behalf. The pope has the ability to shorten someone's stay in Purgatory or cause a person to escape it. This doctrine of Purgatory built quite a few Catholic shrines, but certainly not God's kingdom. The problem with believing in Purgatory is that the Bible doesn't agree.

First, salvation is by grace, through faith in Christ alone, not by man's works, (Ephesians 2:8-9). If man could gain Heaven by his works, (before or after death,) then the work of Christ on the cross was not necessary. Christ *"appeared once for all at the end of the ages to do away with sin by the sacrifice of Himself,"* Hebrews 9:26b.

Second, *"Man is destined to die once, and after that to face judgment"* Hebrews 9:27.

Third, because of Christ's blood, believers are *"without stain or wrinkle or any other blemish, but holy and blameless,"* Ephesians. 5:27b.

Fourth, the wicked Rich Man and the good beggar Lazarus, the "Rich Man" was immediately *"in Hell, where he was in torment,"* from which there was no escape, Luke 16:23, 26. Believing we get another chance is Satan's lie. Purgatory is a false hope and a false doctrine.

Prayer: Lord, thank You that even the thief on the cross who perhaps never did a good work in his life, was with You immediately after death, because he had faith in Jesus. Our Lord Jesus Christ is our only hope also. In His name we pray. Amen.

October 12

"Now we see but a poor reflection as in a mirror; then we shall see face to face. Now I know in part; then I shall know fully, even as I am fully known. And now these three remain: faith, hope and love. But the greatest of these is love." 1 Corinthians 13:12-13

Will we recognize others in Heaven?

The worship of the Father, Son, and Holy Spirit will be our number one joy in Heaven. We will also have joyful reunions with our loved ones too. We will recognize Biblical characters we have never seen before. A number of verses show this fact: *"We know that the One who raised the Lord Jesus from the dead will also raise us with Jesus and present us with you in His presence,"* 2 Corinthians 4:14.

David said to his servants after his child died, *"But now that he is dead, why should I fast? Can I bring him back again? I will go to him, but he will not return to me,"* 2 Samuel 12:23. David looked forward to seeing his little son again. In Luke 16, the rich man recognizes Lazarus and Abraham. He had never seen Abraham before. In Matthew 17:3, Peter, James, and John recognize Elijah and Moses. The disciples had never seen them before!

Paul said, *"For what is our hope, our joy, or the crown in which we will glory in the presence of the Lord Jesus when He comes? Is it not you?"* 1 Thessalonians 2:19. Paul was looking forward to being with those he had ministered to! *"Now we see but a poor reflection as in a mirror; then we shall see face to face. Now I know in part; then I shall know fully, even as I am fully known. And now these three remain: faith, hope and love. But the greatest of these is love,"* 1 Corinthians 13:12-13. If there is love in Heaven, we will recognize one another, the objects of our love. We know that we *"will neither marry nor be given in marriage,"* Matthew 22:30b. But that is because there is no need of procreation in Heaven since we will never die. But we will still recognize one another in Heaven.

Prayer: O great God of relationships, we know Heaven is wonderful beyond description. We thank You that not only will we see You in all Your glory, but others in all their glory also. For You said, *"I am the God of Abraham, the God of Isaac, and the God of Jacob."* In Christ's beautiful name we pray. Amen.

October 13

"Jesus said to them, 'I tell you the truth, at the renewal of all things, when the Son of Man sits on His glorious throne, you who have followed Me will also sit on twelve thrones, judging the twelve tribes of Israel. And everyone who has left houses or brothers or sisters or father or mother or children or fields for My sake will receive a hundred times as much and will inherit eternal life.'" Matthew 19:28-29

Are there degrees of glory in Heaven?

All saints will be in Heaven by the grace of God alone. We will glorify and enjoy Him forever. Yet still, the Bible shows there are degrees of glory and responsibility in Heaven. "*A certain nobleman* (Jesus) *went into a far country* (the earth) *to receive for himself a kingdom and to return. So he called ten of his servants* (us), *delivered to them ten minas* (a responsibility to be faithful and serve the Master), *and said to them, 'Do business until I come.'*" "*When the Master returned, the first servant said,* (before Jesus in judgment) '*Master, your mina has earned ten minas.'*" The Master said, "<u>Well done, good servant; because you were faithful in a very little, have authority over ten cities.</u>" The next servant's mina "*earned five minas,*" and the Master said, "<u>You also be over five cities.</u>" "*And another came, saying 'Master, here is your mina, which I have kept put away in a handkerchief.'*" The Master said to him, '*You wicked servant*' and the Master took away the one mina and said, "*give it to him who has ten minas,*" Luke 19:12-24 NKJV.

There are reasons for degrees of glory in Heaven. First, the grace of God gives different gifts/abilities to people. Who can argue about that? Secondly, man's demonstrated faithfulness is rewarded by God in Luke 19, and again in the Matthew 25 parable. If any doubt this, then answer a few questions. Are all angels in Heaven plain angels, or are some archangels? In Revelation 4:4, "*Surrounding the throne were twenty-four other thrones, and seated on them were twenty-four elders.*" Faith is rewarded. "*Some were tortured, refusing to accept release, so that they might rise again to a better life.*" Hebrews 11:35, ESV.

Prayer: Lord, we thank You for encouraging us to endure hardship and even disgrace now, for Your name. Lord, we deserve death and You so lovingly give us abundant life. Lord, we praise You for Your grace. In Christ's name we pray. Amen.

October 14

"They will throw them into the fiery furnace, where there will be weep-ing and gnashing of teeth." Matthew 13:42

Is Hell a real place?

If Hell were not real, then why was it necessary for Jesus Christ to come to earth, to save us from the wrath of God? Jesus came partly because we were all condemned to Hell. In fact, *"whoever does not believe stands condemned already,"* John 3:18b. Jesus placed Himself on the Cross so that we could escape an eternity in Hell. If God the Father did not spare Jesus the real agonies of Hell, how can we think that God will spare sinners from a real Hell? If Hell were not real, why did Christ cry, *"Eloi, Eloi, lama, sabachthani"?* (My God, My god, why has thou forsaken Me). Hell, fulfills the demands for God's holy justice.

Sheol is the Hebrew Old Testament word for Hell. Hades is the Greek New Testament word. Both words describe the present place of destruction for those who die apart from Christ. After the resurrection, there will be a New Heaven and New Earth created for believers. Gehenna will be the new Hell where unbelievers spend eternity.

Hell, then is the final place where God sends the wicked, in both body and soul, for all eternity. People are not destroyed in Hell. No, it's a place of eternal suffering and punishment. Hell is being com-pletely separated from the love of God. Yet still, Hell is the very presence of God, <u>in all of His wrath eternally</u>. The Bible describes Hell as: *"Unquenchable fire"* - Matthew 3:12; *"Outer darkness"* - Matthew 8:12 NKJV; *"The furnace of fire"* - Matthew 13:42 NKJV; *"Everlasting punishment"* - Matthew 25:46 NKJV; *"Their worm never dies"* - Mark 9:48 NKJV; *"Weeping and gnashing of teeth"* - Matthew 8:12; and *"Tormented day and night forever and ever"*- Revelation 20:10. Hell is very real!

Prayer: Loving Father in Heaven, when we study the doctrine of Hell, we can only praise You for sparing us through the blood of Your Son. Lord, it is quite something to meditate on how Christ saves us from Your eternal wrath! Forgive us for failing to proclaim the bad news of Hell to those who are perishing. We pray that our families and friends are not deceived about the reality of Hell. In Christ's name we pray. Amen.

October 15

"How much more severely do you think a man deserves to be punished who has trampled the Son of God under foot, who has treated as an unholy thing the blood of the covenant that sanctified him?"
Hebrews 10:29

Are there degrees of suffering in Hell?

The Bible indicates there will be degrees of suffering in Hell. Granted, all those in Hell will be there because they did not respond to God's provision of Christ's sacrificial blood for their sins. Nevertheless, our text shows some will be punished more than others. Those punished the most will be those who were brought up in the covenant (in the church), but still rejected the Gospel. According to Leviticus 26:28, they will be punished *"seven times more."* Our text shows why.

There are other verses that indicate degrees of punishment in Hell. *"That servant who knows his master's will and does not get ready or does not do what his master wants will be beaten with many blows. But the one who does not know and does things deserving punishment will be beaten with few blows,"* Luke 12:47-48. The underlined words are clear.

Jesus, in all seriousness, condemns certain cities more. *"Then Jesus began to denounce the cities in which most of His miracles had been performed, because they did not repent. Woe to you, Korazin! Woe to you, Bethsaida! If the miracles that were performed in you had been performed in Tyre and Sidon, they would have repented long ago in sackcloth and ashes. But I tell you, it will be more bearable for Tyre and Sidon on the Day of Judgment than for you. And you, Capernaum, will you be lifted up to the skies? No, you will go down to the depths* (This is the lower parts of Hell). *If the miracles that were performed in you had been performed in Sodom, it would have remained to this day. But I tell you that it will be more bearable for Sodom* (a most wicked city) *on the Day of Judgment than for you,"* Matthew 11:20-24.

Prayer: Holy and just Lord, may we hear Your Word and repent today! Lord, may the truth of Your coming judgment provoke holiness in all of us. Help those who think little of the degrees in Hell, not to be lukewarm to the Gospel. Have mercy on them, Lord. In Jesus' name we pray. Amen.

October 16

"And I say to you that many will come from east and west, and sit down with Abraham, Isaac, and Jacob in the kingdom of Heaven. But the sons of the kingdom will be cast out into outer darkness. There will be weeping and gnashing of teeth." Matthew 8:11-12

Will God punish the pagans more?

A heathen or pagan is usually described as someone who has never heard the Gospel. So then, God will not punish the pagans more. The hottest fires in Hell are reserved for those who have heard the Gospel. In the context of our text, a Gentile centurion came to Jesus and believed, exercising a greater faith than found in Israel. Jesus then said, *"The sons of the kingdom will be cast out into outer darkness. There will be weeping and gnashing of teeth."* Jesus was speaking about covenant Israel. Not just darkness, but, *"outer darkness."* "The sons of the kingdom," are "covenant breakers." In plain language, that is our sons and daughters who are going to church but do not repent and follow Christ. They will be judged far more severely. Why? Because they had the privilege of hearing and seeing the Gospel first hand, and still rejected it. O how we must pray!

God showed a burning bush to Moses, representing His holiness. God did not show this bush to the Egyptians! Moses had to take off his shoes and give respectful worship. If we and our covenant youth think lightly of God's holiness, we will also think lightly of the cross, lightly about lost souls, and lightly of the Savior who delivers us from Hell. In Revelation 3:15 Jesus said, *"I know your deeds, that you are neither cold nor hot. I wish you were either one or the other!"* Because they were lukewarm, Jesus would spit them out of His mouth. If God condemns the pagans to an eternal Hell for not seeing Him in creation, (Romans 1:18-21), then how much more will He condemn those who have been more clearly shown the Creator?

Prayer: Just and holy God, again and again You warn us who have been brought up in the church, to get serious about our faith. In Hebrews 3:12, You warn us, *"See to it, brothers, that none of you has a sinful, unbelieving heart that turns away from the living God."* Lord, help us to see that our time is so short! Turn us to Yourself, we pray! In Jesus' name, hear our prayer. Amen.

October 17

"As Jesus was sitting on the Mount of Olives, the disciples came to Him privately. 'Tell us,' they said, 'when will this happen, and what will be the sign of Your coming and of the end of the age?'" Matthew 24:3

The end of the Jewish Age

Jesus told His disciples that the temple would come down. *"I tell you the truth, not one stone here will be left on another; everyone will be thrown down,"* Matthew 24:2b. Jesus' disciples then asked for a sign. They did not understand that the end of our world and their temple falling (the end the Jewish Age), were not the same thing. Jesus' answer goes on for two chapters. Luke records this same discussion. Jesus tells His disciples, *"The end will not come right way,"* Luke 21:9b. The Jewish Age extends for 35 more years, until Nero.

Then Jesus also discusses some of the signs for the end of the world. *"Then He said to them: 'Nation will rise against nation, and kingdom against kingdom. There will be great earthquakes, famines and pestilences in various places, and fearful events and great signs from Heaven,'"* Luke 21:10-11. Then once again, Jesus comes back to the present generation by saying in verse 12, *"but before all this, they will lay hands on you ..."* and in verse 20, *"when you see Jerusalem being surrounded by armies..."* He is talking to them personally. The sign they asked for is in verse 25, *"There will be signs in the sun, moon and stars. On the earth, nations will be in anguish..."* And the final sign, *"At that time they will see the Son of Man coming in a cloud with power and great glory,"* Luke 21:27.

These were not all signs for the end of the world as many claim. Jesus was also speaking of the end of the Jewish Age. In verse 32, Jesus said, *"I tell you the truth, this generation will certainly not pass away until all these things have happened."* Some of these people were alive when the Jewish Age ended with destruction of Jerusalem, in 70 AD.

Prayer: Lord, you tell us that the end of the world is coming. We see that the Christians at the end of the Jewish Age faced great tribulation and strong persecution. You said in John16:33 that *"in the world you will have tribulation."* May we be found faithful to the end! In Christ's name we pray. Amen.

October 18

"And I saw an angel coming down out of Heaven, having the key to the Abyss and holding in his hand a great chain. He seized the dragon, that ancient serpent, who is the devil, or Satan, and bound him for a thousand years. He threw him into the Abyss, and locked and sealed it over him, to keep him from deceiving the nations anymore until the thousand years were ended. After that, he must be set free for a short time." Revelation 20:1-3

Satan, bound for 1000 years

God's timetable for the end of the world continues. Satan was bound just before the end of the Jewish Age in 70 AD and continues to be yet today. That is true because many are still coming to Christ. Remember, Satan was bound so the Gospel could go out to the Gentiles. The words 1000 years are figurative. With Satan bound for about 2000 years now, the Gospel continues to go out to the Gentiles.

We first see evidence of Satan being bound when the *"seventy-two returned with joy, saying, 'Lord, even the demons submit to us in Your name,'"* Luke 10:17. Evidently, before that, they were not bound. Something big had happened! Jesus' response to them was, *"I saw Satan fall like lightning from Heaven,"* Luke 10:18b. Jesus also reveals in our text that Satan was bound.

The Angel in our text is likely Christ Himself binding Satan. Who else is stronger than Satan? Satan will be bound until the Angel, who is Christ releases him. Why? Christ alone has the key to Satan's chains. Plus, Satan is in a pit with a seal on it that no one can break! This means the Church will have a 1000-year reign of prosperity, before the great trials come. To understand this 1000-year binding of Satan, we also need to understand the 1000-year reign of Christ (also figurative) in tomorrow's message. With Satan bound for a 1000 years, the Gospel goes out for a 1000 years! Now is the time to tell others about the Gospel.

Prayer: Lord, we can see that Satan will soon be let loose here on earth. Then it will become very difficult to be a Christian. When we look at these things we can see Your wisdom in saying, *"Today is the day of salvation."* May we flee to Christ before it is too late! May we be ready to stand firm to the end! In Jesus' name we pray. Amen.

October 19

"I saw thrones on which were seated those who had been given
authority to judge. And I saw the souls of those... they came to life
and reigned with Christ a thousand years." "When the thousand years
are over, Satan will be released from his prison."
Revelation 20:4 & 7

Saints reign with Christ for 1000 years

The 1000-year reign of Christ, also called "the Millennium," began with Christ's birth and extends to His second coming. In the last 3.5 years of the millennium there will be extreme persecution when Satan is let loose. After this, the souls of all the saints in Heaven will appear with Christ on the clouds for the resurrection/rapture. The bodies and the souls are re-united in preparation for The Judgment. This 1000-year reign of Christ (figurative) has also been called, "The Church Age" for 2000 years.

During this 1000-year reign of Christ, John sees the *"souls"* of those who have died and are now reigning with Christ in Heaven. There will not be souls and bodies united together in Heaven until after the resurrection, and the final judgment. The book of Revelation gives pictures of the saints (souls only) that are before the throne, praising God and the Lamb. Ever since God created the angels, as ministering spirits, they too worship God without bodies.

The 1000-year period in our text ends the Gospel Age on earth. This same 1000-year binding of Satan prevents him from stopping the Gospel. God promised Abraham that his descendants would be both Jews and Gentiles. After the 1000-year reign of Christ in Heaven, things radically change. A 3.5-year tribulation period burst forth.

Some people put the rapture of believers before the tribulation. If that's true, can tell those I teach, "You do not need to get serious with God now, because if Christ comes you still have 3.5 years"? Today is the day of salvation because tomorrow may be to late.

Before Satan is let loose for 3.5 years, two other events must happen. The Gospel must be preached to all the nations, and there must also be a great apostasy in the Church, which we will look at next.

Prayer: Lord, we praise You for binding Satan so we can come to You! Make us strong in You, Lord, for the difficult times that are coming. In Jesus' name we pray. Amen.

October 20

"And this Gospel of the kingdom will be preached in the whole world as a testimony to all nations, and then the end will come."
Matthew 24:14

The Gospel is preached in all the earth

One event that must happen before the end of the world is that the balance of the Jews must come into the Church. Even though the Jewish age ended in 70 A.D., still a few branches will be added to complete the number. *"Israel has experienced a hardening <u>in part</u> until the full number of the Gentiles has come in,"* Romans 11:25b. We read that Jesus commanded the angel, *"Do not harm the land or the sea or the trees until we put a seal on the foreheads of the servants of our God. Then I heard the number of those who were sealed: 144,000 from all the tribes of Israel,"* Revelation 7:3-4.

Secondly, we now turn to the completing of the Gentiles. *"After this I looked and there before me was a great multitude that no one could count, from every nation, tribe, people and language,"* Revelation 7:9a. The rest of Revelation 7 shows how the saints will get through the Tribulation, and not be taken out until the end of that time.

Earlier in the Great Commission, Jesus said the whole world must receive the Gospel or have a chance to reject it. The world will surely exist until the very last of God's elect comes into the fold. There will be famines, signified by the black horse in Revelation 6:5-6. There will be pestilences, signified by the pale horse in Revelation 6:7-8. There will be earthquakes, as God said He would, *"shake the wicked out of it,"* Job 38:13b. However, the Gospel must and will go forth, and the gates of Hell will not prevail against it!

Prayer: O Lord who preserves us, may we be faithful in giving Your message to a lost world. Thank You for warning us that it will not be easy to be faithful in the end. Yet, even now, *"we are receiving a kingdom that cannot be shaken, let us be thankful, and so worship God acceptably with reverence and awe, for our God is a consuming fire,"* Hebrews 12:28-29. Lord, we thank You for protecting us for Your Heavenly kingdom. In Christ's name we pray. Amen.

October 21

*"Just as it was in the days of Noah, so also will it be
in the days of the Son of Man."* Luke 17:26

A Great Apostasy comes

There was a big falling away (apostasy) in Noah's time, and then a flood came. *"It was the same in the days of Lot. People were eating and drinking, buying and selling, planting and building. But the day Lot left Sodom, fire and sulfur rained down from Heaven and destroyed them all. It will be just like this on the day the Son of Man is revealed,"* Luke 17:28-30. The end of the world will be "just like this." People were carrying on business as usual. Little care for spiritual things prevailed, which is an apostasy.

There was also a great falling away before Christ was born. There was another falling away at the end of the Jewish Age. The final falling away near the end our present Gentile/Gospel Age will allow the Antichrist to slide into position. It will get really ugly at the end, not better.

"The coming of the lawless one will be in accordance with the work of Satan displayed in all kinds of counterfeit miracles, signs and wonders, and in every sort of evil that deceives those who are perishing. They perish because they refused to love the truth and so be saved," 2 Thessalonians 2:9-10. The falling for a counterfeit religion is happening now! False shepherds are leading many astray through pretend miracles and pretend holiness! *"For false Christs and false prophets will appear and perform great signs and miracles to deceive even the elect-if that were possible,"* Matthew 24:24. Don't be fooled. Miracles and great numbers in churches do not make a true church. Notice, *"The whole world was astonished and followed the beast,"* Revelation 13:3b. Much of the evil assault will come from within the "Church." Nominal church members will find fault, grow weary, and leave. Many will persecute Christians, and think they are doing God a favor.

Prayer: Lord, You are all wise and warn us that the Gospel will not always be preached with great success or liberty. You warned us that false prophets *"will appear"* and lead many astray, setting the stage for the Antichrist. May we cling to You today, while there is still time. We worship You. In Jesus' name we pray. Amen.

October 22

"He threw him into the Abyss, and locked and sealed it over him, to keep him from deceiving the nations anymore until the thousand years were ended. After that, he must be set free for a short time."
Revelation 20:3

The Great Tribulation begins

Satan's short three and a half year season begins now, right after the 1000-year binding of Satan, and almost to the end of the 1000-year reign of the saints in Heaven. Why now? Because the number of the elect is close to complete. The Great Apostasy continues as Satan is let loose and still more fall away. These are not true believers falling, but nominal Christians, churchgoers who have been practicing religion, without Christ, without repentance. They will flee the organized Church. In their zeal to show they have no church connections, they will persecute those who do. *"A son will betray his father and mother..."*

This specific tribulation period includes the reign of the Antichrist, wars, rumors of wars, earthquakes, and global famines. We read, *"Then there will be great distress, (tribulation), unequaled from the beginning of the world until now,"* Matthew 24:21.

In Revelation 7:1, there are 4 destructive angels who are waiting to destroy and literally usher in the Great Tribulation period described here: *"The beast was given a mouth to utter proud words and blasphemies and to exercise his authority for forty-two months. He opened his mouth to blaspheme God, and to slander His name and His dwelling place and those who live in Heaven. He was given power to make war against the saints and conquer them. And he was given authority over every tribe, people, language and nation. All inhabitants of the earth will worship the beast - all whose names have not been written in the book of life belonging to the Lamb that was slain from the creation of the world. He who has an ear, let him hear,"* Revelation 13:5-9.

Prayer: Dear Lord, by Your grace alone, we hear! We worship You. Lord, we praise You that in this difficult time at the end of the world, You will not let anyone snatch a true believer from Your Almighty Hand. Your people will suffer, but we praise You for keeping our souls safe! In Jesus' name we pray. Amen.

October 23

"Don't let anyone deceive you in any way, for that day (the last day) will not come until the rebellion occurs and the man of lawlessness is revealed, the man doomed to destruction." 2 Thessalonians 2:3

What will the Antichrist look like?

Paul did not want his disciples to be nervous about the Lord's second coming. Some had spread rumors that Paul said the end was coming very soon. Here, Paul tries to calm the people down. First, he says, *"the day of the Lord"* will not come until *"the rebellion occurs."* This is the "Great Apostasy" we have been talking about that sets the stage for this next step. The Antichrist here is called *"the man of lawlessness."*

There have always been types of Antichrists down through the centuries: Hitler, Stalin, just to name a couple. They were men of lawlessness who killed millions. In this Great Tribulation, a single even more evil one will arise. He is described in our text as *"the man of lawlessness,"* more lawless than anyone before! He will hate God, hate His Son, hate you as a believer, and hate anything that has to do with law and order. When the Antichrist comes, orderly society will be on the way out. Truth and justice will now become a mockery. Democracy will surely be out, because it is based on law.

When the Antichrist comes, *"He will oppose and will exalt himself over everything that is called God or is worshiped, so that he sets himself up in God's temple, proclaiming himself to be God,"* 2 Thessalonians 2:4. He will not accept the worship of the true God, but only accept those who worship him as god.

"The coming of the lawless one will be in accordance with the work of Satan displayed in all kinds of counterfeit miracles, signs and wonders, and in every sort of evil that deceives those (unbelievers) who are perishing," 2 Thess. 2:9-10a. People are already falling for this kind of theology. It will only get worse. Today is still the day of salvation!

Prayer: Precious Lord, we know from Your Word that You will allow evil to get stronger as the end gets closer. We are grateful that You are still in control. We are comforted that the intense struggle will be over soon when *"by the breath of Your mouth,"* You forever destroy Satan and his followers. In Christ our Savior's name we pray. Amen.

October 24

"When you and your children return to the LORD your God and obey Him with all your heart and with all your soul according to everything I command you today, then the LORD your God will restore your fortunes and have compassion on you and gather you again from all the nations where He scattered you." Deuteronomy 30:2-3

Must Israel return to a world power?

After leading Israel 40 years in the wilderness, God makes a covenant with Israel. He promised them that He would scatter them among the nations if they forsook their covenant agreement. Following that event in Deuteronomy 29, our text appears.

Some people think the Jewish people must return to their homeland before the end comes. But these prophecies may have already been fulfilled before Christ came. True, all Israel must be complete, but most of Israel was complete before the destruction of Jerusalem in 70 AD. A remnant will come to Christ after that. *"Israel has experienced a hardening in part until the full number of the Gentiles has come in"* Romans 11:25b explains the remnant.

Based on our text, how can the reestablishment of Israel in 1948 be a sign of the end of the world coming? Today's Israel does not fit the conditions God gave in Deuteronomy 30:1-10. True faithfulness is required first to have God's blessings and protection. God loves Israel, but not unrepentant Israel. The present Israel is not yet repentant or Christian. *"This is what the Sovereign LORD says: On the day I cleanse you from all your sins, I will resettle your towns, and the ruins will be rebuilt,"* Ezekiel 36:33. God does not change.

Jesus said that Jerusalem would be destroyed in Luke 21:5-6. In verse 7, *"'Teacher,' they asked, 'when will these things happen? And what will be the sign that they are about to take place?'"* The answer of Jesus concerns the destruction of Jerusalem soon after Jesus' death. *"When you see Jerusalem being surrounded by armies, you will know that its destruction is near,"* Luke 21:20. This battle was about 70 AD.

Prayer: Righteous and holy Lord, we know that Your destruction of the world is coming. May we examine our hearts today to see if we are in the faith! Create in us clean hearts, so that we are ready. In Jesus' name we pray. Amen.

October 25

"We believe that Jesus died and rose again and so we believe that God will bring with Jesus those who have fallen asleep in Him. <u>According to the Lord's own word, we tell you that we who are still alive, who are left till the coming of the Lord, will certainly not precede those who have fallen asleep</u>. For the Lord Himself will come down from Heaven, with a loud command, with the voice of the archangel and with the trumpet call of God, and the dead in Christ will rise first. After that, we who are still alive and are left will be caught up together with them in the clouds to meet the Lord in the air. And so we will be with the Lord forever. Therefore encourage each other with these words." 1 Thessalonians 4:14-18

When will we be raptured?

Some Christians actually believe in two second comings. To get around saying this, they call the first coming, the "Rapture," and the second, the "Revelation." In the first Second Coming, they see Christ coming for His saints. They think believers all over the world will disappear, taken by the Lord. Then, for seven years the "left behind," in much tribulation, have another chance to find Christ. In these 7 years, they say Israel is again set-up and the Antichrist reigns. After these 7 years, they see another Second Coming when Christ returns to destroy the Antichrist and then rescues the new Christians from the 7-year period. Examine our text carefully.

The rapture in our text happens very quickly! In just one Second Coming, God brings the souls of all the Christians in Heaven, "*with Jesus,*" to be reunited with their new physical bodies. This happens just before the Christians on earth are "raptured out," not after. Our text says, those who are alive will "*not precede*" the rising of the dead. After that the souls of those "*with Jesus,*" join their new physical bodies. Christians on earth who are still alive are now "*caught up together*" (raptured) to meet up with them in the air. And then, all formerly dead believers, along with "*we who are still alive*", will be with the Lord forever. "*Forever,*" is not returning seven years later to get the rest.

Prayer: Lord, You said we are to "*encourage each other with these words.*" We're encouraged by Your faithful promises! Thank You! In Jesus' name we pray. Amen.

October 26

"The sixth angel poured out his bowl on the great river Euphrates, and its water was dried up to prepare the way for the kings from the East. Then I saw three evil spirits that looked like frogs; they came out of the mouth of the dragon, out of the mouth of the beast and out of the mouth of the false prophet. They are spirits of demons performing miraculous signs, and they go out to the kings of the whole world, to gather them for the battle on the great day of God Almighty... Then they gathered the kings together to the place that in Hebrew is called Armageddon." Revelation 16:12-14 & 16

The Battle of Armageddon

Our text describes the last scene on earth. Armageddon is called Har-Megiddo in the book of Judges. Here the Canaanite kings *"had 900 iron chariots and had cruelly opposed the Israelites for 20 years, they cried to the LORD for help,"* Judges 4:3. Israel was in hiding without any weapons. What Israel could not do to defeat the enemy, God did, in a place called "Megiddo," Judges 5:19.

The final battle of Har-Megiddo is God again destroying the real, and present enemies of His people, when all human possibilities fail. In this final battle, the Antichrist is finished! *"The Lord Jesus will overthrow with the breath of His mouth and destroy by the splendor of His coming,"* 2 Thessalonians 2:8. This last battle will not be won with tanks, planes, guns, or bombs, but by *"the breath of His mouth."* If you doubt God can do this, then read about what happened in the first battle at "Megiddo," in Judges 4-5. The Antichrist will be defeated in like manner, condemned and destroyed. Revelation 17:11 says, *"the beast"* or Antichrist is then sent to *"destruction"* NIV, or *"perdition"* NKJV.

With the Antichrist destroyed, God in the seventh bowl levels the cities and mountains and *"huge hailstones of about a hundred pounds each fell on men. And they cursed God on account of the plague of hail, because the plague was so terrible,"* Revelation 16:21b.

Prayer: Holy and most powerful Lord, how great is Your wrath against evil and evil-doers. How great is Your protection and provision for those whom are Your elect children. Truly You are Abba Father. Along with the angels in Heaven, we shout "Hallelujah!" In Christ's name we pray. Amen.

October 27

"Immediately after the distress of those days 'the sun will be darkened, and the moon will not give its light; the stars will fall from the sky, and the Heavenly bodies will be shaken.' At that time the sign of the Son of Man will appear in the sky, and all the nations of the Earth will mourn. They will see the Son of Man coming on the clouds of the sky, with power and great glory. And He will send His angels with a loud trumpet call, and they will gather His elect from the four winds, from one end of the Heavens to the other." Matthew 24:29-31

Jesus comes visibly in the clouds

This is the last visible sign before the end. Jesus *"will appear in the sky,"* *"immediately after the distress of those days."* There will not be a big gap of time in-between. First, there will be signs in the Heavens with the sun, moon and stars falling. Our Creator God put the sun, moon and stars in place by the word of His mouth. They will fall by His word once again.

"There will be signs in the sun, moon and stars. On the earth, nations will be in anguish and perplexity at the roaring and tossing of the sea. Men will faint from terror, apprehensive of what is coming on the world, for the Heavenly bodies will be shaken. At that time they will see the Son of Man coming in a cloud with power and great glory. When these things begin to take place, stand up and lift up your heads, because your redemption is drawing near," Luke 21:25-28.

You can imagine the scene that Jesus personally tells us about. Like God's flood in Noah's time (judgment), this will be visible for all in the world to see. Believers and unbelievers will see Jesus coming in the clouds. No one will miss it or be able to run from it. Are we ready? Death and the end of the world are sudden events! Hell is filled with people who had good intentions of serving God later! Seek Him to-day! We are here on earth for that purpose!

Prayer: Dear Lord, we do not know exactly when You will come, but we do know You will come and that those living will see it. Forgive us for not being concerned about these things. Forgive us for wasting so much of the precious time You give us. May we live in the light of eternity! In Christ's name we pray. Amen.

October 28

"Do not be amazed at this, for a time is coming when all who are in their graves will hear His voice and come out — those who have done good will rise to live, and those who have done evil will rise to be condemned." John 5:28-29

Two different resurrections in one day

Our text shows us that all resurrected people, are going two different places. One is bound for Heaven; the other for Hell. Interestingly, the KJV and NKJV say, *"the hour is coming."* Sense the urgency of every soul being on the brink of eternity! The one resurrection of the just and the unjust will be at the same time. This fact should clear up a lot of questions about end-times theology!

Now concerning those still living, some believe in a rapture, (which is a resurrection) for believers alone at the beginning of Satan's return to earth. Then later, there will be yet another time of "Christ's return." And then, after 1000 years, yet one more return!

Our text begs us to consider a few questions. How often did Noah's flood happen? Once. How many times was Jesus ascended to Heaven? Once. How many times will He come back? Again, once. Paul confirms this fact in our text and in the following: *"Listen, I tell you a mystery: We will not all sleep, (die before Jesus comes) but we will all be changed, in a flash, in the twinkling of an eye, at the last trumpet. For the trumpet will sound, the dead will be raised imperishable, and we will be changed,"* 1 Corinthians 15:51-52. Note the *"all."* Also, note how fast it will happen to *"all."* Paul was not in doubt about just one resurrection for all, or how quickly everyone would be changed.

Do I tell those I teach in prison, you do not need to get serious with God today, for if Jesus raptures out believers, you still have some time to repent? "No!" Do some people understand the rapture to be a type of purgatory? "Yes!" The truth is, *"We will not all sleep, but we will all be changed, in a flash, in the twinkling of an eye, at the last trumpet."*

Prayer: O Lord and Savior, You comfort believers saying we have *"an inheritance that can never perish, spoil or fade — kept in Heaven for you,"* 1 Peter 1:4b. What hope a true believer has in Christ! It is in His name that we pray. Amen.

October 29

"And I saw the dead, great and small, standing before the throne, and books were opened. Another book was opened, which is the book of life. The dead were judged <u>according to what they had done</u> as recorded in the books. The sea gave up the dead that were in it, and death and Hades gave up the dead that were in them, and each person was judged according to what he had done." Revelation 20:12-13

What will we be judged on?

We are saved by grace, through Christ alone! Make no mistake about that. <u>The Judgment is not to see who is in Christ and who is not</u>. According to Ephesians 1 and Romans 8, God knew all who were His, even before the world was made! What then is, The Judgment? In the above verses, we see that we will be judged on what was *"recorded in the books,"* our good and bad deeds. The books will be opened and played back to us. These "books" of our life are not blank pages! More proof is:

* Ecclesiastes 12:14, *"For God will bring every deed into judgment, including every hidden thing, whether it is good or evil."*

* Psalm 62:12, *"...and that You, O LORD, are loving. Surely You will reward each person according to what he has done."*

* I Corinthians 3:13, *"...his work will be shown for what it is, because the Day will bring it to light. It will be revealed with fire, and the fire will test the quality of each man's work."*

* Matthew 12:37, *"For by your words you will be acquitted, and by your words you will be condemned."*

* Matthew 16:27, *"For the Son of Man is going to come in His Father's glory with His angels, and then He will reward each person according to what he has done."*

Rev. William Hendriksen wisely asks: "In light of Bible teaching on the testing of our works in the judgment, are Protestants at times in danger of underestimating the value of good works?" I think so.

Prayer: O Lord our giver of all good gifts both now and for all eternity, we thank You for Your amazing grace in saving us and for even rewarding us for our good works. May we live each day in the light of eternity! In Jesus' name we pray. Amen.

October 30

"The day of the Lord will come like a thief. The Heavens will disappear with a roar; the elements will be destroyed by fire, and the earth and everything in it will be laid bare... But in keeping with His promise we are looking forward to a New Heaven and a New Earth, the home of righteousness." 2 Peter 3:10 & 13

The New Heaven and Earth - Part 1

Peter began this chapter in verse 4 by reminding us that people will question, *"Where is this 'coming' He promised?"* He then reasons that God not only made the world, but later also remade the world during the time of the flood. In other words, know the Scriptures and the power of God. In like manner, the *"earth... will be laid bare,"* and be made new. Peter said, *"The present heavens and earth are reserved for fire, being kept for the Day of Judgment and destruction of ungodly men,"* 2 Peter 3:7. What power God has to do as He has planned!

It appears that as the old earth goes out, and the new comes, the people will momentarily be out of a place to exist, other than in the clouds with Jesus. *"Then I saw a great white throne and Him who was seated on it. Earth and sky fled from His presence, and there was no place for them,"* Revelation 20:11.

The old is out and the new is ushered in, again, simply by the Word of the Lord. Amazing, that is exactly how the first earth came into existence. *"That day will bring about the destruction of the Heavens by fire, and the elements will melt in the heat. But in keeping with His promise we are looking forward to a New Heaven and a New Earth, the home of righteousness,"* 2 Peter 3:12-13.

Prayer: Almighty and sovereign Lord, we are in awe of Your wisdom and power to make all things new, including us. May all men know that You, the eternal God, by the word of Your mouth, will remake the Heavens and Earth once again! May we be stirred into action with evangelism and discipleship knowing that Your clock for this present world is ticking! We praise You for being, *"patient with us, not wanting anyone to perish, but everyone to come to repentance."* May we turn today so that we do not burn tomorrow. In Jesus' name we pray. Amen.

October 31

"However, as it is written: 'No eye has seen, no ear has heard, no mind has conceived what God has prepared for those who love Him.'" I Corinthians 2:9

The New Heavens and Earth - Part 2

There is a longing in every true Christian for the New Heavens and New Earth where we will be forever with the Lord. We want to know what it will be like. To get a glimpse of the New Heavens and Earth we look at the following passages:

"Then I saw a New Heaven and a New Earth, for the first Heaven and the first Earth had passed away, and there was no longer any sea. I saw the Holy City, the new Jerusalem, coming down out of Heaven from God, prepared as a bride beautifully dressed for her husband. And I heard a loud voice from the throne saying, 'Now the dwelling of God is with men, and He will live with them. They will be His people, and God Himself will be with them and be their God. He will wipe every tear from their eyes. There will be no more death or mourning or crying or pain, for the old order of things has passed away.' He who was seated on the throne said, 'I am making everything new!' Then He said, 'Write this down, for these words are trustworthy and true,'" Revelation. 21:1-5.

God also revealed something about the New Heavens and New Earth to Isaiah. *"The wolf will live with the lamb, the leopard will lie down with the goat, the calf and the lion and the yearling together and a little child will lead them,"* Isaiah 11:6.

Jesus speaks to us through John: *"Do not let your hearts be troubled. Trust in God; trust also in Me. In My Father's house are many rooms; if it were not so, I would have told you. I am going there to prepare a place for you. And if I go and prepare a place for you, I will come back and take you to be with Me that you also may be where I am. You know the Way to the place where I am going,"* John 14:1-4.

Prayer: Faithful Lord, we thank You for providing a way for us to be with You forever. How wonderful to finally be finished with sin, pain and dying. How wonderful it will also be to see You, and how You are *"making everything new."* In Jesus' name we pray. Amen.

NOVEMBER

"Therefore go and make disciples of all nations, baptizing them in the name of the Father, and of the Son and of the Holy Spirit, and teaching them to obey everything I have commanded you. And surely I am with you always, to the very end of the age." Matthew 28:19-20

November 1

"The revelation of Jesus Christ, which God gave Him to show His servants what must soon take place. He made it known by sending His angel to His servant John." Revelation 1:1

Introduction to Revelation

God gave this revelation to Christ. Then Christ, by an angel, gave it to John, who then in turn gives this to the seven churches and to us. The book of Revelation was written by God, to the seven churches in Asia. "Seven" is a perfect number, God's number, God's message to the Church everywhere, for all time. The types of problems in these seven real churches are in our churches today. The Church of Smyrna and Philadelphia were mostly faithful. Ephesus, Pergamus, and Thyatira were partly faithful and partly unfaithful. The churches of Sardis and Laodicea were unfaithful.

The word "Revelation" means the unveiling of God to men. Jesus gives John and us also, a vision of what will soon take place in The Judgment for all people. Jesus gives encouragement as well as rebukes, an important point that many of us need to hear. Both are important in discipleship whether it is with children, workers, students, or church members. Jesus speaks to us so that we can be more faithful in the good things we are doing and that we may also see our errors and make adjustments.

What John saw was real! *"When I saw Him, I fell at His feet as though dead,"* Revelation 1:17a. John, Job, Isaiah, Daniel, and Paul became like dead men when the glory of Christ was revealed to them. Can you imagine what it will be like for anyone who is not saved to face a holy Christ? We, too, will stand before the Christ, the One who *"holds the keys of death and Hades,"* Revelation 1:18b.

There is also a commission in this Revelation, in this unveiling. John's commission was to write about the unveiling of the things to come! Ours is to read, understand, and then respond accordingly.

Prayer: Loving Father in Heaven, we worship and praise You for revealing the things we are doing right and the things we are doing wrong. Lord, we want a spiritual life that is acceptable to You. Help us to understand Your message to the seven churches and to us. In Christ Jesus' name we pray. Amen.

November 2

"He who has an ear, let him hear what the Spirit says to the churches. To him who overcomes, I will give the right to eat from the tree of life which is in the paradise of God." Revelation 2:7

How is your "ear"?

In Jesus' seven messages to seven different churches, two phrases come up seven times. The first phrase is, *"He who has an ear, let him hear what the Spirit says to the churches,"* Revelation 2:7a; 2:11a; 2:17a; 2:29; 3:6; 3:13; 3:22. Why would Jesus say this phrase seven times? One reason is that the Gospel primarily goes into people's hearts by way of the ear. *"How can they believe in the One they have not heard? And how can they hear without someone preaching to them?"* Romans 10:14. The preached and written Word of God is important. Too often people go to church to "see" something or to "experience" something. God gave the two sacraments of Baptism and the Lord's Supper to see and experience Christ.

The pulpit is not a stage to see someone perform.. God's Spirit who wrote the Bible still opens up hearts through the Word, by way of the *"ear."* Have you noticed how the raised pulpit has been replaced by a wide stage? That is not all good.

Christ strongly preaches the seven particular messages that the church and the people of every place and of every time in history need to *"hear."* Since everyone will soon face Jesus in The Judgment, He gives us seven hints here on just what we will soon be judged on in His final Judgment.

What does it mean to *"hear"* Christ's seven messages? Real hearing involves much more than taking sound into the ear. Biblical hearing is a right response to the message that is given. For example, Peter was preaching, *"When the people heard this, they were cut to the heart and said to Peter and the other apostles, 'Brothers, what shall we do?'"* Acts 2:37. Christ also expects us to have a right response to His seven serious messages. May we *"hear"* it, and then react to it!

Prayer: Dear Lord, it is fitting that You end Your revealed Word by showing us gently how important it is to follow You in the way we worship and live. May we be worshipers whom You seek, ones who worship You in spirit and in truth. In Jesus' name we pray. Amen.

November 3

"Then one of the elders said to me, 'Do not weep! See, the Lion of the tribe of Judah, the Root of David, has triumphed. He is able to open the scroll and its seven seals.'" Revelation 5:5

The Lamb becomes a Lion

Many study the book of Revelation and come away with all sorts of interpretations. A certain ten-year-old once read the book of Revelation. When asked what it all meant, he simply said, "Jesus wins. Satan loses." Now that is good theology! We can get so caught up with the various visions of Revelation that we do not see the bigger picture. *"The Lion of the tribe of Judah, the Root of David, has triumphed."* It is a message to meditate on, rejoice in, and praise God for!

Jesus came into the world the first time as a little Baby Boy, the Lamb of God. Humble Jesus came to save people from the wrath of God against their personal sin. At the end of His life, Jesus was led like a lamb to the slaughter. After three days He came back to life, then later ascended to reign in Heaven. Jesus is coming again. This time He will not come as a Lamb, but as a Lion! It was said of Judah, Jacob's son; *"You are a lion's cub, O Judah; you return from the prey, my son. Like a lion he crouches and lies down, like a lioness — who dares to arouse him?"* Genesis 49:9. The original Judah was a "cub;" Jesus is *"the Lion"* of Judah, the true and hoped for Messiah. Aroused, He will strike with a deadly fury. You can be certain that Jesus' former meekness will be fully replaced with boldness when He comes again.

Jesus will come as a <u>conquering</u> King to give a full reward to those who loved and served Him. Not one of His servants will be disappointed! Jesus will also come as <u>reigning</u> King to exercise judgment and crush all those who hated Him and His kingdom. This was said already in Genesis, *"The scepter will not depart from Judah,"* Genesis 49:10a. As a reigning King, Jesus will hold out His scepter to His children, but not to His enemies.

Prayer: O Lord, what hope we have that You, *"the Lion of the tribe of Judah,"* are coming again in power and in great glory to devour Your enemies and ours. We praise You for being our conquering and reigning God and King! In Christ's name we pray. Amen.

November 4

"To the angel of the church in Ephesus write: These are the words of Him who holds the seven stars in His right hand and walks among the seven golden lampstands." Revelation 2:1

The Church in Ephesus

The Ephesian Church was strong, and Jesus commended them for it. In doing so, our Lord teaches us that contending for the faith is important. Jesus did have some difficult things to say to this church. But first, He commends them for a job well done in certain areas. If Christ was only critical, this church could easily think that He did not see their good points. This is a huge discipleship point. We, too, need to commend those we disciple; children, students, workers and church members.

Jesus now tells them what needs to change. Their love had grown cold. How typical of many churches, homes, and people today who know good doctrine! But, *"If I have the gift of prophesy and can fathom all mysteries and all knowledge, and if I have a faith that can move mountains, but have not love, I am nothing,"* 1 Corinthians 13:2. *"If I give all I possess to the poor and surrender my body to the flames, but have not love, I gain nothing,"* 1 Corinthians 13:3. The Ephesian Church lost its first love, a vibrant relationship with the Lord of the Church, Christ Himself. As a result, they lost their love for those in the world also. They became selfish, doing exactly what the Ten Commandments teach us not to do. How easy for all of us to get so caught up in doing our "Christian rituals" and forget to show our love!

On June 22, we looked on the three main parts of Jesus' rebuke of "Remember," "Repent," and "Do." This effective, three-step process for us to change is exactly what Christ ordained for all churches, all marriages, and all believers. Jesus makes the point, *"If you do not repent, I will come to you and remove your lampstand from its place,"* Revelation 2:5b. When repentance is ignored, Christ as Lord of the Church, lets these cold churches fall apart. He will take away their faithful ministers and give them what they really want - the social gospel.

Prayer: Loving Lord, keep the flame of love hot within us that we may love You, with all of our hearts. May we see that "good relationships" with You and others is good doctrine. May we love You until our last breath. In Christ's name we pray. Amen.

November 5

"To the angel of the church in Smyrna write: These are the words of Him who is the First and the Last, who died and came to life again. I know your afflictions and your poverty — yet you are rich! I know the slander of those who say they are Jews and are not, but are a synagogue of Satan." Revelation 2:8

The Church in Smyrna

Jesus as *"the First"* existed even before all people. Jesus is also *"the Last."* When all people are out of the world, Jesus the living Judge will be there to judge all people that ever lived. This everlasting Jesus identifies Himself so there will be no mistake about what will soon happen! He who has the power to create all, will judge all.

1. It's not a sin to be poor! *"I know your afflictions and your poverty."* The all-seeing omniscient eye of our Lord notices the afflictions of His people and their poverty in material things. He reminds them of a more important truth - their rich spiritual condition. We need to hear this to keep a right attitude. What a contrast Jesus' teaching is here, to those who ignore the Word, and teach that it is a sin to be poor.

2. Satan is God's tool. *"Do not be afraid of what you are about to suffer. I tell you, the devil will put some of you in prison to test you, and you will suffer persecution for ten days. Be faithful, even to the point of death, and I will give you the crown of life,"* Revelation 2:10. Did Jesus cast *"the devil"* out here as so many do? No, God uses "the devil tool" here to test His people.

3. Don't "play church." *"Those who say they are Jews but are not."* The organized church has people who are brought up in the covenant, in a particular church, who actually reject God. This was me for many years. Jesus is aware of those who "play church." Problem is, those who are doing this just don't see it. But, no one can fool the Lord who says, *"I know."* Like so many covenant Jews of old, so many are seen by the Lord for what they really are: *"a synagogue of Satan."*

Prayer: All-seeing Lord, we thank You for the encouragement to stand fast and stay the course. You tell us that many will suffer persecution for the sake of the Gospel. Others will die a martyr's death. We praise You for encouraging us to stand just a short time against evil, to be with You for all eternity. In Jesus' name we pray. Amen.

November 6

"To the angel of the church in Pergamum write: These are the words of Him who has the sharp, double-edged sword." Revelation 2:12

The Church in Pergamum

The warning Jesus gives to this Pergamum Church in Revelation 2:12-17 is: *"cut your relationship to the world."* The church was to be an influence in the world, not the other way around. The word Pergamum means, "united in marriage" in the Greek. They were to be united to Christ, not to the ways of the world.

1. Be married to Christ. Christ commends the Pergamum Church. *"You did not renounce your faith in Me, even in the days of Antipas, My faithful witness, who was put to death in your city — where Satan lives,"* Revelation 2:13b. It appears this Antipas was a martyr for Christ, standing against Satan and the world's ways. Yet still, some in this Pergamum Church were married to the world. They loved created things that were passing away, way more than they loved the eternal blessings of the Creator. They were not married to Christ, not serious Christians.

2. Don't be married to the world. *"You have people there who hold to the teaching of Balaam,"* Revelation 2:14b. Balaam was a covetous Old Testament prophet who tried to unite the Israelites with the world. Some teachers still try to unite all the religions, claiming there are many ways to God. Some use their position in church, to make money instead of teaching about truth and righteousness. What about us? How do we view things like materialism, abortion, etc...? Do we have the world's view of these things or Christ's? Do our activities show our love for Christ, or our love for the world? How do we dress? What do we read? What do we do with our time? Would we rather watch TV, sporting events, or seek a relationship with Christ and a life of prayer? What really is the love of our very short life?

Prayer: Holy Lord, You say to this church and to us, *"Repent therefore! Otherwise, I will soon come to you and will fight against them with the sword of My mouth,"* Revelation 2:16. We see that You are even now, today, presently judging our responsibility to be married to You, the Head of the Church! Lord, forgive our wanderings. Help us to be more faithful. In Jesus' name we pray. Amen.

November 7

"To the angel of the church in Thyatira write: These are the words of the Son of God, whose eyes are like blazing fire and whose feet are like burnished bronze." Revelation 2:18

The Church in Thyatira

<u>Jesus sees the good in every church and loves it</u>. Jesus said: *"I know your deeds, your love and faith, your service and perseverance, and that you are now doing more than you did at first,"* Revelation 2:19. Many "good things" were in this church. The all-seeing, omniscient eye of our Lord sees the good we are doing, even when others don't. Be encouraged, continue to do good and loving deeds for the Lord. Unlike the Ephesian Church, this church was doing more. Their love did not cool off. Encourage the "good deeds" in our churches!

    <u>Jesus sees the evil in every church and hates it</u>. The Lord was clear about what needed to change in this church also! Jesus said, *"I have this against you: You tolerate that woman Jezebel, who calls herself a prophetess. By her teaching she misleads my servants into sexual immorality and the eating of food sacrificed to idols,"* Revelation 2:20. We must confront evil in the Church directly, like Christ does. A person in this church was involved in some sexual sin. This otherwise faithful church knew about this evil person and did nothing! They were likely more afraid of what others would say, than what Christ the Head of the Church thought. Christ here clearly says He will judge both the evil-doer and those who put up with it. Christ is not telling this church to cast a demon out of this person. We see a call to confront this person. In 1 Corinthians 5, the Church is commanded to put an unrepentant churchgoer, out of the Church; and hand them over *"to Satan."* The Thyatira Church was unwilling to discipline, as taught in Matthew 18:15 -20. How amazing is God's grace in giving churches time to repent! Our God is holy and hates evil, *"like a blazing fire."*

    God always looks harder at evil in the church, judging it more severely than the evil in the world. Do we?

Prayer: Holy Lord, thank You for being so open to us for our good and for Your glory. Lord, forgive us for not standing up to evil everywhere. Give us Your Spirit to have the courage to lovingly speak up. In Christ's name we pray. Amen.

November 8

"To the angel of the church in Sardis write: These are the words of Him who holds the seven spirits of God and the seven stars. I know your deeds; you have a reputation of being alive, but you are dead."
Revelation 3:1

The Church in Sardis

Christ begins with a strong rebuke. At one time, the Sardis Church was alive. It was perhaps the first church John started. The church had a reputation of being solid. The problem was, they thought they still were! But God saw that this church was *"dead."* There are two warnings here for today's churches, and us as individuals too.

1. Are we glorying in our parent's and grandparent's faith, yet are adrift ourselves? The holy and great, "I know" sees it all. Jesus sees exactly how we live out our "religion." And He is very direct because there's no time to waste. Our life is short. *"Wake up! Strengthen what remains and is about to die, for I have not found your deeds complete in the sight of my God,"* Revelation 3:2. The omniscient eye of God sees everything, in every generation, everywhere! The solid faith of our parents is maybe over! What do we believe and practice?

2. Hear the Word of God and repent! *"Remember, therefore, what you have received and heard; obey it, and repent,"* Revelation 3:3a. Christ has three points. First, *"remember"* what you received and heard from God and your parents. Second, *"obey it."* Real faith "obeys" not just hears. God said, *"Be holy for I am holy."* Third, *"repent."* How seldom this word is heard today, yet Christ used it freely. Without repentance, the beautiful doctrines of grace are but head knowledge and will condemn us! Real grace in the heart becomes grace in deed! Jesus Christ, the most famous man who ever lived said: *"He who overcomes will...be dressed in white. I will never blot out his name from the book of life, but will acknowledge his name before My Father and His angels,"* Revelation 3:5.

Prayer: Lord, the Sardis Church is so like ours today. May we "remember" the call of the Gospel and "obey" it today! May we also "repent" of our cold hearts and cold religion. In Jesus' name we pray. Amen.

November 9

"To the angel of the church in Philadelphia write: These are the words of Him who is holy and true, who holds the key of David. What He opens no one can shut, and what He shuts no one can open."
Revelation 3:7

The Church in Philadelphia

Philadelphia means the city of brotherly love, which this church was. Jesus found no fault with this church. Notice three things.

1. <u>The faithful, with "little strength" will enter Heaven</u>. No one can stop their entrance into Heaven! *"What He opens no one can shut."* Christ says, *"I know that you have little strength, yet you have kept My Word and have not denied My name,"* Revelation 3:8b. The weakness spoken of here is really a strength! How can we ever depend on the Fatherly grace of God if we don't realize how weak we are to keep His commands to love Him and others? God loves humble people who are confessing their sins, looking to Him.

2. <u>Pretending Christians, who claim "great strength," will enter Hell</u>. And no one can get them into Heaven! *"What He shuts no one can open."* Head knowledge without a loving heart is eternally deadly. There are still proud, unloving Pharisees in churches. May we learn from the church in Philadelphia. Any church or church member that thinks they have big doctrine, but have small love, is lost. They are like an instrument that is not tuned. There are also churches that seem very loving, but have so little good doctrine. They are out of tune also.

3. <u>God hates cowards</u>. Jesus said of the Philadelphia faithful, you *"have not denied My name,"* Revelation 3:8b. God hates cowards with a passion. The first evil God will destroy in The Final Judgment is *"the cowardly,"* Revelation 21:8a. We act like cowards when we do not do evangelism or stand up for God's truth. Our practice of *"political correctness"* in the church and world conceals sins, stops confession and ignores repentance. May we all be examples of good believers. May we be found faithful like the Philadelphia Church!

Prayer: Holy and true Lord, You told the Philadelphia Church, "<u>Hold on to what you have, so that no one will take your crown</u>," Revelation 3:11b. Lord, how lovingly You hold us that we may take hold of You. In Jesus' name we pray. Amen.

November 10

"To the angel of the church in Laodicea write: These are the words of the Amen, the faithful and true Witness, the Ruler of God's creation. I know your deeds, that you are neither cold nor hot. I wish you were either one or the other! So, because you are lukewarm - neither hot nor cold - I am about to spit you out of My mouth."
Revelation 3:14-16

The Church in Laodicea

We turn now to the last of the seven churches. Jesus identifies Himself clearly, so that no one can escape the warning. This church is the worst of the seven. Looking at the land around Laodicea, Jesus shows us a fitting picture of the church itself. On one side of Laodicea there were relaxing hot springs. On the other side there were cold refreshing pools. The water in both of these places was useful. In Laodicea, the water was lukewarm and not useful. Jesus draws off this fact to give them a true picture of their own spiritual state. This church did not heed Jesus' warning and repent, and it ended up in ruins 400 years later. Such is the sure wrath of God against the unrepentant.

1. A dead church is not for Christ, but is against Christ. Unlike some of the other churches, Jesus did not commend even one thing in this church. Dead churches don't breathe, spiritually speaking. They are unconcerned about their own spiritual soul and thus are not concerned about the souls of others either. How can a dead man do missions? How many churches are *"lukewarm"* like this today? How many are just going through the motions? Jesus knows.

2. When our other pleasures are a greater joy than Christ, idol worship is practiced. The very One who says, *"I know,"* is the Lord of Heaven and Earth. He will not stand for our lip service, while we freely give the world our affections. He knows.

3. Jesus gives us a fair warning. *"I am about to spit you out of My mouth,"* Revelation 3:16b. Those who are content in their indifference, need to see their guilt. Only the Word and Spirit of God can convict. May we stop the games and hear the Word of God! He knows.

Prayer: O Ruler of God's creation, You created us to worship You more than anything. May we do so with all of our hearts. In Jesus' name we pray. Amen.

November 11

"Now the people complained about their hardships in the hearing of the LORD, and when He heard them His anger was aroused."
Numbers 11:1a

Am I, Mr. Complain or Mr. Trust?

What describes my outlook in life? Who am I? Am I Mr. Complain or Mr. Trust? Most of the time I am more like Mr. Complain. I do not always say my grumbling thoughts, but I think them. I should have learned from the thankless Israelites that God is not pleased with complainers. God plagued the enemies of Israel, and the Israelites still complained. He preserved His chosen people from hunger, thirst, and defeat, yet they complained. He made a covenant with them and gave them loving laws and dwelt among them; He even gave them priests and they complained.

God caused the Israelites to wander in the wilderness because of their bad attitude. How often do we wander in the wilderness of despair because of our attitude? Truth is, we have even more of God's blessings. God's Son is our High Priest, but we complain. Our complaining reveals our hearts. *"For out of the overflow of the heart the mouth speaks,"* Luke 6:45. The rottenness that seeps out of our mouths reveals the garbage in our souls.

We complain when suffering comes, even though we know it is for our good. We know our trials conform us to Christ, yet we complain. We know James said, *"Count it all joy when you fall into various trials,"* but we don't. We know our pain is gain, but we complain. We even pray for God to remove our trials. We should say, "Bring on the suffering Lord," so that we can be more like Christ. But we don't pray like that.

Prayer: O Lord who hears even unspoken words, our complaining shows that we are unhappy with You. Our complaining says, we know more than You about what is best. Lord forgive such ugly idolatry. We know the process from sinner to saint takes a lifetime, yet we demand instant perfection in our parents, our spouse, our children, and others. We want You and others to be patient with us, but we don't want to be patient with You or others. Lord, correct our miserable attitudes! Help us to be more trusting in You. In Jesus, name we pray. Amen.

November 12

"But the plans of the LORD stand firm forever, the purposes of His heart through all generations." Psalm 33:11

God's sovereignty teaches us

God totally cares for the world and for us, *"through all generations,"* Psalm 33:11. There will never be a time the world will operate outside of God's sovereign control. *"Many are the plans in a man's heart, but it is the LORD's purpose that prevails,"* Proverbs 19:21. God has such complete control of the world and those in it.

Many teach bad doctrine about God's sovereignty. Pelagius first taught that God created things and then left things to run on their own. Armenias went further, teaching that man was in control of his spiritual state. The Deist's went still further, teaching that man was in control of the world and his spiritual state. Then Darwin taught there was no God. Soon, the Antichrist will try to set himself up as god. Wicked man pulls down God to elevate himself.

A question needs answering. If God is so perfect and so in charge of everything, how did sin come into the world? The answer is: God allowed sin. Truth is, Adam had a free will, until he sinned. Already in Genesis 6:5 we read, *"The LORD saw how great man's wickedness on earth had become, and that every inclination of the thoughts of his heart was only evil all the time."* Man now has only a will to sin.

God's sovereignty in Genesis 20:6 shows that He can **prevent** sin if He wants to. God can also **permit** sin as Psalm 81:12 and Romans 1:18-32 teach. God can **direct** sin for our good as He did in the life of Joseph, Genesis 50:20. From Job 1, we also know that God can **limit** sin if He chooses. Satan needed permission to afflict Job! God even allowed man to commit the biggest sin ever, the killing of His only Son. Our God is in charge of this world.

Prayer: Lord, how blessed we are that You are a sovereign God. What comfort we have that nothing is by chance, not even an accident! What protection we have that You are all wisdom, all powerful, see everything, and have a storehouse of love and mercy for us, Your chosen children. Give us the courage to face every problem in life with our eyes on You in expectant faith. In Jesus, our reigning Savior's name, we pray. Amen.

November 13

"David inquired of the LORD." 2 Samuel 5:19a

Do we inquire of the Lord?

How often do we have problems with relationships or a difficult decision or task? Do we inquire of the Lord like David? Or, do we just put our head down and plow forward? Perhaps we just ignore the problem, thinking it's no use. Do we see that God allows us to have problems to see if we will trust in Him? The Lord wants us to depend on Him! God is able to help us. The battle is His. The victory is His. If we do not inquire of the Lord, then we have a faith problem. A living faith is dependent on God, trusts in God, for the honor and glory of God.

Since the Lord knows everything before it happens, it is wise to call on Him. That is why David asked God for His thoughts on whether he should go into battle. David knew that he could waste men and resources if the battle did not go according to the Lord's plan. Divine providence and protection are the best weapons in our battles also.

David inquired of the Lord, *"Shall I go and attack the Philistines?"* The Philistines had been bold in attacking the people of God. But now, King Saul is dead and David is the new king. The Philistines knew that in his youth David had slain his 10,000's and Saul his 1,000's. They assembled to wipe out David while his kingship was still in its infancy. Take note! If we have just come to Christ, or started a new direction in ministry, Satan will also attack us in our infancy. He will surely assemble his forces against us. Before salvation we were in Satan's camp. He didn't need to attack us then. He already had us! Will we learn from David and *"inquire of the Lord"* for our upcoming battles?

David had confidence in the Lord or he would not have *"inquired of the LORD."* Do we have confidence in God? Surely we realize, God knows everything, great and small. If the number of hairs on our head are numbered by Him and He knows the needs of the birds, will He not care for us?

Prayer: Powerful and caring Lord, we are so grateful that You show us the nature of the battle we are in. Lord, build our faith so that we run to You and with You, trusting in Your ability to lead us in this hostile world. In Jesus' name we pray. Amen.

November 14

"Therefore, my brothers, I want you to know that through Jesus the forgiveness of sins is proclaimed to you. Through Him everyone who believes is justified from everything." Acts 13:38-39a

Justified today!

When a believer *"is justified,"* there is no longer, ever again, a debt to God for their sin. The believer's "spiritual accounting books" are now, presently and forever balanced. Justified, is an accounting term that God uses for us to understand that He no longer holds our sin debt against us! How beautiful are the words, *"is justified."* The word *"is"* means a present justification, as well as a future one!

Faith does not somehow produce justification at a later date. It is instant. Justification is given to a soul the exact moment that God accepts us, because we now have His Son's innocent blood covering us. All in Heaven are justified. Every Christian on Earth is also fully *"justified"* now. The one thief on the cross next to Christ was instantly just as *"justified"* as Abraham, David, and Paul. Their years of service did not make them more justified. Oh how we need to hear that once forgiven is always forgiven! *"God's gifts and His call are irrevocable,"* Romans 11:29. God will never take back His forgiveness to us. A son or daughter in Christ can still sin, but they cannot stop being a son or daughter!

A Christian is today accepted by God. Today your sins are gone! Today you are washed as white as snow. Your death penalty is now forever gone, today! Christ died for you so that today you are with God! There is not a single sin that God still holds against you. Your soul is clean. Not even one piece of your flesh is offensive to God. God sees you just as He sees His Beloved Son. *"Everyone who believes is justified from everything!"*

Prayer: O Lord, how personal is Your love to us in Christ. How powerful *"is"* the blood of the Lamb! How great it is that, *"there is now no condemnation for those who are in Christ Jesus,"* Romans 8:1. May the present privilege of being Your child today, wake us up to our present duties today also. May we always remember to act like Your child. Help us, Lord, to do this. In Christ's most precious name we pray. Amen.

November 15

"Those He justified, He also glorified." Romans 8:30b

Salvation always brings glorification

If you are God's child today, you will be with Him tomorrow. This verse is a promise built on the very faithfulness of God. What God starts, God always finishes. *"He who began a good work in you will complete it,"* Philippians 1:6 NKJV. Your trials will soon end. Your fight against evil will soon be over. Someday soon, at the twinkling of an eye, you will be with the Church of all ages, in Heaven forever. Just as God is with you today in your trials, He will be with you in glory.

"Now the dwelling of God is with men and He will live with them. They will be His people, and God Himself will be with them and be their God. He will wipe away every tear from their eyes. There will be no more death or mourning or crying or pain, for the old order of things has passed away," Revelation 21:3b-4. There will never be a death of a Christian's soul/spirit. The moment your eyes close for the last time on Earth, you will immediately see the glory of God in Heaven. The gates of Heaven will open to let you in immediately. You will see Jesus and the saints right then, and forever!

"Who shall separate us from the love of Christ?" Romans 8:35a. The answer is no one and nothing in Romans 8:38-39. Hell cannot touch you. Persecution cannot steal your soul. It only purifies it! The very power and voice of God, who called you into a relationship with Him, will again call you to Himself. He may seem distant at times today, but that is because you moved away from Him. We are told He will never leave us or forsake us! In fact, *"The Lord will rescue me from every evil attack and will bring me safely to His Heavenly kingdom. To Him be the glory for ever and ever. Amen,"* 2 Timothy 4:18.

Prayer: Dear Lord, we thank You for Your promises and protection. Your grace is truly amazing! There is no other god like You. Dear Lord help us to trust You more, especially when we cannot figure things out. May we follow Your Word knowing it is not a blind faith, but a living faith that leads to Heaven! In Jesus' name we pray. Amen.

November 16

"I know that my Redeemer lives, and that in the end He will stand upon the earth. And after my skin has been destroyed, yet in my flesh I will see God, I, and not another. How my heart yearns within me!"
Job 19:25-27

"I know that my Redeemer lives"

These words are a great confession of faith by the old saint Job. The definition of faith is, *"Now faith is being sure of what we hope for and certain of what we do not see,"* Hebrews 11:1. With this true Biblical definition in mind, let us look at Job's creed of faith.

First, we must consider the words, *"I know."* Job did not say, "I think," or "perhaps" my Redeemer lives. He said, *"I know that my Redeemer lives."* Job was absolutely certain there was a Redeemer. Secondly, Job was fully convinced that his very own personal Redeemer lived! He said, *"my Redeemer lives."* He had the living Christ in his heart! That is the secret. So many people know about Jesus and that Jesus saves sinners. But is Jesus their personal Savior? That is the real question!

The patriarchs were commended for their faith in the book of Hebrews, even though they did not see what we see today. They only saw in shadows. They saw many sacrifices and the shedding of much blood. They knew this all pointed to a Redeemer that would come some day from the seed of Abraham. But they did not have the New Testament to be able to see as clearly as we can! The patriarchs were, *"sure of what they hoped for and certain of what they did not see,"* Hebrews 11:1. Are you *"certain"* about the Redeemer Jesus?

After losing his children and possessions, Job said, *"Naked I came from my mother's womb, and naked I will depart. The LORD gave and the LORD has taken away; may the name of the LORD be praised,"* Job 1:21. Like Abraham, Job was *"looking forward to the city with foundations, whose architect and builder is God,"* Hebrews 11:10. Are we looking forward to being with God in eternity? Or are we so intent in this world that we think little of the next?

Prayer: Eternal Lord, help us to be more Heavenly minded, so we may be more earthly good! We praise You that you are a personal Redeemer, our Jesus! In His name we pray. Amen.

November 17

"You show that you are a letter from Christ, the result of our ministry, written not with ink but with the Spirit of the living God, not on tablets of stone but on tablets of human hearts."
2 Corinthians 3:3

Is your ministry changing hearts?

Many people in ministry make excuses for their lack of fruit in their work. They say that the kind of work that they do takes a long time to get results. Amazingly, many people accept this. Compare all these excuses to what Paul said in chapter 3, that I do not need a letter of recommendation from anyone for what I do. The same should be true for us concerning our qualifications as the Lord's servant and also our productivity. The way our various disciples live speaks for itself. Paul said to the Corinthians he ministered to, *"You show that you are a letter from Christ, the result of our ministry, written not with ink but with the Spirit of the living God, not on tablets of stone but on tablets of human hearts,"* 2 Corinthians 3:3. Paul's effectiveness in ministry was seen in the lives that were changed by God's Spirit.

When God's inner grace changes a human heart, the same Spirit now changes the thoughts, words, and actions of that person. God's saving grace produces new outward graces! Changed people will become kinder, easier to live with, easier to do business with. The result is as Paul says, *"you are a letter from Christ."* Are our children, students, or church members, a living letter from Christ? If not, then what are we teaching them?

Every Christian is called to "do ministry." One man in India was in charge of 10,000 people in the railways. He wanted to quit to teach 5 pastors. I reminded him that his discipleship of 10,000 was a very important ministry for God. How we relate to others is ministry. Is there any evidence that we are affecting the people God put in our lives, to live God's way instead of the world's way? Or, is the world affecting us to live its way?

Prayer: Loving Lord, use us everywhere for your glory and for the building of Your church. In Jesus' name we pray. Amen.

November 18

"From one man He made every nation of men, that they should inhabit the whole earth; and He determined the times set for them and the exact places where they should live. God did this so that men would seek Him and perhaps reach out for Him and find Him, though He is not far from each one of us." Acts 17:26-27

Created to Worship God

The Westminster Catechism asks, "What is the chief end of man?" The answer is: "Man's chief end is to glorify God and to enjoy Him forever." That truly answers the question as to why we are here in this world. Our text says God, *"determined the times set for them and the exact places where they should live."* Every person is where God wants him or her to be. That should comfort us and motivate us to do what God intends for us to do - live for Him. It is so sad then that so many people want to be anywhere, but where they presently are.

The question before us is: "Are we looking to glorify God where He has placed us?" God did not put us all in the same place, position, or country for a good reason. We would find a lot more contentment if we take it to heart that we must glorify God right where He currently has us. If we have no desire to glorify and enjoy God now, then we are not preparing to enjoy Him in eternity.

We are all responsible to *"reach out for Him and find Him."* Too often the Calvinist tries to sweep this truth under the rug. Jesus said, *"Ask and it will be given to you; seek and you will find; knock and the door will be opened to you. For everyone who asks receives; he who seeks finds; and to him who knocks, the door will be opened,"* Luke 11:9-10. God is not far from each of us. If we seek and knock we will find Him. Granted, God's sovereignty gives us the *"will and to do for His good pleasure,"* Philippians 2:23. Yet man's responsibility in our text is just as true as God's sovereignty. Are we *"seeking"* and *"reaching out"* for God?

Prayer: O Lord, we confess, we are not always content with where You have placed us. We so often want to escape from our relationships and our responsibilities. We have not loved You as we should. We've been selfish. Forgive us for our cold hearts and move us to where we belong, close to You. In Jesus' name we pray. Amen.

November 19

"And I say to you that many will come from east and west, and will take their places at the feast with Abraham, Isaac, and Jacob in the kingdom of Heaven." Matthew 8:11

Christ makes us willing to follow Him

Is salvation the will of God, the will of man, or a little of both? A popular song says, "I have decided to follow Jesus." You may think from this line that it was man choosing the God of Heaven! Truth is, it was the Holy Spirit, God Himself who convicts us to cry to God for mercy. Imagine a Christian couple adopting a baby girl that is blind, diseased, and almost dead. They nurse this baby back to health. After a few years, the child sings to the parent, "I have decided to follow you." Great, but that is the child merely responding to the love of the parent's grace to her. After all, the little girl in the story was almost dead. Way more than that, God, *"made us alive with Christ <u>even when we were dead</u> in transgressions-it is by grace you have been saved,"* Ephesians 2:5.

Our text says, *"many will come"* to the *"kingdom of Heaven."* Yes, and every one of them because God called them and woke them up! Spurgeon says about this text: "The devil says, 'they will not come,' but they shall come. Their sins say, 'you can't come,' God says, 'You shall come.' You yourselves say, 'We won't come,' God says, 'You shall come.' There are many who laugh at salvation, who scoff at Christ and mock the Gospel; but I tell you that some of you shall yet come. 'What?' You say. 'Can God make me become a Christian?' I tell you yes, for here rests the very power of the Gospel. It does not ask for your consent, but it gets it! Christ does not say, 'Will you have Me?' But Christ makes you willing in the day of God's power, not against your will, but Christ makes you willing to follow Him!"

Prayer: Amazing Lord, we are in awe of Your grace! You even planned that we would believe. Then You made us believe! You caused us to be part of the many who *"will come from east and west, and take their places at the feast with Abraham, Isaac, and Jacob in the kingdom of Heaven."* We praise You for Your grace! In Jesus' name we pray. Amen.

November 20

"Blessed is the man who does this, the man who holds it fast, who keeps the Sabbath without desecrating it, and keeps his hand from doing any evil." Isaiah 56:2

Proper Sabbath observance

It is amazing that God created us to know and enjoy Him forever. How can we know and enjoy God if we neglect the Sabbath to meet with Him. If two people say that they love each other but do not want to meet with each other, their love is not very real.

In our text, God here promises to bless the one *"who keeps the Sabbath without desecrating it."* We must admit, the observance of the Sabbath has slipped, but why? Just how do we *"desecrate"* or do *"evil"* on God's Sabbath day?

The resurrection of Christ was on the first day of the week. The disciples continued to gather to worship and glorify the risen Lord on this day. Their practice became ours today. Since God entered into His rest through our Lord Jesus Christ on this first day of the week, God now spiritually bestows that rest upon His church. In worship, we dwell or meet (tabernacle with) God in Heaven, through Christ.

The last day of the week that was formerly set aside for worship at creation, was done away with. We will never again return to the paradise of the first Adam. Now, the second Adam, Jesus, welcomes us into His death and resurrection, He wants to fellowship with us! To fail to worship on the Sabbath is to tell God we are not interested in being with Him and the resurrected Christ. What a serious mistake that is.

"'If you keep your feet from breaking the Sabbath and from doing as you please on My holy day, if you call the Sabbath a delight and the LORD's holy day honorable, and if you honor it by not going your own way and not doing as you please or speaking idle words, then you will find your joy in the LORD, and I will cause you to ride on the heights of the land and to feast on the inheritance of your father Jacob.' The mouth of the LORD has spoken," Isaiah 58:13-14.

Prayer: Wise and holy Lord, we thank You for speaking to us. You are such a practical and loving God. You are so good to invite us to come into Your very presence to know and to worship You for who You are. In Jesus' name we pray. Amen.

November 21

"Then they willingly received Him into the boat, and immediately the boat was at the land where they were going." John 6:21 NKJV

Is Jesus in your boat?

Does it seem like you are rowing your boat against heavy seas? It is really hard going with all the heavy, sinful baggage we carry. With the seas rough and our boats deep in the water, it is also dangerous! The disciples of Jesus went through the same kind of difficulties we go through. Their experience was for our benefit, so that we can get to where we need to go. *"Now when evening came, His disciples went down to the sea, got into the boat and went over the sea toward Capernaum. And it was already dark and Jesus had not come to them,"* John 6:16-17 NKJV. How hard it is, if Jesus has "not come" to us.

In the darkness, problems increase. *"Then the sea arose because a great wind was blowing,"* John 6:18 NKJV. The winds in our lives also try to push us away from Christ and the shores of the Promised Land. What can we do? What did the disciples do? *"So when they had rowed about three or four miles, they saw Jesus walking on the sea and drawing near the boat; and they were afraid,"* John 6:19 NKJV. Jesus is that nearby, even approaching our boat and our storms in life too! Do we see Him? He sees us! The rough seas we have, are like flat water to Him. *"He said to them, 'It is I; do not be afraid,'"* John 6:20. He who is still perfect love, says, "Do not be afraid." I am with you.

"Then they willingly received Him into the boat, and immediately the boat was at the land where they were going," John 6:21. Here it is! We may know who Christ is, but is He in our boat, our lives? We can't row hard enough to get through life without Christ in our boat. Amazing, Jesus walked to them and sought them. We are such passive recipients of Christ and His grace! When Christ finds us, Heaven is as much a present reality as the distant shore was *"immediately"* for the disciples.

Prayer: O Lord who always sees us, we praise You that Jesus calms our storms too. How kind of You to give us a picture of how our human effort cannot get us to the promised land! With Christ in our life, we too are immediately Yours, on the shores of Heaven. Help us to keep our eyes on You, for You are still, the Way, the Truth, and the Life. In Jesus' name we pray. Amen.

November 22

"'You will not need to fight in this battle. Position yourselves, stand still and see the salvation of the LORD, who is with you, O Judah and Jerusalem!' Do not fear or be dismayed; tomorrow go out against them, for the LORD is with you." 2 Chronicles 20:17 NKJV

God sends us with His blessing!

God went out of His way to impress this verse on me when I was very fearful of moving ahead for Him. I knew that God was calling me to do His work in India, but still, I was afraid. My fears were really a lack of faith. It's true, some of the people who should be the most encouraging to us in the Lord's work, are the most discouraging. Our God is not like that! He tenderly pushes us, but at exactly the right rate of speed so that we do not run ahead of Him.

I love God for His encouragement through this fearful time. On Friday, I arrived in India. Then on Sunday, twice God used our text to encourage me. The evening speaker began his sermon by saying that he did not know why God impressed him so strongly all week to preach the same text that was used by the morning speaker.

For the second time I heard, *"Do not fear or be dismayed; tomorrow go out against them, for the LORD is with you."* I knew God was speaking to my fears. The evening pastor even ended with this verse before he said amen. *"And on the fourth day they assembled in the valley of Berachah, for there they blessed the LORD; therefore the name of that place was called The Valley of Berachah until this day,"* 2 Chronicles 20:26. The next day was my fourth day in Madras and I needed to teach on Berachah Road. I was greatly encouraged by God's Word. God went to great lengths to give me this message. In the years to come, God did what He promised, protecting me from terrorists and much more. God is so good in taking away our fears, giving us a much stronger faith and hope in Him!

Prayer: Most wonderful Lord, You are a great comfort to us as You keep Your precious promises to us personally. Even Your last words to us before You ascended were; *"Surely I am with You always, to the very end of the age,"* Matthew 28:20b. May Your name be praised! In Jesus' name we pray. Amen.

November 23

"Watch out for false prophets. They come to you in sheep's clothing, but inwardly they are ferocious wolves. By their fruit you will recognize them." Matthew 7:15-16a

Are you a fruit inspector?

There have always been false prophets in the church. Jesus warned His people, *"Watch out for the teachers of the law. They like to walk around in flowing robes and be greeted in the marketplaces, and have the most important seats in the synagogues and the places of honor at banquets,"* Mark 12:38b-39. Jesus said, *"They devour widows' houses and for a show make lengthy prayers,"* 12:40a. They were so interested in money and reputation that it consumed them! The Scribes and Pharisees sat in Moses' seat teaching the law, yet contrary to the law, were proud, covetous, and wicked. May we not be like them!

False prophets are not that easy to recognize at first! They come to you in *"sheep's clothing."* They may teach the Law of God and talk a good line, but they do not walk a good line. In fact, they are *"ferocious wolves."* Can a "wolf" pray to God for you? No! Their prayers will not even make it to the ceiling. *"If anyone turns a deaf ear to the law, even his prayers are detestable,"* Proverbs 28:9. God does not hear the prayers of fake ministry workers. The blind cannot lead the blind. This fully explains why there is not good *"fruit"* coming out of some ministries. Inspecting the fruit of a ministry is a Christ-recommended way of telling what is real and what is pretend. The Spirit only works with that which is real.

The dead church of the Middle Ages regularly recited good creeds and confessions. Yet, they were outward pretensions and did not come from the heart, so nothing was happening. The Spirit was quenched. Is this also part of our problem today? May the Lord search our hearts and open our eyes to what is going on.

Prayer: O holy Lord who sees everything. You say *"many false prophets have gone out into the world."* Help us to recognize them. How often we look at other qualifications in ministry, other than in changed lives or fruit. Forgive us. May we see a living doctrine in our churches that promotes humility, holiness and love — the fruit of changed hearts. In Jesus' name we pray. Amen.

November 24

"'God, have mercy on me, a sinner.' I tell you that this man, rather than the other went home justified before God." Luke 18:13b-14a

What must I do to be saved?

One man thanked God in prayer that he was a good man. A second man begged for mercy. It was the beggar who was given mercy, because he sincerely asked for it! The beggar realized he was lost. The other proud man thought he had already arrived. The beggar realized, *"there is no one righteous, not even one,"* Romans 3:10b. Yes, only one understood that he was born a sinner and then broke God's holy law on top of that. Only one understood; *"Therefore no one will be declared righteous in His sight by observing the law; rather, through the law we become conscious of sin,"* Romans 3:20.

Many in our churches believe they are Christians because they were born into a Christian family, born good. We all need to see our spiritual problem in a court of law. We are taken to the biggest judge in the country. He reads off a list of 10 laws that we broke. We are guilty of treason because we bowed down to the enemy of our country. We did not honor our father and mother. We murdered our own brothers and sisters (anger and bitterness also count). We were guilty of adultery (lust also counts). We stole from many people. We lied about our neighbors. We set our hearts on the things of others.

In deed, we are wicked and are now standing before a perfect, righteous judge who never took a bribe (Deuteronomy 5:6-21). He must punish sin! What can we do as we stand before God, totally guilty? Can we pretend that we are righteous? The judge knows better! There is only one thing we can do, and that is beg for mercy. This is exactly our situation with our God in Heaven! *"The law* (Ten Commandments) *was our tutor to bring us to Christ, that we might be justified by faith,"* Galatians 3:24 NKJV.

Prayer: O holy Lord, we have not met Your righteous standard and need Your forgiveness! We fall on our knees before You, the perfect holy Judge, and plead, *"God have mercy on me, a sinner."* We thank You that You cover our sins with the perfect blood of Christ and give us His righteousness! In His name we pray. Amen.

November 25

"Religion that God our Father accepts as pure and faultless is this: to look after orphans and widows in their distress and to keep oneself from being polluted by the world." James 1:27

Do I have a faulty religion?

James showed us what "worthless religion" was all about in verse 26. James is clearly concerned that we get our passions in the right order. James now tells us what *"pure and faultless"* religion is: *"to look after orphans and widows in their distress."* Do we hear the cry of the orphan and widow? Does it move us that orphans and widows are in need of our love? Does it concern us that there are widows and orphans in families where the mothers and fathers are still living? Struggling, they are hurt and confused. Do we hear their cry for help? Or, are we too possessed with our own agendas?

God does hear the cries and prayers of orphans and widows in their distress. God's omniscient eye sees their plight. God demands that His people, those whose hearts He has changed, hear their cries also. God desires that His grace, which He put in us, becomes a noticeable grace. Gracious hearts care about what God cares about! Showing grace is, *"to look after orphans and widows in their distress."* Look at this selfishly. Do I want God to hear my cries for mercy? Do I want God to see my suffering with a sympathetic eye? Then I must listen to God's encouragement. *"Blessed are the merciful for they will be shown mercy,"* Matthew 5:7.

There are still better reasons to reach out to the *"orphans and widows."* God is worshiped when we help them because God's righteous character is being displayed through us! The orphans and widows will praise God for sending His help through our hands. Our helping the orphans and widows *"in their distress"* keeps the law of God, for then we love what God loves. Anytime we love God first and others second, we have our love life in order!

Prayer: Merciful Lord, we are selfish people by nature and live to please self first. Forgive us! We see Your heart here. Give us the desire, the strength, and the means, to help the orphans and widows in their distress. In Jesus' name we pray. Amen.

November 26

"The just shall live by faith." Romans 1:17b NKJV

Justification by faith alone

The words of our text rang in Martin Luther's ears and did much to usher in the Great Reformation. These words must ring in our ears too! We all stand guilty and are under the condemnation of God because of the original sin of man as described in Romans 5:12. Justification is an accounting term, central to true Christianity. We all owe God a debt we cannot possibly pay! A Christian's justification is having Christ's atoning blood covering our sins. The many ism's of the world, Catholicism, Buddhism, Hinduism, Mohammedism, etc., teach that our good works can move God to allow us into Heaven. But our spiritual problem is we cannot atone for ourselves in any way. Thus, being justified by faith alone, through Christ alone, is the exact opposite of trying to be saved by our works, by what we do.

"For it is by grace you have been saved, through faith-and this <u>not from yourselves</u>, it is the gift of God, <u>not by works</u>, so that no one can boast," Ephesians 2:8-9. If it were possible for us to be righteous without Christ, then He would not have needed to come to earth! Seeing our spiritual problem, God *"made Him who had no sin to be sin for us, so that in Him we might become the righteousness of God,"* 2 Corinthians 5:21. Jesus, the perfect Lamb of God, took the sin of believers upon Himself. He became the perfect sacrifice. *"It is the blood that makes atonement for the soul,"* Leviticus 17:11 NKJV.

Through faith in Christ, God gives us His righteousness. Justification restores us to the perfect man God once created us to be. Justified, with God's divine justice now satisfied, we are saved from His eternal wrath. Justified, God no longer sees us dressed in our sinful rags, but in the robes of Christ's righteousness. Freed from our slavery to sin, we have God's power to live differently. We do not deserve justification, because we can not earn it. Praise God, *"The just shall live by faith."*

Prayer: Loving Father, we praise You for Your amazing, justifying grace. If You did not take pity on us, we would be lost forever. What a privilege to be able to praise You now, and in our perfect world that will never end. In Jesus' name we pray. Amen.

November 27

"Make it your ambition to live a quiet life, to mind your own business and to work with your hands." 1 Thessalonians 4:11

God's view of work

What great wisdom! Work is not a four-letter cuss word! A main reason we are here in this world, is *"to mind our own business and to work with our hands."* At the very beginning of history, *"The LORD God took the man and put him in the Garden of Eden to work it and take care of it,"* Genesis 2:15. Adam was a farmer, called to work in service to the Lord who made everything. For a good reason, Bible translators often see worship and service as the same. But why is work worship to God? If we take our Christian duty out of our weekly schedule, what is left besides eating and sleeping? It is in our daily activities that we serve/worship the Lord. The Sabbath is a special day set aside for worship.

Paul encouraged Timothy, *"study to show thyself approved unto God, a workman,"* 2 Timothy 2:15a KJV. This is just as true for a woman as is it is for a man. In Proverbs 31, a wife and mother's hard work pleases the Lord, and delights her husband and children. Paul also wrote, *"I urge you, brothers, in view of God's mercy, to offer your bodies as living sacrifices, holy and pleasing to God — this is your spiritual act of worship,"* Romans 12:1. It's an honor to work!

Our work matters now and also in The Judgment. *"For the Son of Man is going to come in His Father's glory with His angels, and then He will reward each person according to what he has done,"* Matthew 16:27. The Biblical theology of work is that the labor of the ditch digger is just as holy as that of a preacher. Adam was a farmer, Noah was a boat builder, David a shepherd, the disciples fishermen, and Jesus was a carpenter. If you think you need to quit your current job to be able to do the Lord's work, you need a more Biblical view of how God has ordained all work.

Prayer: O great God who works all things for our good, forgive us for whining and crying about the fact that we need to work. Forgive us too, for not seeing our daily work as part of our daily worship. We have even done our work to please others before You. Forgive us. May all we do be to glorify you. In Jesus' name we pray. Amen.

November 28

"'They have credited David with tens of thousands,' he thought, 'but me with only thousands. What more can he get but the kingdom?' And from that time on Saul kept a jealous eye on David."
1 Samuel 18:8b-9

Jealousy in the workplace

The ladies sang the song in our text the very same day David killed Goliath. Immediately, Saul was jealous, then fearful, then angrily threw a spear at David. Bitterness consumed Saul the rest of his life and bitterness is called demonic in the book of James.

If bitterness clings to us, then we are just like king Saul, in league with the devil. Surely, Saul thought the ladies made him jealous and fearful and that David caused his anger. Not so. Saul's heart caused his horrible response, and he was the king. If we are known by: *"jealously, fits of rage, selfish ambition, dissensions, factions and envy,"* in Galatians 5:20, 21a, then we *"will not inherit the kingdom of God,"* Galatians 5:21b. Why is that? Our jealous, fearful angry and bitter hearts show there's little or no grace in our soul.

What happened to Saul, will happen to us. Someone will be noticed more than us. What will our response be? That is key for our mental and spiritual health. King Saul *"kept a jealous eye on David."* It wasn't so bad that Saul now noticed David with a jealous eye, but with a spoiled mind, he did not do his kingly duties. A main part of our job on Earth, is to train the next generation. Instead of doing his job, Saul concentrated on David's elimination. Saul spent his energies tracking down David, instead of tracking down the real enemies of Israel. What about us? Has someone received a promotion we wanted? Is someone getting noticed more than we are? The Word of God is so clear. Jealously is a hostile act to hurt others. Jealousy is wicked.

Prayer: Holy Lord, may Your Word shine in the dark corners of our hearts. We have been jealous of others. We have desired their good looks, money, power, prestige and even their position in life. We have not been content with what You have given us! We are sinful. Lord forgive us. In Jesus' name we pray. Amen.

November 29

"Though the fig tree does not bud and there are no grapes on the vines, though the olive crop fails and the fields produce no food, though there are no sheep in the pen and no cattle in the stalls, yet I will rejoice in the LORD, I will be joyful in God my Savior."
Habakkuk 3:17-18

What are you "joyful in"?

A certain man and his wife retired at the age of 50. They had made their money. Their bank account was fat. They had good health. Their children were all settled down in life and were successful. They would visit the best places to eat and buy the latest electronic gadgets. They had closets full of clothes they seldom wore. They collected sea-shells on their morning walks and were very proud of their growing collection. This was their life. In the light of eternity, what a waste. After all, our *"days are like grass; as a flower of the field, so he flourishes. For the wind passes over it, and it is gone,"* Psalm 103:15b-16a NKJV.

We will soon stand before God in The Judgment to give an account of our life. Imagine showing God a seashell collection? Imagine showing God a big bank account or the house we worked so many years to pay for? God will surely say, "I put you on the earth to glorify Me and to be a blessing to others." "You lived to build up your own name, your own reputation, your own bank account!" "There is no reward for that."

Habakkuk understood! Even his unusual Hebrew name means, *"one who embraces or clings to."* Habakkuk clings to God, which we can see in our text. His hope is in God. He is not dependent on having many earthly possessions to try find comfort and fulfillment in them. If all his earthly possessions fail, he still has hope. What about us? What do we cling to for our hope? What do we find our joy in? Will it stand in The Judgment, or will it be burned up?

Prayer: O holy Lord, we want to be like the faithful Habakkuk who said, *"I will be joyful in God my Savior."* Forgive us for looking for our joy in other things, before finding our joy in You. May we not fall to the god of hedonism like the apostate and uncaring people of Israel. Lord give us hearts that beat for You. In Jesus' name we pray. Amen.

November 30

"Although I am less than the least of all God's people, this grace was given me: to preach to the Gentiles the unsearchable riches of Christ."
Ephesians 3:8

The privilege of bringing the Gospel

If our president asked us to work directly for him, we would have a great job. We have an even better job, when we work for God telling of, *"the unsearchable riches of Christ."* Every Christian is a missionary for God. If we think we are not, then we are still a mission field. What a privilege it is to bring the light of the Gospel to those who are in darkness!

As believers, we are *"God's workmanship, created in Christ Jesus to do good works, which God prepared in advance for us to do,"* Ephesians 2:10. The fact that we are selected by God to be His servants must humble us. God arranged our time here on earth and then gave us each a special God-given ability to help build His everlasting kingdom. Did God pick us out from the masses of other people because He foresaw that we would be gifted for Him? NO! There was nothing in us that appealed to Him. By grace God selected us to work for Him, is the context of Ephesians 2:8-10. Paul also wrote in Philippians 2:13, *"It is God who works in you, both to will and to act for His good pleasure."*

May our call to work for God be like it was with the Apostle Paul. He considered himself, *"less than the least of all God's people."* We pray that kind of humility is ours! Paul more than any other, fully realized that if any "good" came out of him it was because of Christ alone. Even in Abraham's case, God saw nothing good in him but appointed him to go to a faraway country. Abraham *"obeyed and went, even though he did not know where he was going,"* Hebrews 11:8b. Paul and Abraham went by faith in Christ, obedient to God's call. May we follow in their steps and be found faithful.

Prayer: Precious Lord, thank You for the privilege of being a servant of Yours to a lost world. Forgive us for crying about the hardships that we face as we tell others about You. Lord strengthen us even more, for Your name's sake! In Jesus' name we pray. Amen.

DECEMBER

"Finally, brothers, whatever is true,
whatever is noble, whatever is right,
whatever is pure, whatever is lovely,
whatever is admirable — if anything is excellent or
praiseworthy — think about such things."
Philippians 4:8

December 1

"How you have fallen from Heaven, <u>O morning star, son of the dawn</u>! You have been cast down to the earth." Isaiah 14:12a

The history of Satan

We can make two big mistakes that glorify Satan. First we can ignore Satan, and second, we can give him too much attention; he is then glorified. We need a Biblical response to Satan. He was first a created angel; his name is underlined in the text. There are angels, archangels, powers, principalities, cherubim and seraphim. They all carry out God's will in Heaven and on earth. Satan, also called Lucifer, was the highest created angel and the most beautiful. *"This is what the Sovereign LORD says: 'You were the model of perfection, full of wisdom and perfect in beauty. You were in Eden, the garden of God; every precious stone adorned you: ruby, topaz and emerald, your settings and mountings were made of gold; on the day you were created they were prepared,"* Ezekiel 28:12b-13. This *"Eden"* was in Heaven.

"You were anointed as a guardian cherub, for so I ordained you. Cherubs covered the mercy seat of the ark, where atonement was to be made between God and man. You were on the holy mount of God; you walked among the fiery stones. You were blameless in your ways from the day you were created till wickedness was found in you," Ezekiel 28:14-15.

Then something happened. Satan sinned and God put him on earth. *"Through your widespread trade you were filled with violence, and you sinned. So I drove you in disgrace from the mount of God, and I expelled you, O guardian cherub, from among the fiery stones. Your heart became proud on account of your beauty, and you corrupted your wisdom because of your splendor. So I threw you to the earth; I made a spectacle of you before kings,"* Ezekiel 28:16-17.

Prayer: Holy and Righteous Lord, we praise you for telling us about Satan's beginnings. We see how he was once the guardian of the Holy of Holies, the very place that atonement was to be made in Heaven. Now fallen, we get a clearer picture of why Satan tries so hard to prevent our holiness. We are so thankful that Christ crushed the head of Satan. Lord, how grateful we are that You protect us from this evil angel. In Jesus' name we pray. Amen.

December 2

"The great dragon was hurled down - that ancient serpent called the devil, or Satan, who leads the whole world astray. He was hurled to the earth, and his angels with him." Revelation 12:9

Satan's army

When Satan was cast out of Heaven, he did not leave alone. It is commonly believed that one third of the angels in Heaven were also cast out when Satan fell, based on Revelation 12:4. Satan is called the father of this world. Our text also shows he *"leads the whole world astray."* However, Satan is not omnipresent, (everywhere at once), like God is, but he does have many demon helpers. Keep in mind that according to Luke 20:36, angels do not die, nor are any new angels being made. The number is the same as when God created them. Also, as spirits, angels do not have bodies.

The word Satan itself means, accuser. As such, Satan is against believers, accusing them before God in Heaven. Satan and his band of angels are also against the other holy angels. When Daniel was praying to God in Daniel 10:12-14, he was informed that God could not answer his prayer, yet. First, Michael a chief, good angel had to come and defeat a high ranking evil angel who was assigned by Satan to the Persian kingdom. More than anything, Satan is against Christ. In Genesis 3:15, it was predicted that Satan would lose to Christ. Satan tried so hard to stop the birth of Christ and His perfect life in Matthew 4.

Adam gave into Satan in *"the lust of the eyes, the lust of the flesh, and the pride of life,"* 1 John 2:16. Christ didn't give into the very same temptations in Matthew 5. We can also overcome Satan, in Christ! The final victory of Christ over the powers of Satan was the Cross. Death kept Adam and everyone in the grave. But because Christ had no sin, the grave could not hold Him. In Christ, we too live forever. As children of Adam, we lack the power to fight Satan on our own! Christ alone sets us free from Satan in salvation and then protects us.

Prayer: Saving and protecting Lord, thank You for teaching us about Satan and how we can defeat him. We praise You that You defeat Satan in every battle. We look to You the Author and Perfecter of our faith, to free us and to protect us. In Jesus' name we pray. Amen.

December 3

"What harmony is there between Christ and Belial? What does a believer have in common with an unbeliever? What agreement is there between the temple of God and idols? For we are the temple of the living God. As God has said: 'I will live with them and walk among them, and I will be their God, and they will be My people.'"
2 Corinthians 6:15-16

Can a demon indwell a true believer?

Can a demon dwell in Christ? No. In three different ways in our text, Paul shows us that a believer has only Christ in the heart. *"For we are the temple of the living God."* There is no example in the Bible where a demon ever inhabited or invaded a true believer! There is no place in the Bible, where we see anyone rebuking, binding, or casting out demons from a true believer! Never does the Bible instruct any believer to cast a demon out of any other believer.

God, *"has rescued us from the dominion of darkness and brought us into the kingdom of the Son He loves,"* Colossians 1:13. *"Thanks be to God, who always leads us in triumphal procession in Christ,"* 2 Cor. 2:14a. John was also so sure a believer has been delivered from Satan's grip at salvation that he said: *"You have overcome the evil one,"* 1 John 2:13.

A person with demon <u>possession</u> is totally unable, in all parts of their life, to live God's way in this world. In many countries, there is much confusion in this area of casting out demons, miracles, healings, etc... Those with real demon possession in our churches today need Christ in their heart and only then will the demon be out! Too often, a "salvation experience," is merely a "feeling," and not a real change of heart. When a person returns to the same evil pattern of living as before their "experience," and are again, lying, cheating, stealing, their "experience" shows that they are not Christian. O how we need the Lord Jesus Christ in our hearts!

Prayer: Dear Lord, we thank You that even though Satan can tempt us, he cannot live in our hearts because You live there. How blessed we are that we are literally the temple where You now dwell. We are the church and belong to You, body and soul. Thank You Lord for Your powerful and holy presence! In Jesus' name we pray. Amen.

December 4

"Our struggle is not against flesh and blood, but against the rulers, against the authorities, against the powers of this dark world and against the spiritual forces of evil in the Heavenly realms."
Ephesians 6:12

Did Job or Paul "bind" Satan?

I write this because some churches are so intent on Satan that they do not concentrate on who God is and what His will is for their lives.

We know from Job 1:8a, that God allowed Satan to afflict Job physically. *"The LORD said to Satan, 'Have you considered My servant Job?'"* Satan's answer accused God of blessing Job too much, and that was why he was so righteous. To prove that Job loved Him, God allowed Satan to afflict Job. One big point is, Job was one of the most righteous men in the Bible. Did he, or any of his counselors, ever attack the devil directly and say, "Satan, I rebuke you"? Did Job ever say, "Satan, I bind you"? Not in 42 chapters is this ever recorded! But you argue, "that is Old Testament theology!"

Paul in the New Testament wrote: *"To keep me from becoming conceited because of these surpassingly great revelations, (He had a view of Heaven no one else did) there was given me a thorn in my flesh, a messenger of Satan, to torment me. Three times I pleaded with the Lord to take it away from me; But He said to me, 'My grace is sufficient for you, for My power is made perfect in weakness.' Therefore I will boast all the more gladly about my weaknesses, so that Christ's power may rest on me. That is why, for Christ's sake, I delight in weaknesses, in insults, in hardships, in persecutions, in difficulties,"* 2 Corinthians 12:7-10a. Did Paul cast out a demon or rebuke Satan? No! He appealed to God who could remove the *"messenger of Satan"* if He wanted to! Later on, did Paul "bind the demon of Rome" for imprisoning him? No. Why? It was God's will to allow this affliction also!

Prayer: Powerful Lord, we thank You that Your sovereign love allows Satan to afflict us, just enough, so we move closer to You! May we learn to love You more than we hate the devil. Help us to endure all affliction for Your name's sake, trusting in You to give us the strength we need each day. In Jesus' name we pray. Amen.

December 5

"Be strong in the Lord and in His mighty power. Put on the full armor of God so that you can take your stand against the devil's schemes."
Ephesians 6:10-11

God's armor is ours at salvation!

God never leaves any Christian defenseless! There are 6 parts of armor that God gives every Christian when they become His soldier. God gives: 1. The belt of truth; 2. The breastplate of righteousness; 3. The Gospel of peace; 4. The shield of faith; 5. The helmet of salvation; 6. The sword of the Spirit. We will study these six pieces of armor. But first, we need to see the words *"Be strong in the Lord."* These words are about courage, for what good is armor on a soldier without courage?

Earlier, we said it's possible to pay too much attention to Satan or too little. Both are defective in doctrine and in life. Too many ignore the six pieces of armor that God uses to protect us from Satan. Instead, they seek after mystical experiences, power encounters, and miracles. Problem is, they concentrate more on what Satan is doing, than in how they are living for God and with God.

Christian courage is what is needed! It is a heart-felt obedience and passion to trust in Christ and His promised protection. We can't fight Satan without the armor of God. Man-made methods of warfare against Satan and his demons are not effective! Actually, it is our wicked hearts that are the problem, not Satan! Thus, the two commands, *"Be strong"* and *"put on"* show it's our personal responsibility to put on the *"full armor of God."*

Why is it that so many of the people who are big into the "spiritual warfare" movement, are noticeably lacking in Christian character? Does not the real Holy Spirit produce holiness in every believer? So then, any man-made weapon of warfare will not be useful to help anyone advance the kingdom of God!

Prayer: Protecting Lord, we praise and thank You that You have provided armor so that we might fight with confidence and have protection. How much we need Your protection from the many adversaries to the Gospel. In Christ's name we pray. Amen.

December 6

"Stand firm then, with the belt of truth buckled around your waist, with the breastplate of righteousness in place, and with your feet fitted with the readiness that comes from the Gospel of peace."
Ephesians 6:14-15

The Armor of God - Part 1

Paul wrote about the armor of God from prison, chained to a soldier. A soldier first puts on his belt, signifying a commitment, acknowledging there is a battle to fight, and a readiness to fight. As soldiers of the Cross, we too must be committed to Christ and His truths. It is God's *"truth"* that sets us free. The Christian life is one of spiritual warfare on this side of the grave. We need God's "truths," not Satan's lies to be able to live God's way.

The *"breastplate"* was necessary to protect the vital organs and bowels in hand to hand combat. The only spiritual righteousness that will protect us is Christ's righteousness imputed to us, justification. Of course, the devil wants us to believe in self-righteousness, thinking we can make it to God and Heaven by our good works. The devil also wants us to concentrate on getting rid of him and the evil we need to put off, instead of the righteousness of Christ we need to put on.

"Feet fitted," shows that the Christian has embraced the Gospel, and is ready to walk with God in a new pattern of living. *"Feet fitted,"* is being able and willing to walk the road that Christ walked. When we walk according to the commandments of God, the Holy Spirit gives us real *"peace,"* according to John 14:15-27. The world's kind of peace, is the absence of problems. God's *"peace"* is trusting in Him, even in the midst of problems! God's *"peace"* is eternal. The world's peace comes and goes. Thus, God gives us a peace the world cannot give.

As we look at the pieces of armor, we can see how God equips us through Christ and His Spirit to stand against evil.

Prayer: Beautiful Savior, King of creation, we so appreciate Your truth in Romans 8:28 *"that in all things God works for the good of those who love Him, who have been called according to His purpose."* May we all accept that You are the General and we are the soldiers. Thank You for fighting the devil for us. In Jesus' name we pray. Amen.

December 7

"Take up the shield of faith, with which you can extinguish all the flaming arrows of the evil one. Take the helmet of salvation and the sword of the Spirit, which is the Word of God. And pray in the Spirit on all occasions with all kinds of prayers and requests."
Ephesians 6:16b-18a

The Armor of God - Part 2

"The shield of faith," is what we rely on to protect us from the blows of Satan. *"Faith is being sure of what we hope for and certain of what we do not see,"* Hebrews 11:1. *"Faith"* is the full assurance that God's promises are true. Our faith will be severely tested in our trials of life! What will we do? If we get eclectic, (adding a variety of belief systems, like psychology) we set aside *"the shield of faith."* God's shield is His Son, Word, and Spirit. A Christian's faith and protection is God! Running from our trials, including using alcohol and pills to numb us from them is a problem, for there's no armor on our backs then.

Salvation is a *"helmet"* that protects our heads, just like the breastplate does the heart. The evil enemy aims for our eyes, which are windows to our souls. Demons throw the darts of TV, pornography, etc... to pluck our eyes out spiritually speaking. God's *"helmet"* also protects our ears. The enemy tries to put evil into our ears to poison our soul. Seeing and hearing Biblically protects our heads. Satan wants us to leave our Christianity in church or at home when we go to school or to work. God's helmet protects our head wherever we go.

The *"sword"* in *"the sword of the Spirit,"* is a penetrating blade for close hand-to-hand combat. That *"sword"* is the Bible! It is made of the best material; it's infallible, without flaw or blemish. The Bible is complete, authoritative, sufficient and effective. We are in a spiritual battle and need divinely empowered weapons. Use the sword or lose the battle! We don't need some special "technique," to deal with the enemy. Jesus said, *"it is written"* three times when Satan tempted Him in Matthew 4. The "sword" has two sides. One side must cut our hearts; the other side must cut the hearts of others in the work of evangelism.

Prayer: Wonderful Lord, You even give us prayer, another weapon. You equip us to fully overcome evil. May we *"put on"* Your equipment, In Jesus' name we pray. Amen.

December 8

"If anyone turns a deaf ear to the law, even his prayers are detestable." Proverbs 28:9

When God doesn't hear us

In giving us the Ten Commandments, God specifically promised He would show *"love to a thousand generations of those who love Me and keep My commandments,"* Exodus 20:6. God has not changed His truth about showing love to His children. God is the same yesterday, today and forevermore.

It may seem that God is rather silent at times while we have some big needs. God probably seems silent, because at times, He is silent. So, we cry a little louder for God to see us, to notice our troubles. And while we are crying, secretly we are a little upset with God for not giving us more of His blessings! Based on our text, is it God's fault when we are not being blessed? Or, is it often own fault? We may go to all night prayer meetings and to church each Sunday. Is it possible that God's silence is a blessing in itself? If we were listening to God and His Word, we would be more obedient than we are at present. God promises us in our text that He will not even *"hear"* our prayers if we turn *"a deaf ear to the law,"* which is His will for us.

God's response to our disobedience is so strong that our *"prayers are detestable"* to Him. When we plug our ears to God, He plugs His ears also. When we are disgusted with His will, He is disgusted with our will to sin. So, God in love starts to heap the blessing of guilt, to convict us of how we have become selfish, the opposite of what His *"law"* teaches. Through conviction, God prods us to confess our sin, so that He can once again hear our pleas and petitions. Why do we go through this rebellion process so often?

Prayer: Holy and compassionate Lord, You are so good in moving us closer to the Cross by Your convicting Holy Spirit. You help us to see our sin so we can confess it and receive Your forgiveness. Lord, how quickly we become so proud and ignore You and Your perfect *"law."* How short is our love for You! May we treasure our relationship with You. In Christ's name we pray. Amen.

December 9

"In this you greatly rejoice, though now for a little while you may have had to suffer grief in all kinds of trials." 1 Peter 1:6

A Biblical view of sickness

Yesterday, I walked by a church and saw a big sign out front, "God will surely heal all your sickness and diseases and bless you." Is this what the Bible teaches? Is it some kind of sin to be sick? Think about the righteous Job! God said: *"There is no one on earth like him; he is blameless and upright, a man who fears God and shuns evil,"* Job 1:8b. Yet God allowed this righteous man to be greatly afflicted.

Are they right who say: "If you have a strong faith, God will surely heal you." What about Joni Erickson Tada? She has been in a wheelchair for 35 years and has greatly witnessed to many people. Is her faith too weak to come out of that chair? Ask Joni about where she is at spiritually? She would surely agree with our text. She would surely say that God's grace is sufficient. What about Jesus Christ? He was beaten, bruised and even offered up on the Cross! If His faith was stronger, would He have not had to endure these things?

A false gospel gives a false hope. Jesus had a stone for a pillow, no house, and few comforts. Jesus' message to His followers was to *"deny yourself, take up your cross and follow Me."* You would think that Jesus had a cross of pure gold the way some people carry on for the sake of money! What is missing is the truth of our text. God allows us to suffer, so that through it, He can bless us! Peter explains the "why" of suffering. *"These have come so that your faith - of greater worth than gold, which perishes even though refined by fire - may be proved genuine and may result in praise, glory and honor when Jesus Christ is revealed,"* 1 Peter 1:7.

May we, with gratitude, think on the eternal blessings our suffering brings, rather than in getting temporary relief from them! God will never waste pain in the life of His children! In our suffering, may we trust the heart of God, and learn what He is trying to teach us!

Prayer: Compassionate Lord, we thank You for always giving us what we need in our spiritual journey. Help us to understand our suffering, so that we, with a good attitude may grow in grace. In Christ's name we pray. Amen.

December 10

"Let no one be found among you...who consults the dead. Anyone who does these things is detestable to the LORD."
Deuteronomy 18:10; 11b-12a

Talking to the dead is *"detestable"*

Nowhere in the Bible does God allow us to talk to the dead. Through divination, many try to seek the dead, for the purpose of looking into the future. Searching for knowledge through such "channels" is a conversation with the devil himself, literally an abomination to the Lord, who speaks to us through His Word and Spirit.

In Deuteronomy 18, God talked about the bad living practices of those in Canaan, Israel's destination. Why not consult the dead? Because the souls of the dead, whether in Heaven or in Hell, can't see or hear the living on earth. When someone tries to call up the dead, Satan answers the phone! He uses this as an opportunity to speak lies and to deceive. Consulting the dead quickly gets into the demonic and the practice of witchcraft. God's Word really shouts to us:

"Do not turn to mediums or seek out spiritists, for you will be defiled by them. I am the LORD your God," Leviticus 19:31. *"I will set my face against the person who turns to mediums and spiritists to prostitute himself by following them, and I will cut him off from his people. Consecrate yourselves and be holy, because I am the LORD your God,"* Leviticus 20:6-8.

Only God's Spirit can help us to know God's will. *"We have a great High Priest who has gone through the Heavens, Jesus the Son of God." "Approach the throne of grace with confidence, so that we may receive mercy and find grace to help us in our time of need,"* Hebrews 4:14a, & 16. Faith looks to God and believes what He reveals concerning the past, present, and future. Consulting the dead is idolatry.

Prayer: Wise Lord, what a blessing is ours, that the one and only High Priest, Jesus Christ knows us. How grateful we are that You are all wisdom, seeing everything, having all power, and working all things for Your glory and our good. We praise You for being such a wonderful active God. In Jesus' name we pray. Amen.

December 11

"Not everyone who says to Me, 'Lord, Lord' will enter the kingdom of Heaven, but only he who does the will of My Father who is in Heaven. Many will say to Me on that day, 'Lord, Lord, did we not prophesy in Your name, and in Your name drive out demons and perform many miracles?' Then I will tell them plainly, 'I never knew you. Away from Me, you evildoers!'" Matthew 7:21-23

More programs or more practice?

In our text, a group of people were tragically disappointed in The Judgment. Jesus did not recognize them as His children. Yet they thought they were His. What went so wrong? What can we learn from this, so we are prepared for The Judgment that is coming?

One of the problems is, many in the church are into programs, events, meetings and much busy-ness. Ministry workers are running around like chickens with their heads cut off, going to all-night prayers, special meetings, miracle healings, meetings to cast out demons, meetings to get the anointing, even meetings to learn how to do soul winning. Something in all this "going" is missing!

A friend of mine shocked me years ago. He told me he could leave a Hindu alone in his office and they would steal nothing from him. But certain people who considered themselves "Spirit-filled Christians," would take things. Does such a person need more "miracle" meetings to attend? Do they need more all-night prayers? No. They need to change how they live.

The solution for us is more practice, not more programs. Jesus followed up the words of our text by saying, *"Therefore everyone who hears these words of mine and <u>puts them into practice</u> is like a wise man who builds his house on the rock,"* Matthew 7:24. God wants our hearts, not more programs. If we love God we will listen to Him. True religion is about relationships. May our eyes be opened to the fact that God is far more interested in what we are becoming than what we are doing!

Prayer: O holy Lord, take our hearts and let them be, consecrated Lord to Thee. Lord, help us to see that without holiness, we will hear the words, *"I never knew you."* Change our hearts Lord. Make us live holy lives. In Jesus' name we pray. Amen.

December 12

"Who will bring any charge against those whom God has chosen?"
Romans 8:33

Presently and forever His!

Think for a minute, about the question in our text. God's children are forgiven, totally guiltless! If God has forgiven a Christian, who can charge them with "*any*" sin? For every Christian, Christ has paid for every sin. He has paid for our past sins. He has paid for our current sins. He has even paid for our future sins. Not one sin remains on our head. All have been transferred to Christ, who has fully satisfied the wrath of God. Forgiven, God is no longer the Christian's Judge, but is now his or her loving Father.

See the reality of our present situation. We are already eternally pardoned from every single sin! That is why God asks us to meditate on this question. "*Who will bring any charge against those whom God has chosen?*" Think about what Christ has done for every Christian. He removes 100% of our guilt! With our guilt gone, our punishment is gone also. God the Father, Son, and Holy Spirit did this judicial wonder of all wonders for us personally. Christian, see the power of God here for you personally. You were dead and unable to move to God, spiritually speaking. Even when you were "*His enemy*" Romans 5:10, God moved to you, pardoning and saving you! Now, you are washed, you are clean, you are purified, and you are preserved for all eternity. You are beautiful to your God now and forever!

It is true that Satan can still make our life miserable, but he is like a snake without a head! Such a snake will wiggle until sundown, but its power to bite and poison is cut off! We are presently saved from not just the guilt of sin, but the power of sin also. There is not a single sin we cannot overcome if we use God's resources. Let us look to the Author and Perfecter of our faith, Jesus Christ.

Prayer: O Lord and Savior, what praise and worship we owe You. You did what no one else could do. You forgave us. We are now clean. So clean that You see us just as if we have never sinned. O how You love us in Christ. Lord, we lift up Your name. Help us to keep our eyes on You, our holy and righteous God. In Jesus' name we pray. Amen.

December 13

"We also rejoice in our sufferings because we know that suffering produces perseverance; perseverance, character; and character, hope. And hope does not disappoint us, because God has poured out His love into our hearts by the Holy Spirit, whom He has given us."
Romans 5:3b-5

How to win over discouragement

It is so easy to be discouraged. All we need to do is follow our natural desires, which is basically, to feel sorry for ourselves. That is the sure road to the pit of despair. Granted, we all have disappointments and setbacks of many kinds! But what is the bigger picture of life and death that our trials and suffering are designed to teach us? Our text shows us some promises, to encourage us. A number of other points and verses are helpful to win over discouragement.

1. Don't give up! *"Our salvation is nearer now than when we first believed,"* Romans 13:11b. Our time in this world will soon be at an end! Our war with sin and pain is almost over! Hang in there! *"Stand firm. Let nothing move you. Always give yourself fully to the work of the Lord, because you know that your labor in the Lord is not in vain,"* 1 Corinthians 15:58. Be a soldier of the Cross, not a deserter who is afraid to fight the good fight of faith.

2. *"Now we are children of God, and what we will be has not yet been made known. But we know that when He appears, we shall be like Him, for we shall see Him as He is,"* 1 John 3:2. Now, even today, we are completely already a child of God.

3. You will someday enjoy perfect health! *"The body that is sown is perishable, it is raised imperishable,"* 1 Corinthians 15:42b. What is a few years in a painful body compared to an eternity in a perfect body?

4. You will be forever happy! *"He (God) will wipe every tear from their eyes. There will be no more death or mourning or crying or pain, for the old order of things has passed away,"* Revelation 21:4.

Prayer: O Lord, You encourage us and give us hope. Help us to keep our eyes on You and all of Your promises. We know that if we resist the devil he will flee from us. But Lord we cannot resist him, until we cling to You. Help us to cling to You. In Jesus' name we pray. Amen.

December 14

"You have heard that it was said to the people long ago, 'Do not murder, and anyone who murders will be subject to judgment.' But I tell you that anyone who is angry with his brother will be subject to judgment." Matthew 5:21-22a

Are you still angry with your brother?

"When my brother or sister are decent and kind to me, then I will love them. Until that day happens, I will ignore them. They have hurt me without any cause. They have said bad things that simply are not true. They have gone out of their way to hurt me." Are these some of your thoughts? Earlier, we studied anger. How are you doing? You really cannot say that you are progressing much in holiness if this still the way you are living.

Many "church" people think it is okay to be angry. Jesus is not joking here! *"Anyone who is angry with his brother will be subject to judgment."* A minister recently tried to justify his anger by quoting: *"Be angry, and do not sin,"* Ephesians 4:26a NKJV. He should have read the NIV that says *"In your anger do not sin."* Better yet, he should have read five more verses in the same chapter. *"Get rid of all bitterness, rage and anger, brawling and slander, along with every form of malice,"* Ephesians 4:31. He should have known, *"A fool gives full vent to his anger, but a wise man keeps himself under control,"* Proverbs 29:11.

What needs to completely grab our hearts is that both anger and bitterness are completely, yes entirely, the opposite of the grace of God. Anger and bitterness are an unwillingness to forgive our brother or sister. Our anger and bitterness are deeds of the flesh in Galatians 5:19-21. Jesus demands, *"If you do not forgive men their sins, your Father will not forgive your sins,"* Matthew 6:15. Our anger is the opposite of forgiveness.

Prayer: O holy Lord, we still have some anger and bitterness in us, and You told us to get rid of all of it. We still say that others make us angry when, in reality, it comes from our hearts. We are still unwilling to forgive certain people. We have been unwilling to pray for them and show them kindness. Lord, correct us by Your Spirit. Help us to take the log out of our own eye. Help us to live with Your life-changing grace flowing out of us. In Jesus' name we pray. Amen.

December 15

"For those God foreknew He also predestined to be conformed to the likeness of His Son." Romans 8:29a

Your enemy makes you beautiful

In a dream, God showed a man a big block of marble saying, "I am going to chip away the pieces until only your face remains." Hands slowly began to chip away! The man cried to God, "faster, faster." Soon the man's face began to appear. He was so happy. God said, "Would you like to see the face of the hands that chipped away the marble?" He said "Yes." And it was his enemy doing the work. God uses our enemies to make us beautiful.

This happened to me and it will happen to you. My number one enemy hurt me by saying and doing things that were very wrong. He took things I said and twisted them around to sound much different. He was jealous of my God-given ability to teach and wanted people to appreciate him, not me. My enemy was constantly negative, angry, trying to remove me from my service to God. This happened to me many times. I was hurt, frustrated, even disappointed that the one who should encourage the work of the Lord, so viciously discouraged it.

As I experienced the pain of all this persecution, I responded with bitterness for a long time. In pain, I began to understand that I also hurt Christ and others much like this person hurt me. God helped me to see that I needed to get rid of all the resentment, the bitterness, and the pain. The whole process forced me to be gentler and more loving to others. <u>I began to pity the one who was hurting me</u>. In the process, my heart became more beautiful. Perhaps, it is time to thank God for His wisdom in giving us enemies to make us beautiful.

Prayer: O most wise and loving Lord, You said, *"Dear friends, do not be surprised at the painful trial you are suffering, as though something strange were happening to you."* But Lord, we are surprised. We think it strange when others hurt us. Yet how wonderful it is that through pain, You mercifully teach us to respond in grace instead of anger and bitterness. Thank You for making us more beautiful. In Jesus' name we pray. Amen.

December 16

"For God so loved the world that He gave His one and only Son, that whosoever believes in Him shall not perish but have everlasting life."
John 3:16

True love is giving!

The "love" in our text is more than a great feeling that God had for us; it is a great action! *"He gave."* We will never learn this kind of love on TV or by watching some movie. There, love is basically what you feel or get. We can quickly fall into this trap if we are not careful. How many times have we heard a person say, "I no longer love my spouse?" Or, "I have fallen out of love." How do we respond to this? Is it possible to "fall out of love"? Real love is a verb, an action, a commitment.

With this introduction in mind, how can we teach little children what love is all about? A child says, "I love my classmates," but then steals their pen or pencil. They also tell stories about their classmates to try ruin their reputation. What will happen if a child continues to follow this kind of upside down love? When the child becomes older, they will say that they love their customers, but then cheat them to get more for themselves. After ten years of marriage, they will want a different spouse, all because the "feeling" is gone. This kind of person is deceived! We think ourselves to be a loving person, but too often our actions tell another story.

It is good to keep our text verse in mind, not forgetting that "love" is giving. God created us to give His kind of love, sacrificially. If we have few friends, it is because we are giving real love to few. We will never figure out what love is until we stop the getting game and follow God's giving theme. *"For God so loved the world that He gave His one and only Son, that whosoever believes in Him shall not perish but have everlasting life."* There are great rewards in this life and the life to come if we will just lovingly give out love God's way!

Prayer: Lord, You know the truth about life. You clearly show us here a very simple but profound truth. You loved us by giving Your very best, Your Son. Forgive us for being so selfish! May we embrace Your Son and then with a new heart, love others Your way. In Jesus' name we pray. Amen.

December 17

"Salvation is found in no one else, for there is no other name under Heaven given to men by which we must be saved." Acts 4:12

Who are you trusting in to save you?

Once in a rural village, a pastor said to me, "These are my believers." After teaching there three days, it became apparent that many did not even understand the basics of confession, forgiveness and repentance. They believed much in their pastor, little in Christ. Our text is clear. *"Salvation is found in no one else."* No pastor can save us. Nor can anyone save themselves by the good they do. If they could, then Christ is not needed. The truth is, *"there is no other name under Heaven given to men by which we must be saved."* Looking for someone other than Christ to save us is not a new problem. Spurgeon wisely said:

"Some are foolish enough to put their confidence in ministers (or priests), I cannot even save myself; what can I do for others? Here is a story. 'There died in London not long ago a man of much wealth. When he came near to death, though I had never seen the man in my life, he asked for me. I could not go. My brother went and after setting before him the way of salvation, my brother asked the man, 'Why did you ask for Charles?' 'Well,' he said, 'whenever I have a doctor, I always like to get the best. And when I employ a lawyer, I like a man who is high in the profession. Money is no object. I want the best.' I shuddered at being so regarded. I was the best possible help he could get? That best is less than nothing, and vanity. What can we do for you if you will not have a Savior? We can stand and weep over you! We can break our hearts to think that you reject the Lord Jesus Christ! But what can we do?"

Look to the Savior, to the One who died for you!

Prayer: O righteous and most holy Lord, we cry to You for forgiveness. Some of us have carried on in ministry as if we were the way to You. Lord, help us to clearly understand Your math; Christ + nothing else = salvation. Dear Jesus, we thank You for giving Your perfect blood to make us right with God. How amazing, we too have Your eternal salvation, now and forever. In Jesus our Saviors' name we pray. Amen.

December 18

"My times are in Your hands; deliver me from my enemies and from those who pursue me." Psalm 31:15

Is God bigger than our enemies?

We may know that God is bigger than any enemy, but what will we do when a very difficult situation comes? Are we sure enough of the bigness of our God that we will not fall into a fear or worry problem? These two big sins fail the test of trusting in God. Jesus called worry *"little faith"* in Matthew 6:30b, and He called fear *"wicked and lazy"* in Matthew 25:26b.

Our experiences in life will teach us about the bigness of God, just as studying the attributes of God does. Our faith in God is tested and grows when we cannot see how some relationship or event in our life will turn out. Then God rescues us, showing us He can be trusted! The truth is; God in His love allows and even designs difficult situations, just so our faith can grow.

What God did for David, He will do for us. King Saul doubted a small, shepherd boy could face a giant. By faith David knew God was bigger than his enemies. *"Your servant has killed both the lion and the bear; this uncircumcised Philistine will be like one of them, because he has defied the armies of the living God,"* 1 Samuel 17:36. In our trials too, the size of our God gives faith instead of fear or worry!

<u>Psalm 31 testifies to our much needed past, present and future faith</u>. In verse one; *"In You, O Lord, I have taken* (past tense) *refuge."* And then in 31:3a, David said, *"You are* (present tense) *my rock and my fortress."* Then David prays, *"For the sake of Your name lead and guide me,* (future tense) *...for You are my refuge,"* 31:3b-4. In three tenses, David appeals to the righteous and holy name of God. David was saying, "I am Your child. I bear Your name. Rescue me." God will honor such a trusting prayer.

Prayer: Almighty Lord, like David in Psalm 31:15, we can say, *"My times are in Your hands; deliver me from my enemies and from those who pursue me."* Lord, You put us here. You changed our hearts. You gave us Christ's name. Rescue us so that we can declare Your name to many who do not know You. And Lord, may You be glorified by our life. Our *"times are in Your hand."* In Jesus' name we pray. Amen.

December 19

"What does the LORD require of you? To act justly and to love mercy and to walk humbly with your God." Micah 6:8

The Lord's requirements for life

The people of Israel gave up their love for God, and then lost their moral compass. Chapter six begins with the Lord asking the people, *"plead your case before the mountains,"* Micah 6:1a. Even the mountains saw how God had blessed them. God here challenges those who are in His service to testify against Him if He was ever a hard and unreasonable Master. God says, *"My people, what have I done to you? How have I burdened you? Answer Me,"* Micah 6:3. God then goes on to say how He delivered His people from slavery to sin (from the penalty and the power of it), yet they returned to it so willingly. God, whom we have offended, and to whom we are accountable, now clearly sets forth His requirements for how He wants us to live.

First, *"to act justly,"* love good and hate evil, according to the Ten Commandments. Do not just think or just pray about those who have suffered unjustly. Act on it. *"Learn to do right. Seek justice, encourage the oppressed. Defend the cause of the fatherless, plead the case of the widow,"* Isaiah 1:17. God said, *"I looked for a man among them who would build up the wall and stand before Me in the gap on behalf of the land so I would not have to destroy it, but I found none,"* Ezekiel 22:30. Will you stand in the gap?

Second, *"to love mercy,"* means we must become merciful in our day to day giving of our abilities and possessions. But, we must first give up our selfishness before we can *"love mercy."* God's mercy reached out to us who were blind, poor, and wretched. "Mercy" is that undeserving. As God's children, God requires us to also give *"mercy"* to undeserving others!

Third, *"walk humbly with your God."* God will not bless us if we are proud, for then we would become more prideful. It is when we humble ourselves that it is safe for God to bless us.

Prayer: Dear merciful Lord, we have not loved or obeyed You as we should. Forgive us and open our eyes to see the opportunities around us. Then, may we act humbly, as You want us to act! In Jesus' merciful name we pray. Amen.

December 20

"Our fathers worshiped on this mountain, but you Jews claim that the place where we must worship is in Jerusalem." John 4:20

The Person, not the place of worship

The context of today's text is John 4:1-42. Jesus is talking with the Samaritan woman. He told her about the past five husbands she had, and about the man she was now living with. She thinks Jesus is a prophet to know these things. The gentleness of Jesus encourages this unbeliever to ask more questions. She asks Jesus, "should we worship on Mount Gerizim where we go? Or, should we go to Jerusalem, where the Jews go?" Jesus corrects her, saying that it is not the place of worship but the Person we worship that is now important. He said, *"Yet a time is coming and has now come when the true worshipers will worship the Father in spirit and truth, for they are the kind of worshipers the Father seeks,"* John 4:23.

The Gospel Age to the Gentiles was beginning. It is no longer the Law and Mt. Sinai, but Christ Himself that is important. *"The woman said, 'I know that Messiah' (called Christ) 'is coming. When He comes, He will explain everything to us.' Then Jesus declared, 'I who speak to you am He,'"* John 4:25-26.

Do we worship Christ, the person? Or is the place of worship more important to us? God gave His Word, the Bible, and His Word the Son for us to hear. Real worship is hearing the Word of God and by faith obeying it. *"For everyone who calls on the name of the Lord will be saved. How, then, can they call on the one they have not believed in? And how can they believe in the one of whom they have not heard? And how can they hear without someone preaching to them?"* Romans 10:13-14.

The Samaritan woman and many of her friends believed in Jesus. They said to the woman, *"We no longer believe just because of what you said; now we have heard for ourselves, and we know that this man really is the Savior of the world,"* John 4:42.

Prayer: O Lord our Savior, when we hear Your Word, it changes us. May we fall in love with Your Person and with the hearing of Your holy Word. You alone are the Way, the Truth, and the Life. There is no other way to God except through You, our Savior. In Jesus' name we pray. Amen.

December 21

"He will cover you with His feathers, and under His wings you will find refuge." Psalm 91:4

Are we *"under His wings"*?

In a rural village in India, I saw a mother hen with her chicks. All were scratching for a living, looking for food to eat. All of the chicks were close to the mother hen, except one. A beautiful, bold, fat and cocky chick wandered far from the mother hen. He was not content to be scratching by mom. I admired this chick, until an eagle swooped down and snatched it up. Up, up, way up, in the sky the fat little chick went, firm in the grip of the eagle.

What an important warning for us who are content to be away from the Savior! It is possible to be suddenly snatched from this life, if we wander far from God. Our Lord here says, *"you will find refuge,"* if we stay close to Him.

The fat little chick was suddenly afraid, but it was too late. He simply had wandered too far. How far have we wandered? *"Covered with His feathers and under His wings"* is very close to the Savior. We may say, "I think I am close." That small chick thought he was close too. He thought he could dive for cover if danger came; after all, he was fast. But he wasn't fast enough! He was snatched from this life in the blink of an eye. Are we acting like the fat and sassy, little chick today?

The Lord invites us to dive for the cover of His wings. God's protection is much better than that of a mother hen. *"His faithfulness will be your shield and rampart,"* Psalm 91:4b. The shield that God gives is above us, around us, behind us, beneath us, and in us. God *"will command His angels concerning you to guard you in all your ways,"* Psalm 91:11. God will do this for us because we are in Christ, His adopted son or daughter. How close are we to God?

Prayer: Dear Lord and Savior, it is good for us to see examples to remind us to flee to Christ and from the wrath to come. Lord, we thank You for Your protection in Christ. You protected Daniel, in a den of hungry lions, protect us also. Daniel said, *"My God sent His angel and He shut the mouths of the lions. They have not hurt me because I was found innocent in His sight."* Lord, we praise You that we are also innocent and protected in Christ! In Jesus' precious name we pray. Amen.

December 22

"Let us hold fast the confession of our hope without wavering, for He who promised is faithful. And let us consider one another in order to stir up love and good works, not forsaking the assembling of ourselves together, as is the manner of some, but exhorting one another, and so much the more as you see the Day approaching."
Hebrews 10:23-25 NKJV

Why go to church?

Sabbath observance is slipping fast. Many think going to church is optional. One excuse for staying away is that there are so many hypocrites there. True, but in The Judgment, will it matter how others lived? Some stay away for "personal reasons." Be careful! Keeping the Sabbath Day holy is about *"His pleasure,"* not ours, as explained in Isaiah 58:13-14. Also, bad habits once started, quickly get worse over time.

A tired church goer complained in a letter to a newspaper, "It makes no sense to go to church every Sunday. I've gone for 30 years now. I've heard over 3000 sermons. But, I can't remember a single one of them. So, I think I'm wasting my time and the pastors are wasting theirs by giving the sermons." This started a huge argument in the newspaper which went on for weeks.

Then someone wisely wrote: "I've been married for 30 years now. In that time my wife has cooked 32,000 meals. But, I cannot recall the entire menu for a single one of those meals. But I do know this, they all nourished me and gave me the strength I needed to do my work. If my wife had not given me these meals, I would be physically dead today. Likewise, if I had not gone to church for nourishment, I would be spiritually dead today."

If you are DOWN and don't feel like going to church, know that God is UP to something! Go, your faith will see the invisible, believe the incredible, and receive the impossible. Thanks be to God for our physical and spiritual food.

Prayer: O Lord, You tell us not to forsake *"the assembling of ourselves together, as is the manner of some."* You tell us that we are on Earth to worship You. May our spiritual engines be recharged on Sunday and on every day for Your honor and for our good. May our worship move us to be a blessing to others. In Jesus' name we pray. Amen.

December 23

"The Word became flesh and made His dwelling among us."
John 1:14a

Why did Jesus have to be fully human?

1. As the second Adam, Jesus had to be fully human to fully identify with us. A man in prison asked me, "Why are there two testaments?" Adam was given a "covenant (testament) of works in Genesis 2:7. If Adam obeyed the covenant perfectly, he and we would go to Heaven. Adam sinned, plunging the whole world into sin and eternal death through his disobedience, Romans 5:12. After that, no one could keep the old covenant because all were born with his original sin. So, God in the Old Testament, provided an innocent animal, to shed its blood, to pay for the sin of guilty man.

In the New Testament, God sent His Son, fully God, fully man, to live a perfect life. He did what Adam did not do, and what we could not do. Jesus was perfectly obedient to rescue the world from sin. *"For since death came through a man, the resurrection of the dead comes also through a man. For as in Adam all die, so in Christ all will be made alive,"* 1 Corinthians 15:21-22. Jesus now offers a new Covenant, a New Testament, saved through His perfect blood.

2. Christ had to be human suffer for us. The Bible says: Jesus *"had to be made like His brothers in every way, in order that He might become a merciful and faithful High Priest in service to God, and that He might make atonement for the sins of the people. Because He Himself suffered when He was tempted, He is able to help those who are being tempted,"* Hebrews 2:17. Christ had to be like us to be our substitute.

3. Christ was fully human to be our High Priest. *"Such a High Priest meets our need, one who is holy, blameless, pure, set apart from sinners, exalted above the Heavens,"* Hebrews 7:26. *"For Christ died for sins once for all, the righteous for the unrighteous, to bring you to God."* 1 Peter 3:18a.

Prayer: O Lord our Savior, how You humbled Yourself! You even put Yourself into a body no one would admire. You were beaten, mocked, scourged and lived as a poor man, to fully identify with us. Your desire was for sinners to know God's forgiveness. We praise You for doing what the first Adam did not do. In Your name we pray. Amen.

December 24

"In the beginning was the Word, and the Word was with God, and the Word was God." John 1:1

Why did Jesus have to be fully God?

We have already seen that Christ had to be fully man. But He must also be fully God. The belief that Christ is fully God, is called the deity of Christ. To say that Christ is not fully God is a main belief of every cult! We will examine three reasons Christ must be fully God, equal to God.

No created creature (man, animal or angel) could possibly endure the wrath of God against sin! The holy wrath of God is such a terrible and crushing burden that only God Himself could possibly bear it! Our sin will surely crush us, if Christ does not take it upon Himself for us.

Wicked people need a Mediator. We need one who stands between two parties that are against each other. *"For there is one God and one Mediator between God and men, the man Christ Jesus,"* 1 Timothy 2:5. In the Old Testament there were prophets, priests and kings who acted as mediators. Even these were pictures of the Christ that was to come. We cannot approach the throne of God without an advocate, a lawyer. Through a new covenant of grace, or the New Testament, Christ forgives and presents us to God, perfect. Now a holy God can receive us.

Slaves need a Redeemer. We need one who will buy us back, to pay the price to free us! We are totally bankrupt, *"without money"* as Isaiah 55 teaches. We read that God *"was appalled that there was no one to intervene; so His own arm worked out salvation for Him,"* Isaiah 59:16b. God Himself shed His own blood to purchase our redemption. Just as God passed over the blood of the lamb in Egypt, so too, God accepts our Redeemer's "perfect blood," to free us from our personal sin. The holy justice of God demanded "a God-Redeemer."

Prayer: Holy Lord, Your perfect holiness could not possibly accept any other creature, man, or angel to be our Mediator or Redeemer. So You sent the only possibility, Your only Son, who was also God. You, *"made Him who had no sin to be sin for us, so that in Him we might become the righteousness of God,"* 2 Corinthians 5:21. In Jesus' name we pray. Amen.

December 25

"For God so loved the world that He gave His one and only Son, that whosoever believes in Him shall not perish but have everlasting life."
John 3:16

You can be sure that God forgives sin

God's gift of Jesus proves His love. Look to the manger. Look to the Cross. Dear friend, you need look no further. Both are undeniable proof that God cares for sinners! See from Christ's life that He did not spend His time rescuing bugs, birds, fish or animals. He did not come to save the earth from destruction. Jesus came to save sinners from the righteous wrath of God. After living a perfect life, Jesus willingly poured out His own innocent blood so that we could be set free from our guilty blood! What more could God do to prove His love for us? God allowed our sin to be the nails that pinned His only Son to the Cross. God allowed our unbelief to pierce His heart of compassion!

Satan wants us to doubt the power of the Cross and God's ability to forgive sin. The first thing Satan said to Eve in the Garden of Eden was, *"Did God really say?"* Genesis 3:1b. Still today, people doubt God's ability to totally wipe out their sins through Christ's shed blood on the Cross. Yet Jesus Christ, and His life as an atoning sacrifice for their sin, is the very heart of the Gospel. For those who doubt God's love, tell them to look to the Cross.

It is sad that today the image of the Cross has been cheapened when it is worn as a fashion statement. Granted there are some very sincere people who wear a cross. But there are many who wear it on their neck as some kind of good luck charm. Would you wear a bullet around your neck to remind you of a family member who was killed by a gun? Would that not be insensitive? The Apostle Paul did not glory in a cross that was an ornament. He gloried in the Cross that saved sinners for all eternity and presented them spotless before God in Heaven. Glory in that Cross!

Prayer: O Lord, what proof of Your love, Your Son is. You freely gave Your Son to rescue perishing souls *"from every tribe and language and people and nation."* Lord, may many see Your love in Your greatest of all gifts ever given. We thank You for Your Son who unites us to You for all eternity. We worship You, Lord. In Jesus' name we pray. Amen.

December 26

"Here is a boy with five small barley loaves and two small fish, but how far will they go among so many?" John 6:9

Jesus breaks the loaves

What a great question the disciples ask Jesus in our text. The many people following Jesus needed to be fed. How was Jesus going to do it? The meaning of this story has far more spiritual implications than the physical feeding of thousands of people.

When you see this story, think about the lives of many suffering Christians who are going through very deep trials in their lives. Each day is a difficult journey of letting go of all that is dear to them on Earth, hanging on the promises of God in Heaven. Their bodies are literally being broken just like the bread and the fish were broken in our text. Out of all this brokenness, Jesus multiplied a spiritual blessing to thousands of people.

The pain of being broken is real and intense. Do not think this so strange or unusual. Jesus' own body was broken to feed many spiritually. We celebrate this fact when we take Communion and remember what Jesus did for us. The disciples who watched this miracle of Jesus in the feeding of the five thousand from the loaves and fishes, were themselves broken in the same way later. Peter, for example was severely tested. Later Peter was able to write, *"Dear friends, do not be surprised at the painful trial you are suffering, as though something strange were happening to you. But rejoice that you participate in the sufferings of Christ, so that you may be overjoyed when His glory is revealed,"* 1 Peter 4:12-13.

When we belong to God, we are His child. God will likely break us some, just as in the story of the Five Thousand. Jesus said, *"let nothing be wasted,"* John 6:12b. Not one broken piece was wasted. Your pain will not be wasted! Your broken prayers for others will not be wasted! Your small words of encouragement will not be wasted. Every crumb of kindness you give, will not be wasted!

Prayer: Dear Author and Finisher of our faith, we are humbled that You allow us to suffer so we can help others who are suffering, for Your name's sake. O Lord, touch our lives with Your nearness, so we can teach others. In Jesus' name we pray. Amen.

December 27

"Love the Lord your God with all your heart and with all your soul and with all your mind. This is the first and greatest commandment."
Matthew 22:37-38

How much do you love God?

Our text shows us this is the greatest of all the commandments. The reason is that it includes the first four commandments. It is easy to claim to love God more than anything, but where is the proof? We could say that the proof is that we go to church every week or we have devotions every morning. Fine, but where is our heart when we worship God? What are we thinking about? Would we rather be doing something else? I only need to look at my own life to know how guilty I am. I often approach my daily job of writing devotionals or articles as my "Christian duty." Many times, I do not feel like sitting and wrestling with the Word of God. Some days I see my relationship with God as more of a duty, than as a love relationship. Surely love includes duty. But where is my heart?

What if a man approached a woman he wanted to marry and said, "I think it is my 'duty' to live for you the rest of my life, will you marry me?" A perceptive woman would surely ask, "Will you love me?" Love is way more than "duty," both to Christ and to the marriage relationship. Our hearts need to be in it, fully. When any relationship places duty before love, it is more like slavery. Neither Christ nor a spouse really wants the kind of love that is not freely given. Love with *"all your heart and with all your soul and with all your mind"* is a love so strong it motivates compassion, obedience, loyalty and yes, even duty.

Prayer: Dear Lord who loves us everlastingly, how many times we have gone to church more out of duty than out of our love for You. Many times we have done things for our marriage that were more out of duty than out of love. Lord, You fully know it and see it all. Change us Lord. Make us love You with our whole heart, mind and soul. May our marriages also reflect this same kind of deep sacrificial love that is completely interested in the object of our love. Train our eyes, Lord, and move our hearts. We pray in the name of Jesus, the true lover of our souls. Amen.

December 28

*"My sheep listen to My voice; I know them, and they follow Me. I give
them eternal life, and they shall never perish; no one can
snatch them out of My hand."* John 10:27-28

Can we lose our salvation?

The grace of God extends throughout all eternity. Our text is Jesus'
definition of *"eternal life."* Would Jesus use words like *"never perish"*
and *"no one can snatch them out of my hand,"* if we could lose our
salvation? The word *"eternal"* by definition means forever. Jesus also
says, *"My Father, who has given them to me, is greater than all, no one
can snatch them out of my Father's hand,"* John 10:29. If someone can
lose their salvation, then these words of the Father and the Son are
simply not true, but we know that these words are true.

There are other verses that show salvation cannot be lost. One
is, *"Being confident of this, that He who began a good work in you will
carry it on to completion until the day of Christ Jesus,"* Philippians 1:6.
The Apostle Paul was convinced he could not lose his salvation. *"The
Lord will rescue me from every evil attack and will bring me safely to
His Heavenly kingdom. To Him be glory for ever and ever. Amen,"* 2
Timothy 4:18. Paul praises the eternal grace of God.

Why then do some Christians think that they could lose their salvation? One reason is that they see people who are born to Christian
parents fall away from the Church. People then assume that this person
lost their salvation. But is a child automatically a Christian just because
they are born in a Christian home? No. Truly, children of believers are
born in the covenant. But is such a person always a Christian? No. God
warns us of such "covenant presumption" in Hebrews chapter three.
The children of Israel who came out of Egypt had the law and the
covenants, yet *"they were not able to enter, because of their unbelief,"*
Hebrews 3:19b.

Prayer: Eternal Lord, help us by Your Word and Spirit to hear Your
voice. For You tell us, *"My sheep listen to My voice"* and *"follow Me."*
We confess that too often we've known only an emotional response
to the Gospel and have not wholeheartedly followed You. Create in
us a clean heart, O Lord, and renew a steadfast spirit in us. In Jesus'
name we pray. Amen.

December 29

"Altogether, Methuselah lived 969 years, and then he died."
Genesis 5:27

"He died"!

We read the long list of names in the genealogies or the historical record in Genesis, and in other places. I used to think, why do we need to read all of these names? I now realize that it is important to see that Christ was a literal, physical descendant of Adam, David, etc... It is also important to trace the covenant faithfulness of God through the generations. It is important to see how great sinners were transformed and then included in the line of Christ.

The words shout to us, *"he died."* We are not immortal, though we might try live as if we are. Death will not somehow spare us if we avoid the subject. Even the 969 years of Methuselah are not even a drop in the oceans when compared to the years of eternity. Some people say we are simply matter, without a soul. They say we will someday just cease to exist. But even the atheist says "O My God," when something terrifies him. An atheist in this life who denies the existence of God, will know the truth in the next life as he will see and experience God, in all of His wrath.

"You will not surely die," that was said by Satan in Genesis 3:4a, is still a lie. A wrong belief on death will never change the reality of it. The wise and faithful Job said about our life, *"You overpower him <u>once for all</u>, and he is gone; You change his countenance and send him away,"* Job 14:20. We also read; *"Man is destined to die once, and after that to face the judgment,"* Hebrews 9:27b.

Someone once said that there are two things for sure in this life, taxes and death. Some people cheat on their taxes, but no one will cheat death. The wages of sin is always death, Romans 6:23. Like "Methuselah," we sinners will die someday soon.

Prayer: O Lord of both Heaven and Hell, You bring us Jesus, the Good News to save us sinners! You tell us that those who are in Christ, are seen by You as totally sinless. We worship You that in Christ, we will never taste a spiritual death. We thank You for telling us that we will die, to sober us up on the importance of how to live. In Jesus' name we pray. Amen.

December 30

"Two of every kind of bird, of every kind of animal and of every kind of creature that moves along the ground will come to you to be kept alive." Genesis 6:20

Noah, a picture of Jesus and grace

In the worldwide flood event, two truths are seen: the righteous wrath of God, and the amazing grace of God. First, the wrath of God is seen. *"The LORD saw how great man's wickedness on the earth had become, and that every inclination of the thoughts of his heart was only evil all of the time,"* Genesis 6:5. That verse is quite some statement! *"Now the earth was corrupt in God's sight and full of violence,"* Genesis 6:11. Because of the corruption and violence God said, *"I am going to put an end to all people, for the earth is filled with violence because of them,"* Genesis 6:13b.

We also see the amazing grace of God. Noah is commanded to make an ark, a picture of Heaven, and Noah is a picture of Jesus. The *"birds," "animals,"* and *"creatures," "will come to you."* Do these animals come of their own will? No, not at all. God made them willing to come, fully grace! Did God call all the other animals and birds to come to the ark and be saved? No. The road to Heaven is a narrow road! Can you picture the procession that God is calling to Heaven? Some come with sins like an elephant, others have sins like a bird. All were called into the ark, to Heaven itself. We must understand our privileged position through seeing God's grace in this flood event. God's grace is calling some of us wicked yet redeemed sinners to Heaven. There was only one door on the ark, and there is one Door to Heaven. Jesus said, *"I am the door. If anyone enters by Me, he will be saved, and will go in and out and find pasture,"* John10:9 NKJV.

Prayer: O Lord, the truth of the ark event is so amazing! We see how You called and compelled the people and animals to come and be saved from Your wrath! Jesus' words in John 15:16, *"you did not choose Me, but I chose you,"* describe Your grace to us. *"Blessed is the man <u>You choose</u>, and <u>cause to approach You</u>, that he may dwell in Your courts."* In Jesus our Savior's name we pray. Amen.

December 31

"As it was in the days of Noah, so will it be at the coming of the Son of Man." "Therefore keep watch, because you do not know on what day your Lord will come." Matthew 24:37 & 42

Are you ready?

Jesus is coming again! *"No one knows about that day or hour, not even the angels in Heaven, nor the Son, but only the Father,"* Matthew 24:36. Even though we do not know the exact time when Jesus will return, we do know that people will be acting just like they did, *"in the days of Noah."* Yesterday we saw that in Noah's time, *"The earth was corrupt in God's sight and full of violence,"* Genesis 6:11. Even in Noah's day, God said, *"I am going to put an end to all people, for the earth is filled with violence because of them,"* Genesis 6:13b. Yet once again, God is going to act in judgment, not with a flood again, but by fire. It could be soon, because we see *"violence and corruption"* increasing and becoming very common.

At the same time, we people will be doing the things that we have always done. *"Before the flood, people were eating and drinking, marrying and giving in marriage, up to the day Noah entered the ark,"* Matthew 24:38. It will be the same again at the end of the world! *"And they knew nothing about what would happen until the flood came and took them all away. That is how it will be at the coming of the Son of Man,"* Matthew 24:39.

The end will be so sudden that, *"Two men will be in the field; one will be taken and the other left. Two women will be grinding with a hand mill; one will be taken and the other left,"* Matthew 24:40-41. Are we ready? Nation is rising against nation. There are many earthquakes, famines, violence and corruption. When Jesus does come, it will be too late to repent and "get right" with Him. Do not be with the many who are putting off seeking God, thinking they can do that tomorrow. Tomorrow may never come. Today is the day of salvation.

Prayer: Dear Lord, You so lovingly tell us to be ready. You tell us to seek You while You may be found. Satan wants us to wait until tomorrow. You tell us that salvation is today. May we seek You and find you while there is still time. In Jesus' name we pray. Amen.